Rural Commercial Capital
Agricultural Markets in West Bengal

To the memory of Sunil Sengupta

Rural Commercial Capital
Agricultural Markets in West Bengal

BARBARA HARRISS-WHITE

OXFORD
UNIVERSITY PRESS

YMCA Library Building, Jai Singh Road, New Delhi 110 001

Oxford University Press is a department of the University of Oxford. It furthers the
University's objective of excellence in research, scholarship, and education
by publishing worldwide in

Oxford   New York

Auckland   Cape Town   Dar es Salaam   Hong Kong   Karachi   Kuala Lumpur
Madrid   Melbourne   Mexico City   Nairobi   New Delhi   Shanghai   Taipei   Toronto

With offices in
Argentina   Austria   Brazil   Chile   Czech Republic   France   Greece   Guatemala
Hungary   Italy   Japan   Poland   Portugal   Singapore   South Korea   Switzerland
Thailand   Turkey   Ukraine   Vietnam

Oxford is a registered trademark of Oxford University Press
in the UK and in certain other countries

Published in India
by Oxford University Press, New Delhi

© Oxford University Press 2008

The moral rights of the author have been asserted
Database right Oxford University Press (maker)

First published 2008

All rights reserved. No part of this publication may be reproduced,
or transmitted in any form or by any means, electronic or mechanical,
including photocopying, recording or by any information storage and
retrieval system, without permission in writing from Oxford University Press.
Enquiries concerning reproduction outside the scope of the above should be
sent to the Rights Department, Oxford University Press, at the address above

You must not circulate this book in any other binding or cover
and you must impose this same condition on any acquirer

ISBN 13: 978-0-19-5691597
ISBN 10: 0-19-5691598

Typeset in Joanna MT 10.5/12.5
by Sai Graphic Design, New Delhi 110 055
Printed at Pauls Press, New Delhi 110 020
Published by Oxford University Press
YMCA Library Building, Jai Singh Road, New Delhi 110 001

Contents

List of Tables	vii
List of Figures, Maps, and Appendices	ix
Preface and Acknowledgements	xi
Professor Sunil Sengupta	xvi

1. Introduction:
   How the Successes and Failures of West Bengal's
   Agriculture are Affected by its Agricultural Markets ... 1

2. Analysing Markets ... 19

3. A History of West Bengal's Food Economy ... 47

4. The System of Rice Markets in Birbhum District in
   the Early 1980s ... 72

5. The Dynamics and Politics of Rice Markets in
   Birbhum District ... 126

6. Institutional Diversity, Price Performance, and
   Power Relations in the Commodity Markets of
   Bardhaman District ... 146

7. The Dynamics of Market Institutions and Market Politics
   in Bardhaman District in 1990 ... 185

8. Liberalization and Institutional Development in the Rice
   Market System in the Early 21st Century ... 213

9. State and Market, 1991–2002: De-Regulation,
   De-Participation, Re-Regulation, and Crisis ... 258

10. Conclusions
    Rural Commercial Capital, Market Systems, and the
    Left Front ... 290

Contents

Appendices 321
Glossary 385
Bibliography 387
Index 411

Tables

1.1a	Production of Rice in West Bengal by Districts	17
1.1b	District-wise Share of Production of Rice in West Bengal	18
2.1	Field Research	40
3.1	Production of Staple Foods Birbhum and Bardhaman Districts 1975-95	48
3.2	A Statistical Profile of Bardhaman and Birbhum Districts 1990s	50
3.3	Rice Mills in West Bengal	55
4.1	The Structure of Control in Rice Markets, Bolpur and Sainthia Blocks, Birbhum District, West Bengal	82
4.2	Loans from Paddy Agents, 1981, Bolpur and Sainthia Blocks	87
4.3	Short-term Crop Loans Issued through the Co-Operative Bank, Birbhum District, 1976-81	88
4.4	Paddy and Rice Value Chain, Birbhum, February–March 1982, Rs/Qtl.	90
4.5	Wealth in Terms of Annual Income of Firms in Circulation of Rice, 1981, Bolpur Region	100
4.6	Income from Agricultural Production, 1981, Birbhum District	102
4.7	Income and Livelihoods, Birbhum District	103
4.8	Agricultural Interests of Agro-commercial firms, Birbhum district	103
4.9	Employment in the Rice Markets	107
4.10	Ownership of Firms in the Rice Markets (%)	108
4.11	Family Size and Type and Social Characteristics of Owners of Firms	108
4.12	Caste in the Rice Markets (by firm)	110
4.13	Wage Rates: Clerks and Mechanics	113
4.14	Wage Rates: Coolie and Casual Labour	114
4.15	Wages in the Cost Structure of Firms in the Circulation of Rice: Birbhum District, 1981 (Averages)	117
5.1	The Organizations of Merchants	137
6.1	Database—Bardhaman District. 1990	148
6.2	Caste, Ethnicity and Religion in Commerce (% of sample)	155

6.3	Market System Structure, Bardhaman District, 1990	156
6.4	Physical Commodity Flows	162
6.5	Storage	170
6.6	General Distribution of Landholding in Bardhaman District, 1984–5	171
6.7	Land Holdings of the Sample of Merchants, Bardhaman District, 1990	171
6.8	Traders' Credit, Bardhaman District, 1990	178
6.9	Co-operative Crop Loans in the Areas studied (Rs lakhs)	180
7.1	Approximate/Indicative Net Profits (Rs)	190
7.2	Causes of Loss (% of Cases Reported for Each Type of Trade)	192
7.3	Institutions for the Regulation of the System of Markets	203
8.1	Contribution of West Bengal to All India Production of Rice	215
8.2	District-wise Share of Production of Rice in West Bengal	218
8.3	Firms in the System of Markets for Rice, 2002	221
8.4	Indicative scales of operation—Birbhum District, 2002	222
8.5	Price Margins in 2002, Birbhum District	223
8.6	Rice Mills in West Bengal	223
8.7	Petty Parboiling, 2002	225
8.8	Kutial business (n=3), 2002	225
8.9	Permanent Unskilled Labour within the Rice Market System (Rs/month, 2002): a labour market?	226
8.10	The economics of processing, 2002, Rs '000	227
8.11	Physical Outturn (% of paddy)	232
8.12	Muri Rice Process	233
8.13	Labour In Rice Processing	235
8.14	Combined impact of Unions and Adoption of Mechanical Drying	239
8.15	Kolkata's Rice Retail Markets, 2000	245
9.1	Domestic Liberalization of Rice	263
9.2	Composition of State-controlled Supply	274
9.3	Quotas and Off-take of Rice and Wheat under the Targeted PDS in West Bengal, 1999–2000	282

Figures, Maps, and Appendices

Figures
2.1	The Physical and Economic System of Circulation	24
4.1	Rice Processing Technologies Birbhum District	73
4.2	Structural Elements of the Rice Circulation System, Birbhum District to Calcutta 1981–82	76
4.3	Paddy and Rice Prices, Birbhum District Rs/Quintal 1977–81	93
4.4	Net Profits, Rs/Quintal, Rice Processing, Birbhum, 1981, (non levy rice)	95
6.1	Commodity Systems Studied in Bardhaman District	149
8.1	Trends in Prices of Different Varieties during 1997–8 to 2001–2	216
8.2	Elements of the System of Rice Markets, 2002	220

Maps
1. S. Asia, India, and West Bengal	xviii
2. West Bengal: Birbhum and Bardhaman Districts	51
3. Calcutta/Kolkata	243

Appendices
1.1	Field Methodology	321
2.1	Marx's Merchant's Capital and its Influence in India	334
4.1	The Processing of Rice	339
4.2	The Process of Accumulation, 1982	351
4.3	Price Behaviour 1977 to 1980	359
6.1	Details of the Official Price Data	362
6.2	Price Integration Models and Results 1988 to 1990	365
7.1	Investment Portfolios in Bardhaman and Birbhum–1990	371
7.2	Collective Action in Markets	375
8.1	Exports and Imports: West Bengal and Other States of India	379
9.1	Price Collapse	381
10.1	Political Parties in West Bengal (% seat shares)	384

Inflators/Deflators

FOOD PRICE INFLATORS / DEFLATORS
Oct 2001	427	100
Oct 1990	194	45
Oct 1980	100	23

GENERAL INFLATORS / DEFLATORS
Oct 2001	449	100
Oct 1990	197	37
Oct 1980	100	22

Notes: Derived from the Price Index for Rural Agricultural Labour, West Bengal. Base years for the price indexes are 1960–1 and 1986–7. To reconcile the two bases, conversion factors of 6.07 were applied to the 1960–1 base for the General Index and 6.49 for the Food Index. These factors were based on the average General and Food Indexes for the entire year 1986–7.

Exchange Rates

RUPEES EXPRESSED AGAINST £ STERLING
1981–2	:	14
1990	:	40
1997	:	57
2001	:	67
2003	:	75

Preface and Acknowledgements

The story of this book begins in 1978 when the path of the late Professor Boudhayan Chattopadhyay, then Director of the ambitious project on *Food Systems and Society in Eastern India*, crossed mine at a meeting on Food Systems held in Queen Elizabeth House, Oxford. Impossible to imagine then that nine years later, I would join Queen Elizabeth House (QEH), and that twenty eight years later I would be finishing research inspired by that meeting. However, by 1978, I had become addicted to the study of markets. Long spells of field work on grain markets in Tamil Nadu, Sri Lanka, Bangladesh and Francophone West Africa had already confirmed the reaction I had had when driving to India to climb mountains in 1969—for which it had been necessary to cross Punjab in the ferment of the Green Revolution. Without markets we don't get to consume food; the drama of accumulation is played out in India in marketplaces; despite the facts that fossil fuel drives global capitalism—and that our food is sodden with fossil energy—food, water and human labour remain the basis of any market economy. So staple food markets are a valuable key-hole through which to view the rest.

In 1981–2, at Professor Chattopadhyay's request, John Harriss and I spent four months in West Bengal as members of the United Nations Research for Social Development Food Systems (UNRISD's) Project, first in Calcutta. I expected to work on data already collected on markets in Kalahandi but there were glitches with some of the eight million punch cards on which the data were recorded. Instead I did first hand field work based in Santiniketan under the guidance of Sunil Sengupta, an agrarian economist who had acted as an adviser to the Food Systems project. I was asked to find out about the extent and kind of autonomy displayed by agricultural markets and how the rice marketing sub-system meshed with the sub-systems of production and consumption. The systems framework was certainly useful as an ordering device, but it was sometimes difficult to distinguish structure from relationship, and endogenous perturbations from exogenous shocks. Was the state endogenous or exogenous? Was money a stock and a structure or a flow and a relation? The 1982 field-work in Birbhum district observed markets at the kink point in the process of agrarian transformation after a long phase of mediocre growth and fluctuation in production.

In 1990, I was able to return, this time to Bardhaman district, thanks to a generous invitation from Professors Amartya Sen and Sunil Sengupta, to spend an intensive six weeks in the field and to participate in their project run from the (UNU) United Nations University's World Institute for Development Eeconomics Research in Helsinki: '*Rural Development and Poverty in Eastern India*'. I was asked to find out what the implications of the ongoing transformation of the marketing system might be for the Left Front Government (LFG). I found that the Left Front Government was preoccupied with the reforms in the structure of production, and had little appreciation of the significance of either radical or reformist policy for markets. Indeed, it had what looked (and still looks) like a cosy relationship with a 'rurban' bourgeoisie far richer and more powerful than the village-level agrarian bourgeoisie and rich peasantry, to whose politics so much carbon paper and toner have been dedicated. Meanwhile, the marketing system was polarized and being wrenched from the rule of law to that of custom, the opposite of what the progressive development of markets is usually taken to involve.

Between 2000 and 2004, I was able to return on short, focussed bursts of field work, and with the help of two young researchers, Sutapa Choudhury and P.K. Ghosh, able to update this work. Professor Sengupta once more ensured that I got off to a good start with research into the Food Administration in Kolkata and even came with me to talk to rice millers in Bolpur. But he died in 2001.

This project has been completed in his memory.

Over these years, I co-directed a Department for International Development (DFID)-funded project on *Trade Liberalisation and India's Informal Economy* in which members of QEH collaborated with a team from the National Council of Applied Economic Research (NCAER), New Delhi. Under the auspices of this project (which compared the insights of field work with those from a CGE model), the impact of the long delayed but now considerable domestic market liberalization on registered rice processing firms could be compared with its impact on informal firms—and the useful concept of informality could itself be problematized (see Barbara Harriss-White and Anushree Sinha (eds), *Trade Liberalization and India's Informal Economy*, New Delhi, 2007, OUP). I was able to conduct rapid research into other parts of the system of markets and, with P.K. Ghosh, could not avoid observing the crisis of poor returns to agriculture, and of paralysis in the public sector distribution system which built up unprecedently mountainous food reserves—a crisis due to the politics of de-regulation. I also supervised Sutapa Choudhury's M. Phil. field research on the non-state, social regulation of rice retailing in Kolkata.

Those who originally invited me knew, and know, how enormously rewarding all these opportunities were, and how much they have been appreciated. First and foremost I am grateful to the owners of hundreds of commercial firms who have spared time to discuss the markets and their business histories with me. I am grateful to UNRISD for meeting the costs of the 1981–2 research, to the World Institute for Development Economic Research (WIDER) for meeting those of 1990, and to DFID, the British Council, the Oxford University Webb Medley and Beit Funds, and Wolfson College, Oxford for meeting those of the period 2000–4. On all three occasions, two people provided all the practical help, friendship, and intellectual nutrition a foreign researcher could ever wish for: Sunil Sengupta and Madan Ghosh, who had spent long periods of their lives working at the Agro-Economic Research Centre (AERC) in Visva Bharati.

I wish to thank Dilip Chatterjee and Pundarik Mukherjee, both students of the Department of Economics, Visva Bharati and P.K. Ghosh (assisted by Swagata Mondal) of the NCAER, for their enthusiastic and capable research assistance under not the easiest of conditions. In NCAER, I am grateful to Dr Abusaleh Shariff for having seconded Ghosh, and to Dr Rupinder Kaur and Ratna Sudarshan for energetically taking on field work on rice processing in Punjab as well as West Bengal, a subject that was new to all of them. I am grateful to Sutapa Choudhury for having chosen to study rice retailing in Kolkata; it has enlivened the second update. I also want to thank John Harriss for being a great co-researcher in 1982 and to remember the late Mrs R. Pubadi, who was willing to travel from Coonoor in Tamil Nadu to care for our young daughter then with much initiative and a keen sense of fun. ('They do speak funny Telugu round here', she observed quizzically in Tamil on the Visva Bharati campus).

I could not have completed this research without help from a number of people whom I cannot name. I am most beholden to them all. They include officials in the Department of Statistics, the Food Department, the West Bengal Co-operative Bank, the West Bengal Finance Corporation, the FCI, and the FCI Employees Union, the Kisan Sabha, and at various levels the West Bengal Rice Millers' Association and the Chamber of Commerce. I also wish to thank the staff of the Rama

Krishna Mission in Kolkata because, as is the case with so many foreign scholars, their International Guest House has been a haven for me ever since my first visit in 1980.

I think that the late Professor Biplab Dasgupta, MP, of Calcutta University knew how much I valued his reactions to my argument, and his advice. I am grateful to Professors Nripen Bandhopadhyay of the Centre for Studies in Social Sciences (CSSSC), Suman Sarkar of Visva Bharathi, Graham Chapman of Lancaster University and Donald Michie; also to Drs Jairus Banaji, Jyotish Basu, Sudipto Bhattacharyya, Pinaki Chatterjee, Sanjib Mukhopadhyay, and D.K Lahiri Choudhury for fruitful discussions, criticism, and all kinds of practical help. I was able to put a line under this project thanks to a Visiting Fellowship at the Centre des Etudes de L'Inde et de L'Asie du Sud, EHESS, Paris. There, Pierre Lachaier, Frederic Landy, Claude Markovits, Jean-Luc Racine, and Denis Vidal spared time to ask and answer some very interesting questions during a distracting month in which French academics took frequently to the streets. They, along with Ben Crow (now at UC Santa Cruz), the Development Policy and Practice team at the British Open University and Ben Rogaly (now at Sussex University), have all helped to put my field work into comparative perspective. Many thanks also to Theodosios Palaskas (then of QEH, now at Athens University) for his lead in collaborating on the innovative econometric analyses of prices; to Dr Wendy Olsen (now at Manchester University) and Susan Erb (now in Darfur) who made the first moves towards transforming the two earliest field reports into the book you may be about to read. I am grateful to Oxford postgraduate students Ravi Ahmad-Haque, Proochista Ariana, Conrad Barwa, Nadir Cheema, Yoon Kim, Emma Samman, and Swagato Sarkar; for excellent assistance from Denise Watt and Rachel Crawford at QEH, and Nigel James at the Bodleian Library Map Room—all of whom have cheerfully helped in the physical production of this book. I also wish to thank the team at OUP, New Delhi, and the anonymous readers who made very useful and constructive comments. Alice Thorner nominated me for the fellowship which enabled me to finish the first complete draft and had been keenly interested in its themes; but Alice died in 2005. I would like to think that the dedicatee of this book would have enjoyed sharing some of this tribute with her. Lastly, insofar as the argument interests an audience wider than that of scholars of West Bengal, it is in large measure due to discussion with—and advice about textual clarifications from—Colin Leys. It would surely not have seen the light of day without his encouragement.

This preface would not be complete without warmly acknowledging the family of Sasanka Mukherjee, especially Saumik and Sumi, who took the project to their hearts. They have helped gather (and translate) research materials and continued to mull over findings originally discussed on Sunil-da's verandah. It is only because my field work was so thoroughly interrogated by him that I have the confidence to present it in his memory. Where I have got it wrong, it is certainly no-one's fault but my own.

August 2007   BARBARA HARRISS-WHITE

Professor Sunil Sengupta
(July 1927–May 2001)

Sunil Sengupta was born on 26 July 26 1927 in Sylhet in what is now Bangladesh, into the family (of nine brothers and four sisters) of Suresh and Bijon Sengupta. After his schooldays, he was admitted to B.M. College, Barisal, where his father was Principal, and immediately was drawn into left-democratic student politics. Having completed his college education, he moved to Calcutta (where his father had had a fine family house built at Lake Place) and was admitted to Presidency College where he read for an M.A. in Economics. Once again he combined studies with political activism in the Student Federation. From there he joined the Communist Party, where he made many friends and comrades and started work both as a political journalist in the 'Swadhinata' (freedom) newspaper and as an activist. Arrested by the British, he endured the experience of a hunger strike in Alipur Jail. In 1953, he was arrested for a second time when covering the mass agitation against the Tram Fare price hike.

In 1954, however, he joined the newly formed Agro-Economics Research Centre (AERC) at Visva Bharati, Santiniketan, one of the networks of such centres covering India which produced much work of lasting importance. He was inspired by Rabindranath Tagore's ideas about rural development and Gandhiji's project to create a Panchayati Raj in order to decentralize power to the villages. He was also impressed by the thought and work of Ashutosh Sen, and had visited Dr. Sen's workplace in Sriniketan. He was to spend most of his career in the AERC (although in fact his working life never stopped) starting out as a Field Investigator and finishing as its Director.

From that moment on, there issued a stream of papers and monographs on agriculture and rural development in West Bengal and adjacent states. For the most part, they were published by the AERC where they can be found in the library and are consulted and used to this day. He visited and studied the Santhal regions of Bihar (now Jharkhand) and Orissa and wrote about tribal economy and society. During his long tenure at the AERC, he came into close contact with Amartya Sen. Together in 1982–3 they researched and wrote an influential paper on child malnutrition and the sex bias, based on field work in Kuchli and Sahajapur villages nearby and published it in 1983 in *Economic and Political Weekly*.

Later in the 1980s, Sunil Sengupta came to Palli Charcha Kendra (Visva Bharati's Rural Development Centre) at Sriniketan, which he directed.

On his retirement from Visva Bharati, he began a new era of research, turning to direct a project (with Amartya Sen as Adviser, financed by the World Institute for Development Economics Research—WIDER—in Helsinki). Housed in Visva Bharati, it examined 'rural poverty, social change, and public policy' and ran for four years, feeding results into *Indian Development: Selected Regional Perspectives* (eds) Jean Drèze and Amartya Sen (OUP 1997). He was to organize and supervize three more projects, one on 'social and natural resource use' for the International Development Research Centre (IDRC, Canada), a second on the 'role of panchayats' for the Planning Commission and last, 'the socio-economic status of vulnerable women in West Bengal' for Oxfam.

Through these projects, many research scholars and social and left-political activists (both from within India and abroad) came into contact with him. They were stimulated by his erudition and wisdom, entertained by his warmth, his mischievous wit and his story-telling, impressed by his stoicism and courage, help in many practical ways. They were always asked to give account of their findings—either at impromptu gatherings of students and neighbours in his home or at scholarly meetings in Visva Bharati. All were encouraged to be critical in their work and were subjected in turn to the most constructive of criticism.

In the year 2000, he was invited by the University of Bath, UK, to deliver a lecture at a seminar on 'Global Social Policy' in Bangladesh. He used the occasion to return to his ancestral home where he and his family were greeted with great warmth. What was special to him was his receptivity, his generosity, and his freedom from any class or caste prejudice. He was a foul-weather friend to his friends and a great sheltering tree to his family.

His wife, Bina, died in 1995. He himself died on 11 May 2001, leaving his daughter Sumita, son-in-law Saumik Mukherjee and grand daughter Sailee.

He is remembered by scholars of rural development worldwide.

SAUMIK MUKHERJEE AND BARBARA HARRISS-WHITE

Source: Bodleian Library Map Collection, Oxford University.

Map 1: S. Asia, India, and West Bengal

1 Introduction
How the Successes and Failures of West Bengal's Agriculture are Affected by its Agricultural Markets

This book is about the way markets for agricultural commodities have influenced, and are important determinants of the performance of agriculture in the state that is now India's leading 'rice bowl', West Bengal. To those directly involved in agricultural production and agro-processing, this is not in the least surprising. But those who make policies in the World Bank, and those who have to pay attention to them in the all-India and West Bengal ministries responsible for agriculture, and numerous other policy areas on which agriculture depends, have not yet grasped the reasons for the importance of these markets, nor have many mainstream economists.

West Bengal's seemingly paradoxical history of agricultural stagnation, followed by rapid advance, subsequently by renewed relative stagnation—and of growth associated with poverty—can only be explained once the nature of the state's agricultural markets is taken into account. The research needed for this task is unavoidably time-consuming and local; for this book it involved three periods of fieldwork spread over more than two decades, most of it in two districts of West Bengal. Generalizing from such local findings is risky, but it is less risky than making policies in ignorance of the way real markets are actually working, as a result of which well-intentioned policies all too often lead to the reverse of what is intended, or hoped for.

This chapter outlines the central argument of the book as a whole. Chapter 2 sets out the main conceptual tools needed for analysing markets, and Chapter 3 provides an outline history of agricultural commodity markets in West Bengal up to the last decades of the twentieth century, when most of the fieldwork for this book was undertaken. The rest of the book consists of three pairs of chapters, one for each period studied (that is 1980–1, 1990, and 2000–2), and concluding with Chapter 10, which brings all the findings together and outlines their implications for government policy, as well as for economic theory.

West Bengal has gone from being a fertile but deficit state, which was the site of the worst South Asian famine in the modern era, (see the contrasting accounts in Sen, 1981 and Chattopadhyay, 1991a) to being the top-ranking rice-producing state in India, with a surplus for export (Government of West Bengal, 2002; Ghosh and Sudarshan, 2003). Yet, despite the Left Front Government's early resolve to bring relief to deprived sections of society, West Bengal is still low in the ranking of India's states in terms of poverty, nutrition, health, and education.[1] Those who argue that the prime mover of growth has been Left Front Government's agrarian reforms of the 1980s have to explain West Bengal's persistent and multi-dimensional agrarian poverty. This has much to do with the character of its markets for staple food. The firms that control the journey of the marketed surplus from farms to the metropolitan consumer have had a declining interest in land and every interest in encouraging new agricultural technology once it became available. But the way in which they have controlled the marketed surplus has prevented agrarian poverty from being reduced.[2]

West Bengal's agricultural markets are the manifestation of a persistent form of commercial capitalism, in which agricultural production is controlled through money advances. The system of circulation and post-harvest production is polarized: on the one hand, there is a large sub-circuit of petty trade, and on the other, a numerically small sub-circuit of large rice mills. Petty commodity production and trade has mostly taken the form of seasonal livelihoods which are essential not only to the system of circulation but also to the survival of petty production in agriculture itself. Meanwhile, the big mills have increasingly become the property of non-landed fractions of the business class. Using money advances to preserve their indirect control over the primary production structure, and to tie their suppliers to themselves so long as agriculture grew rapidly, they were able to stave off any threat to their supplies that might have arisen from small-scale traders buying from the producers.

Not only have the reforms in production not been matched by any reform in the structure of control in rice markets, but for most of the last quarter century, the Left Front Government has been reinforcing the old pattern. While attacking the elite agricultural producers and redistributing resources to the agricultural poor, it was at the same time protecting the privileges of the agro-commercial elite, and actively penalizing the agro-commercial poor. Its interest in protecting the agro-commercial elite lay in keeping down the costs of state procurement and trading. Meanwhile, the agro-commercial elite actively developed its 'clientelage' to the state to a point where it exercised decisive power over its 'patron'.

West Bengal is not exceptional in this respect; it is only exceptional in having been ruled in a stable way for three decades by a democratically elected Communist front, which has been dedicated to eradicating middlemen as well as poverty. As a result of this political accommodation, petty trade has been actively prevented from developing in such a way that it could threaten the agro-commercial elite. This elite has not just reinforced the dependence of petty trade on itself, but has also made sure that price margins keep the returns to most petty production relatively low. Only after West Bengal went into surplus, did this structure undergo rapid change, and then not as a result of the political dynamics of the Left Front Government but due to pressure from the 'National Democratic Alliance' (NDA) in New Delhi, and lobbying from local agri-business interests.

The public distribution of food, under the control of both state and central governments, has had an ambivalent track record. Since India's Independence, it has been successful enough in provisioning the cities and staving off famine; but it has been unable to vanquish under-nutrition in West Bengal in the period under consideration. In the 1980s, for instance, the decade of land reforms, the proportion of adequately nourished village children increased from an appalling low of 12 per cent to a mere 21 per cent.[3] If the Left Front Government had not capitulated to the dominant agro-commercial class and had developed a coherent policy (linked to but separate from production policy) for the agro-commercial petty bourgeoisie that was emerging in rural areas, then the gains from trade would have been spread more equally, and much more widely—and the balance between returns to agro-commerce and returns to production might also have been less disadvantageous to production.[4] Production incentives would have been enhanced, conditions would have been created for agricultural labour to claim a higher proportion of the distributive share,[5] and the agricultural miracle would have had a manifest impact on rural poverty.

The story of a decade of sustained agricultural growth in West Bengal, after decades of backwardness and mediocre performance, only to be followed by a relapse over the period of liberalization, is well known. Between 1965 and 1980, agriculture grew at an annual average of 2.3 per cent. Then, over the period 1983–4 to 1991–2, the annual rate of growth increased to somewhere between 4.3 per cent and 6.9 per cent,[6] but slumped back to an average of 2.4 per cent in the 1990s (Banerjee and Kundu, 2001). The Left Front Government in West Bengal is rightly acclaimed for its achievements in rural economic and political development, notably through land reforms (*Operation Barga*), the decentralization of local government (panchayats), the provision of production credit and the enforcement of a gender-blind minimum wage,[7] and most analysts have attributed West Bengal's success in increasing production to one or more of these policies.[8] But the key to making sense of the pattern is agricultural markets. To some extent, the state's growth occurred despite them, but in other ways markets were crucial determinants of growth. With a focus on markets, this book offers a different account of these years, with different policy conclusions. It builds a critique—intended to be constructive—of the Left Front Government's policy towards markets for staple food.

West Bengal's Agrarian Transformation and Agricultural Achievement

Accounts of West Bengal's backward agriculture and poor performance have exposed its peculiarly fragmented and miniaturized landholding structure. When the Left Front Government was voted into power in 1977, 70 per cent of land holdings, twice the all-India average, were under 1 ha even though the landholding structure was already considerably less unequal than that of the country as a whole (Government of West Bengal, 1988–9; Sengupta and Gazder, 1998, pp. 133–42). It goes without saying that the mass of small cultivators were pauperized. A decade into the era of the Left Front Government, 'nearly three-fifths of the rural population... [still] lived below the poverty line' (Sengupta and Gazder, 1998, p. 129). James Boyce has argued convincingly that it was inequality coupled with the fragmentation of land holdings which prevented collective action necessary for the establishment of the forms of water control needed to propel agriculture out of its backward state (Boyce, 1987).

This structuralist explanation of West Bengal's agricultural underdevelopment did not end there, however. West Bengal was also the epicentre of a type of rental tenure, sharecropping, in which up to 75 per cent of the crop went not to the tiller but to the land-owner. Sharecropping has been the subject of a great variety of theories, (Byres, 1983; Majid, 1994), few of which were empirically verifiable and most of which rested on a stylized simplification of the widely varied conditions under which sharecropping was, and still is, actually

Introduction

practised, but few people have doubted that it was one of the key causes of rural poverty. In West Bengal, however, the sharecropper was also at the base of a 'sub-infeudated' rental hierarchy, topped by a parasitic *zamindari* class (established as tax collectors early on under British rule). Zamindars were abolished shortly after Independence in 1951, but a class of landlords-cum-moneylenders retained a stranglehold over land, labour, money, and commodity markets. This comprehensive interlocking of markets, it was argued, not only discouraged sharecroppers from adopting new production technology but also kept them at a subsistence level of poverty.[9]

Another strand of explanation found fault with the state. The synergy between public investment and private capital formation is well established, so the state's failure to develop canal irrigation and drainage and other infrastructure, such as rural roads, electricity, credit, marketplaces and agricultural extension, was said to have contributed to agrarian backwardness.[10] There was also no relevant high yielding variety (HYV) technology of rice for rainfed conditions in general, or for the main *aman* (monsoon) season during which 75 per cent of West Bengal's rice crop was produced. As a result, there was a relatively low level of both supply and demand for fertilizers at a time when other regions of India were being transformed by the Green Revolution (J. Harriss, 1982).

The decade before the Left Front took power was, moreover, a period of rural political strife as movements for land redistribution gained strength and direct actions took place, including the 'outing' of landlords' concealed holdings, land seizures, and violence against the landed elite. Once in power, the Left Front Government had to deal with this unrest as a matter of urgency and set about a programme of agrarian reforms that contained elements of redistribution, transformation of production, and democratic participation.

Between 1981–2 and 1991–2 foodgrains output grew faster in West Bengal than anywhere else in India (Sengupta and Gazder, 1997; Saha and Swaminathan, 1994). Estimates of the annual growth rates vary between 4.3 and 9 per cent.[11] There is a significant body of research devoted to explanations for this change in the trend and for discrepancies in the estimated rate, because the change happened under Left Front Government rule. Differences in the base-line and end-periods within which the rates are calculated make a difference to the resulting growth rate. The conventional base-line of 1981–2 was a time of very low rainfall when production was affected by drought, so adopting it exaggerates the subsequent rate of growth. Changes in the way crop production estimates have been made over the period are also thought to have led to an overestimation of growth.[12] But growth certainly occurred, and there is no doubt that it was due to increased yields in the main *aman* (*monsoon*) and minor *aus* (June–September) seasons, and to a massive increase in the acreage cultivated in the dry *boro* season (January-May) (Government of West Bengal, 1995–6; Table 5.2).

The fast growth of the years 1981–92 has been chiefly explained as the result of a bundle of reforms in agrarian structure. Two factors have been credited to the Left Front Government : land reforms and decentralized local government.[13] Although land reforms had been initiated under the Congress Party and United Front rule, and nearly 630,000 acres had been distributed to nearly one million households, another wave of redistribution of land in excess of the legal ceilings— a total of 140,000 acres—took place in the early years of the Left Front Government. From 1977 to 1983, land was assigned to just under half a million households, and during the years 1983–91 to just over half a million more (60–70 per cent of landless labour households, the majority being Scheduled Castes and Tribes, were provided with plots of 0.3 acres each).[14] In addition, house plots were allocated to 250,000 agricultural labour households. And even more redistribution took place through sales and purchase than through redistribution by the state.[15] Yet, despite these unprecedented property transfers, the Gini coefficient of landholding inequality only declined from 0.65 to 0.63— that is, a decline not much better than the all-India trend (Rogaly et al., 1995).

Over the same period, under Operation Barga, some 1.4m of an estimated total of 2m sharecroppers (*bargadars*) had their tenures registered. This had two important consequences: first, the terms of their share tenure were reduced and fixed at 33 per cent, and second, registration made sharecroppers eligible for production credit from co-operatives and state-regulated banks. But these changes in security affected only 8 per cent of the net sown area, and only one third of that changed status under the Left Front Government (Bandhyopadhyay, 1993, 2003). By themselves these reforms could not possibly have accounted for the doubling or trebling of the growth rate that was achieved.[16]

As for local government, from as early as 1978, the government pioneered a decentralized form of political representation and governance via a hierarchy of panchayats (a *gram panchayat* for every

10 villages, a block panchayat for 100, and a district panchayat for roughly 1000), so by the mid-1990s half the outlay in the State Plan was being administered through panchayats. (Kohli, 1987; Thorlind, 2000). But they had limited powers to raise and spend revenue. The panchayats were not responsible for negotiating the contentious reformed and standardized sharecropping ratio, and they could not improve the electricity supplies necessary for private irrigation. They did organize improvements to roads, and roads have a clear (though little-celebrated) effect on agricultural productivity (Wanmali and Ramasamy, 1994). The government also made panchayats responsible for enforcing district-level minimum wages, to make sure that the distribution of gains from agricultural growth included agricultural labourers (Westergaard, 1986). Minimum wages set the basic terms of agricultural employment for six to eight months of the year.[17] They are undercut, however, by the prevalent use of non-local migrant labour. (Rogaly, 2002; Rogaly and Rafique, 2003; and Rogaly et al., 2003). But the literature on the role of panchayats in agricultural growth emphasizes representation and participation by the mass of peasant smallholders, which is said to have had a positive impact on total factor productivity. This worked through an 'x-efficiency' factor created by politicization and by striking improvements in people's access to resources. Claims could now be made by small producers for electricity, agro-chemicals and the state credit targeted at poor households, and for increasing their assets under the Integrated Rural Development Programme (Swaminathan, 1994). Much of the funding for such development projects came from the central government, so the panchayats gave villages in West Bengal a direct link to New Delhi. (Whether this link is properly understood as decentralization or is the very opposite is still being questioned) (Basu, 2002, p. 344).

The Left Front Government's rural development project was of course not confined to changes in structure and government. It extended systematically to all the major 'factors of production' and their markets. Land registration made the newly secure tenants eligible for credit. Credit for agricultural production was directed to the poor not through producer co-ops but through co-operative banks (Ramachandran, 1997; Basu, 2002; p. 329). As in other parts of India, this credit was captured by the producers of the marketed surplus, some of whom were both landowners and sharecroppers. New HYV rice became available for the main aman season. Fertilizer and pesticide distribution networks were established. Real wages for agricultural labour increased and there was a dramatic and widely-noted surge in investment in private irrigation wells. But none of these interventions make a convincing explanation for the doubling of growth. West Bengal's uptake of agricultural credit was found to be 'disproportionately low', as was its use of agro-chemicals—in fact it was lower in the 1980s than in the 1970s, though the balance between nutrients may have improved.[18] And the introduction of HYVs was not as important as the extension of production to the two smaller seasons—boro and aus. Rice yields persisted in following the all-India average.[19] While there is no doubt about a rise in agricultural wages, the nature of the relationship between wage levels and agricultural output is unresolved, for the real rise in wages is about the average for all-India, while agricultural growth has been much above the average. (Rawal and Swaminathan, 1998; Sarkar, 2006). Did wages rise because of the power of local panchayats to enforce a district-level, gender-blind minimum wage? Was the minimum wage a distant goal for struggle rather than a policy enforced by the Left Front? Did the rise in wages translate into a rise in incomes sufficient to act as a production incentive? Answers to these questions remain inconclusive. Could the 17 per cent increase in public irrigation between the arrival of the Left Front Government and 1995–6 have triggered the massive development by the agricultural elite of Shallow Tube Wells (up 130 per cent in 1981–7) and Deep Tube Wells (up 50 per cent between 1989–96)?[20] Neil Webster, who investigated the emergence of waterlords, found that private irrigation and water markets were dominated by large cultivators who used these transactions as a way of renting land from pauperized producers (Webster, 1994). Moitra and Das, in state-wide research on private investment in groundwater, provide evidence that casts doubt on the taken-for-granted public-private synergy. They find that the relation in West Bengal is complex and 'not robust' and depends crucially on geophysical conditions. In some regions, reliable canal water is actually a disincentive to private investment.[21] Attempts to examine all these factors suggest that the sharp change in growth rates cannot be generally explained by either infrastructure or inputs alone (Mukherjee and Mukhopadhyay, 1995).

So major debates persist over how much change there was, and how much of the change was due to which of these factors. Did the rain-fed agriculture of the poverty-belt of north East India (of which West Bengal was the emblematic state) merely lag behind, or was growth actively obstructed by structural factors?[22] Was the lag in public

Introduction

and private sector agricultural research induced by low factor prices, or did it proceed on its own slow, autonomous track to find solutions to low insolation (cloudy) harvests (in aman), to wet harvests (in boro), and to the simultaneous incidence of drought and flood? Was the unprecedentedly sustained increase in agricultural wages, which accompanied the growth of output, a labour-market phenomenon resulting from a tightening of the labour market due to increased demand for labour in boro and aus? Or was it due to state action and the implementation of the minimum wage in support of organized agricultural labour? To what extent was it political stability itself, rather than particular government policies, which released growth (since higher growth also occurred in Bangladesh and other adjacent states of eastern India)? Could the participative politics of panchayats really have empowered the mass of peasant smallholders, irrespective of their party-political composition? Why were panchayats run by the Left Front Government found to be patchy in their effectiveness? (Williams, 1999). Middle castes and classes have been shown to have benefited from decentralization to a far greater degree than the mass of Scheduled Caste/Scheduled Tribe (SC/ST) landless agricultural labourers. (Ruud, 1999; Bhattacharya, 1999). No consensus has emerged, not the least because many important lines of enquiry have proved researchable only at a micro level, from which it is not easy to generalize.[23]

The debates over agriculture have also focussed on rice, but while rice production rose, and the debates on the causes of the rise gathered pace, major changes in land use diversification also occurred. Land granted to other cereals, dry grains, pulses, and gram shrank alarmingly. But in the period from the start of the Left Front Government to 1990–1, oilseeds production increased 6.4 times, jute 2.4 times, and vegetables 2.8 times, due to increases in both area and yield.[24] Vegetables meant potatoes. In Bardhaman district, for example, potato production expanded at 10 per cent a year throughout the 1980s, and by the early 1990s, West Bengal was recording the highest potato yields in India (Saha and Swaminathan, 1994; 150 per cent of the all-India average).

In the 1990s, West Bengal surged to self-sufficiency in rice, and in 1992–3 achieved its first, fragile rice surplus. Over the tenure of the Left Front Government, West Bengal's share in India's total rice production more than doubled, from 7 per cent to 16 per cent. By 2001–2, the state was producing 15 m tonnes and had become India's leading rice-producing state (Government of West Bengal, 2002). Yet from 1992 onwards, the growth rate in rice production faltered, dropping back to at most half the rate that had been achieved in the 1980s. While there was a very small increase in canal irrigation in West Bengal over the years 1980–95, the two rice bowl districts we studied recorded declines. (Government of West Bengal, 1996; Table 5.13; p. 95). Despite a rise in the proportion of total agricultural labour that was hired, the growth rate of hired agricultural labour decelerated. Over the decade of the 1990s, the share of total agricultural income taken by wage labour fell from 30 per cent to 26 per cent, and the elasticity of absorption of hired labour headed towards negative. (Abhijit Sen, 2002; p. 402–4). Ominously, given these trends in agricultural production, West Bengal was also recording decelerating growth rates of rural non-agricultural employment, worsening income distribution, an increase in the headcount under the poverty line,[25] and an unimpressive performance in other sectors of the economy.[26]

Yet scholars searching for the causes of slowing agricultural growth rates have focussed neither on the structural factors reviewed earlier, nor on the more general failings of the local state. Instead, they have pinpointed the reforms instituted by the central government during the time in office of the Congress from 1991 to 1997 and the National Democratic Alliance led by the Bharatiya Janata Party from 1997 to 2004.

In 1993, the central government decontrolled fertilizers and lifted the subsidy from two of the three major nutrients. This had such a catastrophic impact on the balance of nutrients—with a multiplier effect on yields—that subsidies were restored (Landy, 1997). Capital investment in infrastructure has also seized up. It is not that there is no longer a synergistic relation between public and private investment and productivity; it is that public investment has atrophied, and the kind of private investment substituting for it hardly qualifies as 'rural development'. In the case of private irrigation, for example, over-pumping has actively undermined rural development by pauperizing those unable to gain access to the water table and by releasing arsenic in soluble form from the seasonally dehydrated clay aquifer.[27]

State-directed rural credit was also hobbled by the central government: liberalization allowed rural banks the freedom to retreat from the countryside to the towns, and from those regions which had gained most from bank nationalization; to reduce their lending to agriculture; and to small producers; and to raise real interest rates (Ramachandran and Swaminathan, 2005).

Liberalization has also involved the piecemeal removal of domestic and international 'movement' (trade) restrictions, as well as discrepancies between domestic and world market prices. While in the late 1990s, the export of non-aromatic rice was still controlled by the parastatal Food Corporation of India (FCI), the world market was undergoing a collapse due largely to the assiduous protection of US domestic rice farmers at times when world market prices were undercutting domestic US ones. The backwash of this protectionism on the thin and volatile world rice market, in the shape of the wave of supplies caused by simultaneous liberalization in South East and South Asia, slashed prices. This then reinforced the conditions giving rise to domestic protection in the US, and entirely reversed the 25 per cent rise in nominal domestic rice prices achieved over the decade of the nineties (Gulati and Narayanan, 2002; Vakulabharanam, 2005; p. 977).

The study of agricultural poverty carried out by Madan Ghosh in West Bengal in the late 1990s notes two further factors: first, the drying up of funds for—and the signal failures in the implementation of— the central government's main 'anti-poverty policy', the Integrated Rural Development Programme which subsidized agricultural assets for poor households; and second, the severe degradation, privatization, and informal commercialization of common property resources such as forests and culturable waste which provide dietary supplements. These are not part of the official process of liberalization and not controlled by either central or state governments, even though they ought to be. He concludes that agricultural poverty is 'intractable' (Ghosh, 1998). So there are at least five plausible reasons why agricultural growth faltered and agrarian poverty persisted.

Commodity Markets

These debates on West Bengal's remarkable transition from deficit to surplus status, and the rise and fall of the agricultural growth rate, are notable for one glaring omission: they pay no attention to the system of commodity markets through which this transformation occurred—or at best they take them into account as 'stylized facts'; not as empirically analysed processes. Actually-existing markets are ignored, and it is the aim of this book to repair that omission. But while explanations for agricultural growth may be incomplete in not incorporating the role of commodity markets, does that make them wrong? Does the introduction of commodity markets into the analysis change the explanation?

I argue that it does, for the following reasons. The established agro-commercial elite mounted no serious opposition to the Left Front's reforms. Once a commodified production technology had been developed which was appropriate to local agro-ecological conditions, the agro-commercial elite made no attempt to prevent its diffusion. They were already moving some of their assets out of agricultural production proper to be invested in other sectors of the economy. But in respect of what remained, they had a keen interest in supplies, and in the continued defence of their capacity to control supplies and prices, they did so through webs of money advances. To this end, throughout the entire period of Left Front rule, the primary interest of the agro-commercial elite lay in the defence of their access to state-regulated and private credit which ensured their supplies, the reduction of commercial risk, and the defence of the price margins which ensured both their profits and control of labour. Meanwhile, agricultural growth staved off the threat that their supplies would be undercut and diverted by petty trade.

The last point was crucially important, because petty trade in food staples expresses a powerful dynamic. The combination of an immense metropolis, whose own great industrial bases are unravelling, together with local agrarian structures has served to concentrate the extraction of physical and financial surplus and shift them to Kolkata, or to other regions. West Bengal has unusually few market towns, and the local non-farm rural (or 'rurban') economy has not been well developed. The rice and other staple food markets constitute one of the very few local outlets for small-scale savings and investment. This petty trade is unlicensed, socially regulated, and often seasonal. Rather than being supplied by capitalist retail food firms regulated by the state, significant proportions of the populations of Kolkata and the other cities of the coal belt become dependent for their most basic food supplies on a myriad illegal petty traders and the shadowy wholesalers they are forced both to sell to and to buy from.

Under the Left Front, petty trade has not just been passively neglected; its development has been actively thwarted by a reluctance to legitimate or finance it. The rice mills, on the other hand, have been actively protected, because several interests have been satisfied by this protection. The state has had an enduring interest in minimizing the costs of procurement for its public food distribution system. Local commercial capital has an enduring interest in capturing state finance and infrastructure, which is a major way of reducing business risk.

If the dominant commercial class had an interest in agricultural growth, the 1990s saw it caught in both an ideological and a practical bind. Because of its interest in increasing supplies and in protecting its rates of return, and its returns to scale, it worked politically towards deregulation, but not at the expense of protected access to state credit for new technology, or of contracts which minimized commercial risk. Unable to prevent the destructive aspects of deregulation and decelerating growth, it worked politically to secure a structure of intervention, which continues to protect its interests by making it difficult for petty trade to grow. Petty trade does grow nevertheless, but its growth is constrained due to squalid and makeshift market sites, limited access to state-regulated finance and petty incomplete, and arbitrary forms of social regulation.

The analysis of agro-commercial capital may thus advance the theoretical understanding of agrarian transformation in two ways. First, agro-commercial capital must be seen not as a passive receiver of the impacts of either political regulation or liberalization, but as an active shaper of both. Second, when the state fails to impose regulations, agro-commercial capital evolves its own institutions of social regulation. These are of two types. One consists of consciously-designed regulative forms of 'collective action' that is, business associations or guilds. The second involves reworking of non-market institutions such as caste and ethnicity (which also express culture and identity) into economic regulators. These must not be regarded as semi-feudal relics, archaic residues from the colonial era, destined for the scrap-heap of history, in reality they are manifestations of a thoroughly contemporary capitalism, with its own forms of market authority and undemocratic 'market-driven' politics.

This book aims to show the role planned by these markets in accounting for stagnation, growth, and then deceleration in West Bengal's agriculture and the related questions of how new markets for other staple foods have been created and grow and why poverty remains so widespread despite this growth. Since markets are a key element of the agrarian structure, to understand their effects requires a systematic analysis of the ways markets are instituted,[28] and a conception of both circulation and production as being integral parts of a food *system*. The next chapter reviews the analytical tools we need for this purpose.

Notes
1. When the Left Front Government assumed power, West Bengal had the

dubious distinction of having the highest proportion of the population below the poverty line. From NSSO data, the proportion of West Bengal's population under the poverty line was 27 per cent greater than the all-India average in 1987–8 having declined from being 32 per cent worse in the early 1970s. In the quarter century before 1987–8, illiteracy progressed from being 20 per cent worse than the all-India average to 12 per cent worse; the decline in infant mortality rate was fractionally above that of all-India; and although village level evidence shows that moderate to very severe weight for age scores had declined by 22 to 30 per cent during the 1980s '(t)he overall level of [nutritional] deprivation has remained extremely high' (Sengupta and Gazder, 1998, pp. 171; 191;187; 198). In 1999–2000, it remained one of the poorest states with a head count of 44 per cent according to the Government of India's Expert Group—and the Government of West Bengal, 2003—and 28 per cent according to the World Bank (Sen, 2002, p. 442–3). West Bengal's human development ranking (9th among Indian states) has been unchanged over the decades 1981-2001. Its female participation rates have been extraordinarily low until recently when a dramatic doubling of the proportion of women in wage work brought West Bengal in line with other low ranking states (Ghosh, 2002; Macroscan, 2003b). The supply-side defects of the primary education system have been analysed by Rana et al., (2003) and provide structural incentives for both private tuition and dropping-out. The latest East India Human Development Report shows West Bengal as still having a low human development score, with poor scores in nutrition, education and rural consumer expenditure, and averagely mediocre indicators for health (NCAER, 2004, pp. 273–4). The West Bengal Human Development Report for 2004 records rural-urban consumption differences as being 'one of the highest of the major states'. It also shows lower than All-India average ranking for housing, elecriticity, and income-poverty (14th) (Sarkar, 2006, pp. 342–4).
2. These firms can control the prices of inputs too, see Moitra and Das 2004.
3. This is from village level evidence for the period 1983–9 (Sengupta and Gazder, 1997, pp. 188–190). For the atrophication and reversal of land reforms in the 1990s, see Sarkar, 2006, pp. 344–5; and for evidence for persistently poor nutrition, see NCAER, 2004, pp. 273–4.
4. Apart from evidence in this book, see Mitra and Sarkar, 2003, for these mechanisms at work in the potato economy.
5. This is the relation between total wages and profits in gross value added. Despite unionization and strike threats, agricultural wage rates in West Bengal have dropped below the all-India rate and '(t)here is no evidence of an additional upward pressure on wages due to increased bargaining power' (Sengupta and Gazder, 1997, p. 177).
6. The rates are disputed (Gazder and Sengupta, 1999; Rogaly, Harriss-White and Bose, 1995). See also Sengupta and Gazder, 1995, pp. 163–69; Government of West Bengal, 1995–6, Table 5.0a. The data used for estimation come from two agencies with two different methods of collection. Changes

Introduction

in the necessary adjustments to these data may bias estimates upwards (Datta Ray, 2002) or downwards (Saha and Swaminathan, 1994). Some scholars estimate that the rate was even less in the 1970s. Boyce (1987) suggests 1.74 per cent with the main aman season at 0.24 per cent. Rawal and Swaminathan calculate a less than 1 per cent growth rate in the 1970s (1998, p. 2596). Chattopadhyay et al. (1993) researching the timing of the kink found none at all. Mukhopadhyay and Sarkar, 2001, criticising the deterministic curve-fitting exercises, discovered that West Bengal's agricultural production series for the entire period of the last half century is difference-stationary rather than trend deterministic, with a stochastic trend and an upwards drift and no acceleration in growth. Disaggregating for rice, however, even their method reveals a sharp acceleration in growth in the early 1980s, within the general model of difference-stationarity and drift.

7. See Sengupta and Gazder, 1998; Rawal and Swaminathan, 1998; and Rogaly, Harriss-White, and Bose, 1995 for detail on these achievements.
8. Moitra and Das, 2004 are exceptions in arguing that the driver was private investment in wells, permitting the expansion of the boro crop, but exploiting producers to whom water is sold through widespread collusive pricing.
9. Bhaduri, 1983. This argument has received criticism for the narrow parametric bands within which it is valid. In an alternative formulation due to Cheung, landlords, having monopoly power, can re-negotiate shares and enforce adoption of new technology (Majid, 1994).
10. RBI, 1984; Boyce, 1987; Mukarji and Sanyal, 1995; Rawal and Swaminathan, 1998
11. See footnote 6; Banerjee and Kundu (2001) estimate 5.4 per cent; Rawal and Swaminathan (1998) 6.4 per cent; Sen and Sengupta (1995) estimate 7.6 per cent for rice in the 1980s and the high estimate of 9 per cent is for the boro season (Rogaly et al., 1995 p. 1868, footnote 2.
12. The kink point is variously placed in 1981–2 (e.g. Sen and Sengupta, 1995) or 1983–4 (Banerjee and Kundu, 2001) but Chattopadhyay et al. (1993), testing for a kink, found none at all and furthermore suggested no higher growth than other states in north east India. The implication of there being no kink would be to challenge West Bengal's exceptionalism.
13. Dasgupta, 1995; *Business India*, June 1994, Interview with the Chief Minister Jyoti Basu; Mukherjee and Mukhopadhyay, 1995; Banerjee, Gertler and Ghatak, 2002; and Rawal and Swaminathan, 1998.
14. Buddhadeb Bhattacharya, 1997, *Frontline* 8, p. 79; Frontline, Vol. 8, No. 8, p. 79. Sengupta and Gazder, 1998, pp. 142–8; Bhattacharyya, 2003; Ruud, 1999; Bandhyopadhyay, 2003,
15. According to an analysis carried out through the Institute of Marxist Studies, W. Bengal; see also Bandhyopadhyay, 2003.
16. See Leiten, 1990 for this argument; see Rogaly et al., 1995, and Basu, 2002, for critiques. See Baruah, 1993, for an early case. There is also an argument that the weak implementation of land reforms was due not to opposition from landed elites but rather to the Left Front Government's having allowed

land reforms to lose its political priority because the logic of redistribution could not be extended into non-agricultural assets. Confining it to agriculture becomes increasingly arbitrary. Even in agriculture it must also be supplemented by other 'pro-poor' policies.

17. The instrument of grassroots agrarian politics, the Kisan Sabha represents petty producers as well as labour and tilts to the interests of the former. There is no CPI(M) trade union for agricultural labour. Regular strikes brokered by the CPI(M) even serve to stabilize relations between landowners and wage workers and thereby serve the interests of employers (Bose, 1999; Rogaly, 1999).

18. Mallick, 1993, p. 212; Agrawal et al., 1997; Rawal and Swaminathan, 1998, pp. 2587–2600; and Banerjee and Kundu, 2001, p. 31.

19. J. Harriss, 1992; 1993. For yields, see Government of West Bengal, 2003: Now the proportion of rice production is about 53 per cent in aman, 7 per cent in aus and 29 per cent in boro (Government of West Bengal, 1999, p. 15).

20. The synergy between public irrigation and private wells has been established elsewhere—Harriss-White and Janakarajan, 2004; see Bandhyopadhyay, 2003, p. 880.

21. Moitra and Das, 2004, p. 123, p. 134. This research also reveals variations in the regional diffusion of wells, diversity in water market contracts, the renting-in of land by waterlords and widespread reports of collusive pricing of water, for which they give a theoretical rationale.

22. Sen, 1985; J. Harriss, 1992; 1993 refers to them as 'the depressor'.

23. Agrarian research has suffered from the hammer blow struck against Village Level Studies by the withdrawal of interest in, and funding for, such work in the 1990s. Bhattacharyya (2001) Ghosh (1998), and Rawal (2005) are notable exceptions in West Bengal.

24. Government of West Bengal, 1996, Table 5.2, and 5.9. The plantation crops of tea and spices also registered huge increases due to area expansion. During the 1990s, rice yields climbed to 10 per cent above the all-India average, only to slump again to 20 per cent below (op.cit., Table 5.9, p. 91).

25. According to Abijit Sen's analysis of the NSSO 55th Round estimates, rural poverty was at 37 per cent in 1990–1 and 39 per cent in 1999–2000 (2002, p. 432). He writes:- 'West Bengal turns in a relatively poor performance'... Distribution appears to have worsened in West Bengal'. (op.cit., p. 433). A. Shariff also records that West Bengal is poorer *per caput* than 13 other Indian states (NCAER, 2004).

26. The reasons for the latter are outside the scope of this book but evidently lie in the industrial, financial and infrastructural failures vividly described by Banerjee et al. (2002) and endorsed by Bandhyopadyay (2003). See also Rana et al., 2003 for persistent problems in primary education.

27. See Ghosh, 1998 for pauperization and Chowdhury et al., 2000, for evidence for the problem of arsenic toxicity in West Bengal and Bangladesh.

28. 'Instituted' and 'institution' are terms with many meanings but here will be taken to denote behaviour which is patterned (Hodgson, 2001).

Table 1.1a: Production of Rice in West Bengal by Districts

('000 tonnes)

State/Districts	1980–1	1985–6	1990–1	1993–4	1994–5	1995–6	1996–7	1997–8	1998–9	1999–2000	2000–1	2001–2	Index 80–81 =100
West Bengal	7466	7991	10437	12111	12236	11887	12637	13237	13316	13760	12428	15257	
Bardhaman	1003	1013	1420	1642	1694	1669	1742	1929	2145	1859	1571	1931	192
Birbhum	586	578	813	832	799	823	858	1020	1188	1043	796	1157	197
Bankura	593	680	844	913	976	1057	1039	1197	929	997	993	1222	206
Midnapore	1256	1458	1529	2097	2284	2093	2362	2302	2056	2419	2584	2711	216
Howrah	151	190	233	260	218	180	216	243	235	296	224	288	190
Hooghly	509	479	611	700	750	689	649	773	745	767	504	848	166
24 Parganas (N)	444	435	647	749	680	660	679	686	863	830	641	855	192
24 Parganas (S)	479	449	510	706	796	668	791	635	750	933	867	1004	209
Nadia	281	376	695	756	701	721	711	747	844	817	650	959	341
Murshidabad	422	436	785	792	793	738	909	897	994	871	548	1085	257
Uttar Dinajpur	486	530	768	859	848	805	501	489	580	568	629	980	202
Dakshin Dinajpur							430	430	464	423	467		
Malda	287	330	498	552	515	561	553	560	489	519	523	536	187
Jalpaiguri	295	261	250	322	271	312	277	311	286	379	384	410	138
Darjeeling	53	49	65	70	66	50	39	40	39	51	53	59	111
Coch behar	278	291	402	421	341	383	401	369	369	440	517	467	168
Purulia	343	436	373	441	504	477	483	609	342	548	475	745	217

Source: Directorate of Agriculture, Government of West Bengal
Note: Figures for 1980–1 to 1995–6 and 2001–02 of the district Dinajpur, Uttar and Dakshin are taken together.

Table 1.1b: District-wise Share of Production of Rice in West Bengal

(per cent)

State/Districts	1980–1	1985–6	1990–1	1993–4	1994–5	1995–6	1996–7	1997–8	1998–9	1999–00	2000–1	2001–2
West Bengal	100.0	100.0	100.0	100.0	100.0	100.0	100.0	100.0	100.0	100.0	100.0	
Bardhaman	13.4	12.7	13.6	13.6	13.8	14.0	13.8	14.6	16.1	13.5	12.6	12.7
Birbhum	7.8	7.2	7.8	6.9	6.5	6.9	6.8	7.7	8.9	7.6	6.4	7.6
Bankura	7.9	8.5	8.1	7.5	8.0	8.9	8.2	9.0	7.0	7.2	8.0	8.0
Midnapore	16.8	18.2	14.7	17.3	18.7	17.6	18.7	17.4	15.4	17.6	20.8	17.8
Howrah	2.0	2.4	2.2	2.1	1.8	1.5	1.7	1.8	1.8	2.2	1.8	1.9
Hooghly	6.8	6.0	5.9	5.8	6.1	5.8	5.1	5.8	5.6	5.6	4.1	5.6
24 Parganas (N)	6.0	5.4	6.2	6.2	5.6	5.6	5.4	5.2	6.5	6.0	5.2	5.6
24 Parganas (S)	6.4	5.6	4.9	5.8	6.5	5.6	6.3	4.8	5.6	6.8	7.0	6.6
Nadia	3.8	4.7	6.7	6.2	5.7	6.1	5.6	5.6	6.3	5.9	5.2	6.3
Murshidabad	5.6	5.5	7.5	6.5	6.5	6.2	7.2	6.8	7.5	6.3	4.4	7.1
Uttar Dinajpur	6.5	6.6	7.4	7.1	6.9	6.8	4.0	3.7	4.4	4.1	5.1	6.4
Dakshin Dinajpur							3.4	3.3	3.5	3.1	3.8	
Malda	3.8	4.1	4.8	4.6	4.2	4.7	4.4	4.2	3.7	3.8	4.2	3.5
Jalpaiguri	3.9	3.3	2.4	2.7	2.2	2.6	2.2	2.3	2.1	2.8	3.1	2.7
Darjeeling	0.7	0.6	0.6	0.6	0.5	0.4	0.3	0.3	0.3	0.4	0.4	0.4
Coch behar	3.7	3.6	3.8	3.5	2.8	3.2	3.2	2.8	2.8	3.2	4.2	3.1
Purulia	4.6	5.5	3.6	3.6	4.1	4.0	3.8	4.6	2.6	4.0	3.8	4.9

Source: Computed from the data given in Directorate of Agriculture, Government of West Bengal.
Note: Same as Table 1.1a.

2 Analysing Markets

This chapter outlines the conceptual toolkit which I have gradually evolved in the course of rural field work in India over a thity-five year period. It is drawn as far as possible from the work of other scholars in India and elsewhere, but it is also the product of repeated close encounters with agricultural markets, for which the research methods and insights of political economy and economic anthropology frequently proved as useful as those of economics.

In mainstream economics, the market is normally understood as an autonomous and flexible mechanism of exchange based on choice, a mechanism by which prices are formed as the result of supply and demand, and through which scarce resources are valued and allocated. Its efficiency and developmental outcomes are taken to be axiomatic and underdevelopment is then characterized by an incomplete correspondence of markets with productive activity.[1] It is also through the currency of markets that economics deals with capitalism—the system of unceasing commodification under which all factors of production, including labour, are exploited. In the quarter century covered by this book, the process of development has been dominated by pro-market or 'market-friendly' policies.

Yet the mainstream conception of markets has been justly criticized for being abstract, asocial, ahistorical, and de-institutionalized. (See Hodgson, 2001; Caille, 1993; and Crow, 2001). Joan Robinson wrote of them as 'extravagant abstractions' relying excessively on shaky foundations of timeless equilibrium.[2] Information theory and contract theory have made significant inroads into the two assumptions against which she rallied—market reductionism and the treatment of time. But the historical dynamism, institutional diversity, and stable coexistence of a range of institutions without which real markets cannot function—all remain major challenges for explanation in economics. In this context, Indian research grounded in classical political economy has made notable and distinctive contributions to the understanding of the instituted nature of exchange and the relations between production and markets. (see Appendix 2.1 for a discussion of Marx's concept of merchants' capital and its influence in India).

Commodity markets are at the heart of development. Not only do they link production and consumption—without which agriculture does not grow, and without which raw material, wage goods, financial resources, and labour cannot be extracted and supplied to the non-agrarian economy—but they are also the means by which society reproduces itself from day to day and through which it is transformed. Trade involves both processing and transport, so markets are also sites of accumulation and play crucial roles in shaping people's opportunities and well-being. Commodity markets are neither passive reflectors of production structures, nor are they independent of them; they are an active element in the process of growth and accumulation. Commodity markets are also, like most markets, political arenas regulated by society and culture, as well as by formal laws. Their socio-cultural regulation challenges and compromises the regulative role of the state. It also means that markets are unavoidably complex. It is this institutional complexity which gives them their 'character', and requires the empirical specification of them which is so rarely done.

Class and Exchange Relations

Two theories of how markets work in South Asia see what happens in markets as crucially determined by social class. According to Krishna Bharadwaj (1974, 1985), prices are created by the speculative exchange activities of large farmers, who not only are subsistence producers *par excellence*, but also dominate the marketed surplus. Middle peasants are seen as self-sufficient and engaging in sporadic marketing when they have a physical surplus. At the base are two other classes of producers—small peasants and landless labourers—both unavoidably involved in grain markets, as producers after the harvest and as consumers before the harvest, when they have to obtain the means of subsistence in the lean season. Using this model, Suman Sarkar showed that the marketed surplus in Bengal could have three streams, which will respond differently to price changes.[3] Immediately after the harvest, supply consists of the completely price-unresponsive sales of indebted producers. A second stratum of producers with fixed income goals, and risk-minimizing 'instalment marketing' behaviour will respond perversely by marketing smaller consignments while post-harvest-prices rise. And those with holding power will delay bringing crops to the market and speculate on pre-harvest price maxima. In his detailed research in Bangladesh, Ben Crow has verified this pattern of differentiated supply of the marketed surplus, and Ashok Rudra, using

Analysing Markets

a similar productionist model, suggests how such differentiated exchange relations are sufficient to account for the wide pre- and post-harvest price fluctuations typical of agricultural markets. (Rudra, 1989; Crow, 2001).

A second analyst, Amit Bhaduri, also saw semi-feudal tenurial relations and interlocked contracts as determining important structural characteristics of West Bengal's agriculture, which he called 'forced commerce': indebtedness causes producers to part with produce they need for their own subsistence immediately after the harvest on highly disadvantageous terms and to buy it back before the harvest using loans, on terms and conditions under which the risk of default is borne by the borrower. Worse still, contracts for agricultural commodities may be interlocked with credit in ways to depress commodity prices below those which would result from unconstrained transactions, and raise interest rates above those of the 'market'.[4] Distress sales or 'forced commerce', using the mechanisms of interlocked contracts co-exist with normal commerce under a variety of agrarian structures in South Asia.[5] Complex exchange relations like these structure the distribution of returns to production and the gains from growth and new technology in ways which are socially and economically differentiating. An overall rate of growth may conceal the co-existence of growth and stagnation, accumulation and pauperization, transformation and stasis.

These are important analytical advances, but these models of exchange relations are still striking in the way they see markets as residual. In Bhardawaj's model, 'the market' remains unproblematized while in Bhaduri's it is specified only as a strategic alliance between landlords, moneylenders, and traders. But resource appropriation via 'the market' is in reality far more complex than a mere redistribution resulting from buying and selling, and has far more complex implications for production. Surplus may be appropriated, not just from the direct producers or workers, but also by merchants from landowners; and a further expropriation is effected by merchants from the labour they also employ; that is, there may be more than two sites of appropriation of surplus inside a complex agro-industrial marketing system.

The commercial firms which constitute real markets are also rarely pure traders. They commonly employ various methods of extracting surplus, which reflect the complexity of the property relations and productive activity in both production and circulation. These methods include redistribution through the market, usury or finance, rent on land, water, animals or property, and capitalist agro-processing activity. In 1981, Boudhayan Chattopadhyay defined 'conglomerate property' as capital deployed over a range of modes of extraction and investment inside a firm. Referring to the all-India Rural Credit Survey of 1951, he invoked a 'Trinity' which 'commands the land market, commands credit and comes with the transport'. Perhaps also in the context of eastern India, the Trinity may have 'an arm reaching into processing units at one end and urban epicentres of finance, trading, and political-administrative linkages at the other end'. Conglomerate capital is not maximizing a targeted rate of return, but, he conjectures, 'is maximizing a targeted gross margin of revenue over outlays across the range of assets, commodities and instruments of control'. This, he concludes, is 'elusive to research' and not made easier to analyse by the fact that key relationships may embody economic processes acting against each other. For example, Utsa Patnaik has pointed out that moneylending capital has as its purpose the appropriation of a peasant's surplus as interest. It therefore plays a destructive role in agriculture, reducing the returns to production of the direct producer. Traders' moneylending, by contrast, may aim to change the cropping pattern so that production is increased. The surplus appropriated by the merchant through moneylending 'is neither interest nor profit. It is the return on the capital invested by the trader in the production process' (Patnaik, 1981, pp. 31-33). These contradictory roles are resolved only by the domination of one process over the other.

Resources are also commonly appropriated by crime and coercion (fraud on weights and measures, arbitrary deductions, and misinformation about prices etc.), as well as through the evasion of state regulations. (see Janakarajan, 1993; Harriss, 1984; and Harriss-White, 1996 for South Indian examples). The resources plundered in this way may be dissipated unproductively, but they may also be mobilized for necessary and productive investment in commerce or production. This is a primitive form of accumulation. In any epoch when primitive or primary accumulation is occurring, not only are the institutions regulating capitalism being created and capital concentrated, but labour is also being proletarianized. (Banaji, 1977). In many forms of agrarian capitalism, this type of accumulation, whether it is logically prior to productive investment and hence 'primary'—or whether it is achieved by non-market means—and hence 'primitive'—continues to a greater or lesser extent. It promotes differentiation in circulation and non-agricultural production as well as in agriculture. State policy may resist primary accumulation in some respects while encouraging it in others. For instance, in its land redistributivist politics, the Left Front has formally attempted to stop or at least delay the development of agrarian landlessness, while its treatment of agricultural markets and commerce allows primary accumulation, accompanied by fraud and corruption, to grind ineluctably onwards, dispossessing some producers of their land.

Market institutions

Structuralist models of differentiated exchange, such as those just discussed, incorporate some key characteristics of the modes of resource extraction in real markets, but like all structural models, they account poorly for changes in the structures of exchange,[6] and they ignore structural relations that involve non-land assets in the agrarian economy, including non-class institutions necessary to the functioning of real markets.

As regards the latter, markets would not work at all without a complex of other institutions; but as yet there is no consensus on what these institutions are.[7] Market-making institutions have either been researched individually,[8] or in individualistic selections which tend to focus on permutations and combinations of money, banking, and financial institutions, legitimate commodities, property rights, institutions of trade regulation, corporations, unions, and exchange.[9] A systematic conceptualization remains to be established. A few scholars have been sufficiently fascinated by real markets, and provoked by the unexpected practical problems created by liberalization and privatization, to research market institutions in the field,[10] and several attempts have been made to theorize markets as instituted phenomena.[11]

In the analysis of industrial organizations, 'market structure' traditionally referred to a structure of production: 'the market' was not seen as independent of production but as a direct result of it. The firm was the central institution and the distribution of *assets* in a sector was the key element of structure. (Both are clearly derived from competition theory). The central processes of a market agency were *price formation* and *transactions* or *contracts*. However, in conceiving of a market as a 'layer' of buying and selling, and in being restricted to transactions between producers and wholesalers, this approach will not work for agricultural markets where many transfers of property rights occur. It is therefore necessary to think of markets not only in terms of their institutions, but also as *systems of circulation* (see Fig. 2.1).[12]

The concept of circulation refers to the movements of a commodity once it has been produced. The elements of this system are firms. Although market exchange will frequently be the major flow relationship in the system of circulation, it is not the only one. Loan repayments, payments to labour, and rental contracts (all of which may involve payment in kind) are just as much a part of the system of circulation as are buying and selling, processing, transport, and storage. The last three activities, however, transform the commodity in form, space, and time. Storage also minimizes spoiling. These activities link the circulation of a commodity with the circulation of money, and with the exploitation of labour and land. They tie the sphere of circulation

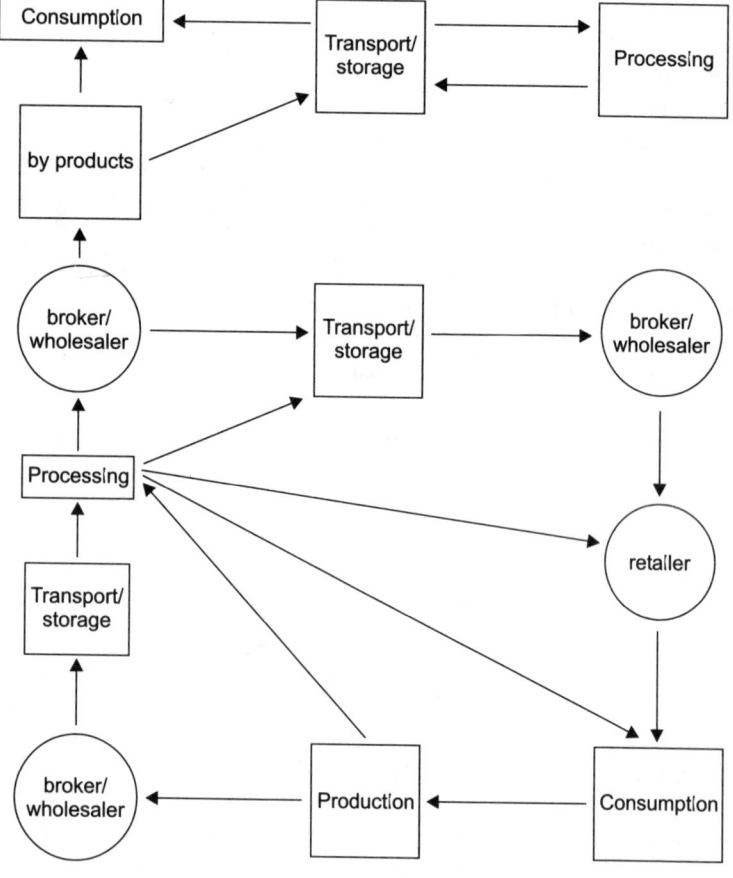

Fig. 2.1: The Physical and Economic System of Circulation

to that of production. Market-making institutions are draped all over this system and the repercussions of change in institutions of circulation are felt in institutions of production.

Market systems are also never in equilibrium. They are dynamized by at least three kinds of forces which are not mutually exclusive on the ground, even if they need to be distinguished analytically: changing market-based relationships (contracts) between the elements (firms), shocks to the system from outside, and changes in non-market institutions.

Market relationships revolve around commodities and price-forming processes. These are the result of contestation between the interests of labour and capital, competition or accommodation between individual capitals, and the collective actions of capitalists as a class as they strive for surplus, for the control over labour, for the infrastructural and political preconditions for market exchange, and for the establishment of order in markets. A system of markets is thus at one and the same time a set of prices sending allocative signals to producers and consumers, and a mechanism for the extraction and distribution of resources. *Shocks* to the system—weather-related, disease-related, life-cycle-related, infrastructural, energy-related or political—will change the elements, relations, and flows in ways which reshape firms and livelihoods (or even destroy them). As for non-market institutions, they are so critical for markets that they call for discussion in a separate section.

Non-market institutions and their diversity

The system of circulation depends implicitly on non-market relationships. Geoffrey Hodgson suggests that they may be usefully analysed in terms of their 'dominance', that is, in terms of their significance for, and the importance of their role in the economy; or their 'prominence', that is, how general they are.[13] To establish which ones are dominant and prominent in any given case, there is no alternative to returning to the empirical literature on real markets and extrapolating from it. This literature records a much greater diversity of institutions than currently imagined in theoretical literature. Research on India's rural markets does nonetheless allow us to identify which are dominant and which are prominent. For the system of agricultural markets in West Bengal, dominant institutions will be those through which capital is accumulated, and prominent institutions will be those affecting labour and livelihoods.

Dominant institutions include at least the following aspects of firms: self-employment, on a petty scale, in a family firm, including petty trading (the commercial analogue of petty commodity production); private firms, with combinations of family labour, permanent and casual wage labour, with private or corporate ownership, with national or international capital; co-operatives, commonly with but sometimes without wage labour, and state-trading institutions, whose ownership varies from complete dependence on the state to part-privately-owned, part-publicly-owned joint stock companies mandated to work independently of the state.

A dominant feature of these institutions is *complexity in activities*. The activities undertaken by firms in real-world markets are not confined to buying and selling. Trading firms may buy, sell, broker, store, transport and process, produce, finance production, and finance trade. There are two to the 9th possible combinations of these nine activities, and there are other activities. (Donald Michie, Pers., Comm., 2003). From the simplicity of vernacular classifications of trading firms, it might be assumed that activity combinations are highly patterned. But this is not so. Wherever activity combinations have been analysed, diversity, complexity, and tendencies to uniqueness emerge, qualifying the conception of a market as consisting of comparable firms. (Harriss-White, 1995).

A further dominant feature of dominant market institutions is *contractual diversity*. Common forms of contract can range from spot contracts (the rarest, although the most likely to be discussed in official documents) through advance, and/or futures agreements, attached, repeated or relational forms, to internal transfers. Contracts affect the transfer of rights of control—not only over tangibles (commodities) but also over 'intangible' social attributes and obligations that are very frequently entangled in the contract (such as reputation of the parties to the transaction, the 'quality' of the goods habitually transacted, and personal loyalty) (Jagganathan, 1987). Contracts may be written but are still usually verbal, and the rules of adherence may be formal and legal, or just customary norms. Contracts entail institutions of dispute resolution. (In general, disputes are resolved privately or through business associations; courts are avoided.)

As for 'prominent' institutions, they must include: a) *commodities* and b) *families*. Commodities are goods produced for mass consumption through markets (Huws, 2003). Their commodity form is not the whole story because after they have been purchased, commodities may be used for other kinds of exchange—tribute, redistribution, and gift exchange being the most discussed (Appadurai, 1988, Vidal, 2003). At each point they carry social meanings; a given commodity such as rice may have a range of meanings, and different meanings at different points in the circulation system. However, the fact that every commodity has a unique word for it, like 'rice', indicates some unique set of attributes. These may be physical (such as divisibility or perishability) or cultural (such as being 'a staple', 'polluting', or 'gendered'). These essential qualities may shape the structure and/or conduct of the market. For example, without technologies of preservation, a commodity with a high degree of perishability requires spot contracts and immediate payments, while low status products are only traded on the physical margins of market places, and only by people of low status.[14]

Then there is also universality of the family. Neither the firm nor labour markets can survive without it. This non-market institution produces labour, which works for wages in family firms under patriarchal authority according to a division of tasks based on age, and a division of rewards based on status within the family. The business family also creates and transfers capital or business assets through kinship alliances. Women are carefully controlled by men, as their private behaviour has an impact on the public reputation and creditworthiness of the firm (Laidlaw, 1995; Harriss-White, 2003; Ch. 6). The business family also subsidizes employees' wages in cases where payments are made in prepared food as well as cash. It also subsidizes apprenticeships by providing board and lodging as well as socialization into work. The productive activity interlaced with trade is also meshed with relations of kinship and politics. Associative life is crucial for alliances and for the control of women in communities which link private reputation to public creditworthiness and capital accumulation. Clearly, markets will be affected by significant changes in the nature of families, as much as by changes in commodities themselves.

Empirical analysis thus reveals the coexistence of diverse and complex institutional forms. Real markets do not reduce to firms with comparable organizational forms, let alone comparable objectives. Market institutions are devoted not only to trading, but to trading and many other activities (Laidlaw, 1994), while markets for a given commodity are actually bundles of separate economic markets, each loaded with social meanings. Despite the fact that institutional diversity and complexity is usually ignored or residualized, it is not epiphenomenal, but as much structuring as are competitive conditions.[15] Since institutions are patterned, habituated thought and behaviour and cultural diversity are another set of institutions that have to be incorporated analytically into the system of markets, and India's economy is remarkable (though not unique) for the close relation it exhibits between cultural and religious plurality and 'communities of accumulation'. The next section explores this aspect of institutional diversity further, because it has received little attention from economists and is important for the argument of this book.

The Relevance of India's Family Business Diasporas

West Bengal's rural markets cannot be understood without reference to this phenonemon in India as a whole. India is marked by having a striking concentration of business assets in family businesses (in 1997, 70 of the biggest 100 firms were family firms, and 70 per cent of total Indian business assets were still in family hands) (Datta, 1997). Even more striking is the control of the economy by a miniscule proportion of the Indian population, a subset of heterogeneous trading castes which have come to be configured socially and politically into an even smaller set of 'communities'. Many are practitioners of minority religions. Shekawati Marwaris, for example, who formed 0.4 per cent of the population in the 1980s, were thought at that time to hold 60 per cent of total investment in the private sector.[16]

Studies of family businesses stress the ubiquity of patriarchal partnerships, the paternalist organization of business-family roles based on status, reward unrelated to effort, and the development of diverse investment portfolios (ibid). These are not at all particularly 'Indian' practices, although family businesses are much more common in parts of mainland Europe—and in China and its diaspora—than in the UK, the USA, Japan or Korea. Family business is the basic building block of capitalism in what Fukuyama calls 'low trust societies' (1995, p. 336), in which strangers are not trusted to cooperate (Dobbin, 1996; p. 202). A second common aspect of the business family/family business is the trading diaspora, characterized by spatial dispersion, social interdependence, and the development of a collective cultural consciousness distinct from that which characterizes the group in its place of origin. 'Marwari', for instance, is a 'multivalent term' forged through migration, trade, and capitalist alliances to define a heterogeneous set of castes. A Marwari identity has been created through the strategic behaviour of these business families in the public sphere, drawing on symbols of kinship, lineage, family, and the 'domestication' of women (Hardgrove, 2002; Ch. 2; p. 8).

Why is capital concentrated in the hands of such a small proportion of the Indian population—Marwaris, Gujarati Banias, Parsees, Kayasths, and Punjabi Hindus? Scholars have shown the central importance of caste and community for restricting control over—and access to—money and private banking.[17] Money can be moved around the country fast and flexibly within a community. The community also controls socialization into business through exclusive apprenticeships (Taknet, 1986; p. 165). Research on Shekawati Marwaris shows how the community provides shelter and support to migrants both en route and at their destination (in the *basa* (the homebase) which doubles as a domestic and a business unit), as well as to the family left behind for long periods in the place of origin. These communities also give collective responses to intra-community disputes. They safeguard collective goodwill by settling debts owed outside the community, and by boycotting individuals who make losses by which that collective goodwill is jeopardized. Communities are formally federated for collective political representation to protect rights, commercial advantage, and status. Public demonstrations of philanthropy are made collectively as well as individually.[18]

Socio-economists have also modelled religious minorities as 'groups', seen as efficient ways of minimizing information and transaction costs; but the collective preconditions for accumulative success which have been given above cannot be reduced to transaction costs. The communities we are talking about are not confined to the economy, but are moral communities which see themselves as shaped by divine authority. Trading communities practising minority religions combine inter-community transactions based on market prices with intra-community transactions on preferential terms; they behave differently and often more harshly towards others, and yet famously treat others to philanthropy. Indian trading communities also cannot be reduced to minorities. Marwaris cut across the Hindu/Jain division, and across the divisions within the Jain religion. Laidlaw writes that 'You can be a Jain without ceasing to be, in the broad sense, a Hindu'.[19]

Diasporic trading communities were necessary in W. Bengal in general, and in rural markets in particular. For centuries, Marwaris migrated to parts of India where there were no native business castes.[20] Their arrival in Bengal is dated to the end of the 17th century (Taknet, 1986; p. 55; Hardgrove 2002). By the mid 19th century—after the collapse of indigo prices in 1834—Marwari traders had put paid to local ones and had consolidated the Bura (big) bazaar in Calcutta both as a money market and as the hub of a far-reaching wholesale trading network. Marwaris came to dominate not just the export of crops—opium, jute, and cotton—but also the trade in basic wage goods—salt, ghee, rice, and wheat. They rapidly moved into large scale finance, manufacturing industry, and insurance. There they developed elaborate monopolies, single business houses with 'direct and indirect control over hundreds of investment and industrial units' (Taknet, 1986, p. 177). Calcutta became the locus of choice for the top Marwari families. Dependent on Marwari money and brokerage, the British reciprocated with business concessions. At the same time, the Raj attempted without much success to regulate trade and to call a halt to periodic scandals of speculation and adulteration. Both before and after Independence, Marwari business houses aligned with the Congress and secured foreign exchange, credit, and industrial concessions, a process which Anne Hardgrove argues has far-reaching consequences. It 'preserves communities as institutions' Hardgrove, (2002, ch 2, p. 4) and thereby encourages modern elite political participation to take collectivist forms. From their dominant position in commerce and industry, Marwaris branched out further into law, accountancy, and other professions, even professionalizing domesticity in home science colleges.[21]

At an early stage, they also moved upcountry into trade in rural Bengal, beginning modestly with basa in every marketplace or river port. Having displaced local long-distance traders, they diversified and controlled trade in wholesale and retail, import and export, stocking and hoarding: foodstuffs, agricultural raw materials, agro-industrial raw materials, transport, and basic wage goods and materials for construction. Saha writes that while abnormally high prices of basic wage goods have been attributed to their practice of hoarding, in addition they regulated imports and raised prices in times of scarcity (2003, pp. 231–6). 'Upcountry Marwaris then moved into agro-industrial processing and from there into manufactures based on wood and plastics...' They will undertake business in any commodity, writes Saha,[22] like rice, wheat, salt, ghee, mustard seeds, spices and candles; tobacco, cloth and jute, forest products and timber; cement, corrugated iron and tin, coal, fuels, auto and transport and all ancillary industries; medical drugs, electrical goods, watches, newspapers, and luxury goods, even fish (Saha, 2003, pp. 227–9). At the time of partition, along with a movement of landed and landless Hindu Bengalis, there was a surge of Marwari migration from East Bengal to *mofussil* (upcountry) sites in West Bengal. Saha's painstaking chronology of Marwari business in Jalpaiguri, Darjeeling, and Cooch Behar shows that even though their hold on local commerce has since been loosened, they still own between a third and a half of all registered businesses in those districts and dominate the chambers of commerce and business associations (Saha, 2003; ch. 7). Although they were precocious in forming community-specific associations (from the 1830s onwards in Calcutta), some 140 years passed before they started creating upcountry cross-community organizations of collective business representation, (op. cit., p. 238). This speaks volumes about the difficulties of wrenching 'business class' consciousness and politics from its embeddedness in community. In 2002, two thirds of the 37 office bearers of the Bengal Rice Millers' Association were Marwaris.

Ethnicity, community, and culture: A summing up
By ignoring ethnicity in India, mainstream economics underestimates the barriers to the mobility of factors of production and overestimates the power of markets in allocating resources.[23] Even in political science, the literature on 'ethnicity' in India focuses on fluid and manipulated markers of religion, language, colour, tribe, dress, diet and, to a much lesser extent, territory (Singh, 2000; for territory see Banerjee, 2004). It neglects powerful networked communities of accumulation such as those of the Marwaris and the question of whether (and if so how) they, like other ethnicities, have been built into the modern structure of Indian politics and the economy. Whatever the status of Marwaris in their heartland, and notwithstanding their individual and associative philanthropy and their linguistic skills,[24] in West Bengal—a state with a strong tribal and Muslim presence and one quite remarkable for its relative lack of communalist tension—Marwari merchants are certainly regarded by landless people and by small Bengali producers of staple foods as a distinctive economic 'other'.[25] But, these 'others' have an insider's complicity with the secular state. For without their private banking, no government in West Bengal could now regulate the economy. As far as I can tell, this is an aspect of Left Front politics unaddressed by scholars.[26]

The importance of the implications of the role of Marwaris in West Bengal's rural economy can thus hardly be over-estimated. While many scholars have stressed the role of sub-infeuduated land relations in agrarian backwardness, in fact two major trajectories of accumulation have competed and dominated. One is that of landlordism discussed at the start of this chapter. The other is that of the trading diaspora. While both involve the control of the mass of small and landless producers through debt relations and interlocked contracts, the significance of there being two streams of accumulation is that one has a direct interest in land, while the other thrives on the marketed surplus. One had a direct interest in opposing land reforms, while the other did not.

The Persistence of Institutional Diversity

It is one thing to acknowledge the need to foreground a fundamental institutional diversity, including that pertaining to culture and identity, but another to explain why it persists in the face of so much confident prediction about the dissolving effect of market—or capitalist—rationality on archaic or pre-capitalist modes of organization.[27] Several explanations are available. For many analysts—well exemplified by Hodgson—diversity is seen as a pre-capitalist relic. Preserved through the 'path dependence' of institutional structures, the diversity of pre-capitalist modes of production makes contemporary capitalism diverse. Hodgson also sees institutional diversity as necessary for the working of evolutionary processes.[28]

But institutional complexity and diversity may also be seen as functional for capitalism by serving to absorb shocks—the greater the range of possible shocks, the greater the diversity.[29] And elsewhere I have shown how, in the absence of effective regulation by the state, non-market structures and ideologies are effectively re-worked, given economic content, and act as social regulators of accumulation (Harriss-White, 2003; 2005 a; Colatei and Harriss-White, 2004). I have paid particular attention to the roles of patriarchy and gender relations, to a plurality of divine authorities and to differentiated caste status, but these certainly do not exhaust the roles of non-market power in the process of capitalist development.

It follows that these diverse structures, ideologies and institutions cannot be regarded as mere pre-capitalist relics but must be understood as fully incorporated into capitalist accumulation and in some sense necessary to it. They are reworked by their market functions, and yet at the same time they require the exercise of forms of power that largely originate and certainly operate outside markets. But to recognize the centrality of yet another dimension of diversity—the diverse forms of social power involved in capitalist accumulation—involves

Analysing Markets

questioning the very widely-held understanding of capitalism as an institutionally homogenizing force. It also involves accepting that the agency expressed through social power in and out of the economy is crucial to institutional change in markets.

Markets and the State

Last but not least, we come to the state—the non-market institution that is pre-eminently seen as dominant—whether or not it is. What state institutions and practices need to be in place in order to develop and reproduce a commodified society such as that of West Bengal? How does the system of food markets fit into these institutions, and vice versa?[30] As we have seen for institutions, so with interventions, there is no consensus about how state regulation is best studied. In *Locked in Place*, a comparative study of the power of capital and state in the industrialization of India and Korea, Vivek Chibber makes the useful distinction that the state's developmental and regulative activity in general has to provide both *incentives* and *discipline*.[31] The state also needs to *co-ordinate* the two kinds of activity and these roles affect the the modes of extraction and distribution of the surplus.

For agricultural commodity markets, the state's incentives include: i) infrastructure—sites, stores, roads, electricity, and communications; ii) subsidies to cheapen capital for investment; iii) directed flows of resources, not necessarily always subsidized, where resources are considered insufficient; iv) protection of sectors, and of desirable types and scales of firms which would be wiped out without protection; and v) security for private property rights.

Its disciplinary powers may be of two general types[32]: i) 'parametric' regulation, on the assumption that capital operates efficiently enough for the state's discipline to be confined to the imposition of norms of trade in the public interest: defining legal sites, types of price formation, contracts, payment and dispute resolution,[33] and ii) 'participative' regulation, in which the state actively substitutes for capital on the assumption that capital will not invest in the market, or that it will invest but is sub-optimally efficient, or that it can only be made efficient by competition with an active state.

In order to reduce the risks of investment and to control the tendency of capital to move to places other than those to which it was originally planned it should go, the state also has to *co-ordinate* both forms of incentivization and discipline, mediate between them and at the same time destroy or buy out hostile interests. With respect to agricultural commodity markets, there is no shortage of state institutions for coordination. In fact, their proliferation is a structural source of tension between the jurisdictions of central and state governments; and within any given state, many different departments are involved with any one sector of the economy. Yet, while many departments and parastatal institutions may have some formal responsibility, their powers may be quite limited.[34] And over and above their quality and their powers, capital needs these institutions to be stable—or at least unstable in a predictable way—which is by no means guaranteed.

By 1977, when the Left Front Government was elected to government, West Bengal's agricultural commodity markets were being regulated by the state in a framework that aspired to cover the entire nation and that remained fairly institutionally stable until the mid-nineties. The key institutions of intervention in agricultural markets had been decentralized and diffused, but were certainly not well co-ordinated as they evolved. Their stated objectives were developmental, transformational, and consistently anti-mercantilist: they were created to curb the power of private trade. They were also populist—repeatedly justified in productionist terms for the benefit of 'small farmers' (Harriss, 1984).

Regulatory incentives included transport and market sites (under the Agricultural Markets (Regulation and Enforcement) Act) with their associated godowns, rural electrification, and roads. Co-operatives and small scale industries were entitled to subsidized credit for new technology. Rice mills could also gain access to working capital from nationalized or private banks, to which other elements in the market system were not eligible. To that extent, certain parts of the system were protected. By contrast, the rice system as a whole was taxed rather than protected, for India's domestic open market prices were usually lower than those on the world market, and (except in the North-West) prices in the state-administered subsystem or circuit were lower still. Last but not least, property rights were vested not only in private individuals but also in joint families. In the latter case, rights were (and still are) assigned on the basis of status and gender.

'Parametric' Disciplinary Institutions included licensing; the specification of modes of price and contract formation, and payment (and therefore of acceptable conditions for competition and, in turn, of market structure); restrictions on movements and on the quantities and periodicity of storage; compulsory purchase at fixed prices and fixed milling out-turn rates for the state's public distribution system. Even

the conditions of issue and sale of open-market and state-traded grains is regulated, through law specifying the display of information about stocks and prices. In the government's 'fair price shops' (FPS), the times of the day and the days in the week when such distribution points would be open, the kinds of other products alongside which foodgrains could be sold, together with the size of the consignment were all specified by law. Throughout the system, weights and measures were calibrated, sack sizes standardized, and information on prices and supplies was required.

As for *participative regulation*, the West Bengal Food Department, the Government of India's Food Corporation of India (FCI), its Storage Corporations, and its price and freight policy enabled the state to intervene actively in the procurement, storage, milling, transport and distribution of rice and wheat. The National Cooperative Development Corporation (NCDC) and West Bengal Department of Co-operation made sure that co-operative processing competed with private capital as well. Later on, panchayats were empowered to procure grain. The state still finances procurement, storage and trading for the public food distribution system, and for employment guarantees, the plantations and the military, emergencies, and food reserves.

This complex and comprehensive structure of regulation clearly required many central and state government departments—not to mention parastatal institutions—to be mandated with regulative roles, some in flat contradiction with others. At the very least, the food markets in West Bengal involve Finance, Revenue, Agriculture, Labour, Food, Electricity, PWD and Co-operatives.[35] Incentives, discipline, and some co-ordination were and are all simultaneously managed by more than one department. (Departments of Food and Agricultural Markets, for instance). Acts themselves have been amended in such a way as to render them internally incoherent.[36] Few procedures establish priority between contradictory regulative jurisdictions, or discipline departmental non-performance or non-compliance.[37] The department centrally mandated with market regulation, the Department of Agricultural Marketing, resembles other departments with dedicated mandates in other Indian states in having limited jurisdiction and weak funding. And no single state institution is responsible for co-ordinating the rest.

Does this structure of institutional diversity within the state itself supply elasticity to the state, and enable it to absorb political shocks, as we argued earlier in this chapter may be the case for diversity in firms? It is not hard to see that the complex and conflicting structure and objectives of a multiplicity of state institutions provides an appropriate structure for a great many different kinds of accommodation—not necessarily corrupt—between capital and the state. With such a structure, it does not have to be stressed that social identities and private social status or political party allegiance regulate state practices, (Sengupta, 1998; Harriss-White, 2003) or that officials engage in predatory activity of the sort that Michal Kalecki coyly called their 'self employment', and Robert Bates calls 'rent-seeking'. Their complex interdependence implies a fact of market life, and so of Indian capitalism. It also makes this multiplicity of institutions extremely difficult to change, or reform, and especially to dismantle. (Harriss-White, 2004a).

Not only is the matrix of state institutions very wide-ranging and contradictory, it has to cope with continual changes in the scope of its operations. Instability is built into the structure of regulation through the rain-dependent nature of the harvest in West Bengal—and harvests in the other major centres of procurement, and this in turn affects the availability of public funds for procurement. Over and above this environmental instability, the regulation of the system of rice markets also suffers contingent instability from sources as varied as the micro-politics of patronage within the administration, and the very unreliable supply of rural electricity.

State regulation also does provide ample opportunities for bureaucratic rent. But rent-seeking is not confined to the state. The protection of market share is a basic aspect of competition in markets. Capitalist competition works actively to protect rents and capitalist interests will connive and collude to try to create conflicts of interest inside the state, so that officials implement regulative policy in such a way that it protects market shares.[38] Further, the practice of regulation not only gives expression to the contradiction between rhetorical policy objectives in the public interest and the private interests of individuals representing the state, and endowed with discretionary power; it also reveals a deliberate design of policies which maximize discretionary power.

'Parametric' regulatory intervention has had conspicuous success in achieving its stated intentions in India only where: i) agricultural marketing is separated from lending of money for production and consumption; and ii) the relations of commerce were already quite competitive. Elsewhere, linkages between money and commodity markets, the institutional diversity and idiosyncracy of agro-ecological regions, the wielding of economic power and extra-economic coercion, and the regulatory activities of mercantile guilds themselves have reduced much parametric disciplinary regulation to the levying of fees, or merely another layer of petty rural taxation.[39] State disciplinary institutions have been infiltrated by merchants and are frequently controlled by them. This is amply illustrated by the case of West Bengal, as we shall see.

State regulation is interwoven with customary norms as attempts are made to put the law into practice, and food merchants benefit from this. Price policy has tended to follow (with lags) the price structures established on open markets, reinforced by both merchants' and producers' lobbies (Clay et al., 1988). Private traders are often recruited to act as agents for state trading corporations. This reduces the costs and risks of private trading, and liberates the financial resources of private firms for trading on their own account. In India, outside the north west, the state does not purchase directly from producers but, even in the era of liberalization, 'procures' by 'levy'—that is, it buys a proportion of the inter-regional trade of private merchants. Certain mills may specialize in this procurement on behalf of other firms, reaping economies of scale in transaction costs, and reimbursed by firms which are informally exempted from such arrangements. Levies or quotas are exacted by the state at a price below ruling market prices, which is experienced as coercive, and market prices are then raised to compensate for these financial losses. Certificates of permission to transport unprocured grain—needed to ensure that the state's needs are not evaded—have been dependent upon compliance with disciplinary regulation, but they may also be discretionally awarded as incentives. Not only are open market supplies reduced when the post-harvest levy proportion suddenly rises, but price hoists may be cumulatively increased over a post-harvest season in an inflationary way, to merchants' benefit (Harriss B., 1977). This process penalizes those who are dependent on the residual markets for their subsistence and who are ineligible for the public distribution system, which in 'surplus' districts often does not cover even quite poor households. The inspection of procurement performance, and of stock (carried out by the revenue and food administrations and the police) allows widespread evasion in practice and is accompanied by institutionalized bribery: the threat of prosecution may act as a sanction on procurement performance but also as a way to enforce an elaborate system of corrupt payments (Mooij, 1999).

Restrictions on inter-regional trade movements (monitored by checkpost forces and the police) are overcome by bribing low-level officials who have discretionary responsibility for quantity decisions, and thus allow excess profit-making by private traders, who take advantage of the difference between the artificially low prices in cordoned-off surplus districts and artificially high prices in cordoned-off deficit ones. Traders sell grains that they can leak out of the system, and entitlements to rations through ration cards may even be mortgaged and traded for profit (Swaminathan, 2000; Harriss-White, 2004c). In agricultural commodity markets, the Indian state—despite its comprehensive formal structure of regulative institutions—leaves very large spaces for non-state regulation. West Bengal is no exception.

We can therefore agree with Kaviraj (1990, p. 13) that 'since major government policies have their final point of implementation very low down in the bureaucracy, they are reinterpreted beyond recognition'. Despite the depoliticized language of much policy-making, there is a strong mutual interest in collusion between elite food merchants and the state bureaucracy. This results in the secondary appropriation of surplus and its distribution via combinations of excess profits and rents, subsidies, the *virement* of state financial resources from their stated purposes to others, persistent weakness of the public sense of obligation to the state, and the strength and progressive reinforcement of obligations to non-state regulative institutions. Throughout most of the period covered by this book, the leading international aid, development, and financial agencies took it as axiomatic that the relationship between state and market was one of conflict. The reverse was actually more typical.

Conclusion

We have argued not only that any attempt to explain West Bengal's agrarian transformation and its transition from deficit to surplus will be *incomplete* if it does not consider the post-harvest system of markets, but also that the cause-effect relationships it aims to specify, and policy conclusions based on them, will be wrong.[40]

It will be wrong because the 'productionist' privileging of the process of surplus extraction through share-rents as the major cause of stagnation, and of land reforms as the trigger for growth, does not accurately describe the relative balance of power between rentier and commercial capital. As a result, it does not accurately describe either the politics of the limited land reforms that were brought about, or the incentives for the use of new growth-expanding technology once appropriate packages had been devised.

A productionist account of development in which markets are reduced to price signals or are treated as a residual—and are by implication competitive—is also wrong because it masks the varied exchange relations through which agrarian classes are formed. Agricultural commodity markets have been both a result of the ongoing process of primitive accumulation and one of its chief mechanisms. So, the use of prices in the evaluation of markets means focussing on their efficiency role rather than their role in extracting surplus. As a result, it fails to explain how the operation of markets (and 'privatization') can intensify poverty and vulnerability, rather than reduce them, as economic theory predicts. Neglect of the range of co-existing exchange relations means that the distributional question—how markets can pauperize certain producers while enriching others—cannot be answered. Yet, this is the question at the heart of any explanation of West Bengal's agricultural achievements and its enduring, multidimensional poverty.

Any account which fails to incorporate the non-market institutions in which accumulation is embedded—and through which markets are socially regulated—will also be wrong because it will fail to recognize the extensive barriers to the mobility of capital and labour, to which the rhetoric, rules, and laws of the state are equally blind. It will fail to see the means whereby social power is mobilized (against the state) in order to shape market regulation and protect market shares and accumulation trajectories, rather than spreading accumulative opportunity more generally. It will be complicit in supporting interventions intended to be in the general interest, such as credit for agriculture and small scale industry on the one hand, and liberalization and de-regulation on the other, which have all had perverse and differentiating outcomes.

It is, therefore, necessary to admit the market system as a crucial part of agrarian structure. This involves understanding three aspects: i) how it works in itself—through its elements—firms, their organization; technologies; sites, and flows; ii) how it works in relation to agricultural production, growth, and the supply of the marketed surplus—in particular labour processes and relations, and the flows of money advances and power relations of payment which lubricate commodity flows throughout the system; and iii) how the system is dynamized, how structures and relations change.

To flesh out this framework is an ambitious project, and this book is in part a record of the development over the last quarter century of my attempts to improve our understanding of markets, production, and state intervention. On this intellectual journey in West Bengal, three sets of questions guided three successive rounds of field research (see Table 2.1).[41]

The first set of questions was theoretical. How autonomous is the sphere of commodity markets and circulation? To what extent was circulation determined by production relations? I asked these questions in 1982 and looked for answers in the rice markets in Birbhum district—a 'food bowl'—straddling an alluvial river valley and lateritic plateau, with a long history of commercial production. Chapter 4 reports the findings of this research introducing the structures which link markets to production, while Chapter 5 describes the forces which dynamize the system.

Table 2.1: Field Research

Date	Places	Staples studied	Sample size	Original objectives of the research
1981-2 Birbhum Dt.	Bolpur Sainthia + Villages	Rice	60 firms	Relations between system of production and system of distribution
1990 Bardhaman Dt.	Burdwan, Gulsi Katwa Memari	Rice Potato Mustard oil	66 firms	Implications of diversification for market system and policy of LFG
2000 Kolkata Birbhum Dt.	Kolkata Bolpur	Rice	50 firms (S. Choudhury) + 18 officials (B. Harriss-White)	Instituted nature of markets/state intervention/technical change
2002 Birbhum Dt. Bardhaman Dt.	Bolpur + Villages Burdwan+ Villages	Rice	50 firms (P.K. Ghosh)+ 16 firms (B. Harriss-White)	Impact of domestic liberalization on formal and informal markets and their regulation
2003–4 Kolkata	Kolkata	Rice	4 Officials	State intervention under liberalization

Analysing Markets

The second set of questions was more practical and were asked eight years later, in 1990, at the start of the era of liberalization in India, when West Bengal's agriculture had been wrested from torpor, undergone structural reforms, and witnessed what few analysts would deny was vigorous and sustained growth. Indeed it was approaching the unprecedented condition of being in surplus, and had even begun to show signs of diversification. I wanted to know how markets respond to rapid changes in land use and agrarian structure; and what policies might the Left Front Government adopt to improve the markets in which small producers sold their old and new staple food crops? These questions required relaxing the exclusive focus on rice.[42] In this round of field research, I looked at markets not only for rice but also for potatoes and mustard oil, in the major surplus district of Bardhaman. Chapter 6 records what I discovered about the elements and power relations of the system of old and new markets, and Chapter 7 the sources of institutional change and the evolving relations of regulation.

I asked the third set of questions in 2000–03, as West Bengal was consolidating itself as India's largest rice-producing state, and as domestic state regulation was being reluctantly and slowly cut back. How had these markets responded to changes in the structures through which markets were regulated? On this occasion, I drew on both my own work and that of others, looking again at rice markets, from 2000 to a crisis of deregulation that occurred in 2002, and following the system of markets right up to the stage of retail sales in Kolkata. Chapter 8 describes the changes that had occurred, or were occurring, in the institutional embeddedness of the system of markets, while Chapter 9 examines the process of political and organizational reform in markets, and the crisis in production which resulted.

The final chapter, Chapter 10 collates the results of these three studies and relates them not only to the specific questions motivating each round of research but also to the general questions with which the first chapter has been concerned. It should perhaps be stressed that this is an account of state-market relations in the central regions of West Bengal, not of the entire state. It is also an account of the engagement of agro-commercial capital with the state during the period of Left Front Government rule, not a study of Left Front Government politics. Observations on the field methods and samples can be found in Appendix 1.1.

Notes

1. The market is one of the three principal denominations in the conceptual coinage of contemporary international institutions of aid and development finance—the others being state and civil society/'social capital'. (Mackintosh, 1990; World Bank, 1997; and Fine 2002).
2. Joan Robinson 1962, the precise written origin of which I have been unable to re-trace. See also Akerlof, 1999, Caille, 1993, Crow, 2001 and Hodgson, 2001 for criticisms of the treatment of markets in neo-classical and new institutional economics.
3. Sarkar (1989) used empirical material re-worked from the Bardhan-Rudra data set on exchange, drawn from 221 villages in West Bengal (Rudra and Bardhan 1983).
4. Bhaduri, 1986: interlocked commerce makes it difficult to define equilibrium or identify a competitive alternative for a subordinate party deprived of choice, or to separate interest and price. Resources may also be appropriated through interlocked rental contracts involving land and/or water and commodities, through triadic exchange involving these and money (Janakarajan, 1993)). The latter's structural model is unique in arguing that the interlocking of markets does not have of necessity to block growth or to stay the technical transformation of agriculture (and evidently it didn't in the South Indian region where it was observed).
5. Distress commerce of this general type has been quite widely observed coexisting with normal commerce under a variety of agrarian structures in South Asia (Nadkarni, 1980; Harriss et al., 1984; Crow, 1991; Olsen, 1991, 1996).
6. The ways in which the transformation of agrarian relations and agricultural growth change the social composition of the marketed surplus and the behaviour of markets has been empirically investigated by Ben Crow in two contrasting regions of Bangladesh (2001). Crow found that in a region where production has been transformed and wage labour has developed, rich peasants dominate the market whereas in a backward region characterized by sharecropping, landlords and mercantile moneylenders prevail. He does not argue that a transformation of agriculture is impossible without a change in market structure in the backward region but he does show how class specific terms and conditions, prices, and seasons of exchange act so as to differentiate peasant society. The different regional market conditions contribute to class formation in different ways.
7. 'There still remains lot of confusion and disagreement on how to theorize the role of institutions, in particular their relationship with the market and the state' (Chang, 2003, p. 41).
8. One has only to look at the exceptionalism of research by economists into the firm (Hodgson, 2001).
9. See for example Chang, 2003, pp. 53–54 and Hodgson, 2001. No research into agricultural markets known to me has ever considered either this list of

Analysing Markets

institutions or considered the criteria that ought to govern the contents of such a list.

10. See exemplary research by Ellis et al, 1991; Spoor, 1991; Bryceson, 1993, Pujo, 1997, Mukhopadhyay, 1998; van Ufford, 1999; J. Basu, 2002, and Larsen, 2004.

11. See the reviews of new institutional economics/transactions cost economics, industrial organization, and filiere/value chains in Harriss-White, 1996 and of economic sociological approaches, politics of markets, and social structures of accumulation in Harriss–White, 2003.

12. In its Anglo-Saxon incarnation, the commodity systems approach has tended to focus on the rationale for vertical integration, on economies of scale, and on institutional responses to market imperfections (Jaffee, 1991; Ellis et al., 1991). The Francophone version ("filieres") traces descriptively the organizational, contractual forms taken by a commodity system, their costs and profits (Pujo, 1997).

13. In his innovative book *How Economics forgot History*—on the now marginalized question of historical specificity in economics—Hodgson (2001) has started to tackle the problem of identifying both the *market-making* and the *non-market* institutions without which markets will not function. Even though he rejects concepts of purity in an economy, he nevertheless needs to call these institutions 'impurities' (Hodgson, 2001, pp. 341–3).

14. Harriss, 1976 b on perishable fruits and vegetables, low status onions, garlic, and meat in periodic marketplace trade.

15. For Hodgson, a 'real' type (of provisioning system, such as capitalism) contains variation and can encompass a variety of forms (p. 343). Lenin had been here earlier : 'infinitely diverse combinations of elements of this or that type of capitalist evolution are possible'—quoted by C.T. Kurien in his review of Geoff Kay's study of merchant capital under colonialism—and of its modes of alliance with the reactionary elements of the pre-capitalist ruling class which blocked the capitalist transition (Kurien, 1977, p. 430).

16. Taknet, 1986, p. 173. see also Dobbin, 1996, p. 3 where it is suggested that Tata (Parsee) and Birla (Marwari) alone controlled 40 per cent of the assets of the top 20 industrial companies in India in 1978; and Hardgrove writes that Marwaris control 60 per cent of the Indian business sector in the current era (2002, Introduction p. 7)

17. See Pache Huber, 2002 on the Maheshwari community and Laidlaw 1992 for Jains.

18. Taknet, 1986; pp. 156–7; pp. 164–8; Lachaier, 2000; Saha, 2003, p. 305.

19. Quoted in Hardgrove 2002, Introduction, p. 3. The reasons for the accumulative success of mercantile diasporas have been sought in a plethora of factors: i) geographical determinism (the harsh environment of Marwar forcing out-migration); ii) genetic superiority (theories of entrepreneurial races, hereditary calling and entrepreneurial personality type (discussed in Taknet, 1986, ch. 6, and critically in Dobbin 1996, ch. 1)); iii) religious

ideologies legitimating wealth, rendering wealth a sacred duty to accumulate, sacralising the means of accumulation and often aligning thrift with personal ascetism (Laidlaw, 1995); iv) distinctive cultures of cosmopolitan modernity, combining the capture of state–allocated resources with a conservative domesticity involving the seclusion of women (Hardgrove, 2002); v) the efficient structuring roles of network organization; vi) histories of comprador agency for (and their finance of) British commercial exploitation, and vii) the pre- and post-independence usurpation of the British managing agencies.

But success has also been seen as due to resistance to any disciplining by British colonial power and the modern Indian state. Datta discusses creative informal accounting the capability of family businesses, and networks to manage capital flight (Dutta, 1997). Hardgrove researched collusive speculation, relating it to gambling within the community and to exploitation across the community boundary. (see Hardgrove 2002, ch. 5 on speculation in wheat, rice, and cotton in the period between 1919 and 1926). 'No means to make profit are forbidden' writes Taknet (op.cit., p 167) and this extends to adulteration. Hardgrove gives historical evidence for the adulteration of milk, ghee, mustard oil, and wheat flour (Ibid.). Taknet records strong intra-community preferences in the circulation of information about prices and production and of knowledge about contacts and finance (Taknet, 1986, p. 157; see also Hardgrove 2002, ch 2. p 8). The intense exclusivity of 'hands-on' management implies a reluctant and delayed incorporation of other castes as professional managers and intense resistence to hostile takeovers (Dutta, 1997).

20. Timberg, 1978; Saha 2003, p. 215 See Taknet, op cit; Timberg, 1978 and Hardgrove, 2002, for the early history of marwaris as landowners and bankers to rulers in N.W India.

21. Hardgrove, 2002, Preface, p. 3; Introduction, p. 5; Datta, 1997; Taknet, 1986, p. 177.

22. Dobbin has explored whether Asian entrepreneurial minorities underdeveloped or developed those who produced the commodities they traded and concludes that it is not possible to generalize (1996, p. 209) and that production conditions at the outset are crucial to the explanation. Taknet observes that marwaris lent money to daily wage earners, peasants and small artisans at any time of the day or night (1986, p. 91) and concludes that every village or small *dhani* speaks volumes of the numerous marwari seths and sahukars whose generosity and philanthropy has made life a little better and fuller for the common man (op. cit. p. 111). By contrast, Hardgrove writes of Bengali resentment of what was seen as their draining the life blood of peasants to the British (2002, 2001, Intro, p. 2) and ruining Bengalis on whom they depended for their livelihood (op.cit. Ch 5, p. 17), adding that 'local Bengalis do the same thing without such denigration' (ibid.).

23. To my knowledge, no attempt has yet been made to describe and theorise the co-evolution of the many dimensions of culture (of which ethnicity is but one) in their role as economic regulators.

24. In West Bengal, it extends from hospitals and higher education (much handed to the state after Independence) to wayside inns, constructions for electricity and hospital buildings, market sites and relief work (Taknet, 1986; Saha 2003).
25. Taknet even uses the adjective 'unassimilated' for them (1986, p 157). Hardgrove examines public attitudes in great depth and shows how the Marwari, identity and public culture in Kolkata has been selectively constructed in relation to these attitudes. In other words, the process of 'othering' is both deliberate and mutually reflexive. Taknet and Hardgrove both note recent anti-marwari disturbances in the north-east states, Orissa, Bombay, and Kolkata (Taknet, op. cit., 169; Hardgrove, op. cit.).
26. Patnaik's critical analysis of the Left Front (2001) does not mention markets, commerce or merchants once.
27. See Myrdal, 1968; Lal, 1988; Mendelsohn, 1993; Panini, 1996; Beteille, 1996 for instances from economics, sociology and anthropology.
28. But that we observe fundamental institutional diversity in markets does not mean that an evolutionary process may be extrapolated to society, with markets 'naturalized' as the mechanism of survival of the fittest. Hodgson's claim to have identified in this a mechanism of transition from one real type of provisioning such as feudalism to another such as capitalism is just as open to criticism as his criticism of Marx's failure to provide transhistorical theory and as is Hodgson's related claim to have solved the problem of agency. The problem for Hodgson is whether mutation or competitive selection are at all appropriate categories or concepts by means of which to account for the change in his key drivers: the non-market institutions from which he argues that the central institutions of modern capitalism have evolved.
29. Further, as with institutions, so with the agency through which institutions change, there will be dominance and prominence. The debates over dictatorship and altruism within the household (Folbre, 1995), over motivation in social psychology (McClelland, 1995), the critique of utility maximisation (Hodgson, 2001) and of public/rational choice theory applied to the state (Green and Shapiro, 1994; Chang, 2003, p. 55) have all made this point (but have not pursued the very far reaching implications for the economics of it).
30. It is out of the scope of this chapter to review the state regulation of agricultural inputs, but see Landy 1997, for the regulation of fertilizer, Moitra and Das (nd./2003) for water and Janakarajan, 2004, for agricultural electricity.
31. Chibber argues that capital mounted an effective offensive before and after Independence to defang the disciplinary regulation necessary to ISI (Chibber, 2003, pp. 14–23, ch. 6).
32. See the schema set out in Gordon White's politics of markets, 1993 which is simplified here.

33. As I write, I have before me a good example of 'saturating' parametric regulation: Iranian pistachio nuts sold in Paris inside a hygienically sealed packet with a comforting label announcing their weight, nutritional values, and the fact that they are manufactured in Belgium, providing information identifying the commodity, its quantity, its places of origin and of manufacture, and its significance as food preserved in packaging conforming to EU phytosanitary regulations.
34. Harriss-White, 2004 a, with respect to agriculture; Harriss-White and Gooptu, 2000, with respect to labour and Harriss-White 2004 b with respect to social security.
35. This study does not move the analysis of the finance of such regulation forward. The relation between tax, revenue, and expenditure on commodity market regulation from capital and current account is out of the scope of this research, as it has been with all research on agricultural markets (and almost all research on development policy generally). However, state legitimacy and accountability depend in no small measure on fiscal capability (Roy, 1996).
36. Mooij, 1999 on The Essential Commodities Act.
37. Contradictions originally identified in studies of Tamil Nadu, Harriss, 1984.
38. See Harriss-White, 2003, chs. 3 and 4.
39. By the 1980s, the cities and politically sensitive rural areas of India as a whole were increasingly covered by state trading, although field studies of state trading are few and far between—see Subbarao, 1978; Harriss, 1984; Swaminathan, 2000. The one detailed comparative ethnography of food policy—Jos Mooij's study of Kerala and Karnataka (1999 b)—shows divergent forms of implementation, not only between states but at different 'levels' of the food administration within these states. The market-driven politics of food system regulation hammer home what was already evident by 1982: *that both markets and states are suffused with institutional diversity*, and that it is through this institutional diversity that accumulation takes place, consumption is structured and classes form.
40. It will be obviously incomplete because it is the market system which links production with consumption; less trivially the market system provides substantial number of livelihoods—many seasonal ones without which the agrarian production structure could not reproduce itself. The post-harvest system is as much part of the agrarian structure as the pre-harvest system. The process of commodity production in agriculture requires the transformation of commodity production in the rural non-agricultural economy.
41. A reflection on field methodology is to be found in Appendix 1. 1.
42. For readers wishing to learn about rice, chapters 6 and 7 may be read selectively.

3 A History of West Bengal's Food Economy

This chapter introduces those aspects of the history of markets, the food economy, and the towns of the region which form an essential background to the three rounds of field research reported in the rest of the book. It describes how rice, and later other crops such as potato and mustard, came to be produced in West Bengal as commodities for sale via long-distance trade. It shows how the market system that operates in West Bengal today is the product of a distinctive combination of factors: the fertility of the land, the proximity of a vast metropolis, Calcutta (later known as Kolkata); the distinctive role played by an immigrant class of commodity traders; dramatic transformations in production technology; and the efforts of post-independence governments, swimming with and against the capitalist current, to pursue policies that would maintain incomes for the rural masses—efforts that did not meet with conspicuous success.

In 1981, a quarter of a century ago, the state of West Bengal had 13 per cent of the total area under paddy in India, and produced 14 per cent of India's rice.[1] But the conditions under which paddy was produced were relatively primitive. Three quarters of the paddy was produced in the monsoon season, aman, with water supplied mainly by rainfall and canal irrigation. West Bengal then had only 10 per cent as many 'energized' (power-operated) wells as Tamil Nadu, for 2.4 times as many acres of paddy. The previous decade and a half (1965–80) had seen only a slight increase in overall productivity. In 1978, yields of 1.42 tonnes of rice per hectare were slightly above the all-India average, but compared unfavourably with those of Punjab, with 2.7 tonnes. Fertilizers were still at the experimental stage in the fields. High-yielding varieties of rice were confined to the IADP district of Bardhaman (Table 3.1).[2] With the exception of 1980–1, total production of rice was in decline—from 7.5 m. tonnes in 1977-8 to only 5.5 m. tonnes in 1981-2.

The state of West Bengal needed 9 m tonnes[3] and so had to import 2–4 m. tonnes of grain needed for plantation regions, the industrial belts, and Kolkata. The bulk of such imports came from trade which was 'free', after a fashion, subject to permits from the government. It

Table 3.1: Production of Staple Foods Birbhum and Bardhaman Districts 1975-95 (index numbers)

Production Cereals (1971-2 = 100)

	Ba	Bi	WB rice	(boro) rice	pulses	mustard oil	potato
1975–6	124	99	110	151	115	103	186
1980–1	127	102	119	145	67	208	227
1990–1	193	138	167	447	53	882	518
1994–5	213	137	196	506	37	784	641

Source: Government of West Bengal, 1996, Table 5.2, pp. 56-62.

also came from the central government's trading operations through the Food Corporation of India (FCI). Local FCI procurement was decentralized, consisting of compulsory levies exacted from local rice mills. Over the five years from 1977—when the Left Front Government came to power—the volume of local procurement had declined by a third, and of West Bengal's total paddy production in 1981, only 1 per cent entered the Public Distribution System (PDS). Furthermore, over half the state's rice mills lay idle. So long as the public distribution system existed in this form, the government of West Bengal was increasingly dependent upon the central government's decisions for the supply of ration rice. But as with local procurement, this source of supply was also declining. Until the late 1970s, an average of 355,000 tonnes of grain had been allocated to West Bengal by the FCI, but in 1979–80, this dropped to 225,000 tonnes, which fed the statutory and modified ration areas (the coal belt and Calcutta, respectively) at state-administered prices.

Why were total rice production, local state procurement, and long distance FCI grain allocations all in decline? The answers are rooted in the marketing system, with which we begin. In this chapter, in order to avoid repetition, the history of the rice marketing system is empirically grounded in Birbhum, the first of the two districts studied, while the description of the contemporary food economy is grounded in Bardhaman, the second district studied (see Map 2). Both districts are traversed by the river Padma, a distributary of the Ganges, and have old alluvial soils in the shallow river valleys and lateritic soil on the dry plateaus which separate them. Both receive 1,500 mm of rain in a normal year but are vulnerable to combinations of drought and

A History of West Bengal's Food Economy   49

flood. Both are 'rice bowls' which had expanded the cropped area under gravity flow irrigation in the 1960s and' 70s. Both are known for sharecropping, although in reality a great range of scales of production, forms of organization of labour, land tenures, and contractual arrangements co-exist. (Chattopadhyay, 1991a; ch. 2). The two districts are a mosaic of agro-ecological and cultural regions marked by distinctive distributions of castes, tribal people, and religions, sometimes known as rural 'clusters' (op.cit., ch. 3). Birbhum district has 3 m inhabitants, is only 10 per cent urban, and nearly 40 per cent of the population is composed of scheduled castes and scheduled tribes (SC/ST). By contrast, Bardhaman district now has a population of about 7 m, of which one third is urban while over one third consists of scheduled caste and scheduled tribal people. While Birbhum district has relatively high fertility, high infant and child mortality, and low human development indicators; Bardhaman is more human-developed (NCAER, 2004; p. 275). Table 3.2 provides a statistical profile of the two districts in the 1990s.

Development of the System of Markets for Rice in Birbhum district from 1850 to 1977

Birbhum district (Map 2) produces about 10 per cent of West Bengal's rice and wheat. For well over a century, it has been a surplus-producing district and for well over half a century a net donor to the state system.

Rice was commercialized on a large scale in the wake of commercialization of crops such as indigo, jute, and mulberry after the Permanent Settlement, but it was carried out by the Indian rather than British capital.[4] In the struggle between merchant and landlord 'trying to pluck the same goose', merchants amassed wealth (Ghosh and Dutt, 1977, pp. 33–52). The origins of these mercantile firms are treated obliquely by historians; Ghosh and Dutt say only they were 'self-made men', entrepreneurs, investing profits in land and mercantile property. Patnaik called them 'independent' (1981)—meaning neither rich peasants nor landlords. Their origin is shrouded in the mystery in which the Left leaves *Marwari* capitalists, whose history was described in Chapter 1 and whose extended diasporic migration enabled them to dominate the rural economy.

The development of long-distance trade in rice was greatly facilitated by the construction of railways. In 1859–60, a line from Hooghly reached Bolpur (the town at the centre of our field research in 1982

Table 3.2: A Statistical Profile of Bardhaman and Birbhum Districts 1990s

	Population 2001 (m)	% urban	% sched. castes	% sched. tribes	% net sown	% cultivated area per agricultural worker (ha)	index no production 1972=100	% rural population cultivators (1991)	% rural population agricultural labourers (1991)	literacy M	literacy F
Bardhaman	7	36	27	6	68	0.5	237	21	29	71	51
Birbhum	3	9	31	7	68	0.6	141	32	35	59	37
West Bengal	80	27	23	5	62	0.5	206	27	23	67	46

	% WB's elec consumption 1983-4	% WB's elec consumption 1991-2	Banks 1981	Banks 1995
Bardhaman	25	20	184	363
Birbhum	0.7	1.2	93	174
Kolkata	62	62		

Sources: Government of West Bengal, 1996, Table 14, pp. 205–7; Table 2.1, p. 147; Table 9, p. 152–3.

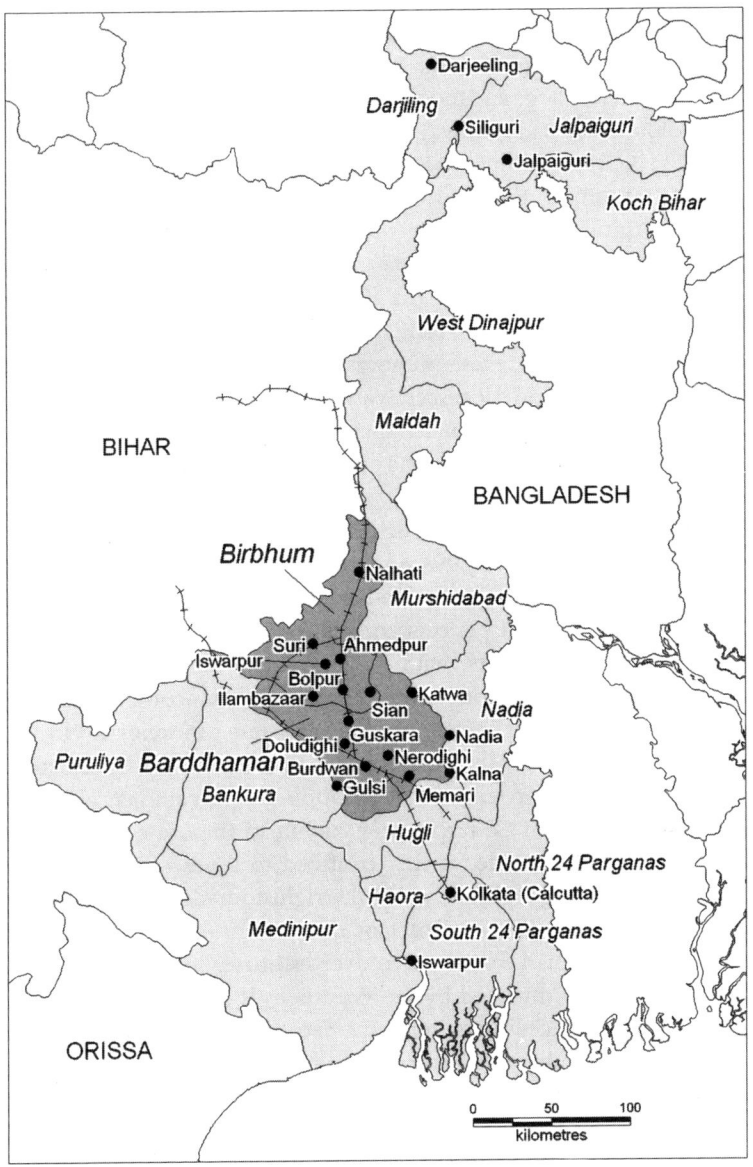

Source: Bodleian Library Map Collection, Oxford University.

Map 2: West Bengal: Birbhum and Bardhaman Districts

and 2000/02), and became the sole artery of supply because of the region's isolation, cut off as it was by the Ajoy river. By 1876–7, the *Report of the Burdwan Division* mentioned that 'trade in rice is unprecedentedly large and most traffic poured into Ahmadpur, Sainthia, and Bolpur faster than railways have been able to carry it away' (see Map 2). By 1900, Bolpur was the chief rice exporting town in the district, a position defended throughout the 20th century. It is also clear that throughout the 20th century, rice wholesaling firms were to be found in small towns, with links of credit to the rich peasant traders in the countryside. In 1946, the towns of Bolpur and Sainthia each had 28 dealers, Suri 17, and Nalhati 7. But during the immediate post-independence period, these numbers increased rapidly; in 1961 they were 84, 46, 49, and 19 respectively (Mukherjee, 1996; Chaudhuri, 1979). Many of these rice merchants probably also controlled textiles, tobacco and hides, which were the other important traded commodities (Government of India, 1960; p. 142). The post-war period saw a large wave of migration of Rajasthani Marwaris and Gujarati Baniyas into rural West Bengal. In the ten years, 1951–61, the proportion of businessmen from other parts of India in Bolpur's population increased from 2.5 per cent to 11 per cent and contributed to its unprecedented growth. These merchants, with no direct connection to local land, reinforced the indirect commercial control of production by creating their own networks of agents, working a system of money advances.

The 1960s also saw the beginning of polarization in the structure of commercial enterprise. The concentration of agro-commercial capital encouraged the then Congress government to impose controls over the paddy and rice trade, at first confined to times of drought and scarcity, conferring legitimacy and the right to trade on a handful of licensed rice millers. The impact of this system of licensing on the structure of rice markets is hard to over-estimate. Some of the effects cannot have been intended by the West Bengal government. It led to much evasion of licensed trade, to the decentralization of transactions and to an influx into trading of large numbers of farmers with investible surpluses. Their applications for trading licences far exceeded the number granted. Hardly surprising then that they diversified, and that the number of parched-rice and paddy husking machines also increased. By 1967, Uma Lele, who made an important study of rice markets in the region, could conclude that 'the grain trade is overcrowded' (1971, p. 66).

From then onwards, the process of polarization intensified, exacerbated in all probability by state controls on the movement of rice, which made spatial price differences alluring to smugglers. Substantial numbers of landless and small holding peasants began to enter rice marketing, at least on a seasonal basis. Just as petty commodity production had come to dominate the agrarian economy, petty traders swarmed into the marketing system. The proliferation of small intermediaries in the 1950s and 1960s was possible because of the wide price margins between paddy and milled rice, and a cost of production of paddy that was 20 to 30 per cent lower in West Bengal than in other major rice-producing states, such as Madras (Government of India, 1961; p. 101).

Over the long term, however, there was little overall increase in productivity. The diversion of the surplus into the support of this increasingly polarized system of commercial capital must be an important element in the explanation of West Bengal's subsequent agricultural stagnation. By the early 1980s and the time of our first fieldwork in Bolpur, such was this diversion that the number of rice merchants had drastically declined, from a one-time maximum of 84 to about 13.

By then, however, not all the capital in marketing was purely mercantile. A thin layer of industrial capital had formed, for paddy had to be converted into rice. 'Processing industries are even more powerful disintegrating factors in agriculture than in trade in raw commodities...because...they take away from the cultivator a number of operations formerly closely integrated to agriculture, thus increasing his under-employment' (Ghosh and Dutt, 1977, p. 52). Or rather, it led to increasing the underemployment of his wife and daughters-in-law.

The husking machine (adapted from a coffee grinder by a Scot, Lewis Grant, in 1898, and still the most common mill in South Asia over a century later) allows cultivators to transform paddy into rice mechanically. It has put paid to the back-breaking pounding of paddy using the dekhi, a foot-operated pestle. The diffusion of the husker went unnoticed in official records. In 1951, there were apparently 500 licensed machines in India as a whole (Government of India, 1954); by the mid 1960s, Uma Lele records the existence of 6,000 licensed and 6,000 unlicensed machines (1971, p. 73). In 1961 there were 51 husking machines in Bolpur's surrounding villages, and this number was expected to double in less than five years (Mukherjee, 1965).

The diffusion of the small-scale husking machine was and is regarded by rice millers as a threat to their paddy supplies. The first phase of its diffusion appears to have been the 1950s and '60s. It predates the era of stagnation in production and is most unlikely to be causally related to it.[5] It is during the period before the 'green revolution' that an estimated 1.2 million livelihoods, largely those of women, were lost from dekhi processing in the north-eastern region of India. Near Bolpur, Sahajapur village alone saw a reduction in employment from 102 dheki jobs in 1950, when the first husker was installed, to two full-time and six part-time jobs by 1956 (Bhattacharjee et al., 1958).

Large-scale rice mill technology spread from Burma to Madras (now Chennai in Tamil Nadu) and thence northwards to the present West Bengal. The proliferation of large-scale rice mills also had a destructive effect on the local labour used for the dheki processing of commercialized rice. Agro-processing was always the most inviting way for agro-commercial capital to move into the industry. The political acceptability of wide price margins between wholesale paddy and retail rice enabled rice mills to generate relatively high returns, even when up-country towns were surrounded by relatively large numbers of mills.[6] Unlike husking mills, rice mills also developed their own integral parboiling facilities and drying yards, and came to dominate the agro-processing stage, gaining control of the growing part of the marketed surplus that was destined for consumption outside its region of production. In Birbhum district, of the 53 firms registered under the Factories Act in 1944, 47 were rice mills (Ghosh and Dutt, 1977; p. 54). The labour on which parboiling, drying and milling depended was plentiful and cheap.

But the accumulation of mercantile and agro-industrial capital did not trigger a technical transformation of agricultural production. The existence of rice mills was not a sufficient condition for the further commercialization of rice. Nonetheless, expansion in the number of mills did accompany a slow increase in the marketed surplus (Table 3.3).

In the late fifties, the marketed surplus was estimated at between 31-33 per cent of production (Government of India, 1960, p. 132,; Bhattacharjee, et al., 1958; p. 86). By the early 1980s, it had increased to about 40 per cent (Ghosh et al., 1983).

A History of West Bengal's Food Economy

Table 3.3: Rice Mills in West Bengal

Date	Number
1953	298
1960	494 (19 in Bolpur)
1962	515
1967	729
1969	741

Notes: The data for the recent period are 1990; 412 rice mills, 1995: 477; 2000: 514; and 2001: 562 rice mills
Source: Office of the District Controller, in Kaur, Ghosh and Sudarshan, 2007.

Rice mills rapidly developed trading activities of their own, challenging the independent wholesale firms. As early as the 1940s and 1950s, millers succeeded in being licensed as commission agents for government procurement operations at times of food controls, and with each periodic relaxation of controls, they became more strongly entrenched (Government of India, 1960; p. 128).

Yet by the early 1980s, rice mills, like rice wholesalers, were far less numerous than they had been earlier. Indeed, fewer than half the 741 mills of the late 1960s—about 300—were working. The industry was widely thought to be in decline, but it was actually just becoming more concentrated. A transfer of ownership had accompanied the initial numerical expansion of rice mills. In his conclusion to a study of paddy purchases in Bolpur between 1933–4 and 1961–3, Mukherjee noted that 'the control of the mills has largely passed on to financially stronger parties, mostly of Calcutta, having a wide inter-state network of procuring and storing centres' (1966, p. 248)—another allusion to Marwari and Baniya capital. The fact was that the investment in rice processing capacity had been excessive, and it was inevitable that, given the static production of the 1970s, there would be a weeding-out.

Locations and Flows

For most of the first half of the twentieth century, the sites of trade had been decentralized because the development of long-distance transport of rice to Kolkata preceded the development of large-scale mechanized processing technology. After Independence, commerce and processing became increasingly urbanized, until the election of the Left Front Government, after which a new army of landless petty traders started to decentralize it once more. Seasonal wayside marketplaces emerged in response to official controls.

Although Birbhum and Bardhaman districts have long been in surplus, Bengal in the 1930s as a whole passed from being a net exporter of rice to a net importer. At first rice came from Burma, later to be replaced with imports from other regions of India. The per capita availability of rice throughout this period of change in flows is thought to have remained roughly constant, having already fallen to a low level in the 1920s. Though the availability of foodgrains remained stable, producers' access to food was changing. Small farmers who had to work as sharecroppers and labourers to earn income from rice became increasingly vulnerable to the vagaries of two key markets—rice and labour (Mukherjee, 1981; Sen, 1981).

Commodity flows consisted of two types: local and long distance. In the late 1950s, it was estimated that 42 per cent of production was for subsistence; payments in kind to labour accounted for 14–15 per cent, and sales for 33 per cent (Government of India, 1960; p. 132). While about 70 per cent of this marketed surplus was sold between December and April, only half of the annual total reached Calcutta during these months (Lele, 1971; p. 129). This meant that much of what was sold consisted of distress sales, and a few speculators stored grains in rural areas. In times of drought, rural hoarding could seriously disrupt the operations of both rice mills and long-distance trade, putting 'surplus' districts into apparent 'deficit'.[7]

Moneylending and Price Behaviour

In 19th century Bengal, an 'independent' merchant-moneylender class developed an indirect control over agriculture by means of money advances. The *zamindars* did not generally collect rent in kind and then sell it in order to pay taxes in cash to the government; it made tenants sell their grain and pay rent in cash. The intricate hierarchy of rent collectors, however, ultimately cost zamindars their power over the process of production. It was now not the landlord but rather the merchant who lent money for production, and it was in the mercantile class and the marwari community rather than among either landlords or *ryots* (peasant producers) that increases in wealth were concentrated. Anticipating the near-bankruptcy of their landed clients, some marwaris diversified their mercantile and moneylending activities and invested in land, to the extent that after independence, marwari mercantile intermediaries were considered by scholars to be effectively fused with the class of landlords and *kulak*-traders (Ghosh and Dutt, 1977; pp. 1–33; pp. 133–41). A typical trader, banker, and landlord would own in the region of 50 acres of land.

The Government of India's *Report on the Pace and Pattern of Market Arrivals of Foodgrains* in 1960 offers this account of the process of vertical integration using money advances, which has persisted into the twenty-first century:

Some (of these wholesaler miller-farmers) also own grocers' shops and some others are dealers in fertilizers. In both these capacities, they often extend credit to the smaller producers on condition that the repayment is effected in paddy after harvest. It is in this way that the big producers and some of the ex-zamindars started to acquire command over paddy stocks after harvest. Recently they have also entered the field of trade and milling of rice. This has led to the emergence of a new type of imperfection in the rice markets, particularly in the areas where transportation has been well developed (Government of India, 1960; p. 148–9).

It was precisely such intermediaries who invested in transport, so that in the rainy season it was less and less difficult to send supplies from the villages to the mills.

Lele's work (1971, p. 52) reminds us that the extension and retraction of traders' finance of production forms cycles, each for different reasons. In the mid-1960s, for instance, competition from nationalized banks and the higher levels of risk attached to traders' money-lending (because of intermittent and unpredictable state controls over trade) had encouraged a withdrawal of traders' money advances and a transfer of capital to experiments in agro-industry. But then land reforms and the inexorable subdivision of large landholdings put paid to the land-base of these commercial capitalists, so by the early 1980s, their direct financing of tenants' production was again declining, along with the reported lendings by paddy purchase agents.

Throughout this period of technical change and expansion in milling, price behaviour did not change much. Little of the impact of the upheavals in structure is betrayed in surviving crude indicators of performance. Ever since the 1950s—and possibly earlier—the rice market of West Bengal had been marked by more exaggerated price fluctuations (between pre-harvest highs and post-harvest lows), and by wider distributive margins, than elsewhere in India (Government of India, 1961; p. 142). Furthermore, while the seasonal amplitude of all-India rice price fluctuations increased—widening from 11.1 per cent above and below average to 22.8 per cent during the 1950s (op cit., p. 66)—these variations increased more greatly in West Bengal than in any other major foodgrain-producing region. Lele's study of returns to storage in West Bengal in the late '50s and early '60s showed that in 7 out of 10 years, the seasonal price increase was 'moderately high' to 'excessive' (Lele, 1971; p. 113; p. 136).

Lele's claim, however, that this behaviour can be explained only as a result of government restrictions, with millers moving rice stocks to terminal markets as early in the season as possible so as to avoid seizure (op. cit., p. 59), was probably wrong, given that the practice of rural stocking was of long standing and that storage capacities at rice mills could hold two thirds of their annual turnover (op. cit., p. 191). Millers were well able to store and to speculate on pre-harvest price spikes. Other reasons advanced for the unusually wide margins in West Bengal include the prevalence of collusive oligopolies at key points in the marketing system; the fact that a far larger proportion of traded rice was procured at less than open market prices by state-trading institutions for the public distribution system than elsewhere in India, resulting in a compensating hoist to open or residual market wholesale prices (Harriss, 1997); and inter-regional trade restrictions, depressing prices in surplus districts and raising them in deficit districts.

Despite her verdict that rice markets were efficient and competitive, Lele's detailed price analyses reveal spatial price differences that were irregular in ways which do not look 'competitive' and need more explanation than she gave. For example, between December 1955 and December 1958, prices in Burdwan (later called Bardhaman) and Guskara were higher than in Calcutta: anyone trading rice from the former to the latter would have made a loss. During the years 1959–63, the difference in price was commonly less than Rs. 4/- per quintal. Similarly, in six of the eight years between 1955 and 1963, farm prices in Bardhaman district were declared to be at the same level as, or greater than, local wholesale prices, and in five of these years in Birbhum too (Lele, 1971, pp. 44–117; pp. 86–9). To conclude, as Lele did, that this reflects 'the costs of movement between primary and terminal markets' (ibid., p. 177) begs further questions and prompts further conjectures. These types of spatial disjuncture might suggest a system where grain is first funnelled into centralized storage and then returned to outlying market places; Lele's data certainly show high returns to storage. Or they could be a product of the conditions of production of

A History of West Bengal's Food Economy

the *data* which, supposing they are not defective, may be averaged in such a way as to mask short-term variations from which merchants make some of their profit (Harriss-White, 1996). Even if we accept the limitations of data on prices and costs, in the absence of evidence about flows and stocks, it is hard to see that the conclusion that the markets were competitive is justified.

Technology
The history of technological change in the post-harvest system for rice since Independence has made nonsense of the apparent objectives of planning. As late as 1955, only seven years before the first modern solvent oil extraction plant for rice bran—still the most advanced technology for its purpose today—was installed in West Bengal, a central government Committee was set up to determine the extent to which processing rice 'by hand' (or by foot pounding in West Bengal) could meet the needs of the country! Recapitulating the principles of the First Five Year Plan, the Committee recognized that 'a programme of village industries has to be supported both by specific measures of assistance as well as by appropriate state policy...for a common productive programme between large scale and cottage industries... with special emphasis on employment' (Government of India, 1955, pp. 317–8). The committee concluded that for reasons of nutrition and employment, the 'Government should formulate a programme for the replacement of the huller type of rice mills by the organized hand pounding of rice' (Government of India, 1955, pp. 103, 43–7 and 322).

These aims accorded with those of the First Five Year Plan, which envisaged a co-operative condominium of organized cottage industries as the goal of development. The committee approved production subsidies for hand pounding and the imposition of capacity constraints on large rice-processing industries. It forbade further expansion of large-scale industry in food processing. Rules and regulations on the statute book reflect this vision to this day, but material conditions rapidly evolved to render them unimplementable. The displacement of labour that occurred due to technological changes in rice, pulse, and oil processing during the 1950s and 1960s must rank, in its disintegrative effects on household livelihoods, with the more widely researched displacement of labour from rural textiles manufacture under colonial rule (Harriss and Kelly, 1982; Roy, 2002).

Yet by the mid-1960s in West Bengal, milling capacity was suffering, as we have seen, from massive private over-investment. The investment had been a response to the existence of an investible surplus, wide distributive margins, and ignorance on the part of individual investors about the aggregate effect of many investing at once. Even Lele concludes that the expansion of the number of rice mills occurred without this industry becoming more competitive (1971, p. 188). The variable costs of rice mills revealed that milling was predominantly a trading operation where the major component of value added came from storage and only a minor component was added in the production of rice from paddy (op.cit., p. 191). This minor component attracted petty processors and covered their subsistence requirements, out-competing the mills.

As aggregate capacity was expanding as a result of the growth in both the numbers and types of mills, the capacity utilization of individual mills dropped sharply. Paradoxically, the new sheller technology which was introduced in the late 1960s also reduced the out-turn of rice from paddy (from 69–70 per cent to 64 per cent). Seasonal peaks and slumps of activity were evened out, since the new parboiling technology made the mills less and less dependent upon sunshine. The ownership of assets in the industry continued to become more concentrated, while the diffusion of small husking mills threatened the household-based manual processing of rice more than it threatened the big rice mills.

Labour

In 1954, the Director of Statistics, West Bengal, produced a memorable comment on public-sector planning and on the consequences of change in mill technology:

The net result [of the installation of rural rice mills] was that thousands and thousands of rural people (especially women) lost their avocations as rice huskers all over the state. The logic of this rationalized practice can only be termed as twisted, twisted deliberately by a handful of organized capitalists and labourers in the sole purpose of appropriating the entire value added by this important food industry to themselves, depriving scores of thousands of small producers of their means of livelihood (Government of India, 1955, p. 5, para 3.6).

But West Bengal government's resolve to resurrect the "professional class of hand pounders", reorganize them in co-operatives, and extend them credit was a pipe-dream.

A History of West Bengal's Food Economy

If organized capital had the capacity deliberately to twist the policy agenda, labour did not, for in the 1950s, it was not yet well organized in unions. Referring to 1961, Mukherjee pointed out that rice mills in Bolpur provided employment to Santal-tribal women and to long-distance migrants who did not belong to unions and had few links with local townspeople. These are the kinds of labour easiest to control. While employment in mills declined further, the millers' capital was invested in industrial, commercial and residential property, indirectly providing a small quantum of wage labour and local livelihoods in urban services.

In sum: From the period after the famine in 1943 until the era of the Left Front, production not only stagnated but was unstable, following fluctuations in the rainfall feeding the irrigation systems. The system of markets was an arena for triangular struggles between rice millers and wholesalers, small-scale traders, and the state. The state imposed and withdrew various combinations of price controls and movement restrictions; it also experimented with procurement from farmers, but found it costly and relied instead on the small class of rice millers to provide supplies for the public distribution system. Procurement declined from 3.5 per cent of production in 1977 to 1 per cent by the time of our first field study in Birbhum during 1981–2 (Chattopadhyay, 1991a; vol. 1; p. 112–3). The national Public Distribution System (or PDS) failed to move the foodgrains surplus of the Punjab to centres of need among India's rural landless agricultural labour force. Supplies fluctuated from year to year and Calcutta was prioritized.

Production and Markets in the Bardhaman district during the Era of the Left Front Government (1977 to the present)

"This is a very disturbed region—the delivery room of our Marxism" (a miller in Memari).

Bardhaman district of West Bengal (with a population of 4.8 million in 1981, and 7 million in 2001) has been the vanguard region for commercialized agricultural production, particularly for rice, where it now ranks first. Its very name means 'increasing' or 'developing' (UCO Bank, 1990; Bose, 1987; Government of West Bengal, 2003). The district was selected in 1961 for inclusion in India's Intensive Agricultural District Programme, and in 1975 for the High Yielding

Varieties (HYV) Programme. For several decades, its agricultural growth rate has been 50 per cent higher than that of West Bengal as a whole.

Vast tracts of paddy land lying in shallow valleys of the Damodar and Ajoy river basins are irrigated from major canal networks. During the 1980s, groundwater started to be exploited using private wells, and water markets started to develop (Moitra and Das, 2004). As a result, the multiple cropping of HYV rice gathered momentum, particularly in the boro (hot, pre-monsoon summer) season. Rice production increased from 449,000 tonnes in 1966 to 1,409,000 tonnes in 1989, with a remarkable 44 per cent increase in yields over the ten years 1979–1989.[8] Production also diversified remarkably, rice being rotated in the boro season with intercropped HYV 'jyoti' variety potatoes and with pumpkins, or with wheat or mustard, according to the prevailing water conditions.

Potato had been introduced as early as the 1920s. Its production received a boost from army demand during the Second World War, but settled into an erratic pattern of production, neglected by the state until the era of the Left Front Government (AERC, 1969). In 1966, the production of potato in Bardhaman district stood at 137,000 tonnes. In the late 1970s, however, it shot up, reaching 733,000 tonnes in 1980–1 and 1.03 million tonnes in 1989. With a mere seven per cent yield increase over the decade, this represented a radical change in land use (UCO Bank, 1990). In West Bengal as a whole, production shot up from 1.2 million tonnes in 1980–1 to 3.5 million tonnes in 1986–7, predominantly on the holdings of smaller producers using family labour. By 1990, production stood at 5.6 m tonnes and in 1995 it reached 7 m tonnes (Government of West Bengal, 1996; Table 5.2, p. 62). HYV 'jyoti' potato has been cultivated using relatively high levels of mechanized inputs (sprayers, seed drills, and power tillers) with relatively high cash production costs (involving, as for rice, HYV seed, fertilizers, pesticides, water, and labour). Rates of return for potato were ten times those for mustard, but the production process has always been fraught with risk. Potatoes are vulnerable to uncertain water supply during their growth and are highly perishable after being dug up (Choudhary and Sen, 1981).

Mustard production also increased, from a low base, in response to local demand. In West Bengal as a whole, production jumped from 35,100 tonnes of seed in 1960–1 to 176,900 tonnes in 1986–7 and 349,000 in 1990, before settling at 317,000 tonnes in the mid 1990s.[9] In Bardhaman district, 46,000 tonnes were produced in 1989, with a

29 per cent increase in yield in the decade from 1979 (UCO Bank, 1990). Mustard is grown on all sizes of production unit. Production is at risk from pests and from relatively high winter temperatures, and from moist weather conditions (Boyce, 1987).

Agrarian Structures

Historically, the Bardhaman region has been a major centre of sharecropping. In 1940, this tenurial form applied to 30 per cent of all land and as late as 1984, 13 per cent of the district's agricultural population were registered as being sharecroppers. The distribution of landholdings has remained relatively highly polarized. While six per cent of operators with over four hectares controlled 23 per cent of cultivated land, 52 per cent of operators with less than 1 ha each were confined to 17 per cent of the land (Webster, 1989). Bardhaman and Birbhum districts accounted for 10 per cent of the land in West Bengal's tenure reform, Operation Barga.[10] Share-cropping continues to co-exist with a variety of forms of production and landlord/labour contracts, including petty commodity production, capitalist forms, and (absentee) landlordism with cash rents. Despite the capital and scale bias of the new agricultural technology, it was widely adopted in Bardhaman district, and for a number of crops. Perhaps because of the structural and institutional reforms of the 1980s discussed in chapter 1, there is no evidence of further polarization of land control and the highly complex agrarian relations in place after the reforms seem to have remained stable (Kohli, 1987; Webster, 1989; Williams, 1998).

But exchange relations characterized as 'distress commerce' are thought by many scholars to have a tenacious hold in both regions. Analyses of the 19th and early 20th century depict the marketed surplus as sporadic, being secured through combinations of rent and money advances at usurious rates via dependent hierarchies of trading intermediaries. Such conditions are a classic example of the way the landed-mercantile elite exerts an indirect control over production so that the producer, while appearing independent, is actually a disguised form of wage labourer (Banaji, 1977). Other interpretations have, however, stressed the comparative rarity of these money advances, the productive uses to which they were put, and the independence of the trading capital financing the highly inequitable product markets (Bose, 1987).

Coercive marketing conditions certainly persist, but they are widely reported to be on the decline (Rudra and Bardhan, 1983; Crow, 2001;

Olsen, 1991; 1996). Sarkar's important reinterpretation of the famous Bardhan-Rudra data set on exchange relations shows how different agrarian classes tend to: a) market produce through different intermediaries; b) market in different locations; c) market under different contractual arrangements; and d) receive different prices (under *ceteris paribus* conditions depending on what kind of intermediary they trade with). Under these conditions, some producers do not engage in voluntary transactions, while larger scale producers stand a significantly greater chance of being able to sell at higher prices (Sarkar, 1981; p. A107). The Agro-economics Research Centre study of rice marketing in Bardhaman and other districts in the early 1980s put distress sales at only 10 per cent of the production of those holding under two hectares, and it also showed how the volume of marketed surplus was dominated by larger producers who would not be selling under duress and would receive higher prices (Ghosh and Chowdhury, 1983). In the mid 1980s, however, despite a massive infusion of co-operative production credit, Webster found that crop marketing in Bardhaman was still associated with complex exchange relations between poor peasants and small- and medium-sized landlords in which pre-harvest paddy loans at money interest rates of 10 per cent per month could also commonly be tied into forward contracts for produce, as well as to land and labour contracts (Sarkar, 1981; p. A107, Webster, 1989).

The empirical evidence thus shows an agrarian structure with a great range of production and exchange relations, but one in which the returns to poor rice producers are lower than those to other classes. We conclude this discussion with brief comments on the history of two specific commodity markets in Bardhaman: rice and potatoes.

Markets for rice
As in Birbhum, so in Bardhaman, paddy and rice have been marketed through a highly polarized system. The process of capital-based technical change from huller to rubber-roll sheller milling, and the associated modernization of parboiling machinery, were accompanied by a concentration of ownership and of control over capacity. Capacity utilization has been chronically low (at between 21 and 45 per cent over the years 1965-83). Wider distributive margins than elsewhere in India provided an open invitation to lower capacity, technically efficient, and employment-intensive husking mills to enter the market.

A History of West Bengal's Food Economy

Between 1966 and 1982, an estimated 13,000 of these were installed in rural Bengal, all but 1,000 of which were unlicensed and illegal but which appeared to reduce the concentration of control over commodity marketing during the 1980s (Ghosh and Choudhury, 1983; Harriss, 1976).

Uma Lele's correlation analysis of rice wholesale prices for Bardhaman markets in the early sixties led to her influential conclusion that markets were very highly integrated, well organized, and competitive (Lele, 1971). Yet in the seventies, marked spatial dislocations in price levels and behaviour were recorded by Ghosh and Chowdhury (1983). In the 1980s, the Left Front Government relaxed its tight control over markets. From 1980–8, the quantities of local rice procured by state trading agencies in Bardhaman dropped from 143,000 to 48,800 tonnes of rice. Inter-regional movement restrictions became less draconian. West Bengal was still heavily in deficit, and became increasingly dependent on grain from north-western India (Chattopadhyay and Spitz, 1987). The import of rice through the public distribution system increased from 649,000 tonnes in 1980–1 to 842,000 tonnes in 1987–8 (Government of West Bengal, 1989). Seasonal price fluctuations narrowed again.[11] This marketing system was already being 'liberalized' in the 1980s, and was expected to be more price-integrated as a result.

Markets for potato

The expansion of potato cultivation meant that the 'old market mechanism under which 90 per cent of the crop was immediately disposed' (AERC, 1969), and under which a major proportion was said to have perished, was replaced by a new system, an 'oligopoly of cold stores', whose locations are highly concentrated. By 1981, Bardhaman and Hooghly districts together had 70 per cent of the state's cold stores and could store half the entire crop. Forced sales were common, but the lowest post-harvest 'floor' price was rising, and physical waste was declining. 'Allowing for necessary charges for transport storage and handling and interest on capital blocked on inventory, off-season price rises should not exceed 30 per cent', Choudhury and Sen concluded. Yet, off-season price rises were 108 per cent of post-harvest lows in 1960–1, 147 per cent in 1970–1, and 70 per cent in 1980–1 (Choudhury and Sen, 1981, p 70). They drew the conclusion that wide price fluctuations between the post- and pre-harvest seasons were being exploited by cold stores owners who had discovered how to evade statutory limits on the ownership of stored stock.

Then, in the late 1980s, a massive increase in the scale of interregional flows altered trends in the seasonality of supplies and prices and the price system appeared to have lost what stability it ever had.

So, while the post-land-reform agrarian structure was still marked by strong and enduring class differentials in production and exchange relations, the combination of growth, diversification, and a relaxation of regulative restrictions in the 1980s led to some changes. It appeared to reduce price instability in rice, but to do the opposite in the potato sector, suggesting the strong influence of the different market institutions that existed for the two crops.

The market towns
The final part of this chapter is intended to convey something of the character of the towns where these markets operate.

In 1982, and again in 2000/2, Bolpur was the base for our research in Birbhum district. In 2001, it was a congested and not too clean market town of some 62,000 people, servicing the consumption and transport needs of a university—Visva Bharati—and of tourists and pilgrims honouring its two Nobel prize-winners, Rabindranath Tagore (Thakur) and Amartya Sen. It also acts as a central place for its rural hinterland. Although well connected by rail, the poor quality of its rural roads is a revelation. Bolpur's economic base is dominated by retail commerce and the milling and wholesaling of rice. This sector is in turn dominated by a set of entrepreneurial Marwari business families, with close access to the political arena in Calcutta, and to private banks. From these families, webs of credit spread into the surrounding villages. If it is the 'Prussian path' to capitalist transformation that dominates most visibly, an 'American path' can be discovered in the villages around, in which small husking machines and trading firms have proliferated.[12] And an altogether different 'road' exists, made up of indigent landless labourers-turned-petty traders gambling on free transport, travelling ticketless on buses and trains. Recently they have squatted on several patches of waste ground in and around Bolpur, turning them into market-places.

Of the three towns studied in Bardhaman in 1990, Memari was a hive of activity of some 16,000 people, about 30 km south east of Burdwan town. In the 2001 census, it logged a population of 35,000.

A History of West Bengal's Food Economy

It had and still has a relatively well-developed communications infrastructure, sitting astride the Grand Trunk Road and the Calcutta-Delhi railway line, and in 1990 already had good STD telephone connections.[13] Agro-processing plants of various kinds are scattered throughout the rather squalid town. The first rice mill pierced the sky over Memari in 1959, the first oil mill was built in 1960, and the first cold store early as 1962. It was not until the late seventies and early eighties, however, that a precocious expansion of mercantile activity and agro-industrial investment burgeoned in Memari, based on agricultural accumulation largely from local land rent. As a result, by 1990, the region suffered from excess installed capacity in post-harvest processing plants. This, together with chronic irregularities of power supply, and a disputatious local labour force, restrained further large-scale expansion.

But the relentless growth of the marketed surplus led to the entry into trade (particularly of grains) of thousands of petty intermediaries. By the end of the 1980s, over 200 husking mills had been installed within 10 miles of the town. An enclosed and secure rice retail market had been developed (which functioned as a petty wholesale market for about 50 traders), supplied by an estimated 3,000 paddy rice processors. Physically congested, it spawned further new market-places on the edge of town.

By contrast, Katwa is a larger centre, with approximately 60,200 people in 1991 and 76,000 in 2001, sited some 50 kms to the north of Burdwan. It is a centre of Krishna consciousness and has for many centuries been a place of pilgrimage as well as a centre of administration and consumption, though its historic centre is in gentle decay. Located in the elbow of the Ajoy river at its confluence with the Ganges, and in 1990 without a bridge, it had an exceptionally poor communications infrastructure. The very narrow congested streets meant that buses and lorries were not permitted inside the town. There was no through traffic and very little motorised transport to the north and east. To the south was a single-track road. Katwa is linked to Burdwan (and Memari) by a narrow-gauge railway. By 1990, the telecommunications infrastructure had degenerated to the point where it was next to impossible to make or receive long distance telephone calls. Its isolation contrasted vividly with Memari's accessibility.

Katwa thus lies in a rich and diversified agricultural hinterland and had backward forms of trade, despite superficial indications of expansion. In 1977, there were reported to be three cold stores and 14 potato wholesalers, while in 1990, there were 10 and 22 respectively. Potato cold storage was a Marwari monopoly and excess capacity in the local stores had forced the development of long-distance potato imports. The two general wholesale markets are owned by the family of a local ex-zamindar, sited in enclosed and protected spaces behind vegetable markets. Oil mills (3 in 1970, 20 in 1990) give the appearance of a crowded market. Only two were trading firms, however: the rest carried out custom milling. Yet this apparent local oligopoly was actually outclassed by mustard oil imports controlled from Calcutta. Rice milling was also dominated here by Marwari migrants from East Bengal, the first of whom had arrived in Katwa towards the end of the 19th century. These well-established traders had a tight control over large-scale agro-processing and production credit. Local petty trading also provided livelihoods for Hindu economic migrants and refugees from East Bengal, as did the entirely unregulated and rapidly growing local trade in vegetables. Perhaps because trade is regulated through caste and ethnicity, which act as barriers to entry, the number of firms in trade was growing less rapidly in the town than in its environs. Katwa had just five rice wholesalers who could legally purchase rice from rice mills and only 36 rice retailers in the privately-rented legal market, while only 15 traders encroached upon public land nearby. The rice market, an architectural warren from which the town is principally provisioned, is the site of complex relations of accommodation between the CPM Municipality, the police, the Food Control Office, legal and illegal traders, and political parties. We describe this further in Chapter 6.

In 1990, the third settlement, Gulsi, was a village complete with a TV retail outlet and videocasette library. At that time, its population was estimated at 14,000, but it was invisible in demographic statistics, not being classified as a municipality then. Located 25 kms north-west of Burdhaman in a paddy bowl, it is a halting place for long-distance lorry traffic on the Grand Trunk Road. The main railway line passes within three miles. Its telecommunications are as well developed as those of Memari.

In contrast to Katwa (where potato trade is being developed from a local trade to a long-distance one), the agro-commercial economy of Gulsi (with 20,000 people in 2001) was 'localizing' to serve the demands of distress purchasers and the growing non-farm economy. Three of its four rice mills were owned by one person: 'the King of Rice'. In 1990, supply to each mill was managed through a network of 40–50 non-mutually-exclusive agents who redistributed both credit and trading risks from the mills. Twenty of them were located in Gulsi itself. The place was a small agro-industrial cluster. Pre-harvest credit, sometimes lent in kind as fertilizer, was still used to bind post-harvest suppliers to buyers. While in 1970 there were thought to have been four small paddy-rice processors, by 1990 there were 40, some of whom operated relatively large businesses. Like Katwa, Gulsi itself was provisioned by this petty trade. Some of this was 'distress commerce' of a new type—traders being forced by poverty into seasonal and unregulated trade. Established traders made efforts to resist such new entrants to Gulsi's marketplace. 'We use unfair tactics to nip them in the bud', said one established petty trader.

In 1990, Burdwan town was also included in the analysis of price performance, though no field work was carried out there except data collection from government offices and discussion with the *zilla sabhadhipati* (the district's chief political officer). In 1990, the town had an estimated population of 194,000, which by 2001 had grown to 285,000. A cosmopolitan university city, it is the headquarters of Bardhaman district, a substantial retail market centre and wholesale entrepot with concentrations of agro-industry and storage, a transport and communications node on the Grand Trunk Road, and as the main Calcutta-Delhi rail link, with rolling stock maintenance depots. Its role in communications and information, as the local base for Calcutta, is well-established.

This brief introduction to the history, food economy, and towns of the region shows that stagnation and instability in production, which persisted well into the era of Left Front Government rule, was accompanied by a dramatic weeding-out of larger commercial firms plus labour displacement in the rice mills, together with a proliferation of seasonal, subsistence-oriented small-scale trade, much of which appeared to be dependent on webs of credit. The state had shied away from local procurement and depended ever more heavily on supplies from north west India.

The era of diversification and growth of the 1980s did not affect the agrarian structure so much as it provided commercial elites with new opportunities for investment in agro-processing and storage. The state's continued experiments with regulative laws and rules were implemented in the face of the elite, which challenged the state's autonomy and capacity. Through the periods of both stagnation and growth, the gains from wide price fluctuations and instability could be captured by firms with storage, mills, access to transport, information, finance, and contacts. The case of Katwa shows how accumulation trajectories reflected a combination of the spatial distribution of such firms, assets, and networks every bit as much as the distribution and quality of communications infrastructure.

In the following chapters, we explore the development of a post-harvest market system polarized in size and operational scale, which gives highly differentiated returns to producers and where firms of widely varying sizes, with widely differing types of operation, transport and processing technologies, and labour processes, co-exist. That such institutional diversity can persist in such a stable fashion also strongly suggests that the markets are socially regulated in ways that set constraints both on competition and the lowering of rates of return—and resulting improvements in efficiency—which might be expected to result from competition.

Notes

1. Paddy is un-milled rice and weighs 1.5 times more than rice. In this form it is inedible. The process of milling removes the hard outer husk together with the inner oily layer of bran—and it polishes the nutritious kernel. The latter is known as raw rice and needs to be boiled or fried. Throughout the eastern region of India, paddy is also soaked, parboiled and dried *prior to milling*. Such pre-milling processing is a legacy from times when rice milling was affected by rain. These processes have long been commercialized. Rice treated this way is known as parboiled rice. Rice may also be crushed for flakes or puffed after milling. See Appendix 3-1 for details.
2. The Intensive Agricultural District Programme, one of the early precursors of the Green Revolution in the 1960s in which new varieties were piloted in a small number of districts with assured water supplies.
3. It now needs 15 million tonnes (Government of West Bengal, 1999, p. 1).
4. The history of West Bengal's staple food markets has to be told from a series of Government of India reports on the marketing of rice. Four will be used here: with the 1954 *Report on the Marketing of Rice in India*; the 1955 *Report of the Rice Milling Committee*; the 1960 *Report on an Enquiry in the Pace and Pattern of Market Arrivals of Foodgrains*, and the 1961 *Rice Economy of India*. Little critical attention seems to have been paid to the origin of their statistics (which in the early reports were frequently recognized to have resulted from more or less informed guesswork). Furthermore, these reports were provoked into existence by burning issues of practical policy and it is not always easy to squeeze their evidence into other analytical moulds. Nonetheless, this material is deployed here to examine the evolution of the system of markets—through its structural elements,

relationships, and sources of disturbance. The pioneering research on markets in the contemporary era deployed the historical sources in a very general manner. Lele (1971) and Ghosh and Dutt (1977, p. 45–52) both use the 1954 report to represent conditions in the 19th century.
5. The dating of the spread of husking mills is supported by the evidence for Sahajapur village (Bhattacharjee et al., 1958; pp. 9, 93), as well as by the histories revealed during field work in the region.
6. Between 1895 and 1914, Bengal had witnessed a proliferation of cotton gins, oil presses, timber and rice mills, as well as small flour and oil mills.
7. Sarkar, 1979. see also Chattodpadhyay, 1991a, ch 1, especially p. 38, for a detailed account of the Bengal Famine which lays emphasis on inflationary war finance, withdrawals of local grain to the war economy, and local hoarding and speculation.
8. Webster, 1989; UCO Bank, 1990, p7. By 1994-5, production had reached 1.69 m tonnes in Bardhaman district – and had risen in Birbhum district from 0.6 m tonnes in 1980–1 to 0.8 mt in 1994–5.
9. Government of West Bengal, 1989, Table 5.6; Government of West Bengal, 1996, Table 5.2, p. 59.
10. 9 per cent of the state's *Bargadars* were in Bardhaman and 7% in Birbhum districts (Government of West Bengal, 1996, Table 5.18a, p. 102.
11. They had grown from 22 per cent in 1960–1 to over 40 per cent in 1970–1, falling back to 18 per cent in 1980–1.
12. The 'Prussian' path refers to a process of capitalist transformation dominated by merchants while the 'American' path consists of the expanded investments of peasants.
13. See Table 2.1 and Appendix 1.1 for a review of the sample size and population size of traders in this research.

4 The System of Rice Markets in Birbhum District in the Early 1980s

This chapter describes the rice markets of Birbhum district as they were in the early 1980s, when the fieldwork for this book began. Here the reader is drawn into the complexity and diversity that are so characteristic of these markets, though by the end of the chapter the outlines will have clearly emerged, and the complexity will have become familiar. It may help, all the same, if the way the material is organized is indicated at the outset.

The first part describes the structure of the market—the firms involved, from the smallest to the largest, their sites of operation, and the flow of rice upwards from the paddy fields through the mills to the wholesalers, long-distance traders, and transporters. The second part looks at how accumulation takes place—who enters the rice markets, how they make a surplus, and who gets what. The final part examines the labour process in the rice markets—family labour, wage labour, and rates of exploitation and productivity. Any reader in need of an overview can also look at the conclusions to the following chapter, Chapter 5, in which essential features of the overall market system revealed by the 1980-1 fieldwork are briefly summarized.

Like all field research, the work on which this description of the rice markets is based, was undertaken with specific questions in mind. As Chapter 1 has already explained, by 1982 (five years into Left Front Government rule), agriculture in West Bengal was at the end of a long period of stagnation. We wanted to know how far commodity markets might be playing an independent, autonomous role in this—or, conversely, how far production relations determined the system of circulation of rice. Or to put it still more concretely, how had the market system been affected by the prolonged period of stagnation in production? These questions lay behind the field work and conclusions to this chapter give our answers to them.

In approaching the study of markets for rice, some general features of rice as a commodity in the early 1980s must be borne in mind. Although rice is a basic wage good, it was by no means fully commercialized (that is, solely bought and sold for cash) in that era (see Fig. 4.1). Most of the paddy was harvested, threshed, winnowed,

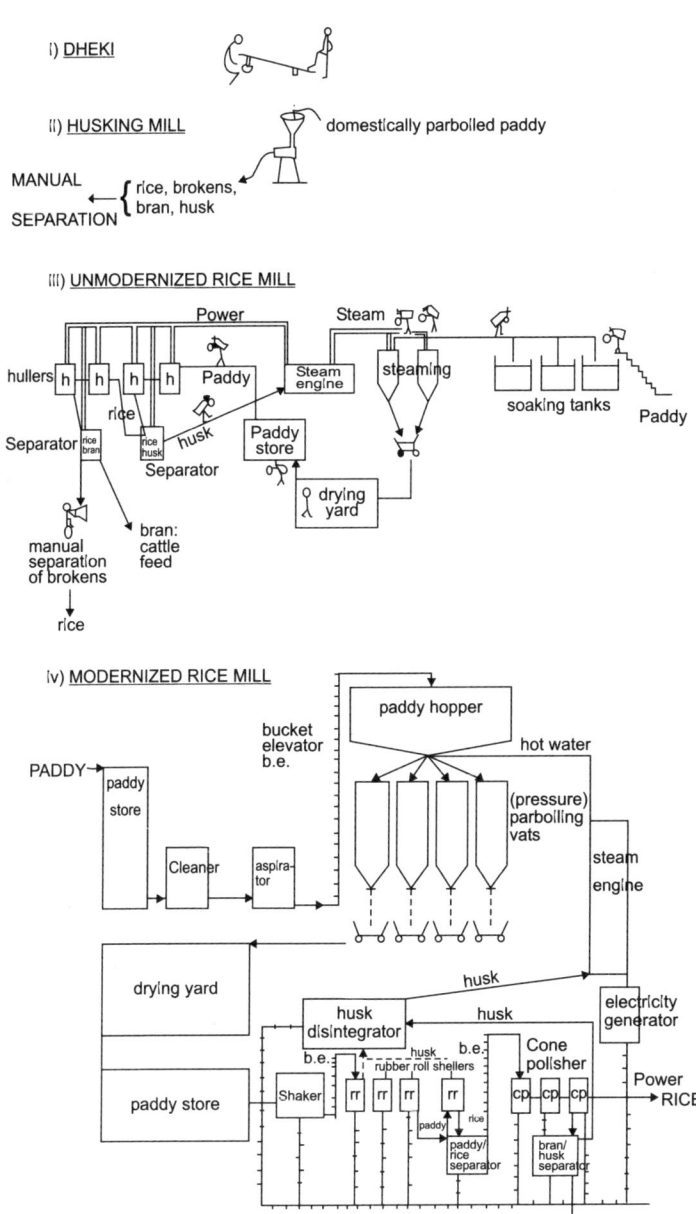

Fig. 4.1: Rice Processing Technologies Birbhum District

cleaned and stored at home, and then taken from the store when required either for sale or consumption. Before husking (milling), it was double parboiled, separated by a soaking of 24 hours, and then dried, using the technologies discussed in Appendix 4.1. Most domestically-consumed rice was custom-milled at small husking mills, and all the by-products were taken home. The commodification of rice began in these mills.

By 1980, husking was slowly becoming less seasonal. Most small mills were open all year round. However, the six-month period beginning in mid-November saw four-fifths of the annual output husked. About 20 per cent of paddy milled by husking machines belonged to small traders and arrived in lots of between 2 and 25 quintals a week. The destination of most of this rice was said to be retail traders in Bolpur, Ahmadpur and their environs. But petty traders also sold directly to the itinerant agents of wholesalers in Murshidabad, Durgapur, Bardhaman, and Kolkata itself (Map 2, page 51).

By-products were a key element in the post-harvest system, but were mostly still at an early stage of commodification, or not yet commodified at all. The whole paddy plant was used. Straw was used as cattle feed, litter, thatch, and rope, and was the raw material with which domestic rice stores were constructed. Rice was single-hulled (that is, passed once through the husking mill) so that some bran was left on the kernel to be consumed as roughage. The rest of the bran and some husk were separated from the rice by winnowing or shaking. This bran was used as cattle feed. Husk was used as fuel, and the ash and manured straw litter were combined and used as organic manures. Husk was also widely used as a binding material in mortar. It was beginning to be commodified as fuel for the boilers of steam engines, which was still the main energy source in most mills. It was also sold as a general purpose fuel or for litter in a local potato cold store in Birbhum. Ash was a free good, taken by farmers for manure.

Bran, from rice mills, was separated for its high oil content (20 per cent), and was being fast commodified at the time of our research. To minimize the free fatty acid content (a high level of which renders bran oil inedible, and useful only for soap, etc.), bran was chemically stabilized. Otherwise, and more usually, it was quickly transported to solvent extraction plants in Ahmadpur, to Konnagar, and Midnapur near Calcutta. From there bran oil was sold to Unilever and other manufacturers of *vanaspati* cooking oil.

There were few 'brokens' (broken rice grains) from rice mills (or rather, few millers ever separated brokens from whole grains). Brokens were sold at a low price directly to retailers for ultimate consumption by humans, cattle, and poultry. The process of commodification of products and by-products in which waste or production for direct use was increasingly physically transformed for sale took different forms in each sub-circuit—but it was being led by rice mills.

Structure of the Rice Marketing System

The structure of the market system is extremely complex (see Fig. 4.2.) and any diagram will be a simplification. In unravelling this system, we begin in the villages and follow the flow of rice sacks towards Kolkata.

Firms

The system of markets is bifurcated into one 'dominant' circuit of commercial capital—dominant in terms of capital and assets—and another of dispersed but very 'prominent' firms, in terms of the labour and livelihoods involved. In the early 1980s, there were four categories of prominent village firms:

Rice retailers

The rice retailer was often also the village grocer. The number of such firms increased greatly in the seventies, reducing the previously dominant position of *urban* groceries in the agrarian economy. The barter exchange of groceries for paddy had also opened up the possibility of such grocers becoming bulk suppliers to rice mills, or acting as paddy suppliers to unlicensed paddy-rice traders. The increase in the number of village grocers does not necessarily imply increased competitiveness. It simply marks the growing pervasiveness of retail sales on credit, to be repaid in paddy—and may allow the debtor a greater choice of creditors.

Paddy purchase agents

The paddy purchase agencies or firms were legally authorized to buy paddy on behalf of a rice mill to which the agent was attached. This authorization did not prevent this type of firm from illegally selling paddy to other rice mills on its own account.

Rural Commercial Capital

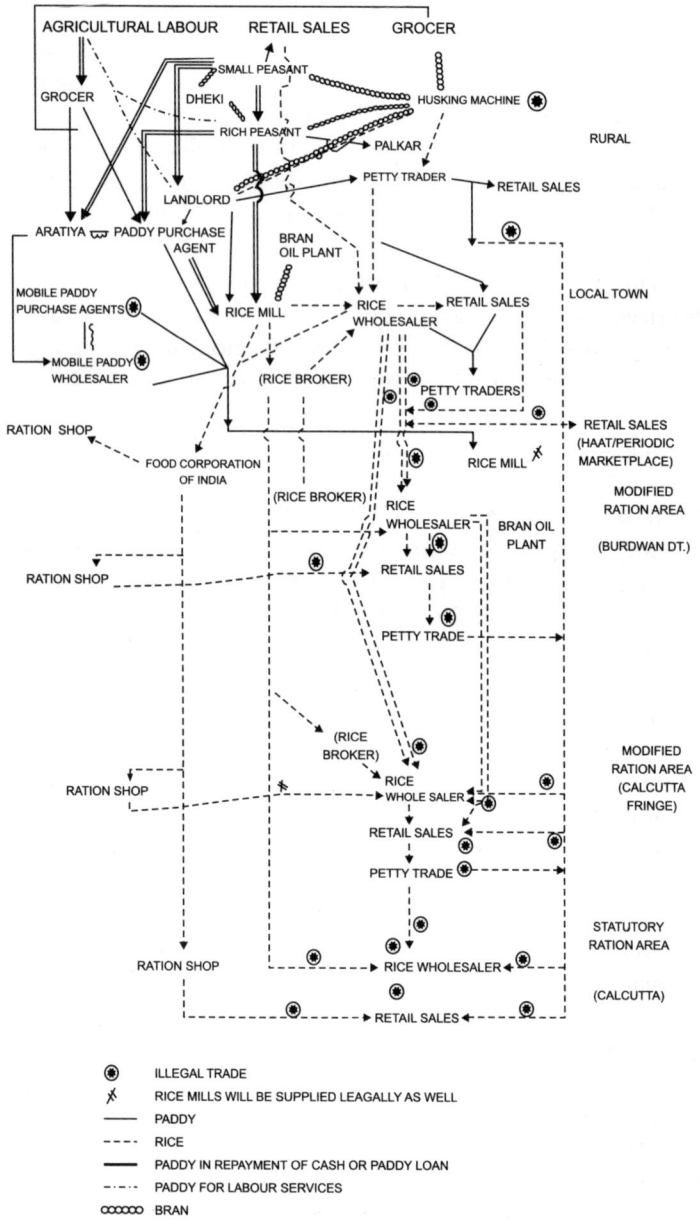

Fig. 4.2: Structural Elements of the Rice Circulation System, Birbhum District to Calcutta 1981–82

Rice Markets in Birbhum District in the Early 1980s

Petty traders

Petty traders were of two types. One type obtained paddy, processed it domestically and /or at local husking mills, and sold the rice. The other just bought and sold rice. Some petty traders did both. Estimates of their number were obtained from husking millers (for petty traders are unlicensed and not regulated by the state). On an average, six petty traders milled their paddy via each husker, and 20 per cent of all paddy milled belonged to such traders. A few were *regularly* attached to peri-urban huskers. They tended to queue up wherever rates were low and electricity supplies were functioning.

Husking mills

The fourth type of firm, the husking mill, did not control paddy but controlled its processing. The sample survey showed that 23 per cent of them were unlicensed. If our sample is representative (see Appendix 1.1) the two blocks may have had some 86 mills between them, and the district 506, an increase of some 50 per cent over the first five years of the Left Front Government. Most new firms were unlicensed, but unlicensed huskers were not penalized by District Magistrates, provided it could be shown that a licence had been applied for. Rules on the spacing of mills restricted them to one per *mouja* (the village revenue unit). But applications that were surplus to this rule were not rejected; instead they were generally put on hold, so the new mills were condoned in practice, if not by policy. A policy requiring the modernization of husking mills was also observed in the breach. All unlicensed mills used 'unmodernized' technology. Electricity was also obtained without a licence. It was often installed for a flour mill or an oil rotary, prior to the start-up of an unlicensed husking mill. These mills operated openly, without any constraints except for erratic electricity supplies and the need to bribe Food Department inspectors. They were an integral part of the process of decentralization of ownership in the circulation of rice.

However, at the same time, this system was concentrated and centralized. There are three 'dominant' elements.

Rice mills

Rice mills were large-scale, commercial firms with a legal monopoly over their attached wholesale supplying agents. They also had integrated parboiling and drying facilities. In Birbhum district, while the number of village husking mills had vastly increased, the number of rice mills had declined, from 55 in 1978-9 to 46 in 1980-1, nine of them lying idle for reasons which are elaborated below. In contrast to the husking mills, the rice mills still in operation were long-established, the average starting date of the firms that were operating in 1981 being 1964. Unlike husking mills, the rice mills were all in or near towns. Indeed, the very existence of rice mills has led to economic multipliers and urbanization.

Rice brokers/wholesalers

Brokers do not take ownership of commodities but they organize transactions. In Bolpur, there were only seven of them. Several were branches of a very small number of controlling families. This did not imply monopolies, since rice brokerage was mostly peripatetic, coming from destination regions, or done from there by telephone. Rice brokers were also under direct competition from rice wholesalers, whose numbers were sharply declining. Wholesaling was also carried out in an itinerant manner by agents or employees of wholesalers based in the centres of consumption. These firms, located outside Birbhum district, were increasing their power over commodities within it. This financial power, together with stagnation in the local supplies of rice at that time, was wiping out smaller local brokers and wholesalers.

Retail firms

By contrast, retail firms were estimated to have doubled in number, to 200, within the first five years of the Left Front Government, proliferating unlicensed at stalls in the urban weekly markets. In Bolpur and Ahmadpur, the state-controlled rice-ration shops were in the hands of families who did both rice wholesale and informal of retail trade rice. Petty rice retailers were often the petty traders of the villages, having transported their stock to town by cycle, bus or cart. Rice was also sold in retail quantities to other petty rice traders who transported and retailed it 'illegally' to consumers living in the statutory rationed areas, including Kolkata.

Sites

While rice mills define towns in this region, the smaller firms do not necessarily define villages. Paddy purchase agents and husking mills are also characteristic of the urban fringe, to which a branch of a successful rural firm commonly migrates. The decade of the 1970s saw notable increases in the number of husking mills and petty traders based not in the main centres of production but near major administrative-political borders. Of course, most purchasing agencies and husking mills were located close to all-weather roads.

Virtually no rice is traded through the network of rural haats (or periodic markets) in this region. The reasons for this, since these are commonly used elsewhere in India for the sale of rice by and to poor rural consumers, are not known. Perhaps landless purchasers of rice could no longer afford to buy consignments to tide them over three to four days between the dates of accessible markets. The situation was different in Bardhaman district, where rice was bulked from landless petty traders in haats by wholesalers who sold it in the industrial towns of the coal belt.[1] In a few Birbhum haats on the border with Bardhaman district, landless traders bartered rice for vegetables and spices during the lean, pre-harvest season. Government ration shops were overwhelmingly located in towns in the study region, posing problems of access for rural ration-cardholders.

Spatial Flows
From village to purchasing agents
The average radius of the area from which a paddy agent typically drew supplies was about 8 kms., the transport costs being borne by the farmers. After the main aman season, from December to April, farmers were the main sellers, and four-fifths of all paddy purchased, much of it of the lowest quality and coarsest varieties, was bought directly from them. Out of the major marketing season, small traders and larger farmers were more prominent as sellers; the quality of paddy actually improves as a result of storage and the finer varieties, with higher costs of production, would be sold at peak prices to maximise returns.[2]

Rice mills
Some mills not only secured supplies from their licensed purchase agents, but also dealt directly at the millgate with elite producers, those who could marshal bulk consignments. By February or March, in the marketing season, pressure would be placed on the District Magistrate to permit the import of large batches of paddy from other states (in particular from regions in Andhra Pradesh and Uttar Pradesh, where different patterns of seasonality of agricultural production might mean prices as much as Rs 50 per quintal—32 per cent—below local prices in Birbhum).[3] Even though a third of the weight of paddy is lost in

milling, so that it makes economic sense to mill at the place of origin, when movement restrictions were lifted, mills in Birbhum district were supplied not only from the two states mentioned but also by brokers as far away as Karnataka, Bihar, Rajasthan, and Punjab.

Rice wholesalers

While large firms purchased their supplies from rice mills in Birbhum and Bardhaman districts, small rice wholesalers obtained rice more cheaply from producer-traders, and from small paddy-rice traders who rented husking machines. Wholesalers paid for transport; and in the case of small traders, it came by bicycle, rickshaw or cart. This supply was destined to be retailed within the district.

Long-distance trade in rice

Rice flowed from Birbhum to the plantation regions to the north, to the Bardhaman colliery settlements and to wholesalers on the periphery of Kolkata, and on the state borders. An unknown proportion was black-marketed in the metropolis, where official supplies had been declining under the Left Front Government because ration rice was being purchased neither by the rich, who preferred the higher quality of the black market, nor by the poor, who could not afford to buy the minimum consignment of a week's supply. As a result, from 1979–80, a large black market had blossomed under conditions of low-level police harassment. Petty traders, who are usually landless, purchased rice from retailers in the environs of Kolkata and transported it into the city by the basket- or sack-load via bus, train or rickshaw. Petty producers from all over West Bengal carried small consignments to the metropolis by public transport. Transport costs were minimal, since the bribe given to ticket collectors for not demanding a ticket was reported to amount to about 15 per cent of the cost of a 2nd class ticket. Rice also 'leaked' from lorries passing through Calcutta on their way to regions south of the city.

Transport

The market for lorries, however, had a specific local structure. Almost every rice mill had one or two lorries, but general purpose lorries were also an independent urban business activity. In Ahmadpur, apart from mill lorries, there were two owners of single lorries and two owners with two lorries, while in Bolpur there were, besides a transport broker, 25 to 30 lorry owners; few had more than two lorries, although one had a fleet of six.

To sum up, the major characteristics of the elements of this system of markets in the early 1980s were three. First, its complexity. Paddy and its by-products were only partially commodified, and not only bought and sold in markets but also exchanged in kind for labour services and for earlier loans, or produced for immediate consumption. Second was its concentration. A large ('dominant') edifice of capital, labour, and technology was being supported by the appropriation of paddy surpluses from rural areas, with three broad levels of stratification in terms of size and power. In terms of gross output, Table 4.1 indicates that while the average value of the businesses of rice millers and rice brokers was between Rs 75 to 98 lakh, the average value of the businesses of the paddy agents, husking mill owners, and rice wholesalers was Rs 6 to 8 lakhs. In stark contrast to both, small traders had an average turnover of only Rs 25–35,000.[4] The paddy trade of village grocers was also of this last order of magnitude. The third characteristic was the illegality of much of the system and, so far as could be ascertained, the informal organization of the finance of this system of supply, on which much of the population of one of the world's largest cities, an important industrial region, and a plantation belt increasingly depended.

These features have implications for the question of the degree of autonomy of these markets from agricultural production. The first five-year period of the Left Front rule, during which agricultural production had stagnated and/or fluctuated, had witnessed a proliferation of rice retailing and petty, but long-distance, inter-regional trade, and an expansion of unlicensed commercial husking mills, which milled paddy both for use and for exchange. Meanwhile, the rice mills which dominated the commercialized circuit of the system were able, when permitted, to mobilize supplies from sources far from the local agrarian region. While these facts confirm that the structure of the market system is continually being contested, it is necessary to look more closely at the relationships between circulation and production to explain the extent to which these changes were determined by production; and if not by production, then by what. In the rest of this chapter, we examine the *relations of accumulation*, first of capital and then of labour. In Chapter 5, we examine the dynamic forces that disturb the system, in the shape of state interventions and the organized political response of firms.

Table 4.1: The Structure of Control in Rice Markets, Bolpur and Sainthia Blocks, Birbhum district, West Bengal

Category	Sampling Fraction	Number Sampled	Turnover 1980-1 (av.)			Average Business Size			Storage (av) tonnes		
			Paddy tonnes	Rice Tonnes	Value Rs. lakhs[1]	Fixed Assets Rs. '000	Own working capital Rs. '000	Maximum money borrowed Rs. '000	Maximum Business size	Paddy	Rice
Rice Millers	55	10	4900 (11000–2000)		65 (146.3–26.6)	14,33 (30,00–7,00)	8,00 (25,00–4,00)	23,66 (50,00–5,00)	46,00	900 (3000–500)	215 (400–150)
Rice Brokers	66	4		4100 (13200–400)	97.6 (314.6–9.5)	37 (60–12)		7,00[2] (20,00–2,00)			
Rice Wholesalers	30	4		285 (500–165)	6.8 (11.9–3.9)	72 (150–15)	40 (50–20)	n.i.	7,37		(50) 20 (25–15)
Husking Millers	20[3]	17	630[4] (1106–360)		8.4 (14.7–4.7)	56 (100–25)	v.little	n.i.	1,12	v.little	
Paddy Agents	2[5]	13	440 (900–140)		5.8 (11.97–1.9)	28 (150–5)	22 (150–4)	44 (200–5)	56	20 (35–10)	
Unlicenced Paddy/	n.i.	2[6]	25 (36–15)		0.33 (0.48–0.2)	1.0[8]	0.3	0.2	94	n.i.	n.i.
Rice Traders	20	130[7]	19 (46–6)		0.25 (0.64–0.08)	1.0[8]	0.2	n.i.	1.5 about 1.6-2.0	about 1.0	n.i.

Notes: Maximum and minimum are set below averages and bracketed.   n.i. = no information.
(1) Based on 1981 annual averages for Birbhum distrit (Dept. of Agric. Mktg.; Suri) of Rs. 1330/tonne for paddy and Rs. 2338/tonne for rice.
(2) Amount for which broker can stand as guarantor.
(3) Calculated from number of licenced huskers + 23 per cent factor for unlicenced huskers derived from field work.
(4) Quantity milled by husker but not owned by miller.
(5) Calculated from average of 30 agents per mill, derived from field work, and 19 working mills.
(6) Derived from one interview in Sian and one interview about 10 petty unlicenced rice retailers in Bassa Para.
(7) According to statements of husking mill owners.
(8) Costs (annual) of parboiling equipment, averaged from 3 interviews.

Relationships of Accumulation in the Rice Markets

In order to decide how far markets are independent of production we must study accumulation as it occurs in major different kinds of firms, tracing its course from its origins, through the profitability and growth of firms, to the destinations of the capital that is accumulated.

Market Entry

Capital is not the sole constraint on market entry. Rice brokerage, for example, required information, skills, and contacts which were costly to build prior to entry, but required no equipment except a telephone. Petty trade in rice, which required parboiling equipment, working capital to cover transport, husking charges and stock, almost certainly required more initial capital than did brokerage, but much less sophisticated contacts and information. A paddy purchasing agency had higher entry costs, for it needed a mud and thatch store capable of containing one lorry load—10 tonnes—of paddy, plus increasing amounts of one's own working capital, because, as the numbers of such agents increased, the structure became more competitive and rice mills became less willing or able to give advances for purchase. A miller's decision to authorize an agent was increasingly based on the latter's site and financial resources, and less on the older criterion of loyalty. In this way, ascribed characteristics were yielding to acquired ones. Indeed, purchasing agents were becoming anything but loyal, changing mills regularly—on an average once every two or three seasons. Every time a purchase agency realigned itself, it needed more capital under its direct control.

A wide variation in the entry costs of husking reflected variations in buildings and equipment, the value of land, and the number and type of machines. Many small rice millers had small wheat and oil mills as well, which made separating the costs related to paddy milling subject to error. Licences, whose official cost was Rs 500, had a black market value of Rs 35,000 in the 1980s. Furthermore, a licence was not necessary for the installation of electricity. The latter took about two years from application to installation and could only be speeded up unofficially, at a cost.

The Origins of Capital in the Rice Markets [5]

The sources of capital for investment in husking were varied. They not only came chiefly from agricultural profits, but also from agricultural rent, and loans from relatives. Sales of jewellery were another source which was closely, if indirectly, based on agricultural rents, profits, and savings. The sale of land was a rarely chosen source of starting capital.

While agricultural rent was an early source of funds for the older paddy purchasing agencies, the centre of gravity shifted over time from small landlords to rich peasants and small capitalists: savings from agricultural production were the main source of capital for the new agencies. Rice wholesalers and rice brokers invested the profits from earlier wholesale trading in agricultural products and, to a lesser extent, profits from groceries and agricultural rent.

Both the oldest and the newest rice mills derived substantial starting capital from other investments in rice milling. In Birbhum, only rice milling could generate the surpluses necessary for further expansion in this type of firm. The large-scale wholesaling of agricultural products has also been a constant source of capital.

In sum, the largest firms, the controllers of the markets of rice, obtained their funds from the sphere of circulation itself, while more rural intermediaries, husking millers, and paddy purchase agents obtained theirs from their own agricultural production or from agricultural rents.

Contractual Behaviour: Payment Systems as Power Relations

Accumulation sufficient to allow lumpy, long-term investments was achieved through countless small cycles of buying and selling. When market payments are delayed and/or asymmetrical, characterized by varying periodicities, then an intermediary either requires commensurate resources of working capital or has to rely on loans, involving extra costs. Asymmetries of power make it possible for one firm to delay payments to another for its purchases, while repayment by the second firm for its purchases must be prompt. If the asymmetricality is regular, not only can the beneficiaries speculate, using these short-term funds, but they can even lend them to others.

Among petty traders, payment for rice transactions commonly took the form of immediate cash. Transactions for husking, rice broking, and wholesaling were in cash, or on credit for a maximum of 7 to 10 days. The Food Corporation of India also paid within seven days from the completion of laboratory testing on its rice purchases. All these transactions were fairly symmetrical.

Matters were different when it came to agents. Paddy purchase agents had three kinds of contractual arrangements. Commonly they gave farmers long-term advances of production credit, typically for four months, to be repaid in paddy; they would also make short-term advance payments for paddy 7–10 days before delivery. But they might delay completion of payments to farmers for their paddy by up to one to two months. These modes of payment reflect different exchange relationships. The first could signify distress on the part of sellers, while the last could indicate distress in the buyer's finances. Depending on their positions in the rural economy, the purchasing agents used payment tactics to maximize secure supplies. While in the 1970s payments to the agents by the mills had been though money advances, by the time of our survey, mills were generally paying in cash after receipt, and sometimes even with delays of up to 20 days. Occasionally, paddy agents used the mills to place their savings, especially out of season, since the physical security of cash was higher at mills than in villages. These 'goodwill' deposits provided rice mills with some of their working capital, especially useful in the off-season when the speculative profits to be made from storing and milling were highest.

In sum: in the system of rice markets, rice mills and some paddy agents were net beneficiaries of the payment systems.

Commercial finance
Borrowing

The literature on agricultural credit focuses on pre-harvest production loans to the exclusion of loans within the post-harvest system. But lenders can reap high speculative returns on post-harvest markets through careful timing of their purchases and sales. The whole paddy crop has to be milled, and there was intense competition to secure supplies of paddy because of overcapacity in the milling sector. Loans within the system of markets ranged from delayed payments on individual consignments (in effect a loan to the buyer) to pre-harvest advances for onward lending. Given the payment systems, it is not surprising that the main borrowers of money, the purchasing agents, and rice millers were also the main lenders. Purchasing agents' borrowing was erratic in time and varied considerably between the firms (Table 4.2). Only a small minority borrowed from farmers and from relatives—such loans accounted for less than 1 per cent of estimated total borrowings. The rice mills provided paddy agents with half of all the money they borrowed. There was no obvious relationship between the quantities borrowed and declared business size.

By contrast, rice mill owners' access to money was very broadly correlated with gross output and assets. Thirty per cent of all their declared borrowings came from banks, on pledge or hypothecation at interest rates between 18–19 per cent, with 45 per cent of the value of their stock as collateral. A similar proportion came from the private money market in Bolpur, where other rice millers could place any spare funds, or was raised by *Marwaris* on the marwari money market in Kolkata through relatives or brokers. Security for these loans was personal; interest rates, at 12–15 per cent, were very low. Lastly, eight per cent of total borrowing was from farmers, for periods of up to four months, at a disguised interest rate of only 9 per cent.[6] This borrowing principally financed the storage of paddy for periods of four to six months. Millers benefited disproportionately from this, relatively to the benefits received (in interest and prices) by their agricultural lenders. Rice brokers were forced on occasion to stand as guarantors for wholesalers who were unable to repay rice mills within the stipulated time. The source of such funds is similar to the borrowings of rice milling firms.

Lending

In this case, only one paddy agent denied lending money. Each firm had a large number of petty debtors, since the main objective of money lending was to secure supplies in crowded markets. Agents referred to this loan relationship as *dadon* (Table 4.2). Money could be lent for periods of up to 12 months, but was commonly lent either for production over a period of two to four months pre-harvest, for the expenses of the *Durga Puja* festival in October, or for the costs of the main aman harvest. A loan in cash was repaid in paddy at the market

Table 4.2: Loans from Paddy Agents, 1981, Bolpur and Sainthia Blocks

	To number of farmers	Maximum to any individual	Average to individuals (Rs)	Total lent out per agent (Rs)
Maximum	400	5000	500	50,000
Average	95	1500	200	15,000
Minimum	22	100	40	3,000
N=11				

Source: Survey in 1982. N=No. of respondents

prices reigning after harvest, ostensibly carrying no interest charge at all. If this loan had been used to purchase paddy at the seasonally highest prices before harvest for domestic consumption, or for payment in kind to labour, and was repaid in kind at the seasonally lowest prices, then in the period October 1981 to January 1982, the disguised interest in this system was 30 per cent over four months. We even observed one exchange where the debtor had to accept Rs 10 below the mill rate for his paddy. Dadon loans from the older purchasing agencies were drying up, not only because of competition from new agents, but also because of both massive default and competition on less punitive terms from state production credit. The latter was, however, in dramatic decline following the increase made immediately after the Left Front Government came to power (Table 4.3), and reports from paddy agents suggested that a proportion may have been diverted and lent onwards to fund trade by landed paddy agents eligible for such credit, rather than used for their own production.

Rice millers also lent money, and on a scale 25 times greater than paddy agents. Only 11 per cent of all the money lent went directly from the mill to the farmer. The vast majority of loans, 89 per cent, were money advances to paddy purchasing agents. This practice was said to be on the decline. One miller admitted charging 20 per cent over about two months on such loans. Some rice wholesalers lent money in their other capacity as paddy purchase agents. They lent for the purchase of paddy rather than rice. So, by and large, money used for buying and selling was fused with money lent at high interest in order to secure supplies.

Competition was forcing husking mill owners to offer milling services to customers on seven-day credit. On an average, Rs 1,100

Table 4.3: Short-term Crop Loans Issued through the Co-Operative Bank, Birbhum District, 1976-81

Year	Total Quantity issued(Rs. Lakhs)
1976–77	317.7
1977–78	2443.2
1978–79	244.1
1979–80	138.5
1980–81	107.3

Source: District Co-operative Credit Bank, Suri

per miller was lent out in this way. Losses from casual default were high. But no difference could be made to the husking charges in order to compensate for such loans—a powerful indication of the pressures on small mills caused by structural overcapacity.

Price formation
In a given marketplace on a given day, far from there being a single price created by the interaction of supply and demand, there is a range of prices determined not just by variety and quality but also by exchange relations and the incomplete and socially-regulated circulation of information about what is happening in other places. Structuralist theories of exchange relations, which predict wide intra-seasonal price fluctuations, the co-existence of a variety of supply behaviours, and a wide range of prices in markets, were reviewed in Chapter 2, but there is very little empirical research on farm-level price formation. The most meticulous and revealing research is undoubtedly that of Ben Crow, Firdous Murshid and their team in Bangladesh in the late 1980s (Crow, 2001). In the work reported here, we were unfortunately unable to research this sensitive question, for it requires a level of detail on production and the marketed surplus that was outside the scope of our field work, which was restricted to the process of price formation within the system of rice markets.

Technologies of information
For markets to perform their roles as efficient allocators of resources, information is supposed to stream from consumption centres back to producers and is assumed to be the basis on which production decisions are made. But in the system of markets which we observed, information was socially regulated, leading to informational monopolies. Local rice mills, although they could influence local rice prices, certainly could not by themselves alter rice prices in the destination towns. The broker's telephone was the main medium for communicating rice prices from Bardhaman, Midnapur, and the environs of Kolkata to brokers in the locality; from there it flowed by phone or word of mouth to rice mills, and thence to local rice wholesalers. Price information was also disseminated more slowly and generally by radio and newspapers. Information on paddy prices circulated from mills to agents.

Paddy prices were determined independently of rice prices through collusive relationships between the rice mills and their suppliers all year round, but were being increasingly complicated by competition from petty trade via the huskers during the four months after harvest.

The price surface

Table 4.4 shows the prices in a value chain from Birbhum to Calcutta. It illustrates the considerable uncertainties resulting from this system. There was a considerable gap between paddy and rice prices, caused not just by competition from petty trade centred on husking mills, but also by the fact that at this point in the post-harvest season, the rice mills were forced to sell 60 per cent of their production to the state at fixed prices. In both February and March 1982, local sales were unprofitable, but rice sales in February to the environs of Kolkata were profitable. In March, no sales were profitable in any direction. This kind of price structure had two important consequences. First, it made it necessary to store paddy and rice across the seasons in order to make profits; and second, mills had to rely on political lobbying to get a reduction in the percentage levied later on, in the off-season. The fact that rice was circulated in two separate markets, one through the rice mills, the other via huskers, at two sets of prices, is also evinced by the fact that rice could be purchased in rural areas surrounding Bolpur and Ahmadpur at Rs 10–15 per quintal below the prices charged by the mills.

Table 4.4: Markets Paddy and Rice Value Chain, Birbhum, February–March 1982, Rs/Qtl.

Markets	February 1982	March 1982
Local market price of paddy	145	165
Local price of rice	290	295
Retail rice price in deficit districts	340	350
Retail rice price in Calcutta*	450–675	400–350
Procurement Price of Paddy	119	119
Procurement Price of Rice	193	193
Local Conversion Price+	240	270
Levy loss (on 60%)	47	77
Non levy compensation (on 40%)	70.5	115.5
Cost covering price at local mills	310.5	385.5

Notes: *Lake Market "black" prices obtained from CRESSIDA staff.
+ Calculated (as by rice wholesalers) as: paddy price plus Rs. 15/quintal of paddy to cover processing and transport x 1.5 to cover out-turn of rice from paddy.

Prices: variety and quality

Prices also varied according to rice variety. Locally there were five main types: IR-8 and *Pankaj*, counted as coarse; *Kalma*, the most common variety, which is classified as fine; and *Lagusol* and *Sitasol*, which are superfine, and in which the rice mills preferred to do their private trading. Rice mills were interested in cheap coarse rice as a medium for the requirements of the levy in order to minimize the losses they made on it.

Paddy prices also varied according to quality. Official data are for fair average quality with 3.56 per cent impurities. We observed paddy agents' staff routinely inserting stones and chaff in 65 kgs. bags of paddy to bring them down to this standard. At the mills in Birbhum, it was promptly cleaned out again; and if impurities exceeded this standard, millers made deductions from the agent's commission accordingly[7]. The rice mills in Bardhaman district had more relaxed quality standards and this was a potent incentive to smuggle paddy to mills there. The very existence of these two paddy markets, separated by the district border, with different quality standards and different levels of government vigilance, meant that within a village on any given day, the price for paddy could vary by Rs 6/quintal (four per cent).

The roles of mills and agents

In 1982, not all paddy agents were in telephone contact with rice mills. Rice mills fixed their purchase prices for paddy each week. As and when agents visited the mill to negotiate the transport of consignments, they were informed about prices. Should prices change suddenly, mill employees were sent out to inform the agents. In the increasing competition between paddy agents, commissions (varying from Rs 1.25 to Rs 2.00 per quintal) could be cut. Competition also encouraged agents to speculate on their own account (which was legal so long as the paddy was supplied to the authorized mill). Yet, agents also sold opportunistically to any mill if the price offered exceeded that of the mill to which they were officially attached.

Special terms were also offered by the rice mills to elite producers selling in bulk. The consignment would be lifted from the 'farmgate' by the mill, the suppliers not having to bear any transport cost and reaping an advantage of up to two per cent. Naturally, this practice was not appreciated by purchase agents.

Prices of by-products

Various price-forming processes play their roles here. Broken rice prices roughly shadowed coarse rice market prices, fluctuating around 30–40 per cent less. Husk was partially commodified, with its price fluctuating between Rs 0-5 to Rs 1.50 per 15 kg. sack according to the season. The price of bran was actually the key to profitability of the rice mills. The necessity for the free fatty acid content to be minimized forced millers to sell immediately, but over-capacity in the solvent oil extraction industry still made it a sellers' market.

While brokens from husking mills fetched the same prices as brokens from rice mills, the other bulkier and lower-value by-products (husk and bran mixed together) from husking mills were still being sold on a small-scale and locally as cattle feed at Rs 20 per quintal—half the commercial price of separated bran—with a modest adverse effect on peasant incomes.

Price behaviour

Crude, month-end prices for paddy, and for wholesale and retail rice, are the summary indicators used to contribute to the cost-of-living indices which are of interest to the Indian state. A run of such prices for four local market centres is given here to indicate the broad contours of price behaviour over the first five years of the Left Front Government (devoid, however, of precisely the detail through which traders make their profits). (Fig. 4.3 and Appendix 4.3, Tables 1 to 3).

Paddy Prices

In any one year there were considerable price differences between places, of up to Rs 16 or over 10 per cent. All the markets had a secular upwards trend, interrupted by regular brief slumps in November and December at the time of the aman harvest. These slumps are abrupt and recovery is quick. But the seasonal difference varied by 30–50 per cent and the difference may have been up to 1.75 times greater in villages because of the much lower post-harvest prices due to informational remoteness, transport costs, and debt-related exchange relations. Fairly predictably, rising prices made the storage of paddy from December until about September relatively risk-free.

Rice Wholesale Prices

There was no obvious evidence of rapid compensating adjustments on the residual 'open market' to the regular post-harvest changes in levy

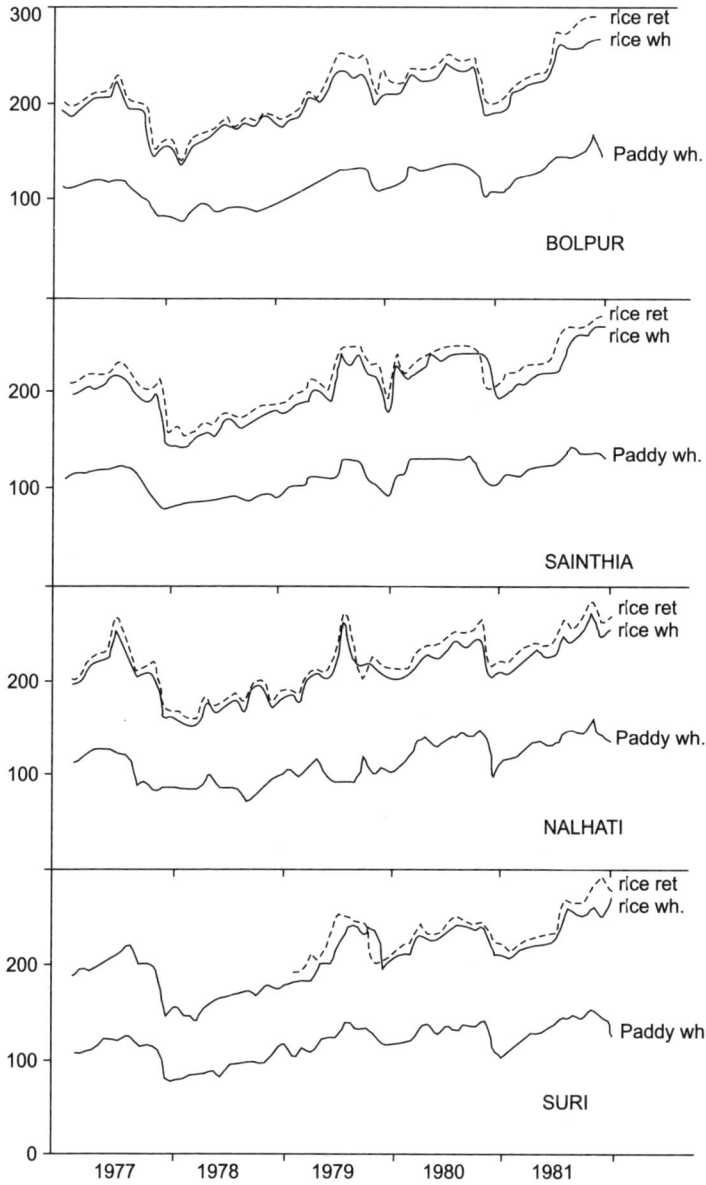

Fig. 4.3: Paddy and Rice Prices, Birbhum District
Rs/Quintal 1977–81

Source: Department of Agricultural Marketing, Suri, monthly prices.

percentages and prices (which were always set at levels below those of the market). However, the gap between paddy and rice prices widened under the Left Front Government (Appendix 4.3, Table 1). It could not simply be explained by increase in milling costs. The difference between paddy and rice prices widened as the off-season progressed. While the spatial price differences were similar, the trend of rice prices had a steeper gradient than that of paddy prices, all of which is suggestive of the independent power of the rice mills. The long-term storage of rice was, like that of paddy, assured of high returns. The post-harvest seasonal slump took two forms: either it lagged behind that of paddy, so that large differences between paddy and rice prices existed for about a month (as in Sainthia and Nalhati); or rice prices collapsed simultaneously with paddy prices, but rose afterwards at a higher rate in the off-season (as in Bolpur and Suri). Short-term price fluctuations were greater for rice than for paddy.

Rice retail prices
Appendix 4.3, Tables 1 to 3, show that retail margins were large and, despite the dramatic proliferation of petty trading firms, widening. Gross margins varied in such a way as to exaggerate wholesale price maxima rather than to cushion their impact. The relative seasonal swing was significantly different from that of paddy and wholesale rice. Scrutiny of the price plots reveals that retail prices could move independently from those of paddy and rice. They were equal to, or below, the level of wholesale rice prices for up to two months, suggesting that retailers are able to practice speculative stocking over such periods of time.

Costs and Returns to Agro-commerce
The returns to agro-commerce are the outcomes of the social process of accumulation at the levels of individual capitals. One way of estimating them is to compare trading and processing costs with the structure of returns indicated by the official price series. Unfortunately, even to discuss this approach, there is no alternative to cutting a swath through a thicket of technicalities and conceptual difficulties. In the light of these issues, let us start with the most complicated type of firm (see also Fig. 4.4, Table 4.1, and the discussion on pages 339–46).

Rice Mills
The cost of milling paddy comprises fuel and power, repairs to

Rice Markets in Birbhum District in the Early 1980s

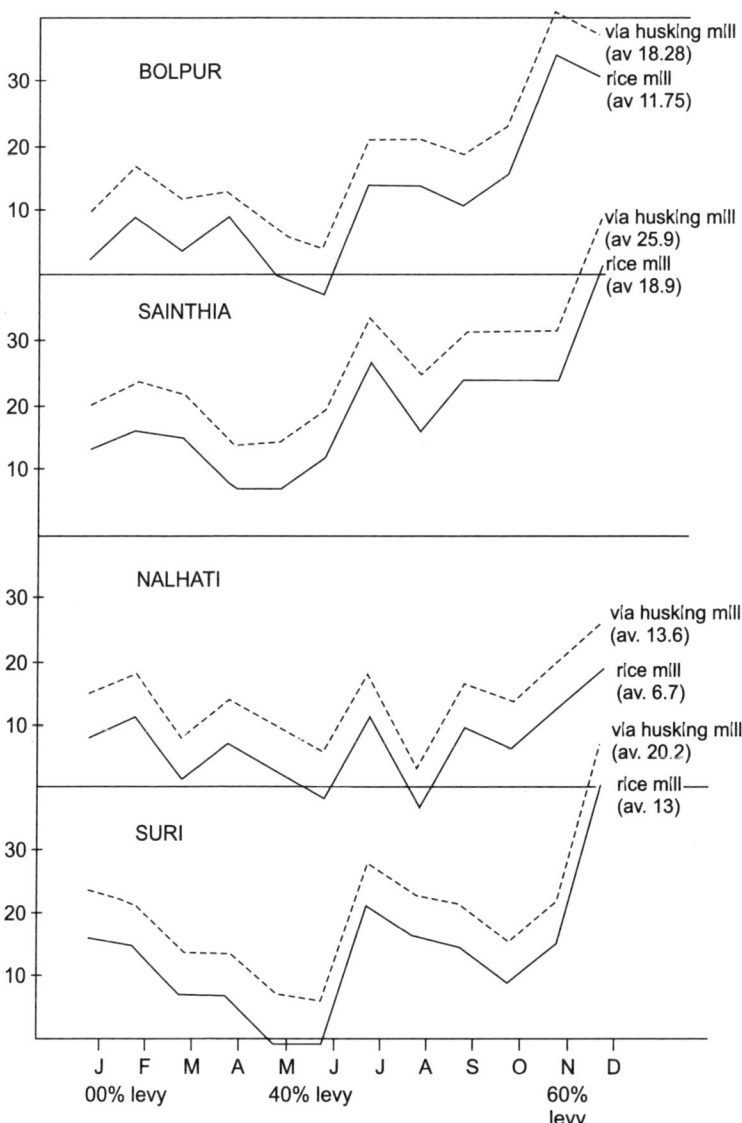

Fig. 4.4: Net Profits, Rs/Quintal, Rice Processing, Birbhum, 1981, (non levy rice)

machinery and plant, labour, interest on loans, and depreciation.[8] The process of milling costed here also includes pre-milling processing.[9]

We have calculated the profit per quintal of rice in the following way:

$$NP = Rx \{1/C[Px + MC]\}$$

where NP is net profit per unit,
Rx is the wholesale price of rice in place x,
Px is the wholesale price of paddy in place x,
1/C is the milling conversion ratio,
MC is the milling cost per unit of paddy.

This is purely the profit from processing. It does not include returns from transport or from storage, or income from the sale of husk, brokens and bran, or the losses from levy rice. Figure 4.5 plots these profits from the data from four towns in Birbhum district over the 12 months of 1981. Profits vary considerably. Fluctuations between market centres were severe during the months of May to August, when net losses can also be observed. Very high profits were achieved at harvest-time in November and December, when rises in the price of rice were matched by drops in the price of paddy. The period of least profitability on processing from May to August is revealed, but would have been avoided by the purchase of paddy early on in the season for milling during these months. The high profits from processing at harvest-time could result from speculation on crop shortages and/or market distortions, to cover the losses made on the 60 per cent PDS levy.

The average net profits from processing are estimated to have varied from Rs 6.7 to Rs 18.9 per quintal of rice. The returns to processing accrued to a relatively small number of firms. These profits would have been enhanced by income from the sale of bran at between Rs 12.4 and Rs 28.5.[10] Returns to transport between Birbhum district and Calcutta are estimated to have netted between Rs 12.5 and Rs 22.5 per quintal of rice.[11]

Returns to levy operations
Without considering transport, storage, and returns from bran, a rice mill would have broken even on levy sales in 1981–2. (Table 4.8).[12] Beyond that, the much greater profits calculated to have been made by mills came from mercantile transactions and through speculating on

Rice Markets in Birbhum District in the Early 1980s

storage. The costs and returns reported suggest that levy evasion was likely to have been substantial—up to as much as 170 per cent of what was actually collected.[13] Evasion will have increased the profitability of processing. It is therefore impossible to do more than calculcate what profits would have been without this—clearly a severe understatement of true profits.

Returns from millers' estimates

Hence we are forced to use millers' own estimates of profitability (only four were obtained from the 10 interviews). According to millers, the average net profit from a combination of purchase, storage, processing, transporting, levy exactions, and non-levy sales of rice and bran in 1981 was Rs 7.8 per quintal of rice. The absolute net profit per mill was estimated to vary between Rs 1.25 lakh to Rs 5.5 lakh and the average net profit per mill was Rs 2.6 lakhs.

The rate of profit can be taken as $\dfrac{O-C}{CS+WC}$

where O is the value of gross output, C is total costs, CS is the value of capital stock (land, buildings, equipment and machinery), and WC is the value of working capital. On this basis the rate of profit from rice milling was 11 per cent, though the value of CS, determined by asking millers for the sales value of their mill, may be exaggerated. The relatively low rate of profit mainly reflected the highly capitalized nature of rice-milling technology, and in this West Bengal was no different from anywhere else in India.

Husking mills

The cost of husking was calculated in a similar way and averaged Rs 1.86 per quintal of paddy.[14] The cost included bribes to Food Department officials (often Rs 80–100 per month). The data also include a case where a substantial part of the electricity supply was stolen by the husking miller so that costs are correspondingly underestimated, but then it excludes the costs of parboiling.[15] Labour is domestic and unpriced. There is little point in imputing labour costs, as virtually no wage labour is used in the unlicensed sectors, even by petty traders. The total average processing costs (husking and parboiling) were about Rs 5.5 per quintal. The weighted average outturn though husking mills was 63.5 per cent, half a percentage point lower than that realized using the modernized technology of the rice mills. Net returns calculated on the basis of the official prices ranged from Rs 13.6 to Rs 25.9 per quintal of paddy; if returns from by-products are factored in, returns rose to between Rs 22.5 and 29.2.[16]

In the same way as for the rice mills, we calculated average annual incomes from husking. At declared rates of turnover, these varied from Rs 2,600 to Rs 24,855 and averaged Rs 7,488.[17]

But husking mill owners also estimated the maximum quantities that they had ever milled. In most cases, these were larger than the state-imposed capacity constraint and related to 'times in the early seventies', or the bumper year of 1977–8. However, if we take these statements of maxima and assume that they actually related (illegally) to 1981, then the absolute profits from husking would range from Rs 5,760 to Rs, 33,750 and would average Rs 10,944. Based on declared gross outputs, the average rate of profit would be 13 per cent; based on 'maximum' outputs, it would be 19 per cent.

These were very high rates of return, and the system of petty trade around husking machines also escaped the claws of the levy. We must not forget, however, that these spoils were divided between a very large number of small traders, husking millers, and the Food Department officials who were paid not to inspect.

The existence of wide net margins thus made possible many livelihoods in the highly employment-intensive, technically illegal sub-system of the rice markets. The margins were kept wide by the minimum quantity requirements of the oligopolistic rice mills. Hence, the small-scale sub-system could attract further entrants without necessarily reducing the absolute profits of individual petty traders.

Not only was the share of the total net profit in the petty trading sub-system which accrued to husking millers small (4 per cent), but it was also declining due to competition and overcapacity. The remainder of the distribution of total net profit accrued almost entirely to the army of petty traders and rice wholesalers.

Other types of firms
Rice wholesalers declared an average net profit of Rs 6.5 per quintal. This would give absolute net profits varying between Rs 8,250 and Rs 20,000 and averaging Rs 13,125. The rate of return on assets would be 12 per cent. The returns from illegal wholesaling (without permits) to modified ration areas were said to range from Rs 8 to Rs 20 per quintal, or on average Rs 12.[18] Estimates of net absolute annual profits, factoring in illegal wholesaling, ranged from Rs 11,000 to Rs 27,000

and averaged Rs 20,143. The rate of return on assets would then have been 19 per cent.

Purchasing agents incurred average costs (depreciation, travel, transport, and interest on stock) of Rs 0.9 per quintal of paddy. Their average rate of profit was low: 8 per cent. We made estimates, in the same way as for rice wholesalers, of the magnitude of the likely 'illegal' trade in paddy, and we also got several explicit revelations of illegal trade. These raised the estimates of gross output from 440 to 558 tonnes, yielding a net profit of Rs 6 per quintal of paddy. The total net profits then ranged between Rs 1,125 and Rs 54,000, and averaged Rs 20,185. The rate of profit was then 40 per cent.

Most rice brokers had average net profits (on their gross commissions of Rs 1 per quintal of rice) of Rs 0.71, their costs being mainly for telephones. Annual total net profits varied from Rs 3,000 to Rs 92,400 and averaged Rs 29,000. Since their owned assets were small, the rate of profit was high: 78 per cent.

Once again there emerges from this discussion of costs and profits the towering strength of rice mills in contrast to other firms in the local system of circulation—see Table 4.5. But these mills were caught in a debilitating contradiction not entirely of their own making. The hoists to open-market prices for rice, made inevitable by generalized losses throughout West Bengal on 'levied rice' procured at administered prices for the Public Distribution System, themselves created the wide margins between paddy and rice, which attracted petty traders into the unlicensed sub-system. The larger the levy percentage and/or the greater the differences between levy rice prices and market rice prices, the greater the diversion of rice away from the 'organized' sector, the larger the number of livelihoods created, the more sporadic the enforcement by the state, and greater the temptation for rice millers to evade the levy. Levy evasion contributed to the non-achievement of levy targets and thus persuaded the Food Department to acquiesce in a further raising of the levy percentage. The contradiction was reinforced.

Commercial Capitalist Accumulation
The growth of individual capitals[19]

It was within this system of varying legality that individual firms waxed and waned. In a short spell of field work on firms in active operation, it proved hard to acquire information about the failure of firms, and thus about the net changes in the local system. We learned, however, that the long-distance rice wholesale trade had been severely threatened

Table 4.5: Wealth in Terms of Annual Income of Firms in Circulation of Rice, 1981. Bolpur Region

(a) Firms Alone	Rice Mills	Rice Brokers	Rice Wholesalers declared	Rice Wholesalers probable (2)	Paddy Agents declared	Paddy Agents probable (2)	Husking Millers declared	Husking Millers probable maximum (2)
Firm no	10	4	4	4	13	13	17	17
Maximum net income (Rs.)	5,50,000	92,400	20,000	27,000	9,000	54,000	24,885	33,750
Minimum net income (Rs.)	1,50,000	3,000	8,250	11,000	1,250	1,250	2,600	5,760
Average net income (Rs.)	2,44,100	29,000	13,125	20,143	4,001	20,185	7,488	10,944
Average rate of profit (1)	11%	78%	12%	19%	8%	40%	13%	19%
Average firm-family livelihood units (2)	24	3.7	0.91	1.4	0.5	2.5	1.02	1.5
Average annual minimum consumption expenditure	10,440	7,920	14,400	14,400	8,010	8,010	7,380	7,380
Average net profit minus consumption	2,33,660	21,000	-	5,743	-	12,175	108	3,564
Average rate of profit minus consumption	9.6%	73%	-	5%	-	24%	-	6%
Average firm-family livelihood units minus consumption	22	2.6	-	0.4	-	1.5	-	0.5
(b) Family portfolios Estimated net income (av.)	9,65,459	1,10,250	65,500	72,518	21,361	37,545	35,000	38,456
Estimated maximum total income	20,00,000	3,03,000	2,00,000	2,13,875	58,800	74,984	1,10,250	1,13,706
Estimated minimum total income	2,00,000	10,000	15,000	17,750	8,625	8,625	12,272	18,72
Average firm family livelihood units (gross)	92	14	4.5	5	2.7	4.7	4.7	5.2
Average percentage of total family income coming from rice firm	25	26	20	28	18	53	21	28

Notes: (1) Rate of profit = $\frac{O-C}{CS+WC}$ for definition of which, see text.
(2) Defined in text.

Source: Data from 1982 survey.

by the imposition of the 60 per cent levy, and also that competition from rice brokers sited in destination marketplaces had cut by half the number of rice brokers operating in the supplying regions. Indeed, no new wholesalers or brokers were established in the regions of Bolpur and Ahmadpur in the 1970s. By contrast, 35 per cent of husking mills, 70 per cent of purchase agents, and 30 per cent of rice mill firms started during that period.

Growth can be measured through increases in gross output, in physical output, and in asset value. Firms were asked about physical output at three points in time: in the year that they set up, in the year of maximum trade, and in 1981.

A minority of rice mills had been in continuous expansion, but most of them declared that they had contracted operations by about a third. Husking mills also declared a present turnover of two-thirds of their historical maxima. These declines could all be due to overcapacity and competition within the expanding sub-system, or, because of the problem of illegal milling, the declared statements may have been underestimates of actual turnover. Rice wholesaling firms had declined by an average of 54 per cent on their maximum trade. *Rice brokering* firms had witnessed a decline in physical turnover of 40 per cent on average. *Paddy purchasing* agencies had by and large grown steadily in the volume stated, even as their numbers increased. Taking the firms as a whole, one group of firms has stagnated, while the other had doubled in size.

The second way of measuring accumulation compares original investments with the present (sales) value of land, buildings, equipment, and working capital. At certain points in this process of accumulation, resources will have been removed from the firms for investment elsewhere; at others, resources will have been put back in for expansion and technological upgrading. This process, which has led to concentration in some plants and idleness in others, is described in Appendix 4.1.

The total starting capital invested in the sample of 10 rice mills was 12 lakhs (in terms of current rupees). Investment peaked in the early 1960s when un-modernized mills changed hands and were modernized. The lower growth rates of assets in the 1970s reflected the heavy capitalization consequent on modernization. The growth of husking mills' assets was both less impressive and more constant. The growth of rice wholesale firms was varied, and probably reflected careful decisions about diversification rather than the vagaries of wholesale itself. The accumulation trajectories of paddy agents were counter-intuitive, with some recently-started firms registering high growth under conditions of increasing competition. In ascending order of assets are ranked the purchase agencies (which tripled in value, being young); husking machines (which quintupled); rice wholesalers and brokers (whose assets grew between two and 15 times); and heading the list, rice mills, whose assets grew by a factor of 19.

Commercial capitalism and agricultural production—relative returns
Firms controlling the circulation of rice have more assets and more investments than are suggested by the grain trade alone. Husking millers made their own estimates (which we have used) of the importance of husking in their family income. Rice wholesalers and rice brokers could be got to declare the relative importance of mercantile activities by declaring the absolute income from other investments, or by giving precise indications as to how this could be calculated. In the case of paddy purchasing *agents* and rice millers, lists of types of family investments were provided, but only in the case of land, lorries and property were any indications given of their quantitative magnitude. We pieced together estimates—surely underestimates—of the likely size of the income streams accruing from investments associated with accumulation in rice markets; and the results are given in Table 4.5. By this means, the returns from agricultural commerce can be compared with those from agricultural production (Tables 4.6 to 4.8).[20]

It became evident that profits from the control of the marketing of rice were in most cases only a minor component of the incomes of the families of the dominant firms. For paddy agents and husking millers, land ownership formed the main income supplement. By contrast,

Table 4.6: Income from Agricultural Production, 1981, Birbhum district

Holding Size (acres)	Gross Income per Acre (Rs.)	Net Income per Acre (Rs.)
2.5–5	1046.2	680
5–7.5	1893.6	1231
7.5–10	1562.9	1015
over 10	1662.5	1080
Weighted Average	1546.8	1005

Source: Bhattacharya et al., 1981, p.56

Table 4.7: Income and Livelihoods, Birbhum district

Average operational holding size 1970–1	3.1 acres[1]
Average operational holding size 1976–7	3.06 acres[2]
Average family size (Bolpur Block) 1981	5.6 [3]
Average net income from agriculture alone	3.1 x Rs. 1005 = 3115[4], [6]
Minimum consumption expenditure for basic needs *per caput*, 1980–1	Rs. 65 per month[5]
Minimum consumption expenditure per family, 1981	Rs. 4,368 per month [5]
Average farm family livelihood unit	0.71

Notes: (1) *Source*: Govt. of West Bengal 1975 *World Agricultural Census 1970–1*
(2) *Source*: Govt. of West Bengal 1979 *Agricultural Census 1976–7*
(3) S.A. Ram, 1982
(4) Bhattacharya et al., 1981
(5) In (eds), Ram and Murthy, 1980
(6) This would be reduced by rent payments and increased by income from agricultural labouring.

Table 4.8: Agricultural Interests of Agro-commercial firms, Birbhum district

	Number	Percentage owing land	Av. size	Max. acres	Min.	Percentage land leasing out	Percentage land leased out	Av. size leased out	Av. size self operated
Rice wholesalers	4	100	11	18	3	50	47	10.5	11.5
Rice Brokers	4	75	7	9	5	100	100	7	–
Rice Millers	10	80	30	100	2	90	83	27	50
Paddy Agents	13	100	11	21	3	9	10	15	11
Husking Millers	17	94	14	25	3	41	49	15	11

Note: Unlicenced petty traders are either without land or small peasants.
Source: Data from 1982 survey

rice wholesaling and brokerage were supplemented by other mercantile activities and the income of rice mills was supplemented by investments in the productive (agro-processing) industry, including other mills. In order of ascending (estimated) total family wealth, first came paddy agents and husking millers, at between Rs 20,000 and Rs 40,000 per family; then rice wholesalers and brokers, at between Rs 65,000 and 110,000; then rice millers at Rs 9.6 lakhs. The levels of family income are very clearly stratified.

In attempting to account for wealth, a problem arises from not having accounted for labour costs of the unpaid labour force where family labour may be a significant input. Net income is thus not pure profit but is partly used for the consumption needs of the entire family. We therefore calculated the annual profit per firm net of its family's livelihood requirements.[21]

Taking the firms in isolation from their portfolios, even if high estimates of output and profits are used, as soon as we subtracted a minimum consumption budget from annual net earnings, husking millers and rice wholesalers fell below the poverty line, and paddy purchase agents were only just above it. The average rice brokerage generated income sufficient for 2.6 families. Each rice mill, however, generated an income stream sufficient to cover the basic needs of 22 families.

The phenomenon of near-poverty results from the very large size of families involved in rice marketing. Average family size, at 11.6, was twice the local average of 5.6 (Ram, 1982). When we assess the family 'portfolios' in terms of firm-family livelihood units, then the average firms were far above the poverty line. Husking millers, paddy agents, and rice wholesalers had per capita incomes four to five times the poverty line. Once again, at 92 multiples of the cost of basic needs, the extreme relative wealth of milling families is emphasized and the stratification within the system is clear.

These figures acquire greater significance when compared with the farm-family livelihood obtained from the average operational holding in Birbhum district. Table 4.7 shows that this was only 0.71 of the income needed to provide for an average farm family. The reproduction of this agrarian class was therefore dependent on labouring and on loans. By the criteria of resource budgeting for basic needs to ensure social reproduction, rice millers were 130 times wealthier than the average producer on whose agricultural surpluses the millers depended.

Investment portfolios

The exact nature of the other investments of firms controlling the circulation of rice now holds great interest, not only in order to analyse the situation of these firms within the local economy, but also to assess the types of productive investment they made. The evidence is set out in Appendix 4.2, Table 2. The most constant elements in their portfolios proved to be the ownership and organization of land.

Ninety one per cent of paddy purchase agents operated land using hired wage labour. They were therefore predominantly drawn from a class of small agrarian capitalists. While all the rice wholesalers and husking mill owners owned land, half of them, generally the larger land owners, rented out their land. Rice brokers owned much less land (on average 7 acres, only twice the district average). They had little connection with this land, almost all the brokers being long-distance migrants from East Bengal. Rice millers owned holdings which were on average ten times the district average. Ninety per cent of millers rented their land out. Milling families were divided between the families of ex-zamindars, owning 50 to 100 acres, and migrant Marwari commercial families who had settled and who had over time acquired average landholdings of 20 acres, which they rented out. So those who controlled the rice markets also formed the dominant agrarian classes. By contrast, the mass of petty traders were usually either landless or small peasants.

But agro-commercial portfolios consisted of much more than land, and also formed the backbone of the local non-farm economy. Apart from agro-commerce, land, and in the case of rice mills, lorries, the average number of other investments was two for husking millers, three for paddy agents, four for rice brokers, five for rice wholesalers, and six for rice millers. Two thirds of the investments by husking mill firms were in productive agro-processing activity. Few trading firms did this, however. Petty traders, being landless or small peasants, had diversified into petty trade in, for example, eggs, mustard seed, and wheat, which may be seasonal complements. The portfolios of paddy agents tended to expand their mercantile activity while those of husking mills tended towards agro-processing (wheat and flour mills), moneylending and land-for-rent.

Rice mills not only had controlling interests in agricultural production, directly through ownership and indirectly through money advances; they also invested in horizontal and vertical integration and concentration in rice (10 families controlled between them 21 rice mills and a bran oil plant, for example) and other agricultural commodities (e.g., wholesale pulses and dal mills).

Commercial firms were thus highly diversified. There could be two kinds of reasons for this tendency, which is unusual elsewhere in India (see Harriss, 1981a for northern Tamil Nadu and 1996 for Coimbatore district). One is that, until recent times, the system of circulation of rice was extremely seasonal, and had quite different structures and behaviour before and after harvest. In situations where supplies dried up, it would have been necessary to have other complementary uses for capital. Diversification would have also been forced on intermediaries such as rice wholesalers and rice brokers as defence mechanisms, in face of the long history of intermittent state intervention and state participation which may have been experienced as economic shocks. At times when their mercantile activities were prohibited, such firms needed to divert both working capital and unspecialized capital assets flexibly and strategically into other activities.

The last extraordinary feature about this table of investments is the relative unimportance of land and agriculture, despite the agricultural dominance of agro-commercial capital. There are ceilings to investments in land, not only ones decreed by land reform laws but also those determined by ecology. Paddy purchasing agents and husking mill owners were predominantly land-based small capitalists and landlords. They were linked to the land by money-lending and the extraction of usurious profits, by surplus value extracted from trading, by processing, and by rentier profits. Paddy agents alone had invested in land improvement. Rice wholesalers and brokers are an intermediate category of landlord-merchant whose dominant source of income was mercantile. Their portfolios contained no investment in agricultural production and were mainly diversifications and consolidations of agro-commercial activity, together with property for rent. As for rice milling families, fewer than 10 per cent had limited their investment to pisciculture and sericulture, to the boring of a tubewell or the purchase of a thresher. Only a minute proportion of the financial resources extracted from agricultural production via the profits made by those controlling circulation was reinvested in agriculture.

Far from being in decline then, the rice mills dominated these markets. Their land ownership, despite being sizeable, was the least important element in their portfolios. Their profits were extracted through money advances, through rent on property and land, and through buying and selling, usually accompanied by processing. Their portfolios were large, capital-intensive and diversified, consisting of agro-processing industry, wholesale commerce, finance and money-lending, transport, and urban property. Rice mill ownership being

Social Structure and the Labour Process in Rice Markets

Surplus is thus extracted from agricultural production through rent, interest on loans, and buying cheap and selling dear. But insofar as traders process goods and transport goods, tendrils of productive industrial activity creep into the sphere of exchange and circulation. Surplus will also be extracted from labour within mercantile firms. Table 4.9 shows the structure of labour in the rice markets in 1981.

Using the sampling fractions from Table 4.1 for the two blocks of Bolpur and Sainthia, it is likely that some 1,670 people worked in rice milling, 1,480 in the purchase of paddy, 1,290 in petty trade and domestic parboiling, 350 in husking mills, 45 in rice wholesaling, and 20 in rice brokerage—a grand total of 4,855. Over half (2,500) of this labour force consisted of owners and family labour; and 20 per cent consisted of permanent employees. A further 20 per cent consisted of female casual labour, and 10 per cent was male casual labour. We have perhaps under-estimated this figure by excluding the gangs of weighing and loading coolies, unattached to the rice mills, who roam the region in search of work.

In the final part of this chapter, the social structure by means of which all this labour is regulated, will be examined. There are three major market-making institutions which shape the labour process: the mercantile family, salaried wage labour, and piece-rate, 'unskilled' labour. Onto these market-making labour institutions, we map the roles of two non-market institutions: caste and gender.

Table 4.9: Employment in the Rice Markets

	Family labour/ Partners per firm	'Salaried' Employees/firm	Casual Labour/firm	
	(male)	(male)	Female	Male
Rice wholesale	2	1.25	–	–
Rice broker	1.25	2	–	–
Rice mill	2.4	17	49	23
Paddy agents	1.5	0.77	–	–
Husker	1.8	1.17	1.17	–

Source: Data from 1982 survey

Commercial families and their labour

The main forms of ownership of commercial firms are shown in Tables 4.10 and 4.11. Richly varied in form, they mimic the heterogeneity of land ownership, although the organization of a commercial firm cannot be read off from the organization of the family farm. The most common or 'prominent' organizational forms were individual ownership or a family business worked by a father and sons or by brothers. In rice mills, there were more joint businesses than joint households. Shares in the mill might be retained in branches of a family scattered throughout the entire country. In husking mills, there was a tendency towards individual management from within a joint household; and a similar tendency existed in rice wholesaling and brokerage. Paddy agencies tended to be individually managed within a nuclear household.

Table 4.10: Ownership of Firms in the Rice Markets (%)

	N	Individual	1–2 members	2–3.9 members	4 members	1–2 Partners
Rice mill	10	10	50	20	20	-
Husking mill	17	47	24	17	6	6
Rice wholesale	4	75	25	-	-	-
Rice broker	4	75	-	-	-	25
Paddy agents	13	54	15	8	-	23

Source: Data from 1982 survey.

Table 4.11: Family Size and Type and Social Characteristics of Owners of Firms

	N	Family Size	% joint family	Av. education	Av. age
Rice mills	10	11.6	70	graduate	40
Rice wholesaler	4	16.00	75	9 years	51
Rice brokers	4	8.75	50	8 yrs	44
Paddy agents	13	8.9	46	9 yrs	41
Husking mill owners	17	8.2	64	10	37

Note: The 1971 census gives average household sizes for Birbhum District as follows: total 5.61, rural 5.62, Bolpur total 5.36, rural 5.34.
Source: Data from 1982 survey.

Although paddy agents were on an average in their early forties when interviewed, they were as a group the youngest entrants to the rice marketing system.

The form of management of agro-commercial firms also changes over time. Many, initially lacking either money or skills, seek partners in order to enter trade. Later on, a partner might be bought out. Within the firm, the number of active family members and the extent of employment of wage labour depend on the household life cycle and the scale and type of the family portfolio.[22] Very large families can be supported by trade.

Earlier in this chapter we found a range of economic entry barriers to the rice markets. Merchant communities create strong social barriers to entry as well.[23] Being a social 'other', an outsider, or a migrant are powerful ways of avoiding the exercise of mercy and local social obligations to redistribute wealth. The political anthropologist, Dieter Evers, has argued that these obligations are as much part of commerce as is the compulsion to accumulate, calling it the 'trader's dilemma' (Evers and Schrader, 1984). Being an immigrant may therefore be a crucial business asset.

Migration

Many Indian business castes are migrants and outsiders. In the sample we studied, 75 per cent of the wholesalers had in-migrated; only one had come from less than 20 miles away. Most of the others had come in the 1930s from Marwar in Rajasthan. Ninety per cent of the rice millers had immigrated, one-third locally and two-thirds from Rajasthan, well before the average start-up date of the current rice mills. Seventy-five per cent of the brokers had in-migrated, one locally and two from an average of 100 miles away in East Bengal (Bangladesh) around 1954. Forty per cent of the purchasing agents had in-migrated, mostly locally, but two from East Bengal in the 1930s. A third of the husking millers have migrated, all locally. Local migration more often than not gives rise to the formation of rural and urban—agricultural and commercial—branches of what the economic anthropologist Scarlett Epstein termed a 'share family'. Long distance migration is much more common in West Bengal than elsewhere in India, not only because it is a feature of north Indian trading castes but also as a result of the political turbulence of the region. In Birbhum district, many castes are exclusively urban; some are migrant; and some practise a different religion from that of the local majority. These features reinforce the social barrier between them and the rural population, a barrier they exploit.

Caste and Gender Structures and Social Exclusion

Table 4.12 gives details of the distribution of caste in the rice markets of Birbhum district. There are fewer castes in trade than have been found in south India: 82 per cent of all the merchants interviewed belonged to only six castes. A third were from *vaisya* (business) castes which are urban, frequently migrant, and segregated socially from agricultural producers. About half of these managed rice mills; the rest were spread between the other types of firms. Nearly half the mercantile families came from two agricultural castes, one of which, Sadgops, was the dominant caste of the 28 castes noted in the surrounding countryside (Ram, 1982; p. 7; Table 2). However, the proportion of Sadgops was already twice as large in trade as it was in agriculture, and they were in the process of becoming urbanized. Brahmins formed 12 per cent of our sample in Birbhum,[24] but only eight per cent of the rural population as a whole. Like Sadgops, Brahmins were in the process of entering business.

Table 4.12: Caste in the Rice Markets (by firm)

	Brahmin	Gondopani Baniya	Agarwal	Marwari	Sadgops	Ugrokshatriya
Caste occupation	priest	business	business	business	cultivation	cultivation
Rice mill	-	2	-	15	7	-
Rice wh	2	2	2	-	2	-
Rice br	-	2	2	-	-	-
Paddy agent	5	5	-	2	15	5
Husking mill	7	5	-	-	15	5
No	6	7	2	6	16	4
Av family size	12.3	8.1	13.5	11.9	9.0	8.3
% joint family	66	57	50	66	56	75
Frequency in villages (% hh)	8.4				13.5	3
Average family-size in Bolpur block	5.8				6.4	4.6

Source: Survey of 26 villages: Ram, S.A. 1982 and own survey of commercial firms (9 would not divulge their caste)

Noteworthy kinds of social exclusion operated in these markets. There was no practical possibility of entering trade for any of the 47 per cent of rural households which, according to Ram's research (1982), were what is now known as *dalit*: tribal or scheduled caste. Nor could women conduct wholesale trade in rice, even though they were known to dominate rice retailing in Kolkata. Three quarters of the local population was therefore socially excluded from the control of rice marketing and processing.

The control exercised by male family labour over all scales of rice marketing firms makes the role of women difficult to observe. Female family labour consisted, in the main, of doing the unpaid domestic labour involved in pre-milling processing for petty trade. On an average, it took 10 women-days to process one tonne of paddy.[25] The female labour used in pre-milling processing in the two blocks was therefore about 128,750 women-days. At 330 days per year, this was 390-women-years of work. The labour requirement per thousand tonnes processed in the domestic/petty trading sector was 70.3 person-years, of which 30 would have been work done by women.

Socialization Into Trade: Knowledge and Skill
To accumulate in commerce requires skills and knowledge, personal contacts, and a business reputation. Rice millers acquired these trading attributes in three ways: first from experience in a related mercantile activity; second through contributing finance to a working partnership which then afforded the opportunity to learn; and third, and most commonly, the present manager entered the family firm after completion of his education and then learned and made contacts through an apprenticeship on the shop floor.

Husking machine owners acquired their knowledge mainly from within the family. A significant minority (35 per cent) learned by employing a mechanic and learning by watching and doing, but we found no mechanic in the sample who had risen to owning a husking machine (which was one trend observable in south India). Rice wholesalers and brokers acquired their experience through groceries, partnerships, and in one case as a rice mill employee. Purchase agents learned as employees of other purchasing agents, of grocers or of rice millers. But when most of them entered the market, their only experience had come from being sellers of produce.

Wage labour

A fifth of all the firms interviewed employed no wage labour at all and were the equivalent in trade of peasant producers. Half the paddy-purchase agents and rice wholesaler firms were of this type. The individual petty firm was of course non-existent in rice mills, and nearly non-existent in husking mills. Even in firms where some wage labour is employed—the majority—the owners were also actively at work. Very few cases of the mercantile equivalent of the (absentee) agricultural landlords were found; they consisted of shareholders in family rice mills.

The permanent labour force

The provisions made for labour by the Factories Act (which covers the rice mills), and by the labour unions, operated as disincentives for secure, permanent employment contracts. In Birbhum district, as in other regions of India where the agro-commercial labour force has been observed, secure, permanent labour is the rarest form of work contract. In Birbhum, nearly 90 per cent of the permanent labour force was to be found in two types of firms: many paddy-purchase agencies and the few rice mills. Of the rice mill labour force, just one fifth had permanent contracts; and the English word 'salaried' was used to refer to them.

The types of labour performed by these employees were very distinct. Generally it was either skilled work, or work requiring a high level of trust on the part of the owner. Clerks, accountants, and price and information scouts do specialized tasks requiring special trust, and distinctions were made between them on the one hand and mechanics and 'engineers' on the other, who might be paid less (Table 4.13). Wages were in cash and kind. The provision of meals was reported to cost between Rs 120–175/month (Rs 150/month has been used for imputing). The value of gleanings for husking mill labour has been imputed at Rs 2–5/kg. of rice. Annual perquisites—one month's pay and/or clothing at the time of *Durga Puja* (October)—have not been included; nor has leave with wages or payment for medicines and medical treatment, which are at the discretion of the employer.

There were three important characteristics of the permanent labour force. First, the labour market was indeed highly segmented and differentiated. Average wages for a given category of permanent labour such as clerks, varied by over 100 per cent, and maximum wages varied even more. Second, to a significant degree, payments were made in

Table 4.13: Wage Rates: Clerks and Mechanics

Firm	Av. per month	Max.	Min.	Notes
Rice Wh.	210	300	150	40 per cent paid partly in kind (meals)
Rice Br.	380	825	300	12 per cent paid partly in kind (meals)
Paddy agency	236	300	175	50 per cent paid partly in kind (meals)
Rice mill	550	1000	250	all cash
Husking mill	234	400	150	66 per cent paid partly in kind as meals and/or gleanings and/or kind payments directly from customer.

Source: Data from 1982 survey

kind. Cash values were imputed for the purposes mentioned in Table 4.14. Third, the minimum monthly wages for 'salaried' employees in paddy purchase agencies, rice wholesale firms, and husking mills were below the minimum wage set at the time by the state (Rs 8.1 per day for men). If we assume 25 working days per month, no salary came below the central government's poverty line (Rs 65/month for rural labour and Rs 75 per month for urban labour). This calculation, however, assumes that salaried employees were providing for themselves alone, and not for their entire families, which is most unlikely.

We were told that virtually every permanent employee was landless and therefore got no supplement from agricultural production.[26] Considering the average wages, and bonuses amounting to an extra one month's pay, it is only in rice mills and rice brokerage firms that the average permanent employee or 'salary earner' would have been able to support the average family, by his own work alone, at above the poverty line.

The piece-rate, unskilled labour force

The operation of rice processing in Bolpur and Sainthia blocks depended on the labour of about 1,000 female casual labourers and 420 male coolies. Together, male and female casual labour constituted 30 per cent of the total labour involved in the circulation of rice in our study region.

Table 4.14: Wage Rates: Coolie and Casual Labour

Job	Sex	Type of payment	Rate	Av. daily take home pay	Max.	Min.	Night
Husking mill							
Manual separation of rice from bran and husk	F	kind	varies from Rs. 0.5 to Rs. 1.3 per quintal separated av. Rs. 1.25	5.9	8.75	3.2	–
Rice mill							
Drying yard and mill work	F	cash and kind	daily wage	7.6	10	5.5	11–12
Parboiling	M	cash	contract or piece rate varying from Rs. 0.15 per quintal to Rs. 0.83 per quintal paddy	8.7	12	6.5	12–13
Various firms							
Loading/unloading	M	cash	contract or piece rate Rs. 0.2–2.5 per bag	about 10			
Weighing and bagging	M	cash	piece rate Rs. 0.20–0.25 per bag	about 10			

Source: Data from 1982 survey.

There was a precise gender division of labour. At most husking mills, one or two women shook or winnowed the mixture of husk, bran, brokens, and rice which poured from the husker. They were always paid by the customers, in kind. In rice mills, female labour tended paddy in the drying yard and checked the passage of paddy through the mills. Men operated the parboiling machinery. They loaded, unloaded, weighed, and bagged paddy and rice. Gangs of 5–6 male labourers, unattached to any rice mills, travelled the countryside to prepare the illegally traded paddy for transport. It was the acknowledgement by paddy agents that they hired this sort of unskilled labour which indicated their illegal trade.

As with permanent labour, casual labour was employed under extremely varied conditions (Table 4.14). The main sources of variation were: first, whether the wage was paid in cash, or partly or wholly in kind, which constrained the circulation of information about wages, since it increased the difficulty of comparison; second, variation in the piece rate; third, variation in the average daily take-home pay; and fourth, variation in 'perks'—subsidized rice, bonuses, and access to money for loans. These variations made the imperfections of the 'market' for coolies and unskilled labour even greater than those for the permanent labour force. Ashok Rudra (1982) observed similar types of 'imperfection' for agricultural wage labour in the villages comprising the clusters of Sian and Ilambazar, and conjectured that relations of production—and hence labour 'markets'—were contained within each village, so that prices for labour could vary between villages. It seems that a big rice mill in Birbhum had some of the same autonomy for wage determination as did Rudra's villages. Despite the Factories Act and the existence of trade unions, it needs to be understood that firm-specific variations in contractual terms and conditions were as much a feature of the labour market as the assignment of different types of contract to different tasks, or the gender division of labour.

On an average, casual wages resulted in daily take-home pay in excess of the minimum statutory wage of Rs 7.6 for women and Rs 8.1 for men. But the minimum wages we recorded were all below this norm. The minimum daily take-home pay for female labour in husking mills could support only 1.2 people at the official poverty line. The minimum for female labour in rice mills could support only 2.1 people, and that for male labour in rice mills only 2.5 people.

In the rice mills, however, labour is not strictly 'casual', although rates of turnover may be high. The male workers in particular were frequently to be found organized into groups of 5–6, each group taken from one village. Employers took labourers on, and laid them off, by gang. Some gangs had gangmasters who negotiated contracts for operations such as parboiling and loading/unloading. Gangmasters got the same wage as the rest of the gang, but their work was limited to supervision.

The social regulation of casual labour

The agricultural economy of West Bengal has long required, and profited from, migrant labourers.[27] Fully half of the male labour force in our sample were long-distance migrants. Migrant labour did not usually come from the same places as the migrant owners of capital but from Bihar, Orissa, and Uttar Pradesh. In rice mills, free quarters were provided for migrants and for any local coolies who needed them. Some got free coal, electricity, and subsidized rice. Wages for migrants were lower than those for local labour, at a minimum Rs 6.5 per man per day. This labour was the easiest to control and to dictate working conditions to on a 'take it or leave it' basis. They were the first labourers to be laid off in the slack season, when they returned to try to find work as agricultural labourers in their places of origin. The demand for this kind of labour has fallen with the demise of the labour-intensive 'chowbacha' system of cold soaking and steaming paddy, for which it was said that 'these tribals have special talents'.

It has been suggested that rice milling has provided few local linkages by way of employment (Mukherjee, 1966). In Bolpur in the 1950s, however, the mills provided employment for 1,550 labourers—a significant linkage. All the local labourers were either scheduled castes or *santals* (tribals). Although local employment for unskilled labour in the rice mills decreased, due to technical changes in the early 1980s, the employment provided was still significant.

Exploitation and productivity

The exploitation of labour may be analysed in two ways: in terms of its physical productivity (in particular the labour intensity of the processing technologies), and in terms of its distributive share (the labour cost component in total costs, compared with profits or returns to the owners of capital), (Table 4.15).

In the 1950s, dheki processing, and the use of domestic labour for pre-milling stages, generated 5.3 times as much employment per unit of output as processing in the rice mills and twice as much employment was generated in the husking mill sector as in the rice mills. Between 1954 and 1981, both of the latter increased their total capacity in our study region. They appeared to have slightly increased their physical labour intensity as well[28]. Chapter 3 revealed how employment in the processing of rice in West Bengal as a whole had been drastically reduced—from an estimated 1,240,000 jobs in 1954 to an estimated 107,250 jobs in 1981–2. An indication of massively-increased physical productivity, this also indicates severe labour displacement. In 1981, the husking mill subsystem generated 2.5 times as much employment as the rice mill sub-system. Every thousand tonnes of paddy processed in rice mills deprived local society of 45 person-years of employment.

Turning to the relationships between labour costs and total value added, and numbers of workers and total value added, Table 4.15 summarizes the distributive share. We have defined total value added as total costs, including those of labour, plus total profits. Wage labour as a proportion of total costs varied from 30 per cent in the 'petty production' of the husking mill (because so little is employed) to 65 per cent in rice mills. Wage labour as a proportion of total value added varied between 10 and 20 per cent for all firms except husking and the rice mills where it is three times as much. The most important feature of this table is that it shows that wage labour as a fraction of the total labour force was everywhere two to three times greater than it was as a fraction of the total value added—and by this yardstick it was grossly exploited.

Table 4.15: Wages in the Cost Structure of Firms in the Circulation of Rice: Birbhum district, 1981 (Averages)

	Rice mill	Husking mill		Rice wholesale		Rice broker	Paddy agent	
		av. est.	max. est.	av. est.	max. est.		av. est.	max. est.
Total value added (Rs)	595,840	7,640	25,536	19,380	25,650	41,000	7,961	28,555
Total costs as % total value added	58	57	57	30	29	45	50	30
Wage labour as % total costs	65	33	23	55	55	41	55	26
Wage labour as % total value added	38	19	13	16	12	18	27	8
Wage labour as % total labour force	98	40	40	40	40	60	34	34
Family labour as % total labour force	3	60	60	60	60	40	66	66
Profits gross of consumption as % total value added	41	42	42	70	77	54	50	70

Source: Data from 1982 survey.

In rice mills, the permanent salaried labour force formed 19 per cent of the total labour force and comprised exactly 19 per cent of total value added. Casual labour also got 19 per cent of total value added, but it formed 78 per cent of the labour force. Family labour made up three per cent of the labour force, but got 41 per cent of total value added. In terms of the contrast between the distribution of sheer numbers and the distribution of rewards, it was female casual labour that received the least. It is clearly in the largest firms that the exploitation of labour generally was highest, that the exploitation of casual labour was highest, and that the exploitation of female labour was highest.

Conclusions

By considering markets in systems terms, as we have in this chapter, the three questions with which we started can be answered. The first was, how far is the sphere of agricultural commodity markets institutionally autonomous? The answer is that it was autonomous, chiefly in the way that non-market institutions—in particular ethnicity, caste and gender—regulate markets.

Although by no means completely, non-local ethnic groups – Baniyas and Marwaris—tended to dominate agro-commercial capital. For several decades, Marwari families in particular had been buying up idle rice mills from the landed Bengali elite. Their starting capital was not mobilized directly from agriculture but by community-specific banks operating throughout India—most particularly in the north—and money obtained from commerce. This finance was used for the long-term intra- and inter- seasonal storage that was increasingly necessary for high-capacity utilization required by the new technology which the state forced rice mills to use. Whenever the Left Front Government lifted trade restrictions, their network of exclusive contacts was rapidly mobilized to secure the long-distance supplies needed to sustain high capacity utilization.

As regards caste, while there is a great range of agrarian castes in the region, only a few of them were involved in the rice trade; for the most part the trade was in the hands of either migrant castes or dominant agricultural castes. Scheduled castes and tribal people had been remarkably successfully excluded from ownership even of small firms, and at best worked as casual labour.

Finally, the system of markets was used to subordinate women. The largest and most exploited element of the casual wage labour force in rice mills was female. They were invisible in local petty trade, even though the labour of women and children was key to the low costs of processing in the petty sub-circuit. No women were found operating firms of any size in the local region. But low-caste women were actively engaged in the large clandestine trade which supplied the coal belt and Calcutta with 'open market' rice.

These three non-market institutions are conventionally excluded from conceptions of the key institutions in an economy, being assumed to be pre-capitalist relics, destined to disappear. In our region, however, they were found to be integral parts of the market structure. On the other hand, they were not merely part of the structure of the markets. They were subject to change arising from challenges in other arenas, particularly production.

Our second question was to what extent the system of circulation of rice was determined by production relations. The answer was, only rather partially, and in the general sense that its supplies ultimately depend on them.

Land was an important source of starting capital in commerce, notably in those parts of the system where the numbers of participants were increasing—paddy agencies and husking mills. With the exception of the newest rice mills, in the rest of the system, the larger commercial firms used rents from sharecropping and cash-rent tenures, as well as profit from agriculture, to enter markets. Indeed, there were few local outlets for local agricultural accumulation other than agricultural markets, and this underdeveloped non-farm sector had resulted in structural overcapacity in sectors such as husking mills. Even at the apex of the system—the rice mills—the system of money advances cascading downwards and outwards from the mills, with the purpose of securing paddy supplies, was a relationship of agro-commercial production, strikingly few of the returns to which were re-invested in agriculture .

Turning from capital to labour, petty trade in the rice markets provides seasonal livelihoods essential to the reproduction of households involved in very small-scale farming. Half the casual male wage labour in rice mills was migrant. Used to depress wage costs in rice mills, this employment also enabled pauperized landless and petty-producing households in other agrarian regions to survive lean periods of employment in their districts of origin, and was essential to the reproduction of the agrarian structure.

All these were significant ways in which markets were linked to production in relations of mutual cause and effect. On the other hand, most of the capital for rice mill expansion, technological upgrading, and ownership concentration was obtained not directly from agriculture but from commercial accumulation in rice markets and from financial resources outside the region. By-product prices, which are important to rice mill profits, fluctuated seasonally but in ways not closely related to the seasonality of paddy prices. The prices at which rice mills sell rice—rice wholesale prices—moved intra-seasonally in a way which exaggerated the price fluctuations for paddy, were not accounted for by storage costs and were suggestive of independent collusive power on the part of mill owners. Technological change in parboiling and milling (described in Appendix 4.1) speeded up the production period dramatically, enabling rice mills to take substantial advantage of rapid price movements, but it also required ever larger production batches to break even, which gave an advantage to firms which had access to large-scale private finance and were free from state restrictions on borrowing. The concentration of power in markets, though parallel to land concentration, was much greater than that in agricultural production, and less and less related to it.

The independent market power of Marwari rice wholesalers operating on the periphery of Calcutta, despite its being severely regulated by the Left Front Government, was also more than a match for the local rice wholesalers and brokers of Birbhum district.

Finally, official price data revealed that the local retail part of the system, although becoming increasingly crowded, exhibited price behaviour which was specific to individual market centres, independent of rice wholesaling, and capable of further exaggerating price fluctuations.

These conclusions bear directly on the answer to our third question, as to how the prolonged period of agricultural stagnation and fluctuation had affected the markets for rice. It did so first through distress entry, and second through the lack of a diversified and dynamic non-farm economy, which meant that there was little alternative to agricultural markets for non-agricultural investments. The sub-system of petty trade through husking mills relied much on labour being implicitly valued at below market rates, or not valued at all, in a process of petty commodity production and trade which was itself controlled through money advances at pauperizingly high rates of disguised interest. These money advances were controlled by local oligopoly capital and were an important means through which it reproduced its conditions of existence. The lack of an alternative to agro-commerce resulted—and still results—in the structure of the system being continually contested. Given the lack of growth, it had also resulted in chronic overcapacity in processing plants of all sizes, and in serious crowding at key points throughout the system—paddy agencies, husking mills, and petty trade. Yet the segmented nature of the market system meant that competition did not drive down rates of return.

In the next chapter, we consider the dynamism of—and disturbances to—this system. The first dynamic disturbance is that from market-driven politics. The second is the political means used to ensure the wide, fluctuating marketing margins which keep returns to commerce decisively higher than those to production.

Notes

1. Haats in the area were privately owned or, like Khujutipara, owned by a temple trust. The Left Front Government encouraged the take-over of the ownership of haats by the village Panchayat, as in Singhi, where the haat was no longer auctioned. The contractor simply took for himself 40 per cent of the rent he collected from stall holders. The Panchayat constructed an all-weather road to attract vegetable wholesalers from Bolpur. Until the 1980s, a small cartel of *Paikars* had bought all the vegetables put up for sales by producers, who found bulk sale at lower prices more attractive than piecemeal sales to local customers. Paikars immediately resold the vegetables, sometimes at 50 per cent mark-ups, having cornered the market. The villagers had on occasions physically threatened these Paikars. They were building a road, and in return hoped to obtain a government grant for a shed for their haat. All these developments were progressive in nature for the production and local consumption of vegetables.
2. There was also a weekly periodicity in paddy sales. Paddy, being a manifestation of the goddess Lakshmi, was generally not sold on those days when the goddess is worshipped (Monday, Wednesday, and Thursday).
3. Such imports took the form of relatively massive consignments such as 1000 tonnes at a time.
4. Prices in this chapter are current prices. See the Table of Inflators and Deflators before the Preface for factors with which to compare past with present prices.
5. See Appendix 4.2 also.
6. Interest rates were disguised when they did not appear to enter a contract at all, but when prices and payment period actually reflected a factored-in interest component.
7. This was one major cause for the high turnover of mill agents. The other causes were prices offered, delayed payments, the size of the commission, rudeness, ill treatment, and the closing of mills.

8. Depreciation is a difficult concept in cases where the sales value and the real value of buildings, land and machinery exceeded the capital cost. By accounting convention, buildings etc. are depreciated at 5 per cent per year, but all the rice mill buildings in our survey were constructed before 1961. Technically they had been fully amortized by 1982. The calculation of depreciation is therefore confined to machinery installed after 1971 at a conventional 10 per cent. In nine mills for which precise data were obtained, a total of Rs 35.5 lakhs of new machinery had been installed. Total depreciation per annum is therefore Rs 350,000 on 287,360 quintals of rice produced: Rs 1.22 per quintal of rice or Rs 0.81 per quintal of paddy.
9. The weighted average cost of milling amounts to Rs 11.2 per quintal of paddy for 1981–2. It ranged between Rs 8 and Rs 15, having doubled from 1977. While the official out-turn specification for rice from paddy is 66 per cent, the actual out-turn obtained by rice mills in 1981 was a weighted average of 64 per cent. This does not reflect engineering inefficiencies so much as the difference between the quality specifications discussed earlier.
10. Bran with an oil content of 20–27 per cent fetched between Rs 1,500 and 2,000 per tonne, with prices varying seasonally after the fashion of paddy. The average income from bran was Rs 7 per quintal of paddy or Rs 11 per quintal of rice. In actual fact, the recovery rate for bran was frequently less than 4 per cent. At declared rates and at declared prices (the mode being Rs 1,600 per tonne), the income from bran was Rs 6 per quintal of paddy, Rs 9.6 per quintal of rice. This would have brought the average net profit per quintal of rice to Rs 12.35 in Bolpur, 28.5 in Sainthia, 16.3 in Nalhati, and 22.6 in Suri.
11. We can make only the most crude of estimates of the returns from transport. We can use the annual average wholesale prices for rice in Birbhum district in 1981 (an average which smoothes out the short-term fluctuations which are the bread and butter of mercantile profits). These ranged between Rs 236 to 240 per quintal. We know that similar average prices in deficit districts such as 24 Parganas and Hooghly ranged between Rs 270 and 280. Transport costs for a lorry containing 150 x 80 kg. bags of rice were between Rs 0.5–1.0 per 20 km. For the distance we are simulating, costs have been assessed at Rs 850 and Rs 900, that is, Rs 6.6–7.5 per quintal. If we use the upper limits for transport costs and prices in the district of origin and the lower price in the district of destination, the net profit per quintal from trading would have been at least Rs 22.5 per quintal. And if we assume the destination prices were retail prices and that the gross retail margin was, as in Birbhum, Rs 10 per quintal, then a wholesaler alone would have still netted Rs 12.5 per quintal at the very least.
12. Using paddy prices as in Fig. 4.4 for Bolpur in 1981, we can plot the monthly losses on the levy. We are assuming, somewhat unrealistically, that a rice mill processes an equal quantity each month. We know that mills actually closed or worked at half rates during the monsoon months, June to August. This is the period when profits on non-levy rice were low, so our simulation

tends toward an over-estimation of levy losses. For each month, we have computed the difference between the open market price and the procurement price for rice for the percentage levied. For the residual, we have computed the net monthly profit. The total annual loss on the levy (without transport) in Bolpur in 1981, on a monthly turnover of 100 quintal, paddy would have been Rs 18,890. The total compensation for the sale in Bolpur of non-levy rice would have been Rs 7,507. The total income from bran would have been Rs 11,520. The net profit incorporating the levy would have been Rs 137. In other words, not considering transport, storage, and seasonality in milling, a mill would break even when it complied with the levy. Beyond that, all profits made by mills would have been through mercantile transactions and through speculating on storage.

13. We developed an estimate of levy evasion from two sources. If we assume that 75 per cent of marketed surplus was milled in the period from October to May, then the weighted average levy for 1980–1 was 51 per cent. Official statistics of procurement from rice mills in 1980–1 are 27,080 tonnes of rice. At a levy of 51 per cent this means that the 46 rice mills should have milled a total of 53,098 tonnes of rice or 82,965 tonnes of paddy. Official data for the output of rice mills in 1980–1 is 118,658 tonnes of paddy. Using official data, some 11,651 tonnes of levy rice must have been evaded: 43 per cent of what was actually collected. My own survey of 10 mills gave an average annual turnover of 4,900 tonnes of paddy—225,400 tonnes for the district as a whole. This is close to the estimate of 240,000 tonnes actually used by the District Rice Mill Association. At this level, the levy evasion amounted to 46,489 tonnes of rice or 172 per cent of what was actually collected.

14. As with rice mills, so with husking mills the real value of the equipment rose over time and exceeds costs. Using the convention of 5 per cent annual depreciation over 20 years for land and buildings, and a 10 per cent annual depreciation over 10 years for machinery, total annual depreciation comes to Rs 13,705 on 107,100 quintals of paddy. This is Rs 0.2 per quintal of rice or Rs 0.13 per quintal of paddy.

15. See Harriss, 1982, for details of the costs of parboiling, estimated at Rs 3.9 per quintal of paddy.

16. Bran from the husking mill was not separated from husk and the two were rarely sold. But on the market they fetched Rs 6 per quintal of paddy and Rs 9 per quintal of rice. If the profits of traded husk and bran are added the net profit per quintal of rice was Rs 27.8, Rs 34.9, Rs 22.6 and Rs 29.2 in the four towns in Appendix 4.3.

17. Few millers willingly acknowledged milling over the level of the Government imposed capacity constraint, which is roughly equal to four hours' operation. Fickle electricity supplies, and competition from new mills, lent some credence to the statements supplied.

18. Estimates of probable un-permitted trade were made from the discrepancies between the declared annual gross output of wholesalers and that output

obtained when they described a profile of their operations during busy and slack periods, and the duration of such periods.
19. See also Appendix 4.2.
20. A detailed discussion of the process of estimation is to be found in Harriss, 1982. The portfolio of investment associated with rice mills was hard to ascertain, not just because of estimation problems connected with investments. The family as a business unit among which features the sampled rice mill, could have up to 50 members, living in several different houses, often with branches in different locations—frequently in Calcutta and sometimes in different states. Land values were calculated through estimates of land owned, and questions about the organization of agricultural production on that land. But with no information on the extent and type of irrigation, the cropping intensity and the cropping pattern, we had no alternative but to use a simple 'average' multiplier for income from land (Bhattacharya et al., 1981, p. 56) and to apply these multipliers to the landholdings of mercantile firms. Land rented out was almost invariably on *krishani* rental terms, where the landlord supplies all inputs except for labour. Share-rent has been taken as a low (but legal) 25 per cent (though it is commonly 66 per cent and occasionally 75 per cent). Income from lorry ownership has had to be derived from two estimates of gross income and total labour, fuel and repair costs.
21. Consumption expenditure was not obtained from mercantile firms, so a hypothetical minimum subsistence budget was prepared for each family using the Planning Commission's estimate for 1980-1 of urban minimum needs: the cost of food (at 2,400 calories per capita per day), the cost of clothing, and rent. Because the consumption of basic goods is highly income-elastic, the subtraction from net income of a 'minimum needs' budget for the family will over-estimate the pure profit of richer families. However, it enables us to examine the element of pure profit in rice trading. It also enables us to calculate the wealth of trading firms in terms of an index representing the number of firm-family livelihood units supportable by the family income. This can then be compared with other sectors of local society. The urban minimum needs budget for 1980–81 was Rs 75 per caput per month (Rangasamy, in Ram and Murthy, eds., 1980; p. 163). Savings and investment will also be derived from gross income but have to be ignored in these calculations.
22. Note that 'family' needs to be differentiated from 'household' in order to operationalise and measure household size and composition. A family can be bigger unit than a household. A family may be a complex unit of capital while a household is a unit for day to day maintenance or social 'reproduction'.
23. Fox, 1969; Hazlehurst, 1966; Harriss, 1981a; Harriss-White, 2003.
24. This might possibly be due to the energies of—and reception to—my Brahmin assistant. However, the problem of bias was anticipated and we did not go out of our way at any stage to meet Brahmin traders.
25. We obtained estimates from eight sets of people on the employment generated in this way. If we were to suppose that the 20 per cent sample of petty

traders had been representative for the two blocks, then the total number of such traders would have been about 515. If they processed an upper estimate of 25 tonnes of paddy a year, then a total of 12,875 tonnes passed through their hands.
26. The minimum monthly wage in a rice wholesaling firm and in a husking mill supported 2.3 people at the poverty line. The wage in a paddy purchase agency supported 2.6 people. The minimum wage in rice mills and rice brokering firms, paid to their salaried labour force, could support 4.6 people at the poverty line. It is only in the last two types of firms that the salaried labour force got a wage which guaranteed the reproduction of a family. The average family size in Bolpur block was 5.3 (Ram, 1982). At the minimum needs standards for rural areas, such a household required Rs 4,134 per annum to reach consumption levels defined at the poverty line.
27. See the research of de Haan and Rogaly, 1996; Rogaly et al., 2001, 2002 and 2003; Rogaly, 2003.
28. Though it is possible that this result derived from differences in sampling; details of the sampling procedure for 1954 were not given.

5 The Dynamics and Politics of Rice Markets in Birbhum District

The institutions of capital, technology, and labour which constituted the system of markets in Birbhum in the early 1980s have been described in Chapter 4. At the same time, thousands of individual agents operating on extremely small scales were creating new 'structures' or institutions and making significant changes to the system. The dynamics of the system, however, also comes from two further sets of forces: state intervention and the collective mercantile political response. This chapter explores the way in which the state and trade associations, both together and antagonistically, sent (and still send) shocks through the system and shape its evolution.

In 1981, Sunil Sengupta argued that 'policy makers upholding market economies have to have two political programmes—one in concession to power lobbies and another in deference to the surging phenomenon of a mass of humanity daily reproducing itself below the poverty line around petty commodity structures' (1981, p. A74). While Sengupta contrasted power lobbies and mass politics related to agricultural production, this chapter does the same with respect to agricultural markets. Together, state parametric regulation and state participation contributed to a nexus of private interests involving state officials and commercial capital, seeking and profiting from rents in markets as well as inside the state. Their social effect was to penalize urban ration consumers (through lower quality), and rural and urban open market consumers (through seasonal price manipulation), to the benefit of millers. Yet they also acted so as to reduce the state-maintained price distortions between surplus and deficit regions. The black market benefited consumers in deficit districts, private officials administering the restrictions, and rice transporters and millers in surplus districts.

The chapter is organized as follows. The first part describes some unintended ways in which state interventions affect the marketing of rice. Then I describe the state's intended interventions in the rice markets, by compulsory procurement, and by various forms of regulation respectively and, sum up the significance of these forms of state intervention. The next section switches to the impact of the political activities of market businesses, describing their trade associations and their lobbying and legal efforts to pursue their interests. The final section pulls together everything that has been described in both Chapter 4 and Chapter 5, summarizing the character of the rice markets as they were at the beginning of the 1980s.

State Interventions: 'Unintended' Interventions

Although policy has to be discussed using the language of sectors and labels, it is an error to assume that a given sector with a distinctive label (e.g., nutrition, a policy-field consisting of education, food fortification, mother–child feeding schemes, and nutrition surveillance), is only affected by a dedicated subset of policies with the same label (that is, Nutrition Policy). A moment's reflection about alcohol in India reveals how fatal this assumption is. Never regarded as part of the Nutrition Policy, and being an important cash-cow for the revenue department, alcohol consumption threatens the food security of households close to or below the poverty line by diverting expenditure which could have been allocated to food, and shared throughout a household, to the empty and toxic calories consumed by the drinker (Harriss-White, 2004c). Yet alcohol has never been seen as relevant either to nutrition policy or to food security.

In the same vein, we begin with two interventions which are *not* directed explicitly at the marketing system but which indirectly affect both its operation and its interventions. One is subsidized 'institutional credit': state-provided or state-regulated credit for agricultural production. Although total state credit declined drastically in Birbhum district during the early period of Left Front Government rule—from Rs. 317 to Rs. 107 lakhs between 1976–7 and 1980–1, and although some of it will have been diverted from its intended use by producers who lent it onwards to others at higher interest than that at which they borrowed, it nevertheless provided an alternative to the production credit given by paddy purchase agents (see Table 4.3). On our estimate, traders' loans could have been of the order of Rs. 210 lakhs in the district as a whole, so they remained the main source of production credit throughout the initial period of the Left Front Government. Nevertheless, in principle, state-subsidized credit freed a significant but declining fraction of agricultural borrowers from oppressive interlocked contracts with paddy agents and enabled them to deal with petty traders. But just as some agricultural loans will have been lent onward, our survey showed that other loans were diverted from production to be used for entry into the very petty trade which challenges the market system supplying rice for public distribution.

The second intervention with an unintended impact on markets and on marketing policy is land and tenancy reform. Operation Barga can be seen as the product of a favourable conjuncture of several social forces—relatively weakened landlords, a metropolitan elite with relatively small stakes in land, and pressure from small peasants and landless labourers, intensified by refugees—as well as being the product of proletarian and peasant confrontations with landlords (Bandhyopadhyay, 2003). Tenurial security has also helped to consolidate the petty commodity character of agricultural production, small surpluses from which were being invested in marketing.

State Participation

The two most important and calculated participative interventions have a long history and work in the opposite direction to the re-distributive impact of credit and tenurial reform. The first are subsidies of 15 per cent on fixed capital for rice mill modernization. These loans were issued by the West Bengal Finance Corporation and were also available—as were other subsidized loans for small-scale industry—from a variety of nationalized banks. The Left Front Government maintained this policy for rice mill modernization. This process would not be able to ensure scale economies and cut production costs unless sufficient supplies could be controlled in order to run mills at high capacity. Mill modernization was not a labour-displacing response to labour unrest and costs, as has often been alleged, because although it was massively labour-displacing, it was the least-cost and least-organized labour that was displaced. It took place as part of the process of lowering the state's procurement costs for the public distribution system. The costs of modernization were thus reduced precisely for the class of commercial capitalists who had the easiest access to large private funds as well (see Appendix 4.1 for details of the process of modernization).

Second, since 1968–9, the West Bengal Commercial Taxes Department has levied a tax of two per cent of the value of paddy purchased by mills. We got no information about the revenue raised in this way which would help to check other official data on the turnover of rice mills. It is not an all-India practice to tax an essential commodity for mass consumption. It has long been abandoned in South India. In U.P., by contrast, a state with a high incidence of poverty, it was being levied at a rate of four per cent in the early 1980s. West Bengal thus practised a fiscal policy with a regressive impact on the disposable incomes of households, mainly urban, which were forced to buy rice in the 'open market'.

Then, above these two forms of direct state participation, there were the compulsory sales of rice to the PDS. As in most other states of India, milled rice was subject to a levy. The operating effectiveness of a levy on rice from mills varies inversely with the proportion of rice levied, and the difference between the state-administered procurement price for rice and open market prices. Except for north-west India, the state price is almost always below the open market price, so that procurement involves an element of coercion. In theory, Chief Ministers have the authority to revise upwards the all-India procurement prices, which are determined by what in the 1980s was called the Agricultural Costs and Prices Commission. In practice, the central government has the power to retaliate by charging a penalizing interest rate on state funds locked up in stock acquired at the higher prices.

Market prices may be distorted upwards by two forces. One is the compensating hoist made to the prices of rice, when traded freely, to make up for losses made on rice levied by the Food Corporation of India (FCI). The other is the result of the cordoning-off of deficit districts (at the discretion of District Magistrates, who often impose a seasonal cordon in the immediate post harvest period). Deficit districts are then supplied on permit, with the inevitable consequence that less rice is 'imported' than that for which there is effective demand. Prices rise in response, markets are spatially compartmentalized, and the price differences between surplus and deficit districts are exaggerated. For any one type of rice, at least three sets of prices may rule: the ration issue price, open market local prices, and black-market prices for imports. By contrast, in surplus states, the imposition of movement restrictions results in local surpluses above what would remain with free trade, so open market prices are lower and procurement is easier.

After November 1981, under a decree of the central government, the levy percentage was relatively high, at 60 per cent, while the procurement price, at Rs. 193 per quintal for rice, was Rs. 100 below the local wholesale price for rice in Birbhum. The Left Front Government was thus forced to operate a set of incentives which in theory turned private firms into state agents but in practice encouraged evasion. In modified ration areas, the issue price of state-administered rice (the price at which PDS rice is sold for consumption—Rs. 2.20

per kg.) might have exerted a downward pressure on free-market prices (then Rs. 3.00 per kg.). On the other hand, the markets for different qualities and varieties of grain were compartmentalized and at the finest and coarsest extremes have been found to function to a great extent independently of each other, so that markets for fine rice will be unaffected by deflationary forces (Palaskas and Harriss-White, 1993).

Mills were inspected daily by representatives of the Food Department, and 'free' trade in non-levy rice to all regions except statutory ration areas required a permit certifying compliance with the levy. This clearly gave the millers an incentive to comply. But 'the state' presented further obstacles to the smooth running of procurement, and thus to the residual 'free' trade. The local FCI store, able to accommodate only two days' supply of levy rice at the 60 per cent rate, was a source of congestion. And although payment by the parastatal corporation was prompter than open market payment (being made within two days after completion of each quality test), its rates of pay for loading and unloading were set at half the prevailing market rates, and the rate it paid for transport was alleged to be one-sixth of the market rate. When millers made losses on both transport and loading on their levy supplies, they effectively gave 'informal' perverse subsidies to the parastatal, which led them to bribe store officials to speed unloading, to 'lubricate' (to reduce the transaction costs of) the procurement system, and so to unshackle their own 'free' trade.

With the most stringent controls over private agro-commerce of any Indian state, this mix of regulative and participative intervention in West Bengal led to the following types of response by rice millers:

i) an attempt to maximize levy payments by using the cheapest types and the lowest permissible qualities of rice, while maximizing the quality, variety, and prices of non-levy rice;
ii) the overloading of lorries for the FCI, to reduce the costs of congestion at the stores;
iii) the use of pressure parboiling techniques for levy rice. These were time- and labour-sparing for the mills, but the rice (appropriate for puffing) becomes extremely hard, takes much longer to cook, and being highly polished, loses many of the nutrients that should be absorbed by the endosperm during parboiling;
iv) the hoarding of both paddy and rice until later in the marketing calendar when the levy was relaxed and the supplies of rice to

West Bengal from other states had dried up. Mills held oligopolistic control of the local marketed surplus and could exert an upward pressure on prices. Such interventions were seasonal and worked to the advantage of firms with access to finance for long-term storage;
v) levy evasion and illegal or 'unpermitted' sales of non-levy rice to the modified ration areas of the coal belt and plantations; and
vi) the illegal smuggling of paddy to cordoned-off deficit regions.

None of these types of response to the incentives and disciplines of regulative and participative intervention is at all unique to West Bengal, nor were they confined to the early 1980s.

Paddy Wholesaling
From 1967 until 1996, private paddy wholesaling was illegal except on the authority of a rice mill. In fact, already in 1981–2, the law was quite widely evaded. Three types of private paddy wholesaling could take place. First, paddy agents could and did buy paddy on their own account and sell it to a mill to which they were unattached but which offered higher prices and/or commissions. They could also do this, at greater risk, with mills outside Birbhum district (bearing the transport and bribery costs themselves). Second, itinerant agents of mills outside the district could and did buy paddy from purchase agents within the district. Third, in 1982, the Left Front Government declared panchayats to be purchasing agents for the Food Corporation of India, each with access to Rs. 1 lakh for this purpose. But in Birbhum district, this policy was a complete failure not only because of the purchases of private agents but also because panchayats had funds but no collective knowledge or motivation.

State regulation
Rice Mills
Three regulative interventions have been implemented in ways which generate pre-emptive responses, the first of which was the Congress government's 1967 grant to rice mills of a legal monopoly over the wholesale paddy trade. A purchaser of paddy could only operate legally as an agent under authority from a rice mill, to which he was attached, using the rice mill's funds. These agents could also purchase paddy lawfully from both outside the district and the state with a permit

obtained from the District Magistrate. But the exporting states had jurisdiction over exit permits, so trade was not 'free'. Price differences for paddy between districts within West Bengal were sufficient, however, to generate a significant flow of illegal wholesale trade by purchasing agents either with mills within the district to which they were not attached, with mills outside the district or with itinerant agents of mills outside the district. Check-post guards were easily corrupted by bribes and vigilance was slack.

For a second example, rice mills must by law store paddy within their perimeters. It is very hard, however, for the state to prevent the decentralized storage of paddy in the go-downs of mill agents, should sufficient finance exist and should anticipated price rises make such speculation attractive. So, off-season storage could be highly decentralized, and a miller could consolidate an indirect control over much larger stocks than were apparent from his accounts.

Third, rice mills are all registered under the Factories Act, which stipulates working conditions and rights for employees. On the whole, office staff and mechanics are protected by the vigilance forces which monitor this Act, but for the casual, *coolie* labour force, it is observed in the breach. Commonly, and despite the unionization of labour, rice millers also do not comply with their obligation to pay the minimum wage, and workers are also laid off and taken on summarily as supplies dictate, rather than with due notice as the law requires. In practice, rice mill labour is regulated in such a way as to differentiate the security and rights of different members of the work-force.

Husking Mills

In West Bengal, holders of husking licences had never been allowed to trade in paddy or rice and therefore to develop into commercial firms. This was easily circumvented by taking trading licences in different family members' names. Licences for husking mills cost Rs. 500 and were heavily restricted in order to discourage the use of such technology, and as a result, were said to have a commercial value of Rs. 35,000. Unlicensed husking mills varied in their illegality depending on whether or not the owner had 'pending' a letter of application for a licence written by a Calcutta High Court Lawyer. (These were costly, and often forged). There was a thriving black market in husking mill licences.

The state also set capacity controls limiting mill operation to the equivalent of about four hours' operation per day[1] to discourage any but the smallest scale of custom milling. This was widely ignored. The State Electricity Board, on the other hand, could rarely maintain more than a fickle supply, which in effect created another capacity constraint. Thus, most husking mills operated as and when current permitted. The unpredictability of the power supply could raise the transport-cost component of processing for petty traders and consumers alike. Shortages of electricity in workshops which manufacture spare parts also caused shortages and raised the price of mill components. The installation of electricity supply to a husking mill was subject to long delays: two years from the time of application was common.[2]

Government rules also forbade the operation of hullers at night, but this too was ignored. In so far, as all these regulations were intended to function as capacity constraints, to curb unsupervizable competition with rice mills, they were ineffective. Vigilance by sub-inspectors of the Food Department was rare, occasional, well-spaced (for example, once weekly), and often very predictable, enabling the 'laundering' of account books (which could seldom be seen being filled while milling took place). Unlicensed husking was profitable, even with the additional cost of bribes (at the least Rs. 80–100 a year from each husker to Food Department officials). Investment and fixed costs were low. Minimum wages legislation (at the time of our survey the minimum wage was Rs. 8.1/day for men; Rs. 7.6 for women) was also frequently flouted in husking mills.

Attempts were made by the state not simply to control the proliferation of husking mills, but also to force the modernization of their technology. The 1979 rules laid down a two-year grace period, after which all huskers should have installed rubber-roll shellers and cone polishers, or else face withdrawal of their licences. But licences had not been withdrawn and no attempt had been made to modernize the husking mills. At least one case is known where the local Food Department *refused* to allow the installation of a modern rice/husk separator in a husking mill.

Thus, various capacity constraints—formal and real—thwarted both the accumulation of capital sufficient for the modernization of machinery (at least Rs. 60–70,000 was needed then) and the economies of scale in operation that would make modern machinery profitable. Rubber-roll shellers cannot easily mill mixed paddy varieties, or small consignments of 2 to 10 kgs, which are the typical demands for custom milling. Continuous operation is necessary, if only to prevent the clogging of bran in shellers. The use of diesel engines to maximize hours of operation would have required changes in the legal capacity controls and would have raised the costs of husking by 50 per cent because of the cost of fuel.

The apparent incentives for modernization in post-harvest processing were completely ineffectual. Indeed, the two objectives seem *prima facie* contradictory—to prevent the spread of labour-displacing husking mills but to make the mills that existed more productive and to increase their capacity.

Rice Wholesaling and Brokerage

Rice brokers were forbidden by law to sell rice wholesale. In practice, the finance of wholesaling by brokers—by standing as guarantors for the purchasers—represents an elision of functions. It is perfectly possible for a broker to trade wholesale on a short-term basis, using money accruing from delaying payments, and using storage facilities at either the point of origin or at the destination.

No wholesaler can survive without a diversified portfolio, in and out of which funds for wholesaling can easily be shifted. Rice wholesalers encounter a number of restrictions, which are intermittent but recurrent. In November 1981, for instance, the sudden imposition of a 60 per cent levy on rice purchased directly from farmers by rice wholesalers (as well as that on rice mills' rice) spawned a trade in false bills of sale from farmers to small traders (without wholesale licences) by means of which wholesalers concealed their eligibility for the levy. District-level movement restrictions meant that while local wholesalers could not sell rice legally outside Birbhum district, rice wholesalers in the adjacent district of Bardhaman were allowed to trade throughout West Bengal. Trading families with kin scattered geographically throughout the region could manipulate these idiosyncratic constraints to trade. Furthermore, rice wholesaling (with or without a permit) to areas south of Calcutta required lorries to pass through Calcutta and this route was a source of profitable 'leakage' to the metropolitan market in rice.

By contrast, petty traders in rice and producers who husked their own paddy, could by law trade directly with retailers. Retailers could legally stock up to 1 tonne at a time. In theory, such an intermediary could legally buy and sell 330 tonnes in a trading year (a tonne per business day), implying a turnover of Rs. 8.25 lakhs. Rice wholesalers could obtain licences to retail, and retailers could separately license several family members. Licensing policy was in the hands of the District

Magistrate and in Birbhum it was liberal. While a wholesale licence was said to cost Rs. 3,000 (Rs. 1,000 as deposit and Rs. 2,000 as bribes), a retail licence could be yours for as little as Rs. 50. So, it is hardly astonishing that the number of rice retailers in Bolpur doubled from 100 in 1978 to 200 in 1982, in a clear response to such legal loopholes. But at the same time retailers were clandestinely storing and selling to wholesalers for smuggling to the modified ration areas of the coal belt, as well as selling to the small army of illegal petty traders who took rice by public transport to Kolkata.[3]

Storage

Lastly, the state had intervened by providing large-scale storage facilities, originally intended to be used by farmers as a way of getting institutional finance for their stock (Harriss, 1984). The Central Warehouse Corporation has a store in Bolpur. It was neither used by farmers, nor was it used by rice merchants because the charge, Rs. 0.20 per bag per month, excluded compulsory extra costs for insurance, stock inspection, and quality checks, which were not imposed elsewhere. As elsewhere in India, the government store was being used by other parastatal institutions. Here again, the intervention did not fulfil its stated objectives and was irrelevant to the rice-market system, surviving on the patronage of the state itself.

State Interventions: A Summing Up

Under the Left Front Government, the implementation of interventions in the marketing of rice took an idiosyncratic form in each district, even though the principles on which state intervention takes place, and pronouncements on food policy were common to the entire state of West Bengal, and in some cases common throughout India. State intervention constitutes a set of profound disturbances to the system of rice markets. The most effective interventions—subsidized credit for larger scale rice mill machines—had not strengthened the system of legal regulation, but led to the creation of price conditions which accelerated the development of a system of petty trading.

The rice mills' state-conferred monopoly on the paddy trade enabled them to continue to control a significant share of the marketed surplus destined for long-distance consumption. This strategically significant sub-circuit—the rice mills—needed to be numerically small in order for the state to minimize its costs of access to rice. It was because of the impacts of levies and movement restrictions on seasonal and spatial price movements that long-term storage by rice mills was encouraged, helped by a modernized technology, which was beginning to be used during the monsoon (and which was also protected by state subsidies and patronage). The state's role in maintaining wide price margins on the residual open markets encouraged a proliferation of rice retailing firms.

Husking mills, on the other hand, proliferated despite the state. It was both because of and despite the state that they failed to modernize their technology. It was despite the state—that is, in disregard of its rules—that the wage rates for much of the casual labour throughout the agro-processing system were determined. It was despite the state that paddy wholesaling expanded. State interventions failed to generate structures of countervailing power sufficient to destroy the existing structures of power. On the contrary, the two existed in tandem, neat expressions of the two sets of political programmes—one aimed at the lobbies and one at the masses—alluded to by Sengupta. The next section suggests how this is possible.

The Political Activity of Mercantile Firms

'We are at right angles to political parties'.
'We are loyal to the party in power'.
'We only unite if there are problems. Otherwise we are selfish.'

These contradictory statements made by merchants in Birbhum illustrate the 'deep structures' of agro-commercial politics. Commercial transactions are competitive and antagonistic. Merchants organize themselves and act in concert for specific purposes, the textbook example of which is collusive oligopoly. In fact, there are many other ways in which merchants act collectively. Table 5.1 shows some of the main ways in which merchants operate in civil society and organize the collective preconditions for competition in markets.

Mercantile firms either tended to avoid any outside social organization at all, or they were highly active. In the latter case, multiple memberships of institutions within one family firm were common. Merchants in Bolpur and Sainthia blocks were much more active socially and politically than were their counterparts elsewhere in India where mercantile politics have been investigated (Harriss-White, 1993). Rice millers, paddy agents, and rice wholesalers all tended to belong to cultural societies. These were town and village clubs, the Hindi Prachar Samiti, the Ramakrishna Mission, etc. Rice millers were also very prominent members of the charitable societies run by business elites

Table 5.1 The Organizations of Merchants

	Numbers of Firms belonging to civil society organizations				
Types of civil society	Rice mills	Husking mills	Paddy agents	Rice wholesalers	Rice brokers
Organization					
Cultural societies	6	4	12	6	2
Charitable societies	10	2	nil	2	2
Co-operative societies	6	11	5	1	2
Panchayat office	nil	5	nil	nil	nil
Commodity associations *other than* that specific to the type of firm	6	3	2	4	nil
Commodity association	10	17	13	4	nil
Total number of firms	10	17	13	4	4

Source: Data from 1982 survey.

(Rotary, Red Cross, Lions, Jaycees, etc.). The significance of these kinds of organizations is twofold. First, they can cement ties between merchants and the middle-level bureaucracy, which are important in the actual implementation of the many policies touching the marketing of rice. Second, they give public displays of redistribution, manifestations of a philanthropy which excuses local extremes of wealth.

Husking millers and rice millers were particularly prominent in local co-operatives for agricultural credit, marketing, consumption, and cold storage. They were members and directors in their capacities as producers, but this also gave them access to information which commercial interests could use to subvert co-operatives. The same was true of the notably close association between husking millers and local panchayats.

Rice millers and rice wholesalers were also active members of other commodity associations in which they had economic interests (for example, associations of lorry owners, oil mill owners, coal dealers, bus owners, etc.), over and above the dedicated associations for their particular types of firms. Rice millers were prominent among the office-bearers of these other associations, which are significant for the power over markets that they may confer.

Finally, all the traders interviewed, with the exception of rice brokers, were members of a commodity association. It is through these associations, not political parties, that merchants exercised political power. The means at their disposal were the lobby and the court case. The most important of them may be briefly described.

The Birbhum District Rice Wholesalers' Association had 28 members. It was formed at the election of the Left Front Government in 1977 and immediately affiliated to the All Bengal Association. The issue which provoked it into existence was the need to confront the state to remove restrictions on movement and to stop the levy on wholesalers. This campaign failed. The local District Magistrate was then lobbied to prevent retail rice traders from buying rice directly from producers and to restrict and reduce the issue of retail licences—also without conspicuous success. However, the association obtained favourable judgements in the High court and the Supreme Court and got a court order to stop the Left Front Government levying rice from huskers (which would have reduced wholesale profits).

The Birbhum District Paddy Agents' Association also came into being under the Left Front Government in 1978–9, and had 125 members (not all paddy agents being members). It was provoked into existence and action by a concerted interest in forcing rice mills to increase their commissions and to give agents discount rates on bulk supplies. In this fight between fractions of commercial capital, the paddy agents had a fair degree of success.

The Birbhum District Husking Mill Owners' Association was set up much earlier, in 1964, and by 1982 had 310 members. The issue provoking its formation was a need to regulate its own market—to call a halt to the huge variations in charges for custom milling that existed within settlements—this failed. Charges in Bolpur and Sainthia blocks varied by up to 100 per cent and within any one village could vary by up to 50 per cent. The association also attempted to regulate local rates and to change them collectively, but in practice these attempts met with resistance.

In 1969, the districts of West Bengal united to form a provincial husking millers' lobby in order to increase their collective lobbying power. They were successful in getting the Calcutta High Court to quash a West Bengal government order which prevented husking millers from accepting money and stipulated that husking services should be paid for only in paddy and at the procurement price. Since the procurement price was below the market rate, paddy owners themselves refused, which added to the power of the case financed by the association. In 1978, the association went to the media and to the High Court, and it lobbied the Electricity Board against the blind eye turned by the government on unlicensed huskers. The sole constraints on unlicensed huskers were electricity supplies and the costs of bribes to inspectors of the Food Department. The Supreme Court stood in favour of the licensed husking millers. The order that all mills must be licensed trickled back to District Magistrates via the courts and the Food Department, which impounded equipment and arrested a number of unlicensed husking millers. This deterrent was short-lived, however. Bribery still ensured the proliferation of unlicensed huskers and increasing competition between the mills, so the court case, which cost each association member Rs. 60, was ultimately unsuccessful.

The association then lobbied against the modernization order which had been passed in 1979 (see pp. 340–6), with a two-year period of grace which expired without consequence. The lobby against modernization succeeded for the same reasons that the lobby against unlicensed mills failed: the reluctance or inability of the state to enforce laws making economic nonsense.

A competing unlicensed Husking Mill Owners' Association was also set up (for the whole of West Bengal) under the Left Front Government in 1978 and by 1982 had some 10,000 members. This association lobbied to stop the harassment of its members by Food Department officials and the Police, and to obtain licences. Husking was profitable, yet the rules passed in 1958 prevented the issuing of licences to more than one machine per revenue village. At the outset, this rule had been inspired by the perceived political desirability of conserving dheki processing. In 1970–1, the West Bengal government had encouraged unemployed people to apply for husking licences, one per village, provided each applicant was prepared to pay a levy quota of 50 quintals a year. Thousands of applications were made using verified lawyers' letters, resulting in lucrative trade. But by 1982, no licences had been issued, because other lobbies had proved more powerful. Unlicensed mills continued, however, to be given electricity supplies. Because it was not illegal to install a mill, cases could only be brought against the owners if mills were found to be running. The costs of such cases were paid for by the association, and the routine subscription of Rs. 6 per month also ensured that members were protected from extremes of police harassment following collective payments from the association.

The Birbhum District Rice Millers' Association was formed in 1940 and in 1982 had 48 members. It is affiliated to the All Bengal Rice Millers' Association and also has connections with the Bharat Chamber of Commerce. For many years, politicians were studiously avoided and lobbying energy was concentrated on government administrators, who were thought to hold more power. By 1982, however, the Association had close and supportive contacts with the media, and frequently lobbied the West Bengal Chief Minister, the Food Minister as well as Ministers of the Government of India in New Delhi. One of its early successes was to reduce the lag in the payment by wholesalers for rice, a delay which had far-reaching consequences for mill finances. In 1982, lobbying was being mobilized around the impact of a high levy in a deficit state, over the economic consequences of pan-territorial procurement prices in deficit and surplus states, and in favour of intensifying the penalties on outlawed, unlicensed huskers (rather than on the illegal paddy trade, which benefits the mills). This lobbying was not conspicuously successful, although in most years the percentage of levy is reduced in the off-season month of May, enabling profits to be made by all those able to afford cross-seasonal storage. The Association also voiced complaints about the capacity constraint on the milling of non-levy rice placed on rice mills by the rampant congestion and slow lifting of levied rice brought to FCI godowns. Without certified FCI sales, the legal trade in non-levy rice, which compensated rice mills for levy losses, could not take place at all.

The millers' other activities included: attempts to regulate the paddy price (not successful); negotiations with the Railways to improve the organization of wagons; and negotiations with the local lorry owners' association (which was, conveniently, presided over by a rice miller) to forbid the use of lorries for purposes other than the lifting of paddy and rice during the main milling season, so as to keep transport charges down and collectively to fix transport rates.

The Rice Mill Owners' Association did not negotiate wage rates with the labour unions, as happened elsewhere in India. Rice mill labour, both office staff and coolies, was organised into unions, but they negotiated rates with individual owners. The CPI-M had organized both staff and coolies, and the CPI-ML and the RSP had also organized coolies. Their political inability to deal collectively with rice mill owners at once weakened their regional strength and forced them to take local action. Strikes had been restricted to one town, Ahmadpur, and to one mill in which a dispute arose. There were two strikes in 1981, one lasting 5 months over the sacking of an 'incompetent' *mistry* (according to the millers); he was not reinstated. The other lasted 8 months and concerned the retrenchment of 102 labourers on the partition of a joint mill-owning family. Again the mill-owners won. The three labour unions for rice mill coolies had applied for registration but it had not been granted. The multiplication of unions, and the informal nature of their authority, did not bode well for the interests of labour.

Collective action: Summing up
Merchants do act collectively—against state intervention, against other fractions of commercial capital, and for self-regulation—that is, a form of social, non-state, regulation of their own markets as well as of derived ones. The pattern of success and failure through lobbies and through court cases has three instructive lessons. The first is that decisions on policy implementation were increasingly being taken by politicians and legislators rather than by the executive. The second is that as early as 1981–2, the judiciary was increasingly important in determining the implementability of policy. The third is that the structure and relations of the marketing system were more powerful forces than those of the state. In regulating the rice markets, the state is market-driven, not the other way round.

Conclusions: The Rice Markets in 1980–2

To conclude, we draw together the findings of Chapter four, which examined the structures and processes of the market system and this chapter which has looked at the dynamics of state intervention and mercantile politics. The system of rice markets can be divided into at least four sub-systems, each affecting the others. One sub-system consists of land relations and agricultural production. Paddy and rice circulate locally in return for cash, as rent, in return for labour services, and as a medium for loans. These loans are to be repaid at a future date in cash, in kind or by labour services. Rice is also a medium for barter exchange.[4] A second sub-system is that of the petty trade surrounding husking machines for local retail sales, or for illegal wholesaling, and long-distance trade. A third subsystem is the sale of paddy for export out of the region. Fourth is the 'official' system of bulking by purchase agents for rice mills who sell a portion to the state in exchange for the right to trade the rest.

Not only is this system far from homogeneous, but some of the elements and relationships in each of the sub-systems are antagonistic to those in others. Furthermore, although the hubs of the sub-systems appear to be agro-processing firms, it is merchants' capital (money used for buying and selling) rather than the productive capital with which it is intertwined that is the prime mover of the system, and the form of capital which gets the highest rates of return.

The largest single fraction of this commercial capital is invested in the network of rice mills. Compared with the structure of agro-commercial capital in South India, these mills are very few in number. They were first built by partnerships of rich peasants or small landlords who had accumulated investible surpluses, or by utilizing the rents of the *Zamindari* families in the 1920s and 1930s. Landlords monopolized the marketed surplus through *dadan* loans at rates disadvantageous to the producers of paddy. For two reasons mercantile firms found it expedient to diversify. Firstly, paddy trading and processing were highly seasonal. Secondly, the intermittent interventions of the state exacerbated the economic risks in the rice markets. These interventions regulated the system, yet were also shocks to it. The possibility of modernization arose in the mid- to late 1960s after the introduction in India, with foreign aid, of modern rice mills. But by 1982, West Bengal was the only region of India in which rice was an important subsistence crop (discounting Punjab, Haryana and Western U.P., where it is a cash crop) and where mills had been modernized on a large scale. While some big mills may have owed their origins to an earlier polarized agrarian structure, such that substantial surplus could be concentrated in few hands, their technological modernization was entirely due to protection by the state. This protection was the most important dynamic element in the system in 1982.

It developed in the wake of a feat of private entrepreneurship: the installation of bran processing technology which conferred a new and high value on the main *by-product* of milling, and altered the cost-benefit ratios of the subsequent modernization of rice mills[5]. The state then subsidized this modernization and protected the rice mills through conserving their legal monopoly over paddy wholesaling. The state had to protect the rice mills because the procurement pricing policy designed to cover the entire nation was being applied in a deficit state with small and patchy consignments of marketed surplus, fetching wholesale prices well above the centrally-fixed procurement price. For a state like West Bengal, to ensure that a substantial surplus was centralized and concentrated at a minimum number of nodes, was an effective way to minimize the transaction costs of procurement.

The modernization of rice mills was accompanied by a widespread change of ownership. Land and credit reforms had reduced the direct power over production of the original rentier-mercantile families. With the proliferation of shares in these firms under the second generation of operators, decision-making inside the commercial dynasties was sometimes slowed down. Languishing mills were then purchased by *Marwaris*, who were even more delinked from agricultural production and who had large, diversified agro-industrial portfolios. It was the Marwari millers who led the process of modernization.

Many unmodernized mills fell terminally ill. But the much-quoted statistic that West Bengal's 700 rice mills had declined to 300 in the early 1980s does not mean that the rice milling industry fell into a moribund state. No evidence could be found for a secular decline in output in those mills that were still working; rather the reverse. Modernization increased the technical capacity of mills in Bolpur and Sainthia blocks from 1.2 to 2.3 tonnes per hour. It also led to an extension of the milling season from 4-6 months to 8-12 months. A process of selection was at work. Ownership became concentrated, with 10 firms controlling 21 mills. Instead of stagnating, the industry concentrated.

If there is a threat to the operation of modernized rice mills, it can only come from the illegal wholesaling of paddy (which, in a deficit state, jeopardizes their supply), and from the rise of petty trade centred on husking machines. Historically, petty trade has always been by far the smaller fraction of commercial capital. In the early 1980s, it was growing in a mass of tiny firms. The network of husking mills differed from that of rice mills not only because of the small capacity of each mill and the lack of on-site parboiling facilities, but also because the ownership of the commodity was separated from the ownership of the processing technology. This sub-system is not a new development. It has evolved in three phases: (i) in the early 1950s when the rich peasantry started to generate regular investible surpluses; (ii) in the late 1950s and early 1960s when big rice mills suffered a crisis of viability, and (iii) in the late 1970s when new mills, unlicensed and rural, appeared in response to West Bengal's distinctively wide price margins. The main threat from husking mills was not in fact to the rice mills but to the dheki. As we have already noted in Chapter 3, as late as 1960, there were estimated to be one million part-time jobs of dheki processing in West Bengal. By the early 1980s, they had been almost entirely eliminated.

The newest market sub-system consisted of a multitude of firms, petty in size, which dealt in paddy and in rice husked by the small mills. These traders were landless or came from the small peasantry.

This sub-system had grown in the response to four sets of factors, which illuminate the process of institutional evolution:

(i) The large difference between paddy and rice prices, created by the oligopolistic control of rice markets by rice mills: the millers have an interest in ensuring conditions in which rice milling is profitable, despite high compulsory levies at procurement prices lower than market prices. The price gap between paddy and rice also reflects the capacity of some merchants to hoard.

(ii) Inter-regional differences in the prices of paddy and rice: within a deficit state, the price differentials between surplus and deficit districts have been exacerbated by paddy movement restrictions and statutory rationing.

As a result of these two factors, the general level of rice prices was higher, and of paddy prices lower, than what they would have been in absence of intervention and with a less oligopolistic marketing system. The gap widened in such a way as to allow large numbers of petty firms to earn livelihoods—or at least a seasonal supplement to livelihoods—as tenants, small producers, and/or wage labour.

(iii) Reliance on unpaid domestic labour in the petty-commodity stages of rice circulation: cleaning, parboiling and soaking, drying, carting, winnowing and separating, weighing and bagging. The petty sub-system generated 2.5 times as many days of livelihood per unit of output as the rice mills. Because these livelihoods deploy family labour, the petty sub-system competes very effectively with the highly capital-intensive stages of modernized agro-processing.

(iv) Consumer preference: the nutritional argument for the modernization of parboiling is nullified by the fact that local consumers want a high polish. The rice processed through the huller with the unmodernized parboiling technology was still preferred, in much of West Bengal, to the extremely hard rice from the rice-mill. The former had a price advantage over factory rice of Rs. 2 to Rs. 5 per quintal.

It is hard to avoid concluding that the domination of agricultural production by petty commodity relations and the persistent relative technological backwardness and indifferent growth of the late 1970s may have resulted from the relative weakness of small agricultural capitalists and small landlords confronting the economic power of the rice mills. Equally, at least some rich peasants, small capitalists, and small landlords had decisive power by virtue of their investment in marketing rather than production. It was the intertwining of production and trade by the commercial capitalist class which created the existence of space for petty production (thanks to their loans) and petty trade (because of the price margins which resulted from their control).

State policy was characterized by significant slippage between stated objectives and actual practice. Intended to concentrate supply, the state's actions led to a centralization and concentration of firms which in turn provided incentives for petty livelihoods. Some of the petty firms were independent and permanent, while others were seasonal or part of a small-scale diversified portfolio. Most were heavily dependent on credit, contracts and information from larger traders. Ultimately, however, these complex circuits of circulation were supported by the 'nutrient base' of rice production. In the absence of an increase in the marketed surplus, such relations of exchange competed with large-scale firms in the marketing system and with all forms of production using wage-labour in agro-industry. Few of the resources extracted from rice producers through the maze-like market system were reinvested in production. By the early 1980s, the marketing system could not evolve further without a growth in production.

Notes

1. 30 quintals of paddy per day for a no. 4 huller; 45 q. for a no. 8 huller, and 60 q. for a no. 2 huller.
2. The Electricity Board's operations were, moreover, not co-ordinated with other departments of the Government and would provide an electricity connection to an unlicenced mill without requiring evidence of legal status.
3. These were finally studied in 2000 (Choudhury et al., 2000). see Chapter 7 for a summary.
4. The manner in which this subsystem ensures the reproduction of different agrarian classes was the subject of a monograph by J. Harriss (1982).
5. The process is described in Appendix 4.1. The rubber-roll sheller technology in the rice mill separates bran from husk and produces a higher quality of bran. In 1988, this fetched a 30 per cent higher price as a raw material for solvent oil extraction than the combined by-product from the husking mill which was used for cattle feed.

6 Institutional Diversity, Price Performance, and Power Relations in the Commodity Markets of Bardhaman District

This chapter and the next report the results of our second study, in the district of Bardhaman, after the 7–8 years of much faster agricultural growth and diversification described in Chapter 1. As we already noted in that chapter, the 1990 study in Bardhaman was not a precise replication of the 1980–1 study of Birbhum. The idea was rather to build on what had been learned in Birbhum and see how far changed circumstances resulting from the shift from stagnation to growth had altered the picture of the way agricultural production affects markets in West Bengal.

Bardhaman also offered the opportunity to study the markets for two other important staple foods that had expanded in the diversification of the 1980s, potatoes and mustard (see Table 3.1), and to see how far the market system in this district was structurally different from the one we had found in Birbhum. In particular, what we had learned about the rice markets in Birbhum encouraged us to try testing the relationship between market places more closely by means of an intensive effort to study the efficiency of price behaviour which is reported on pp. 164–9 of this chapter and in Appendix 6.1.

Bardhaman was and is different from Birbhum in many ways; yet what will strike the reader is how, inspite of all the specific differences between the two places and times, the overall picture presented by agricultural markets in Bardhaman in 1990 is similar to the one presented by Birbhum ten years earlier: a fundamental diversity and complexity; the continued importance of non-market institutions (ethnicity, caste, and gender) in determining market behaviour; growing polarization of commercial assets, with increasing concentration at the top and continued expansion at the pauperized petty-trader end of the spectrum; and a resulting, or at least associated, market inefficiency, at least as conventionally measured.

First we look at the structural elements of the markets for these three products, their physical operations, and the crucially linked, though no less diverse transport markets on which they all depend; then we examine the organization of firms, their activities and their labour processes, the relations between them, and the commodity flows, to see how the system of markets responded to this phase of unprecedented vitality in production, and how the production and circulation of commodities are related. The institutional diversity of these three staple food markets is explored as a plausible explanation of their price performance, since the behaviour of prices is a major indicator of efficiency; we are then able to analyze the economic power by means of which resources are controlled and shifted between sectors. Table 6.1 shows the size of our sample relative to the estimated numbers of rice mills, oil mils, cold stores, and other trading agents/firms.

Elements of the System of Markets for Potatoes, Rice, and Mustard

Classifications need to suit their objectives. The purpose of the field research in 1990 was to examine the impact of growth in production on the components and relations of these market systems. So, position within the system was the most relevant classification. Figure 6.1 illustrates this. It also indicates the sizes of the samples studied and the likely sizes of the local population from which they were derived. It shows the type of activity carried out at the points in space and time at which the spot price data used here had been reported to the Department of Statistics. These points considerably oversimplify these systems. The rice system in particular bifurcates close to the start (into petty and large scale circuits), to merge again only at the finish. Real spatial configurations show a deep structural diversity, which is a fundamental trait in the Indian economy generally, one which economists have been reluctant to acknowledge or attempt to explain. For example, trade ranges from the local exchange to trade which originates in Bihar, Andhra Pradesh, and Rajasthan, and goes to destinations in Bihar and Punjab. Enterprise sizes and numbers vary greatly at different points and places in the post-harvest system, as do the degree of specialization and the degree of vertical integration of firms. Routes through these commodity systems will depend on social and economic institutions which are described later. No single intermediary is likely to view the system as a whole in quite the manner represented here. Even at the points where prices have been recorded, many different types of exchange are carried on.

Table 6.1: Database—Bardhaman district. 1990

	Memari[1]		Katwa		Gulsi	
	Population	Sample	Population	Sample	Population	Sample
Rice Mills	3	1	4	3	4	3
Husking Mills	6	3	8	6	12	1
Paddy Agents[2]	-	-	-	-	20	3
Rice Wholesale/CA/	50	1	no info several '00	9	42	3
Kutali	several '000	2				
Potato Cold Store	9	4	5	5	-	-
Potato Wholesale/CA	20	5	22	4	-	-
Oil Mill	6	4	17	6	2	2
Bran Oil Factory	1	1	-	-	-	-

Total for 3 Market Towns

	mapped population	sample	fraction(%)
Rice Mills	11	7	64
Husking Mills	26	10	38
Paddy Agents	20	3	15
Rice Wh/CA/ret	several '00	13	-
Kutali	several '000	2	-
Potato Cold Store	14	9	64
Potato Wh/CA	42	9	21
Oil Mill	25	12	48
Bran FactoryTotal interviewed	1	166	100

Notes: 1. Populations were mapped by the author and Pundarik Mukherjee in 1990.
2. Mostly rural.

Diversity in Operation

Potatoes

Until the later 1980s, potatoes were either stored 'in the field'—that is, left underground—or they were lifted and kept for four to five months buried in either sand or straw. The increase in the scale of production and in the volumes of marketed surplus that we noted in Chapter 3 led to the introduction of other technologies. In the first harvest ('the poor man's harvest') from January to February, potatoes were lifted and sold directly onto the market until May.[1] The output of

Institutional Diversity, Price Performance, and Power Relations 149

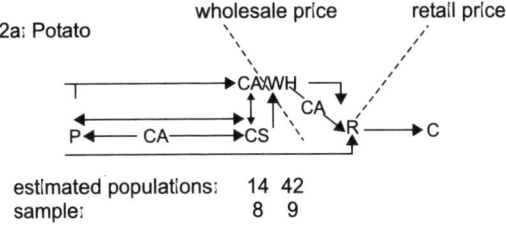

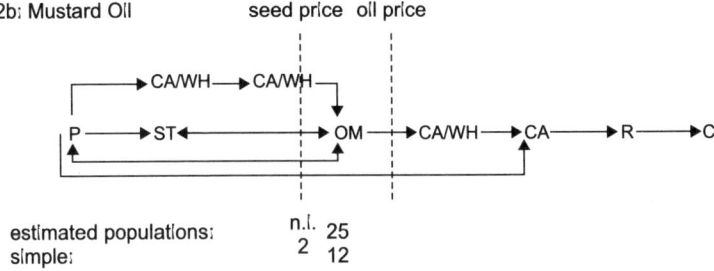

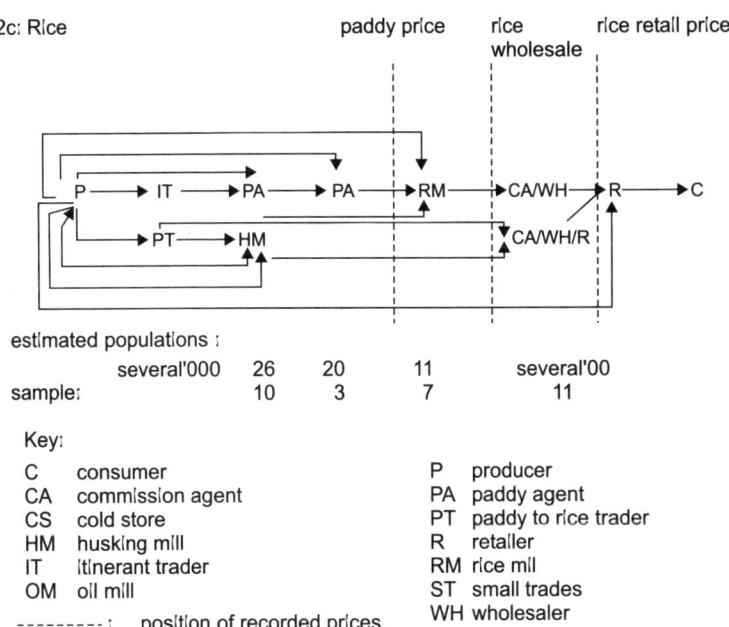

Fig. 6.1: Commodity Systems Studied in Bardhaman District

the second potato season ('the rich man's harvest') was lifted in March, cold-stored until May, and marketed from then until the end of January.[2] It is in this latter set of production and exchange relations that relatively large-scale commercial capital started to confront relatively small-scale production capitals. A variety of air-cooling technologies (involving ammonium compression) and a range of sizes of cold store co-existed, but in all cases break-even capacity utilization was high—between 70 and 80 per cent, extremely high by Indian industrial standards. Although comparatively large agro-commercial capital faced small-scale production, there was intense competition between cold store firms for supplies. The producers of this perishable product adopted a variety of strategies to minimize their risk. These included overbooking cold store space and maximizing the number of cold store sites in which space was booked in advance. This led to opportunistic trading in excess space by both producers and cold store owners when the state-determined closing date for these stores approached. To avert the risks involved in the marketing of space, producers commonly sold their potatoes (sometimes on advance contracts) to agents or wholesalers. The latter operated on cold store owners' finance, bore the transactions costs, and had superior access to market information.

At the cold store, the stages of the preservation process were sequenced and gendered as follows:[3]

- unloading from lorries (male),
- grading (female),
- weighing (m),
- bagging and labelling (f/m),
- controlled refrigeration at 36 degrees Fahrenheit, during which period potatoes could not be lifted from the stores, but the ownership of potatoes was often transferred,
- unloading (m),
- controlled re-climatization under fans for eight hours (f),
- grading (f), and
- bagging, weighing, and loading (m).

There was no by-product, but 'cut-pieces' from bad potatoes were used for wage payments, given to indigent people, or sold at 50–70 per cent of the price of whole potatoes.

In 1990, the average casual labour force working in a cold store numbered 162, a third of whom were female. The casual male and female labour force varied in size, not only seasonally but from day to day—a typical range within a firm was from a minimum of 10 to a maximum of 170. A relatively large managerial and technical maintenance staff (some of them skilled engineers) is needed for cold storage. As a result, labour contracts within one firm varied from arrangements which were fully protected under the Factories Acts, at the secure extreme, to illegally underpaid or bonded labour at the other.

Mustard Oil

Local demand for mustard oil far exceeded local supply, which has long been highly prized both by consumers for its quality, and by millers because the out-turn yielded by local seed is 38 per cent rather than the 35 per cent obtained from imported mustard. Even so, the local market was dominated quantitatively by imports from north and north-west India. It was also dominated socially by *Marwari* traders whose economic network radiates outward from Rajasthan, where mustard is produced.

Demand for mustard oil has been seasonal. Its peak occurred during the festival months that run from *Durga Puja* in October onwards through to the harvest celebrations in February.

The processing of mustard oil involved combinations of several transformation technologies:

- unloading (male);
- drying down to 12 per cent moisture content for storage (female);
- decortication (m); and
- milling using one of two technologies: a rotary (a metal pestle and mortar) or an expeller, the oil from which has further to be filtered through cloth (m/f).

The by-product, oil cake with 6 per cent oil content, is used by local farmers as cattle feed and organic manure.

Compared with rice and potato processing, the casual labour force was comparatively small—on an average eight labourers per firm—and was supplemented by permanent managerial and technical maintenance staff.

Rice

The sustained rise in local rice production in the 1980s had forced its complex post-harvest system to evolve. Several processing technologies continued to co-exist:

- Traditional hand-operated pounding of paddy using the *dheki* (though by 1990 this was only retained for rare ceremonial occasions) (female).
- Small-scale rice processing by (male) 'kutials' using a pre-milling parboiling technology comprising mud pots and a mud stove fired by paddy husk, bamboo stores, small drying yards, and cement soaking tanks. Paddy was soaked for 24 hours and boiled for 2½ hours. When dry, the parboiled paddy was taken to a husking mill, which passes paddy down a revolving screw within a perforated casing through which rice grains are centrifugally forced, shedding their outer husk and inner bran layers in the process.
- Larger scale rice mill technology, which involves:
  - soaking paddy in tanks for 24 hours (male),
  - steaming for three minutes (m) and repeating this sequence,
  - carting to the drying yard (m),
  - drying (female) for between eight hours and four days, depending on the weather,
  - bagging paddy at 12 per cent moisture for storage (m),
  - paddy separation, double milling (m/f), and bran separation (f),
  - polishing (m), and
  - bagging (m).

The process took a minimum of 40 hours and could take up to 10 days in rainy weather.

Parboiling can be understood not only as a process which increases the whole rice out-turn and improves the oil and vitamin content of rice (See Appendix 4.1 and Harriss, 1976 for details), but also as a response to the need to store paddy during rainy or cloudy conditions (characteristic of the post-*boro* season). The by-products are husk and bran. In 1990, husk was being used for fuel. Mixed husk and bran were used as feed for pigs, poultry, cattle, fish, and ducks. Bran, if transported before decomposition, was also used as a raw material for solvent oil extraction, resulting in edible products such as *dalda* and *vanaspati* and other products such as soap, paint, and lube. In 1990, the sale of bran was the key to profitability of a rice mill. Broken rice was also sold at two-thirds the price of whole grains. Sometimes sweepers were allowed to clean broken rice.

In Bardhaman district, thanks to the procurement and storage strategies of millers, and the reduced seasonality which results from multiple cropping, rice milling was developing into a continuous industry. A larger casual labour force was required by each mill: on an average 117 people, a third of whom were female. In addition, a skilled work-force was needed for the management of finance, trading and stock control, and a technical maintenance crew was permanently employed.

Linked and Derived Markets—Transport

Evaluations of agricultural markets which reduce evidence of their performance to the co-variation of prices either ignore derived markets altogether, or residualize transport as a cost-coefficient in regression analyses. But the transport markets serving the system of food markets are market systems in their own right and have evolved in response to the expansion of trade not only in staple food but also in other local products. As a result, they have local idiosyncrasies.

While small-scale consignments of rice and potatoes were carried in sacks by ticket-less train travellers (thereby evading transport costs altogether), the long-distance commodity flows based in the town of Memari depended on road transport. For the most part, this was owned and controlled by operators outside the region, and accessed via a single freight agency. Truck ownership carried low social status. Only 30 trucks and five lorries were owned locally, while the long-distance wholesale potato trade alone was reported to require a permanent fleet of 300 trucks. Local truck ownership was relatively unconcentrated, the largest enterprise controlling five trucks. Rates were set elsewhere and varied seasonally.

Transport in the town of Gulsi was similar (10 owners controlled 12 lorries). So was that of Katwa, the third market town we studied, but the local transport base was much larger, with about 100 owners controlling about 150 trucks and lorries. Rice mills had their own small fleets of trucks, the biggest firm owning five vehicles. Haulage rates in Katwa varied with demand for local non-agricultural products—bricks and riverbank sand. These rates were highest during the months of November to June. In both Memari and Katwa, mustard seed and oil were rarely transported by train because of the high risks and costs of pilferage.

Local, small-scale trade used a great variety of means of transport: rickshaw, rickshaw vans, and bicycles in Memari, and buffalo and bullock carts, rickshaws, tractor-trailers, and boats around Katwa. All these forms had developed rental markets. Many of them were collectively regulated and had fixed rates (e.g., for freight cycle rickshaws in Katwa), which resulted in spatially compartmentalized markets. Villages on the eastern edge of Katwa were separate markets because they had relatively high transport costs. As all motorized traffic was prohibited in the centre of Katwa, transport rates were low and rickshaws were the only type of freight transport allowed to ply in the heart of the town. In Katwa and Gulsi, rates in 1990 varied from Rs 0.3–0.4 per quintal-mile for mechanized transport, to Rs 1–1.3 per quintal-mile using animal or human power. They also varied according to return loads and the condition of the roads (permanent versus seasonal). Absurdly enough, given these costs, the Food Department was allowed only Rs 0.15 per quintal-mile for the lorry transport of grain.[4] Coercive subterfuge was necessary for the Food Department to gain access to transport.[5] It should now be clear that transport costs vary much more than has been allowed for in econometric studies of spatial integration.

Structural and Institutional Diversity
Diversity in Firm Organization
While family businesses predominate, the ownership of firms is varied. In 1990 individual firms where the owner was the manager were the norm for small scale rice trading and processing. The joint family, in which siblings, or more than one generation, work together, was the commonest kind of organization. It allows specialized management of complex activities (and the speediest decision-making in reaction to changing market conditions). Much the same is true of partnerships, which are quite different from family firms and consisted of investors from a given caste. Co-operatives, which may exploit economies of scale but where decision-making is decentralized and where a salaried management may be expected to be risk-averse, were only found in the cold store sector, and even there they had not proved successful.

Diversity among the Owners of Firms
All the owners of firms were male. Table 6.2 gives the caste composition

Institutional Diversity, Price Performance, and Power Relations 155

Table 6.2: Caste, Ethnicity and Religion in Commerce (% of sample)

Caste	Potato Cold Stores	Potato WH	Oil Mill	Rice Mill	Husking Mill	P/P–R/R Trades
Ugrokhatriya (military trade)	17	11	33	14	11	6
Muslim		33	8	14	11	12
Marwari	33		17	43		
Saha (wine trade)			17		22	18
Sadgop	17	22		14	11	
Ghandobanik ('assumed' caste)	17	11				18
Teli (oil trade)	17	11	17			
Brahmin (priest/ professionals)				14		18
Ghosh (milk trade)						18
Namashudra (ag lab (SC))					22	
Tantubai (spinning)			8		11	
Vaisnav (service)		11				
Gorai (trade)					11	
Debnath (cloth trade)						6
Baisha-Kapale (ag: trade)						6

Source: Field research, 1990.

of the traders interviewed. Respondents found it embarrassing to comment on their caste.[6] There appeared to be a wider variety of castes involved in trade in Bardhaman district than in the earlier case in Birbhum. Husked rice was being handled by a wide range of castes, from scheduled castes to Brahmins.[7] Roughly half the traders interviewed came from 'trading castes', but they were far from performing the trading occupations with which their names have come to be associated. Cloth- and wine- selling castes were busy with rice, for instance. Despite this diversity, two business castes dominated: *Marwaris* and *Ugrokhatriyas*. Ugrokhatriyas could be found throughout the system, while nearly half the rice mills and a third of the potato cold stores were owned by Marwaris. Caste operates as an entry barrier not so much to trade as within trade, and power is controlled not by the landlord elite, as theorized by Bhaduri (1983), but by the specialized commercial Marwari diaspora.

Diversity in the Labour Process

Labour processes also showed great variety. Table 6.3, which shows the organization of firms, also summarizes their activity combinations. Family labour was unwaged (though not unremunerated) and not

Table 6.3: Market System Structure, Bardhaman District, 1990

Firm Type	Average estimated present value of assets Rs '000 (1990)	Ownership (% sample)			
		single owner	joint family	partnership	cooperative
Cold stores	16,913	–	50	25	25
Potato wholesale	563	22	55	22	–
Oil Mills	437	25	66	9	–
Rice Mills	4,271	–	85	15	–
Paddy Agents	140	–	100	–	–
Husking Mills	111	20	80	–	–
Paddy Rice processors	78	100	–	–	–
wh/ca/ret	84	45	55	–	–

Activity Combinations (% of firms)

	buy	sell	broker	store	process	transport	finance trade	finance production	co-efficient of combinatorial uniqueness
Cold Stores	63	63	75	100	–	13	50	50	1.0
Potato wholesale	100	100	100	44	–	44	90	44	0.66
Oil Mills	83	83	–	58	100	25	50	50	0.66
Rice Mills	100	100	–	100	100	57	100	100	0.29

(contd.)

Table 6.3 (contd.)

Paddy Agents	100	100	100	66	–	100	100	33	0.66
Husking Mills	30	100	–	60	100	10	60	10	0.70
Paddy–rice processors	100	100	33	100	100	66	33	66	0.66
wh/ca/ret	100	100	82	91	–	18	100	18	0.36

Organization of Work

	Average work force	% female labour	% unwaged family labour
Cold Stores	162	30	2
Potato wholesale	7	–	40
Oil Mills	8	–	35
Rice Mills	117	30	2
Paddy Agents	4	–	50
Husking Mills	4	20	30
Paddy–rice processors	3	30	80
wh/ca/ret	–	–	70

Source: Field Research, 1990.

easily substitutable.⁸ Wage labour took many forms, ranging from a permanent salariat paid on conditions specified in the Factories Acts, through daily, seasonal contracts, to piece-rate labour paid in a mixture of cash and kind. A range of contractual forms co-existed with varying degrees of tying brought about through the manipulation of debt. The labour process was closely related to firm size. Family labour firms were restricted to petty-scale rice processing (where female labour is crucial to the parboiling and sun-drying processes), and to rice trading. Firms with mixtures of family and hired labour predominated, except in rice milling and cold storage. In the latter two sectors, management by family members provided relatively few livelihoods and the great bulk of the work-force was hired. Female labour made up a third of this wage-work. There was a detailed and gendered division of tasks so that labour substitution was far from easy.

In Memari and Gulsi, the local labour market was reported to be 'tight'. By this traders meant that labourers had the alternative of working on their own small landholdings. The unionization of labour had also succeeded in making wage rates sticky downwards. As a result, the employers' preferred arrangement for casual labour was gangs on contract. Yet, gangs made for a lumpy labour supply for activities like the preparation of potatoes before and after cold storage, where significant day-to-day variation in demand for casual labour was the rule. Contract labourers came, for periods ranging from two to three months to many years, from elsewhere in West Bengal (the districts of 24 Parganas and Howrah) and from Bihar and Orissa.⁹ They were recruited and screened through networks based on caste, religion or locality, by agents attached (sometimes in hierarchies) to contractors. Contractors were encouraged to avoid recruiting whole families and were reported to select for age (though children slipped through), physique, sex (according to the numerical requirements of the gender division of tasks), and physiological state (though pregnant and lactating women labourers might be recruited for lighter work at lower rates). Contracts were issued by employers for work carried out for a given period by the entire gang. Out of the contracted sum, the contractor and agents took at least 14 per cent. Their payment of labour took a variety of forms—monthly or daily, with or without food. Food was restricted to ingredients purchased by labourers on credit by agreement between the contractor and particular shopkeepers.

In 1990, payments varied between Rs 7–10 per day with meals for women, and Rs 20–40 without meals for men (See the Glossary for price inflators/deflators). With the legal minimum wage then at Rs 300 per month, women were clearly earning less than the minimum wage, while men were paid above it. Contracts varied in specificity, but the terms and conditions were invariably unwritten. The very idea of the 'contract' was gradually displacing the customary relations of wage work, which had been characterized by an unspecific (and exploitative) 'trust'. 'Faith between *malik* and workers is being ruined by contracts,' was how one miller described the changing employment relationship. Under relations of 'faith', labour, especially female labour, could be bonded by debt for an unspecified period of time and be obliged to work seasonally in the employer's factories and fields.

By depriving workers of family life, and by imposing restrictions on economic and social behaviour, employers ensured that the lives of migrant contract agro-processing labourers were dominated by work—more than if they were doing agricultural labour in their home villages. Tasks and living conditions were sex-segregated. People lived on site in purpose-built *coolie* tenements. Ben Rogaly has argued that the radically different sociality imposed on migrant agricultural workers challenges caste norms and exports new social relations to the regions of origin. The structural conditions which led to such 'institutional change'—gender segregation, control of commensality, and restricted spatial mobility—were even more exaggerated for migrant agro-industrial workers than they were for migrant agricultural coolies. Lodgings might be 'free', but the conditions of work were the opposite of liberating. The absence of any rights to social security, and the lack of enforcement of minimum wages, made migrant contract labourers extremely vulnerable in times of need, whether through accident, illness, or a crisis at home. They were dependent for help on the contractor, the shopkeeper or one another. Sickness was not compensated. 'No work, no pay. I am not responsible for illness,' declared one contractor. Incentive bonuses at festivals were at the discretion of merchant-employers. Indebtedness to contractors was common. 'My labourers are not very bonded,' protested one of them.

Resistance to these conditions took the form of absconding (rates of which were said to be high), slothfulness, etc, even though under time-bound contracts, there were severe constraints on such resistance. But resistance was also formalized in unions. As in Birbhum in 1982, there was a multiplicity of unions among the agro-commercial labour force, though the CITU (Centre of Indian Trade Unions) dominated the organization of labour in cold stores, rice mills, and street-loading gangs. Contractors sometimes actively encouraged unionization, since unions were associated with higher wage claims, upon which their own commissions depended.

In Katwa, the local labour market was said to be less tight, and migrant contract labour was certainly less common. The normal arrangement here involved gangs, recruited from within five miles, moving between fields and factories. At least one such gang was organized and controlled by a merchant: the Secretary of the Local Chamber of Commerce, a corporatist arrangement undermining the political power of labour (Basile and Harriss-White, 2000).

Diversity in the Activity of Firms

Trading firms are assumed to buy and sell. In practice they also perform other activities: brokerage, storage, processing, transport, finance of trade, and the finance of production. There are $[(2^8)-1]$ or 255 possible combinations of the eight activities listed above. It might be reasonably hypothesized that activities would be patterned and that such patterns would correspond to the conventional vernacular classifications of firms. This is not so. In an earlier study in South India, 149 mercantile firms displayed 108 different activity combinations, most of which were unique (Harriss-White, 1996). There is a similar, though less marked, tendency in West Bengal. Among 60 firms studied in Bardhaman, 20 had unique activity combinations, including the simplest and the most complex. Two firms had five combinations, three had four, and four had two (the combinations being (buy/sell/store/process/transport/finance production/finance trade), and the same minus transport). One combination was found in 10 instances: (buy/ sell/ broker/ store/ finance trade)—a purely mercantile combination. There was patterning only in rice milling and general rice wholesale/ commission agency/ retailing firms. Otherwise, the activity structure of firms was both highly diverse and complex, with a tendency to uniqueness. Unique activity combinations mean that agricultural markets are composed of more dissimilar entities than is the case with agricultural production. Elsewhere we have argued that the diversity of the activity mix of an agricultural market may be a systemic defence against environmental and political shocks (Harriss-White, 1995).

Diversity of Flows

As with activities, so is it with physical commodity flows. There were marked differences not only between settlements but also between commodities, as seen in Table 6.4. Potatoes were supplied to the stores from the local region. Memari's potatoes reached their final destinations through a wide and diversified network. They were traded locally, sent to Calcutta, and shipped as far as Assam, Bihar, Andhra Pradesh, and Uttar Pradesh. Much of Katwa's potato supplies were destined for markets in north Bengal. With respect to oil, both Memari and Katwa imported most of their mustard seed from states in the north-west of India. Both in turn supplied local markets, but Katwa also exported to north Bengal.

Even though paddy agents supplied rice mills with local consignments, paddy was also supplied to the rice mills from increasingly far away; in 1990 mostly from other districts within West Bengal, although Gulsi and Memari's accessibility enabled rice mills located there to import paddy also from Bihar and Uttar Pradesh, which Katwa's mills were unable to do. In turn, all three places supplied a great range of destinations: to Siliguri and Guwahati in the north-east, and Kolkata and 24 Parganas in the south. Local demand, moreover, was not met from local rice mills, but in all three settlements it was the preserve of the semi-legal system that had proliferated around husking mills. Small paddy-rice processor firms used these mills on a custom basis and supplied rice to unspecialized, small-scale wholesaler/broker/retailers. Not only did the latter organize local staple food supplies, but they also increasingly supplied semi-legally at long distances: Memari to Bardhaman and Calcutta; Katwa and Gulsi to Calcutta, east to Nadia and even west to Bihar (see Map 2 page 51).

Trading transactions were therefore not activated by information alone, but developed around patterned networks of regular contacts and transport. As a result of such social embeddedness, the spatial commodity relations of each settlement differed. Places get to have particular characters. Within one commodity system, that of rice, there were two scales of commodity flow—local and state-wide—as well as spatial specialization structured around social networks. One powerful insight from this systemic diversity and the uniqueness of its elements and spatial relations is that the operational efficiency of the various firms constituting these markets cannot be compared. A de-institutionalized market which could act as a yardstick for the evaluation of efficiency does not exist.

Table 6.4: Physical Commodity Flows

% of total physical flows:	Origin			Destination			Estimated average physical output tonnes
	Within district	Outside district but within state	Other states	Within district	Outside district but within state	Other states	
Town/Firm							
Memari							
Cold stores	92	8	–	19	41	40	11,500
Potato Wholesale	100	–	–	3	31	66	29,780
Oil Mills	26	–	74	100	–	–	132
Rice Mills	14	16	70	–	100	–	4,039
Paddy Agents	100	–	–	100	–	–	1,000
Husking Mills	100	–	–	100	–	–	231
Paddy Rice Processors	100	–	–	100	–	–	66
wh/ca/ret	100	–	–	–	100	–	720
Katwa							
Cold stores	94	6	–	3	75	22	6,400
Potato Wholesale	100	–	–	44	56	–	1,350
Oil Mills	31	–	69	75	25	–	152
Rice Mills	40	60	–	4	96	–	8,300
Paddy Agents	100	–	–	100	–	–	1,100
Husking Mills	100	–	–	100	–	–	742

(contd.)

Table 6.4 (contd.)

Paddy–rice processors	100	–	100	–	–	120
wh/ca/ret	100	–	23	62	15	663
Oil Mills	100	–	100	–	–	45
Rice Mills	75	20	5	45	50	4000
Paddy Agents	100	–	100	–	–	1670
Husking Agents	100	–	100	–	–	1500
Paddy—rice processors	100	–	100	–	–	2000
wh/ca/ret	100	–	20	–	80	1250

Source: Field research, 1990.

Diversity in Price Behaviour

In both the 1982 study in Birbhum and Bardhaman in 1990, prices were conceived of as the product of varied social relations in the market system. In Chapter 1, it was pointed out that empirical research—such as Ben Crow's (2001) study of exchange relations and rice markets in Bangladesh—which demonstrates this variety is rare. Here, however, we have been confined to official data, which are far from satisfactory for research into exchange relations and prices. Weekly prices for common and fine paddy and rice, potatoes, mustard seed, and oil in Burdwan, the district capital, Katwa and Memari over the period October 1988 to August 1990 have been summarized in Appendix 6.1, Table 1. Weekly prices are either spot contracts—which are actually the rarest kind of transaction —or averages, which mask daily fluctuations. Either way, prices are estimates given to local officials of the Government of India's Department of Statistics, or to West Bengal's Department of Marketing (Harriss-White, 1998).

The plots, means, and coefficients of price variation show that:

i) Prices for high-yielding common quality paddy and rice tended to move discretely, while those for fine grain tended to move over a price continuum;

ii) Procurement prices were never high enough to serve as support prices, and were usually considerably below market prices;

iii) Burdwan's rice prices were above procurement price levels. Since prices on the Burdwan rice wholesale market were formed by supplies from rice mills rather than from petty trading, they may have included a hoist to compensate rice levy suppliers for the losses they made on state procurement;

iv) For both fine as well as common grain there was a close correspondence between Burdwan's rice prices, Katwa's paddy prices, and Memari's paddy and rice prices. But there was no such relationship between Burdwan's rice prices and those of Katwa, either for fine or common varieties of rice;

v) Potato price movements all showed close co-variation and revealed the unexpectedly low minima in the 1989–90 seasons, with no recovery to previous levels; and

vi) Oil prices in Burdwan diverged most from both seed and oil prices in Katwa at the seasons of maximum prices in the former district.

Institutional Diversity, Price Performance, and Power Relations

In separate methodological research, existing ways of evaluating market efficiency under conditions when there is no alternative to working with price data alone have been critically reviewed (Harriss, 1979; Palaskas and Harriss-White, 1993; 1997). A new method (developed from applications to financial markets) has been proposed, developed, and applied by others (Basu, 2002). It involves identifying base and dependent market places, then testing pairs of base and dependent price series for co-integration, evaluating the co-integration coefficient and testing for the identity of the parameters of error correction models. (see Appendix 6.2 for details of the price data and the quantitative results).

We applied this method to weekly Department of Statistics data for common and fine wholesale paddy and rice, for wholesale and retail potato, and for mustard seed and oil in Burdwan, Katwa, and Memari. Burdwan was identified as the price base for rice and oil and Memari the base for potato, since traders recognized them as such.

Even using these crude summary prices, this econometric exercise has revealed paradoxical behaviour within the system of markets:

i) the co-existence of general long-term price integration with a marked price inefficiency in all commodity markets in all locations over the short term of a week;

ii) the long-term co-integration, integration, and high velocities of adjustment of potato prices during the years 1988–90, which was a period of rapid spatial change in commodity flows, and of marked changes in the trend and seasonal minima of prices;

iii) the lack of full co-integration, lower degrees of integration and much greater sluggishness of price adjustments towards equilibrium for paddy and rice prices compared with other commodities, during a period of *de facto* liberalization; and

iv) the lack of co-integration in both the paddy-rice and mustard seeds markets between Burdwan and Katwa (but not between Burdwan and Memari).

Whether spot or average, the estimated weekly prices fail to capture certain types of price variation. Variation due to exchange relationships could not be explored in our field work. However, as Appendix 6.1, Table 2 shows, the price variation reported by different classes of traders often occurs within the span of a day, due to exchange relations, debt, or changes in demand. One informant in the oil market explained that price variations in excess of 17 per cent were possible as compensation for debt, and variations of up to 30 per cent could be attributed to exchange status (caste, holding size, urgency of need for cash, etc.). For the most part, daily variations were 6–7 per cent and were easily outweighed by variations for quality differences (keeping variety constant), which ranged from 5–25 per cent.

In explaining this price behaviour, a number of factors thought elsewhere to be important for the explanation of imperfect integration can be eliminated. One argument is that the youth of the commercialized commodity system is likely to lead to distortions owing to underdeveloped systems of contacts and information. In Bardhaman, both potatoes and mustard oil have been commercialized on a grand scale relatively recently, yet both these crops show greater price integration than does rice. Similarly, variations in physical infrastructure and in information costs cannot by themselves explain the lack of integration because Katwa's potato market does not show the short and long-term perturbations so apparent in its rice and oilseed prices. Attempts to account for the idiosyncrasies of price behaviour cannot avoid being specific to place and crop.

With respect to the finding that the potato market is co-integrated during a period of seasonal price fluctuations, the wholesale prices collected by the Directorate of Marketing were discovered not to be the prices for first sales, but prices formed' somewhere up the commodity system at a point where ownership and economic power was at its most concentrated. The potato market was controlled there by fewer and larger intermediaries than at any other point in the system. At this point, prices were formed under conditions of collusive oligopoly by a powerful Memari syndicate, which controlled a network of local information intermediaries and had privileged access to the media and telecommunications. The control exerted by this oligopoly over the highly concentrated regional trade would appear to be the most likely institutional factor accounting for the observed high levels of long-term price integration.

The second idiosyncrasy, that is the low levels of integration of the paddy-rice price system, needs to be considered along with this system's tendency to show relatively sluggish adjustments to base-price perturbations. Rice had a highly complex system of distribution, but one marked by a bifurcation into two subsystems patterned distinctively in terms of entry barriers, assets, technology (of storage, processing, and transport), activity combinations, spatial flows, price formation, access to information and finance and—last but not least—contractual forms. Information in one branch of the system was not available to the other. Paddy prices used for our study were taken at mill gates. By contrast, rice prices in peripheral marketplaces were taken from crowded, small-scale wholesale markets supplying local settlements and not fed by the output of rice mills. It is likely that the price-forming processes differ in the two branches and that they will be less well-integrated than prices in a unified marketing system, such as that for potato.

Specific forms of state intervention will also reduce price integration. After the 1970s, the rigour with which compulsory procurement and movement restrictions were implemented diminished. This *de facto* liberalization was accompanied by intense, technically illegal competition from the subsystem of petty trade. It was in the 1980s rather than the 1970s that the viability of the rice mills was challenged. By 1990, rice mills were no longer able to enforce the hoisting of 'market' prices by amounts that would at least compensate millers for the real losses incurred by the coerced sales of levy rice at relatively low administered prices. The result was a necessary accommodation with state-trading institutions, involving the replacement of proportional procurements by fixed quotas. The latter gave incentives to the rice mills to maximize paddy purchases from producers at post-harvest price lows (or even lower), via contracts tying pre-harvest credit to post-harvest paddy, and to speculate through long term intra- and inter-seasonal storage, a practice which certainly can exaggerate local seasonal price fluctuations .

Next, consider the third problem of the lack of co-integration of the rice and oilseeds markets of Katwa with its assumed price bases in Burdwan. Katwa's remoteness, its costlier and lagged supply of information, its poor physical infrastructure and worse tele-communications, and its formidable caste barriers to entry and caste control over trading finance and storage cannot explain why one market (potato) was price-integrated while the markets for the other two crops were not. We have provided some institutional reasons for the high integration of potato prices. The behaviour of the other two crops needs separate explanation. Here we can only speculate. In the case of oil seeds, Katwa's oil market supplied a spatially distinct final destination compared with the Calcutta-centred system into which Burdwan and Memari are fitted. The spatial compartmentalization of the oilseeds market may explain its price behaviour. Yet Katwa's rice market, even more dislocated in price, did not supply different final destinations from Memari's. The paddy and rice prices are taken from different subsystems in which prices are formed in distinctive ways and it may be that Katwa's relative remoteness, poor infrastructure, conditions of contractual insecurity, and the physical and economic harassment under which petty trade operates, mean that price formation in the small-scale subsystem was not related to that in the large-scale subsystem, as it was in accessible locations such as Burdwan and Memari.

The results indicating a systemic tendency towards long-term integration are consistent with comparatively well-diffused information and comparatively well-developed transport infrastructure and communications. Despite state regulations, the barriers to entry into petty trading were not high enough to prevent a proliferation of intermediaries at the base of the structure. Reports of the de-linking of previously attached paddy trading agents, of competition (albeit limited) for commercial credit offered by nationalized banks (UCO Bank, 1990); of rapidly expanding long-distance flows and of the replacement of some verbal contracts by written documents, all point to a gradual freeing of conditions of exchange, well before the era of liberalization.

Such developments notwithstanding, in the short term, price behaviour in all the crop markets was inefficient. It is possible that part of the reason for this can be attributed to factors which have had to be considered exogenous but which could, with better data availability, be endogenized. The influence of by-product prices is an obvious candidate for such an explanatory factor.

Structural attributes consistent with pricing inefficiency include the high polarization of assets, particularly of control over storage, and high entry barriers (economic, social, and informational) into the 'power points' of the commodity systems. These structural characteristics make for micro-monopoly conditions. Similarly, the institutions of collective action, which have emerged privately to regulate transactions (discussed later in this chapter), are necessary to the development of markets, yet they also restrict entry and facilitate collusion. Equilibrating trade flows are hampered not only by physical barriers (such as large rivers and variations in rail gauges) but also by economic and state-imposed ones. In 1990, these included the co-existence of multiple markets for road transport, the effects on transport rates of the distributional requirements of other commodities in other places, and the state's prohibition of motorised vehicles in

Katwa. Furthermore, at any one point in time, a multiplicity of exchange relations co-existed throughout the system. There is evidence of repeated transactions between small subsets of intermediaries; of interlocked contracts where the dependent party faces a monopoly; and of 'power premia' enforced when one party transacts under conditions of constrained choice, exacerbated by debt. Even the most voluntary transactions were made after private negotiations. Lastly, the remarkable complexity in the activity combinations of the firms surveyed means that some market prices were actually bypassed inside vertically-integrated firms. Although the weighting of all these types of contract will vary seasonally, one thing is clear: spot contracts—the stuff of official price data—are not very common forms of transaction.

Our analytical framework for the empirical analysis of markets has therefore generated evidence which is useful in accounting not only for generalized phenomena such as the co-existence of long-term integration with short-term inefficiency, but also for the highly particular features of three economic markets, each of whose price system has been shown to behave in quite distinctive ways. Access to transport and price information (the most commonly stressed exogenous factors in the explanation of less than perfect co-variation of prices) are far from being the only or even the most important influences on price behaviour. Other types of information (notably about the nature of the trading contract) and other types of infrastructural barriers (physical or administrative) need to enter the explanation. The way price data are collected privileges certain places and time periods. It masks price behaviour which is specific to class relations, and/or types of firms. Even so, it is evident that markets are differently structured in different places, that collusive power and micro-monopolies affect price behaviour, even when prices are exposed as aggregate summaries of the varied exchanges in market-places. In the last part of this chapter, an attempt is made to map this institutional structure, in particular that pertaining to place, caste, and class, onto the material and non-material resources through which markets are constituted and the commercial capitalist sector develops.

Economic and Social Power
Control over Assets
Table 6.3 presents our best estimates of asset distributions in 1990. The disparity in asset ownership was at least 200 : 1.[10] By the

conventional yardsticks of industrial organization, characteristics of large scale combined with high degrees of polarization revealed in this table are not those of effective competition. The table also shows capital barriers to entry, even into petty production and trade, where in 1990 nearly Rs 1 lakh was necessary. These barriers were compounded by social factors. Caste constrained entry into the largest scale trading firms. In Katwa, Marwaris alone owned the largest firms in all three commodities. Gender relations prevented women from running firms in all but the most petty trading activity. Asset ownership was both highly concentrated and highly specific.

There were also considerable differences between places in terms of the physical capacities and the scales of commercial enterprises (see Table 6.5). Memari's potato cold stores were almost twice as large as Katwa's, and potato wholesaling and brokerage firms in Memari were on an average over twenty times as large as Katwa's. The physical output of Katwa's large rice mills and small paddy-rice processors was on an average more than twice as large as that of mills and huskers in Gulsi and Memari. Gulsi's oil mills were three to four times smaller than those of Katwa and Memari, while its husking mills and paddy agents operated at much larger scales. Each commodity's marketing system is spatially and economically specialized; and in sites where a given activity was clustered, the scale of enterprises was largest and ownership was most concentrated.

Table 6.5: Storage

	Average capacity (tonnes)	Estimated average maximum storage period (days)
Cold Stores	7,763	135
Potato Wholesale	as for CS	5-30 days after contract
Oil Mills	33	7-360
Rice Mills	503	120
Paddy Agents	25	30
Husking Mills	11[1]	5
Paddy-rice Processors	5	20
wh/ca/ret	6[2]	12

Notes: 1. Storing other traders' paddy.
2. 2 respondents (not included) had 40 tonnes and could store for 2 months.
Source: Field research, 1990

Institutional Diversity, Price Performance, and Power Relations

This tendency towards distribution of assets that are specific to a given commodity and place, scaled and patterned in fractal forms, has been observed elsewhere in India (Colatei and Harriss-White, 2004; Harriss-White, 2003; Ch. 8). The economic clout of the largest firms is likely to be contested *outside* the local region, in arenas where other fractions of commercial capital compete for political influence in state or national capital cities. Within the region, where the economic power of all the firms controlling staple food markets (whether it is measured by output or assets) is generally greater than that of the agricultural producers, these trading firms are the masters of the countryside.

Merchants' Control Over Land

Table 6.6 shows the average landholdings of the various categories of merchants, while Table 6.7 gives the distribution of holdings overall in Bardhaman district.

Although the smallest paddy and rice traders we encountered were landless and/or sharecroppers, and although small paddy-rice processors known as *kutials* were drawn from the lowest strata of agrarian society, husking mill owners came from the top 25 per cent of the

Table 6.6: General Distribution of Landholding in Bardhaman District, 1984–5

Acres	% holdings	% area
0–2.5	51	17
2.5–5	25	25
5–9.5	18	35
over 9.5	6	23
Total	100	100

Source: Webster, 1989

Table 6.7: Land Holdings of the Sample of Merchants, Bardhaman District, 1990

	Estimated Averages (Acres)
Potato CS	25
Potato Wh	15
Oil Mills	9
Rice Mills	10
Husking Mills	5
P/P-R/R trades	1.5

Source: Field research.

land-holding distribution. All the other traders had land equivalent to the holdings of the top 6 per cent. Despite the Left Front Government's land reforms, this 6 per cent still controlled 23 per cent of the cultivated area (Webster, 1989). Holdings in excess of 50 acres were still being operated by agro-commercial families as single social and economic units, no matter how they were registered, and however much they were apparently subdivided in share rental agreements. Nevertheless, the wealthiest commercial households had for some time been investing in urban, rather than rural, land.

Control Over Storage
'Hoarding is the key to profit.'
'Mine is a business of hoarding.'
'Rice is a hoarder's business, so a small trader remains small.'
(Rice millers)

The capacity to store enables those who control stocks to prevent physical deterioration, and to sell when prices are highest. Most merchants attempt both to store and to profit from future price changes. 'Hoarding' is the deliberate withholding of stored commodities so as to push prices above the cost of purchase plus storage. Hoarding is difficult to distinguish from storage; it depends on historical information on inventory prices and costs. Even then, the costs of the inevitable physical losses in storage will vary with crop type and moisture, with periodicity and with the storage technology used; and the costs of money locked up in inventory will vary with interest rates in credit markets, which are also socially fragmented and compartmentalized. In all the markets studied, however, the state stipulated maximum quantities and periodicities for storage. Hoarding was locally understood as inventory behaviour in breach of these laws, and this is the sense in which the term is used here.

There were no regional differences in store sizes; but storage technologies and practices were highly differentiated (Table 6.5). Cold stores and rice mills not only represented large-scale holding capacity, their stores (together with their financial arrangements) made it possible to hold commodities over quite long periods of time. For rice, this was over more than one season. By giving pre-harvest credit, rice millers also had property rights over the paddy destined for them. Cold storage firms commonly acquired direct rights gradually, through instalment purchases over the storage season, although this practice was illegal.

Oil mills had smaller stores, but enough working capital to store for long periods. All these firms, occupying commanding positions in their respective commodity systems, had the capacity to 'hoard', and the quotations from their representatives at the head of this section confirm that it occurred. In other types of firms both quantities and periodicities were quite limited, most of all with respect to the traders attached to illegal husking mills.

Information: Its Generation, Control and Costs

Poor physical infrastructure and defective information are factors commonly introduced as explanations for lack of price integration. Here, under markedly contrasting conditions (accessibility and low cost information in Memari; remoteness and high cost, and so lagged information, in Katwa), neither factor appeared to be sufficient to explain the particularities of price behaviour.

Potatoes are perishable, and information about them flows fast and may change quickly. The study region's information about potato prices was controlled by six large wholesalers who operated a pricing syndicate in Memari itself. This group was informed in turn by a small number of brokers who controlled supplies Kolkata (where demand is seasonally inelastic). The syndicate fixed prices each morning. Their price was understood to be a referent for other market intermediaries. It circulated by phone to a network of agents, some itinerant, who passed it on by word of mouth. It reverberated on the radio and in the newspapers. The oligopolists creating the daily price spent about Rs 2,000 per month per firm on post and telecommunications.

There were differences in the costs and flows of information between Memari and Katwa. Despite local differences in communications infrastructure and information costs, and despite polarized market structures, the Memari syndicate ensured widespread access to their price information. Price was important information for both cold store owners and wholesalers in Memari, and was given at low-cost or free for client firms. Price information was much costlier in Katwa where the underdevelopment of telecommunications meant it could not be obtained by long-distance phone. Instead, price information was obtained by using travelling messengers (paid about Rs 1,000 per month, and given another 2,000 for costs). In Katwa, other kinds of information were just as crucial as price to the operation of the market. Break-even points for cold storage were high—at 70–80 per cent of capacity—so crucial information about production, the credit needs of potato suppliers and cold store space was circulated by small traders and agents, often on a commission basis. As the post-harvest storage season developed, even information about reservations of space in cold stores became a marketable commodity.

With respect to oil, a set of 30–40 wholesalers, stockists, and brokers in Calcutta provided reference prices for mustard and its substitutes throughout Bardhaman district, and they also supplied data about production conditions in the north-western states of India.[11] In Gulsi, information about Kolkata prices arrived via Guskara and Sainthia, towns considerably to the north where there was a subsidiary mustard oil cartel. In Katwa, information about prices throughout West Bengal arrived in the evening, by telegram or by bus. The cost of this information, paid for privately by merchants, was at least six times greater than in Memari. Lack of infrastructure increased the cost and decreased the velocity of diffusion of price information, with—as seen earlier in this chapter—a serious negative impact on price integration.

For rice, the information system was also complex, and none too transparent. Several modes of price formation co-existed. Burdwan was the reference location where 34 rice brokers, through whom the rice millers dealt, were information sources. There was easy telecommunication to and from Memari. For Katwa, information was retrieved physically, using messengers. Paddy prices were calculated by rice millers backwards from rice prices, on a cost-plus-profit basis. These prices were also circulated by physical means. Some local rice millers admitted colluding over the formation of paddy prices. The production process took a minimum of four days, so there was a small unavoidable uncertainty about short-term future price movements.

Husking mills and attached traders got to know paddy prices by word of mouth from rice mills. But local market prices for rice were widely reported to be created on a cost-plus basis, from paddy prices, via local commission agencies. Other intermediaries, paddy and rice processors, and farmers, would all calculate backwards from local rice wholesale prices. There was a considerable variation in knowledge about the velocity of price formation. One third of the traders reported no price variations during a day. The majority reported daily price variations of one to eight per cent. In addition, pervasive debt relations between sellers and buyers on apparently interest-free terms—to secure supplies—actually depressed the daily selling price by an average of 1.5–2 per cent.

Contractual Behaviour and Economic Power

'The entire trade runs on verbal contract.'
'A known face is the only one I do business with.'
'Among equals we behave differently from how we behave with weaker parties.'

(*Oil, potato and rice traders*)

The terms and conditions of contracts, particularly their payment systems, reflect the distribution of economic power within the system of markets. In the market for potatoes, complicated contractual forms and ownership transfers were common. Brokers advanced seed potatoes and information together with money on the verbal condition that supplies were then tied to them. Cold-store space could also be traded using verbal futures contracts. Brokerage services and interlocked contracts between suppliers of inputs of fertilizers and suppliers of potatoes might or might not be reflected in prices to producers, depending on competitive conditions at the village level and the social relations between producers and cold-store owners. If production conditions were unfavourable, cold-store owners tied agents by lending them working capital. They would also advance seeds and pesticides in order to guarantee their supplies.

Once potatoes were safely in store, a certificate (or 'bond') would be issued by the owner. The bond is a form of security used by producers for obtaining bank credit. It could also be used for forward trading for up to 30 days. But it was often purchased outright by cold-store owners for speculative purposes in defiance of the law; or it might be acquired in an unclear transfer of rights, via a legal loophole which worked as follows. Cold-store owners had the statutory authority to remove 'rotting' potatoes within 48 hours of notification. Payments for these kinds of sales might be remitted much later, when 'prevailing' market prices were lower than at the time of sale, and would reflect those prices. Payments were rather slow throughout the system, sometimes as late as six months. Although such late repayment might be compensated for (at a surcharge of around two per cent per month), the asymmetry of timing between payment for the producer's own purchases and the repayment of his sales ensured that the seller of this perishable commodity remained financially vulnerable.

In the 1980s, growth in local potato production for storage, and of long-distance trading, increased the use of written documents. By 1990, although the majority of contracts remained verbal ones, traders often kept a written note of instalments paid off by them, and instalments paid to them.

Open disputes over these contracts were resolved by the potato syndicate in Memari. The default option was the CPI(M) committee in the Panchayat office. The courts were avoided, because of costs, delays, and, it was alleged, corruption.

In the case of mustard oil, uncertainties of production both locally and at long distance led to the widespread use of brokers to concentrate the supply of information and to bulk up consignments. Both activities reduced transaction costs. Oil mills and wholesalers always used a small number of known brokers ('two to three', 'eight to ten') to minimize the risks associated with non-payment. The lags in repayment after transactions averaged 20–30 days throughout the system; sellers were compensated at 1.6 per cent interest per month for periods longer than this. This slow velocity was not determined by technical factors. There were two types of short necessary lags, one of about five days between transaction and possession, caused by the transport of mustard seed from north-west India, and a second of two days caused by processing. The slow velocity was instead the outcome of power relations. Written contracts were necessary only for inter-state transport and for repayment by instalments. Otherwise, verbal contracts were normal. Disputes over ownership were resolved by the brokers.

The contractual arrangements for the two branches of the commodity system for rice need to be considered separately. Rice mills could receive direct consignments of paddy from large farmers whom they paid directly and instantly. Some mills had hundreds of regular suppliers of this type. These suppliers were not always indebted to the mills. Nevertheless, 'power premia' existed and irrespective of debt, weaker sellers might be paid at prices two to six per cent below those 'ruling'. At the same time, most mills secured supplies via a mill-specific network of some 15 to 30 agents. As explained in Chapter 4, these intermediaries used to be licensed and attached to a single mill and would operate using money lent by the miller. By the late 1980s, however, they were de-linking, and operating independently of their accredited mills, using their own accumulated capital and diverting rice mill advances to their individual business where possible. Advance credit was extensively given to rice producers on a range of terms and conditions, using verbal contracts.

Examples include cash at 10 per cent per month interest and tied sales; cash at no interest but with a five per cent reduction in paddy price and a forward sales commitment; credit in cash and kind (fertilizers) with tied post-harvest sales. Rice wholesalers buying from rice mills made written contracts and would usually pay within 30 days.

The petty trading system had markedly higher velocities of repayment on verbal contract and most closely approached spot trading, since traders have small reserves of working capital. Normal repayment was two to seven days. Repeated transactions between regular parties were usual. Credit of up to 30 days could be obtained on a friendly basis by a paddy-rice processor from a husking mill owner, and by a consumer from a retailer.

Disputes in both branches of the rice market system were resolved either on a one-to-one basis or by a local trade association.

It is apparent that advance contracts and long-term, regular, patterned, and personalized trading relationships peppered these commodity systems and reduced the cost of transactions within them. The enduring nature of verbal contracts made on a one-to-one basis testifies to the importance of information about reputation as much as about prices. Goodwill, for most parties, depended on reliable payment. As we observed earlier in South India (Harriss-White, 1996), so here in these commodity markets also, debt behaviour is more highly charged in moral terms than is credit behaviour.

Finance and Credit

'We give large scale finance via agents.'
'We finance commission agents on a large scale.'

(Potato cold store owners)

The capacity to guarantee supplies is one of the most important elements of economic power. While occasionally this is done coercively, for example, by the transport cartel operating in and around Narkhadi in Bardhaman district, it is most easily achieved in West Bengal by interlocking money markets with commodity markets. Interlocked contracts are also deployed within commodity systems in order to subordinate dependent parties and deprive them of choice.

Table 6.8 shows the scale of agro-commercial borrowing and lending. The data can be assumed to have been under-declared. Potato

Table 6.8: Traders' Credit, Bardhaman District, 1990

	Average Borrowed (Rs Lakhs)	Sources (in order of importance)	Average Lent Out (Rs Lakhs)
Potato CS	30.5	nationalized banks/co-operative/ private lenders/kin	26
Potato Wh	5.4	banks/cold store owners/ producers/'friends'	4.63
Oil Mill	1.1	traders/banks/farmers	2.1
Rice Mill	3–75.0	banks/private lenders/kin	10.6
Husking Mill	0.24	kin/friends/private lenders	0.18
P/P–R/R trades	0.39	private parties/traders/farmers/IDRP	0.46

cold-store owners borrowed extremely large sums from state financial institutions and *'mahajans'* (private lenders), most of which they lent onwards through networks of agents. These intermediaries disbursed pre-harvest credit and post-harvest, pre-sale credit on conditions which ensured repayment in kind and which tied the producer to the lender's store. Potato wholesalers borrowed from state-regulated banks, and lent 'backward' to producers from whom they purchased, and 'forward' to traders who purchased from them on the long-rolling periodicities described earlier.

The finance of rice milling and trading cannot be usefully described using averages. In Bardhaman district, borrowing ranged from an extreme of zero, in the case of Marwaris using their community-exclusive funds, and 'borrowing from farmers' who were forced into agreeing to delayed payments of up to three months; to the other extreme of medium (Rs 3–7 lakhs) and large (Rs 10–75 lakhs) loans from state banks. Smaller-scale, but similar, behaviour was shown by oil millers. Lending went through a network of agents in which elements of uncompensated 'goodwill' were transformed into explicit interest rates of up to 10 per cent per month.

By contrast, husking mill owners either did not need to borrow, or borrowed relatively small amounts from relatives and friends at no interest, passing such funds onwards to paddy-rice traders as a means of attaching them to the mill. Paddy and rice trading centred on husking mills was carried on at varied scales. While a fifth of traders never borrowed money, the rest used 'private parties' (at interest rates of 5 to 10 per cent per month). Or they delayed payments to traders and

Institutional Diversity, Price Performance, and Power Relations

farmers (sometimes compensated in an *ad hoc* way at Rs. 1–2 per sack for a delay of 15 days). All traders lent out. About half tied production or consumption loans to post-harvest supplies. All traders accepted repayment lags of up to 30 days from agents or other traders.

Three conclusions about trading credit can thus be drawn. The first is that it was only the most asset-powerful firms that had access to state finance. The most numerically common firms all lacked that access. Firms that borrowed from nationalized banks and state-run finance corporations had long been effective credit agents. Provided they had good repayment records, they boosted the credentials of the banks as 'priority sector lenders' at minimum supervision cost and minimum risk to the bank. They then supplied the 'non-institutional', 'informal' sector with funds in a cascade of onward lending at ever higher rates of interest.

The second conclusion is that the least economically powerful firms (whether measured by assets or by gross output) faced sharply differentiated credit terms, either at no interest or at about 10 per cent per month. In the former case, the return they gave for the loans they took was the benefit of providing secure supplies to the lender. In the latter case, their lack of any alternative source was penalized.

The third conclusion is that, despite the seasonality of the agrarian calendar, lending and borrowing are not seasonal but are carried on all year. It was the purposes for which money was locked up with commodities—or otherwise circulated—that varied seasonally. It is therefore justifiable to annualize interest rates.

With great caution we can attempt to place these financial flows in context. There may be elements of double counting in our survey, and thus possible over-estimation. Against this is the near certainty of under-declaration of credit and under-estimation of the population of firms. In addition, our survey is neither representative nor random, but there is no good reason to suppose that our data on loans are *over*-estimated. Supposing the data are representative, and supposing the estimated population numbers for the market system in Table 6.1 are accepted as realistic, then the credit distributed by cold store owners, potato wholesalers, rice and oil millers, and sundry grain traders in the six blocks comprising our study area would amount to some Rs. 7.31 crores. This can be compared with certain kinds of state finance to production and trade. Cooperative loans on potatoes in cold storage in the entire Bardhaman district amounted to Rs 2.3 crores in 1988,

Rs 3.5 crores in 1989, and Rs 4.4 crores in 1990, according to the Bardhaman District Co-operative Central Bank. Co-operative production credit was allocated as shown in Table 6.9.

In 1990, then, so-called informal credit (albeit fuelled in part indirectly by nationalized and co-operative banks) was likely to have been the dominant source for the finance of production as well as that of trade.

From the 'Lead Bank's' district credit plan (UCO Bank, 1990), we can see that the accommodation between local agro-commercial capital and the nationalized banks is an example of 'unintended outcomes'. Local financial policy was clearly oriented to rural lending for purposes of poverty alleviation. There was meant to be no lending for trade, except for very specific purposes. These included:

- 'marketing entrepreneurs in consumer goods' (UCO Bank 1990, p. 69);
- 'support for small-scale agro-based village and cottage industries' (p. 76);
- to 'augment facilities for modern (sic) storage, processing and marketing of agricultural produce' (p. 91);
- to 'strengthen the public distribution system with working capital credit to fair-price shop owners and co-operative stores' (p. 91); and
- in order to break the link between traders and producers, produce marketing loans can be given to producers on condition that co-operative production credit was obtained earlier (p. 98).

But from Table 6.8 it can be seen that it is only petty, not large-scale, trade which is prevented from gaining access to formal sector loans. The loophole for large-scale trading firms is glaring.

Table 6.9: Co-operative Crop Loans in the Areas studied (Rs lakhs)

	1987–88	1988–89	1989–90
Memari block I and II	195.26	209.45	162.0
Gulsi block I and II	67.8	69.92	17.9
Katwa block I and II	29.5	32.4	16.42
Total	292.8	308.77	196.32

Source: Bardhaman District Co-operative Central Bank Ltd, 1990.

Yet at one and the same time the plan declares priority sector lending 'not successful' (pp. 55–6) because lack of recovery creates demand constraints. Among factors including delinquent behaviour, the misuse of funds and defective sanctioning mechanisms, this lack of recovery is also attributed to 'lack of marketing facilities' (op.cit., pp. 63, 69, and 78)!

Party Political Power

In previous studies of the political activity of traders, they were found to behave in risk-averse ways by financing all political parties and by rarely being active in party politics (Harriss, 1981a; Harriss-White, 1993; and see Ch. 5 also). Sometimes systematically and sometimes opportunistically, political power is exerted through commercial lobbies which put pressure on all aspects of the policy process: on agenda formulation, on the making of laws and procedures, and crucially on state allocations and the implementation and practices of intervention. At the same time, power is developed and displayed locally in the domination of local institutions of culture and philanthropy by prominent merchants.

In 1990, Bardhaman district's market-shaping politics conformed to what had been found elsewhere. The political behaviour of the largest firms differed greatly from that of small firms. Cold store owners subscribed to all political parties and some individuals subscribed to every one of them. Among the merchant elite we encountered vanguard supporters of the Bharatiya Janata Party (BJP) as well as benefactors of the Left Front Government. Merchants active in party politics also tended to be office holders in local business ssociations, and in state-level institutions. Among the 60 respondents were the local leaders of all the major political parties. Not only was there a Co-operative Society president but also several officials of temple committees among the merchants who talked to us. Much financial support was given to temples, schools, and hospitals, on whose governing boards these merchants were well represented. Potato wholesalers, some of whom ran the price-fixing syndicate, also subscribed to parties but were not openly active politically. By contrast, 'the king of rice has friendly contacts with all political leaders', said one trader, referring to an influential miller operating out of a peri-urban site. Rice millers could also be found supporting all parties financially and one was a local BJP leader. Rice and oil millers were found to be Presidents of Town Trade Associations and of the local Lions Club.

In complete contrast, the elements of the commodity systems which were: a) small-scale and b) partly illegal avoided party politics and kept a low political profile, although there was greater voter support for the CPI (M) and Left Front Government among their ranks.

Some of the most economically powerful agents in these markets were politically opportunistic, while others were openly politically engaged and committed, more often in opposition to the Left Front Government than in support of it. Open opposition had costs (physical intimidation, being the focus of strikes), and these capitalists had made protective, pre-emptive investments in private security and in political contacts, with access to the police and the local administration. Local mercantile magnates were also active in business and commodity lobbies. The site of this type of politics is usually outside the locality, in Kolkata.[12]

We conclude that despite the mass politics of the Left Front Government, those who were locally economically powerful had developed ways of exercising political leverage too.

Conclusions

In two important respects, the markets for rice, potato, and mustard oil in Bardhaman district in 1990 resembled the market for rice in Birbhum district in 1982: first, in their similar economic structures and second, in their diversity, complexity, and idiosyncrasy.

Both market structures were polarized between a small number of firms controlling the marketed surplus, and a large number of petty firms which eked out an existence between the price margins created by the elite. In Bardhaman district, control over commercial assets, especially storage and credit, was highly concentrated. So too was control over information, not just about prices but also about supplies and contacts. In both districts too, the way in which this distribution of power was mapped onto the distribution of towns was idiosyncratic and particular.

In every aspect of market structure, complexity and diversity were to be found. The economic law which states that a single cost-minimizing (and welfare maximizing) technology always predominates was persistently flouted—in processing, storage, and transport. Firms were characterized by a great range of forms of organization and labour processes. Contracts for casual workers ranged from particularistic combinations of cash, kind, debt and open-ended obligations, to cash piece-rates for gangs. The activity combinations of firms also had

Institutional Diversity, Price Performance, and Power Relations

tendencies to uniqueness. Commodity flows were highly patterned, but differently in different places. Interest rates varied from zero to 12 per cent.

The co-existence of such varied forms of accumulation has to be explained in part by the regulative roles of non-market institutions. In this chapter, for instance, ethnicity, particularly Marwari ethnicity, is revealed as structuring the commanding heights of the commercial economy, but in different ways in different places. By contrast, gender relations effectively exclude women from all points in the market systems except casual labour.

These insights have been used to help account for price behaviour. The econometric analysis shows that all three commodities—rice (fine and coarse), potatoes, and mustard oil—manage to combine long-term price integration with short-term price inefficiency. The detail of this price behaviour cannot be explained away by invoking a general lack of information or lack of transport, as is conventionally done. The explanations have to be specific to place. Our explanations have focussed on particular structural factors: collusive oligopoly in the instance of potato, the co-existence of two separate sub-systems of markets in the case of coarse rice, and physical isolation and social segmentation in the case of rice and mustard oil.

Whether or not these particular explanations seem convincing, the reader of this chapter, and the two preceding ones, can hardly avoid being struck by the extreme simplifications involved in speaking, as so many policy documents do, of 'the firm', given the extraordinary diversity of firms that actually make up the commodity markets in both places—as if all of them will respond similarly to a given signal or incentive; or of 'contracts', as if most contracts were written and explicit, rather than verbal, and not full of hidden, more or less coercive, clauses; or of 'prices', as if the spot prices on which most official statistics are based were the prevalent kind of prices, instead of being exceptional. It is not surprising that policies written at this level of abstraction so often fail to produce the expected results.

Notes

1. Small amounts may be stored domestically for up to 3 months (Mitra and Sarkar, 2003).
2. The loading of cold stores is carried out in March and April and unloading proceeds from May onwards.
3. The gendered labour process is described later in this chapter.

4. Prices in this and the next chapter are those current in 1990. See the Table of Deflators and Inflators before the Preface for factors with which to compare across the time periods covered in this book.
5. For instance: discovering and threatening owners known to have broken the law unless their lorries hauled Food Department grain.
6. By contrast, South Indian traders studied over the years have been willing to speak of ways caste maps onto commercial capital (see Harriss-White, 1996).
7. Rice was hardly ever to be found retailed by Scheduled Caste traders in South India (ibid.).
8. It may be expected to supply itself beyond the point at which the marginal product would equal the return, but neither can be measured.
9. de Haan and Rogaly, 1996; Rogaly et al, 2002; Rogaly, 2003 , Rogaly and Rafique, 2003.
10. Larger firms were most likely to underestimate their assets; and smaller firms were under-represented in our field research.
11. No price data could be obtained for Memari where the costs of telecommunications averaged Rs. 300 per month for a trading oil mill.
12. In the case of rice mills, the state level associations are federated to an All-India apex organization which put lobbying pressure on the central government in New Delhi.

7 The Dynamics of Market Institutions and Market Politics in Bardhaman District in 1990

Similar to the second chapter on Birbhum in 1980–1 (chapter 5), this second chapter on Bardhaman in 1990 also looks at the dynamics of the commodity markets whose structures and price behaviour were described in Chapter 6—at how they changed, and what drove the changes. In Bardhaman, however, we also had a more specific policy focus: besides wanting to find out what institutional changes had taken place in the system of markets during the period of agrarian reforms, growth and diversification, and what had driven them, we also wanted to see what the Left Front Government would do to improve the system for the mass of producers. The overall conclusions of our research were focussed on this, and are reported in the two concluding sections of this chapter.

The first task, however, was to describe what institutional changes had occurred, and to explain them. There is no consensus in the existing literature about the causes of institutional change. The 'new institutionalists' explain it in terms of the market, stylized as prices and competition, which are seen as shaping and reshaping the system of incentives within which institutions are embedded (North, 1989; Hodgson, 2001). Theorists of institutional change in markets themselves, on the other hand, have privileged exogenous factors. One such factor is the technical characteristics of crops and marketing technology; another is changes in the technology and/or the level of production.[1]

But the operations of marketing analysed in the previous chapter clearly show that the technical characteristics of the crops did not prevent a variety of technologies of marketing and transformation either from developing or from co-existing in a persistent and stable fashion. The inherent perishability of potatoes, for example, has no essential implications for market structure. The polarized control over cold storage capacity that existed in Bardhaman was also not an inevitable result of the technology available. A variety of types of cooling systems and sizes of stores co-existed. In the rice markets, while parboiling started out as a domestic response to the perishability of paddy harvested during rainy seasons, it developed as an industrial process because of other nutritional and engineering advantages as well. In practice, a wide range of types of parboiling processes, and associated technologies and institutions can be observed.

Likewise, with respect to changes in agrarian structure and production in this region of India, the massively polarized and concentrated economic structures of agricultural markets described in Chapters 4 and 5 are associated only in part with the concentrated land distributions of the past, for they are also the result of the mercantile diaspora. So while the inter-locked contracts between intermediaries within the market system reflect similar practices imposed by traders on producers,[2] the economic 'power-points' are nonetheless controlled by the network of *Marwari* merchants whose wealth has been accumulated from trade and finance, often outside the region.

For analysing the relationships between changes in production and changes in the institutions of marketing, it is not possible to disentangle the influence of two types of agrarian change. One, tenurial reform, could be expected to lead to a reduction in the obligatory rent-in-kind component of the marketed surplus (because this would be lowered and stabilized by the new law), and secondly to an increase in on-farm consumption (due to a reduction in agrarian poverty). Both would reduce market supplies. On the other hand, technical change, assisted by production credit, was expected to lead to increases in production and the marketed surplus by freeing producers from tied contracts and by 'shifting production functions outwards'. In aggregate, as the data from Bardhaman district showed, this second effect prevailed; and there has been a marked increase in the production and marketed surplus of all major staples. What has been the impact of this change on the markets?

In the 1980s, growth in the marketed surplus was certainly accompanied by an explosion of petty trade. Three lines of explanation for the emergence of petty trade link it with changes in the relations and forces of production. One emphasizes transaction costs: when the marketed surplus is generated in the form of extremely small consignments (e.g., half a 60 kg sack), then a system of bulking is necessary. Such a system has emerged, and could really only emerge, under petty commodity arrangements where the labour costs of bulking do not take the wage form (and will not obey the laws of marginalist economics). The other two explanations are drawn from political economy. One stresses that petty trade is the outcome of the poverty-induced search for seasonal livelihoods by poor landless labourers and marginal peasants (Vaidyanathan, 1986; Chandrasekhar, 1993). The other (introduced earlier in chapters 1 and 6) relates the emergence of investment in petty trade to the decentralized agricultural accumulation process that has been energized by the Left Front Government's agrarian reforms—not only Operation Barga, but also rural credit, the minimum wage, and the 'total factor productivity effect' of those empowered by the decentralization and politicization of the local government. Together, these factors generated agricultural profits, which were used not only for consumption but also for investment—and not only in agriculture. All these explanations may have some validity; but field research confined to markets is unable to distinguish their respective weights.

The debates on the capacity of changes in agrarian structure to catalyze growth have ignored the roles of institutional change in agricultural markets. Over and above the sheer expansion of petty trade, two further aspects of such change are particularly easy to see in the case of rice. One is the increasing internal institutional intricacy—or what the anthropologist Clifford Geertz called the *involution*—of the sub-system centred on rice mills (Geertz, 1970). In defiance of the law, in Bardhaman district by 1990, rice mills were being supplied by a far greater diversity of intermediaries than in Birbhum in the early 1980s, and this was not a matter of regional variation because all the intermediaries interviewed in 1990 spoke of it as happening widely in West Bengal. The mills' legal monopoly over paddy trading had become obsolete. '*Mahajans*'—rich farmers and moneylenders—were using agricultural profits to lend in cash and in kind (fertilizer) before the harvest in order to scoop up paddy at harvest at prices 8–10 per cent below the prevailing ones, in turn in order to supply rice mills. The number of new itinerant traders was also expanding. They had no fixed costs and no wages to pay but did have their own funding. They tied their contracts with producers—in the way described for mahajans—and bulked consignments up to truckloads of paddy (10 tonnes) to supply a rice mill. Paddy agents, with whom these intermediaries were in competition for supplies, were meanwhile developing independent trading finance from savings from their commissions. Rice mills were also increasing the number of paddy agents to whom they gave loans in an effort to attach them.

The second type of institutional change is *evolutionary* (emerging from earlier forms) and occurred in both the formal (rice mill) and the informal (husking mill) sub-systems. Peasants with less than two acres of land, landless agricultural labourers, and economic migrants from East Bengal (some of whom had imported capital which was far from petty) had entered the paddy, paddy-rice, and rice trades. Many of the poorest were not independent traders, but either traded the supplies of mahajans or bulked on behalf of them as 'disguised proletarians', to whom the risks of price fluctuations were transferred. The English words 'labour' and 'sackman' referred to petty agents who, for a commission, transported a small set of sacks of parboiled paddy to husking mills by bicycle. They also transported rice to other petty agents in the rice markets. Apart from its dependence on money advances, the important feature of this process of evolution was the interpenetration of productive activity with trading.

Three other forces besides agricultural growth and decentralized agrarian accumulation of the 1980s can be seen to have affected the market system. One was the effect of accumulation in commerce itself. Profits made from paddy and rice trading were used by trading families to hive off new firms. Competition from new processing plants in distant regions where production had expanded threatened the older installed capacity in the oil markets of Bardhaman. And the influx, especially at cold store unloading times, of imported fresh potato from as far west as Punjab, as far south as Tamil Nadu, and as far north-east as Assam, also affected trends, levels of seasonal minima, and irregularities in prices, leading to the restructuring of exchange relations.

A second additional force was state regulation which shaped, often pre-emptively, the institutions of the market. State-subsidized finance, for example, had been instrumental in transforming total installed capacity in the cold stores we studied from 3,000 tonnes in 1960 to 75,700 tonnes in 1990, with a doubling of capacity between 1985 and 1990 alone.

The third force was the development of institutions of collective action for market regulation. These had significant effects. As markets evolve, certain institutional preconditions for competitive activity have to be met. If the state does not meet them, other forms of collective regulative authority move into the institutional vacuum. In the rest of this chapter, these three processes of institutional evolution are examined more closely.

The Accumulation Dynamic

Appendix 7.1 summarizes the business histories of the firms studied. The origins of starting capital are listed on the left, and destinations of trading profits on the right. The size of starting capital is set on the horizontal logarithmic scale left of the central time column, and an estimate of present value is to the right. Potato wholesale firms are distinguished from cold stores, and husking mills from rice mills. The omission in our study of the smallest trade, and the use of current rather than real prices, introduces some distortion in these diagrams.

Origins of Capital

Our sampling fractions are unknown and this is likely to be especially distorting for petty trade, entry into which had accelerated during the 1980s, where in any case our samples were smallest. Twenty per cent of the firms studied had set up between 1985 and 1990, and 55 per cent had started after 1975. This left a quarter of the firms—and a majority of the largest firms—which were long established. This was especially true in rice milling, where nearly half of all the firms were set up during an early phase of investment in what is now called the 'rural non-farm economy' during the pre-Green Revolution period of IAAP/IADP planning, between 1958 and 1966.

With respect to cold storage, the state has always been a key source of the large amounts of capital required. In potato wholesaling, the principal sources of capital were agricultural rents, profits, and agricultural trade itself. In oil, trading capital came from the profits of agricultural trade, and this was also crucial for the older rice and husking mills. The new rice mills relied on state finance and Marwari banking finance, and the newer husking mills used agricultural profits. Small-scale grain trading drew its initial capital from a wide variety of sources, much of it borrowed. Employment in trade, profits from trade itself, and agricultural profits were also significant sources of starting capital.

Estimates of net returns were supplied by a number of traders and are assembled in Table 7.1. They show a certain amount of clustering and an unambiguous amount of concentration. Small-scale traders using family labour netted on an average under Rs 20,000 per year,[3] while husking mills, rice wholesalers, and oil millers got net returns of between Rs. 40,000 and 95,000. Finally, rice millers, potato wholesalers, and cold store owners averaged over Rs 2.5 lakhs.[4]

Table 7.1: Approximate/Indicative Net Profits (Rs per quintal)

	Potato Cold Store	Potato Wholesale	Oil Seed Agents	Oil Mill	Custom Mill	Oil Agents	Paddy Agents	Rice Mill	Husking Mill	Rice Agent	Rice Wholesale	Rice Retail	Kutali
Margin net of cash costs\q	3-7	3-8	11	25-50 (seed max=100)	5 (seed)	10 (oil)	1-4 (paddy)	3-6 (paddy excl bran)	2.5-10 (paddy)	4-6	5-20	4-10	8-25 max=60 (paddy)
Potential net income from estd average	450,000	825,000		41,000			37,500	250,000 (min)	50,000		93,750	21,000	16,500
Output (tonnes)	(9,000)	(15,000)		(109)			(1250)	(5500)	(800)		(1250)	(300)	(10)

Note: q = quintal
Source: Data from 1990 survey.

The Dynamics of Market Institutions and Market Politics   191

Rates of Profit, Growth and Investment

The massive increases in the value of older firms (Appendix 7.1) reflect the ploughing-back of profit into commercial expansion. The owners of most of the older firms explained that they used trading profits to expand and diversify their investment portfolios, a process which concentrated, differentiated, and stratified commercial capital. Only two out of 17 petty grain trading firms had a present value in 1990 in excess of Rs 80,000, and neither of these exceeded Rs 2 lakhs. Nor did any husking mills. By contrast the largest coldstores, oil and rice mills had average present values of Rs 1-3 crores.

The investment portfolios of cold stores firms were massive and diverse, particularly in the case of firms established before 1970. The owners of these firms had broken the barriers to non-agricultural investment, which has proved very difficult elsewhere in India.[5] They set up in other industries and industrial-commercial activities, as well as investing in rural and urban land and real estate. Potato wholesaling was not in the same league. From the mustard oil market, there had emerged one property tycoon. Otherwise the investments of oil traders went into agro-commerce and other kinds of agro-processing—horizontal and diagonal linkages rather than vertical ones. The owners of rice mills had portfolios similar to those of cold store owners, though with relatively fewer cases of industrial investment and relatively more in transport. Husking millers had invested in land and property. Smaller scale grain-trading firms ploughed profits back into the grain trade.

The eight biggest commercial firms declared control over the following assets, over and above the assets of the firms included in our study:

15 large rice mills
12 cold stores
2 oil mills
13 wholesale businesses
8 non-agricultural industries (including nails and screws, cardboard boxes,etc)
12 lorries
a large amount of urban property and storage space
at least 140 acres of land, some sharecropped out but mostly owner-occupied and farmed using wage labour (some also on contract to cold stores and rice mills).

We did not ask for data on finance, or for expenditures on education, dowries or (foreign) travel, but would expect these also to have been significant. Even in their absence, these eight firms and their money advances remind one of Lenin's expression, 'masters of the countryside'.

Losses and Risk

Given that contracts were mostly verbal and not easily legally validated, that produce underwent multiple transfers of ownership (not always face-to-face), and that information asymmetry and opportunism were commonplace, it is hardly surprising that almost every firm had experienced losses and several faced temporary bankruptcy. The causes of 83 episodes of loss in marketing, volunteered somewhat haphazardly in the course of our interviews, have been tabulated (Table 7.2).

It is indeed the case that the operation of 'the market' led to losses. Cold stores all declared large losses: for example, Rs 4 lakhs lost on 60 truckloads of potatoes detained in Assam; Rs 21 lakhs on non-repayment of credit; and Rs 125 lakhs on speculation.[6] Default on payment was also commonly mentioned as a cause of loss, but so were technical failure (for instance generator breakdown or the collapse of a cold store) and environmental hazards. Rice milling was vulnerable to failed speculation, defaults on credit and payment, theft, and opportunistic adulteration (which was surprisingly commodified),[7] but also to rain and flood. The state was another major source of loss to unlicensed firms, by virtue of swinging summary fines imposed by vigilance forces, and fickle electricity supply.

The State Regulatory Agenda
The Spirit and Letter of the Law

In terms of agenda and intention, and in procedure and law, the staple food markets are quite extensively regulated. The state's regulative aspirations can be inferred from its parametric laws and institutions, and can be compared with what happens in practice. We saw in chapter 5 that the legal framework had been in place (though continually altered) since long before the Left Front Government came to power. The intention was to set severe curbs on private accumulation through trade and markets; to define the scope of technology; to tax agricultural trade; and to endow the state with strong powers of enforcement. With respect to potatoes, the West Bengal Cold Storage (Licensing and Regulation) Act and Rules enacted in 1966–7 set out rules for the regulation of licences, technical standards, and the reservation of space by various categories of landowners. Rents were fixed by law, as was

Table 7.2: Causes of Loss (% of Cases Reported for Each Type of Trade)

	Poor Judgement on Price Expectations	Default on Contract	Technical Failure	Theft	Rain/ Flood	Adulteration/ vermin/ pests	Damage from Load Shedding	Civil Unrest	Govt Fines
Potato CS and Wh	26	21	21	10	–	16	–	11	–
Oil Mills	23	41	–	4	9	14	9	–	–
Rice Mills	18	18	–	9	27	27	–	–	–
Paddy Agent	–	33	–	–	33	33	–	–	–
Husking	–	14	–	–	–	–	28	–	57
Paddy Rice Processing	–	14	–	14	28	–	–	–	42
Petty wh/ret/ca	–	21	–	14	7	–	–	–	57

Source: Data from 1990 survey.

the timing of the cold storage season. Limits were put on the ownership of potatoes by cold store owners, on their finance of production, and on their trading on own account. Potato wholesalers were regulated through licensing. Oil and rice mills were regulated through licensing and security deposits, through the specification of technical standards and through storage restrictions. Both oil and rice trading were subject to inspection by the Commercial Taxes Department. Oil was taxed at two per cent while the tax on rice had been halved to one per cent.

Rice milling was also heavily regulated both parametrically and through state participation. As we saw in chapters 1 and 5, under the Rice Control and Levy Order of 1960, a prescribed proportion of traded rice (50 per cent in 1990) had to be sold to a state trading corporation at administered prices which were always below prices on the open market. Paddy agents were regulated by licence and were attached to specific rice mills. Rice wholesalers were also regulated by licence and had protected access to the un-procured residual output of rice mills. Rice retailers were regulated, under the Food Control Order of 1967, by licence and by restrictions on the volume of operation (75 kg per day) and storage quantities (10 quintals). Husking mills were regulated by licence, conditions for which involved stipulated technology and a legal power supply.

Under the Regulated Markets Act (which covers the first post-harvest transactions between producers and traders), requirements are laid down for investment in physical infrastructure for marketing, for standardised cost-reducing procedures for transactions (weights and measures, open auctions, and unlagged payments), for the democratic and participatory management of market-places. In return, a single fee charged on the first post-harvest transaction replaces what used to be a series of local cesses and arbitrary deductions. The fee income then finances the management of 'regulated agricultural marketing'. This institutional formula, which—decentralised, democratic and participatory—sounds so fashionable, was in fact imposed by the British on Indian provinces from the 1930s, based on a prototype (which in fact had been unsuccessful) in London's Smithfield meat market (Harriss-White, 1995).

Trading and processing co-operatives were also introduced in order to regulate private trade by offering competition. They were financed by the West Bengal Co-operative Federation, the West Bengal Finance Corporation, the World Bank, and EU-assisted National Co-operative Development Corporation. They were intended to provide distributive services to local village co-operatives, and to service state-trading institutions at fixed prices and rates.

State Regulation in Practice

How did state regulation work in practice? The points where practice departed from the letter and spirit of the law reveal power relations between the regulative bureaucracy and agro-commercial capital. With respect to potato marketing, certain aspects of its regulation were implemented as laid down in law. The dates of closing and opening cold stores were randomly checked, as were inventory, temperatures, and the physical conditions of the potatoes. But other aspects of the regulatory framework were creatively reinterpreted out of all recognition. State-decreed rental levels in stores had evolved into a market in which prices fluctuated. State-administered labour laws fixing minimum wages were flouted by using non-local migrant labour on contract. Official rules about the allocation of cold store space to various categories of farmers, traders, and owners not only changed regularly, but also underwent further transformations through the development of active markets in storage space, and through the neglect of the rules stipulating the minimum and maximum size of consignments.

Two regulatory loopholes which we touched on earlier in chapter 6 also enabled cold store owners to engage in trade. First, although owners were constrained from trading on their own account, other members of their joint families were not. The consignment certificate or 'bond', which acted as collateral for state-regulated credit, was transferable and farmers were legally allowed to sell consignments while their potatoes were in store. The transfer of ownership of potatoes to cold store owners who had access to the formal sector credit had thus become common practice. Second, cold store owners were legally required to remove rotting potatoes within 48 hours of having notified their owners, and any payment received from the disposal of unsafe potatoes was subsequently to be remitted to them. 'Rotting' was widely alleged to be faked by cold store owners and 'maximized' at times of maximum intra-seasonal prices. Remittances were delayed, and then often made at current prices if these were lower than those at which the 'rotting' potatoes had actually been sold.

Excess capacity in the sector as a whole had resulted from investment decisions by a variety of funding agents authorized by the state, but in conditions of incomplete information, so that the result was unplanned. Together with the high break-even capacity levels already mentioned, this structural over-capacity intensifed the incentives for cold store owners to ignore the disciplining aspects of the regulative law.

Rice mills operated under a state-protected monopoly, the idea being that in return the state could transfer to the private sector the transactions costs involved in bulking the supplies needed for the public distribution system. As explained in chapter 5, the mills were able to inflate the residual open market prices by sums that compensated them for their actual losses on rice sold to the state. But the explosion of the subsystem of petty trade in the 1980s, which was exempt from procurement because it was illegal, meant that this compensating price hoist had been undercut and was increasingly hard to make. In the late 1980s, the state-trading agency made a response to the collective representation of rice millers, a response which was appropriate to the threat to rice mill profits, but which was nevertheless illegal. Proportional levies were commuted to fixed quotas, negotiated verbally with each mill on the basis of its drying yard capacity, and based on the assumption of only 15-20 days of operation per month. In 1990, the lifting of levy rice was also being restricted to the period October to April. This change reduced supervision, information, and transaction costs for both the millers and the agents of the state. It enabled them to get procurement back on the targeted track (increasing from 29,000 tonnes in 1987–8 to 63,200 tonnes in 1989–90 (Evidence from the District Supply Office, Bardhaman, 1990). But the arrangement also intensified the incentive for rice mills to purchase stock immediately post-harvest at the lowest prices, so as to minimize the uncompensated losses on procurement. An incentive had also been created to ignore both quantitative and time-based restrictions on stock. The behaviour of off-season prices, and the logistics of off-season paddy supply (which can be controlled by millers), and of off-season electricity supply (which cannot), became crucial to maintaining profitability.

At another point in the system, the legal monopoly of paddy traders and their stipulated attachment to specific mills had broken down. Paddy agents had accumulated sufficient capital of their own to trade on their own account and their attachment could no longer be enforced by either the mills or the state. Elsewhere, a certain amount of further pre-emptive structuring could be observed. The operation of commercial tax checkposts, which in the late 1970s did not prevent paddy trade across district and state borders, was more effectively enforced by 1990, so that traders lost more in bribes than they gained from inter-regional price differences. This restriction on the movement of rice encouraged local processing.

The rise of small-scale commercial activity was not only a response of petty accumulation resulting from land reforms, technical change and other state policies for production: it was also a response to the perpetuation by the state of the wide distributive margins maintained by the large-scale circuit in the rice markets. It was, besides, a response to state-administered constraints on regional trade flows provoked by a procurement system which effectively acted as a tax and set up incentives for petty traders to smuggle. If legally-regulated market circuits generated informal petty trade, what happened to this and other kinds of petty trade in markets outside the scope of legal regulation?

Small-scale paddy/rice processors are known as 'Kutalis'. ('We are illegal and invisible to everyone except to the police", said one of them.) In 1990, Kutalis were unlicensed. They rented unlicensed husking mills to mill the paddy that they had parboiled and dried, using domestic labour. In some locations, Kutalis encroached onto wetland to construct drying floors. Turning an official blind eye to this activity had two major consequences. One was to make this sub-system comprehensively vulnerable to the coercive wing of the state, perpetuating institutionalized bribery and harassment. The other was that it remained ineligible for state-subsidized credit, and had to depend on informal credit markets that often operated under local, socially stratified monopolistic conditions at rates of interest exceeding 10 per cent per month. Only two formal-sector trading loans were reported from the field research into this subsystem. Both were IRDP loans obtained on false pretences by Kutalis who were members of the CPI(M).

Much the same sort of relations characterized petty rice traders, (who could sell rice wholesale or retail, or work on commission for others). In one rice market, only one wholesale licence had been issued. Groups of traders coalesced around this licence which rotated among them as necessary—that is, to fend off harassment by police and agents of the FCI and Food Department Inspectorate. Local CPI(M) politicians mediated the institutionalized extortion from which this rather desperate practice arose.

The Electricity Board regulated the power supply to husking mills by enforcing a minimum spacing of two kms between them. In the

1982 study in Birbhum, we saw that this penalty to late entrants was evaded by using diesel engines and/or by poaching electricity supplied for a less stringently regulated purpose (e.g., flour or spice milling). Husking mill licences were also conditional upon the technology used, and the law stipulated a sheller technology inappropriate for local factor endowments and for the local material culture of rice (see Appendix 4.1). For parboiled rice, the prescribed sheller technology was not superior to the huller in engineering terms. At the levels of gross output typical of a husking mill, the capital, fixed, and variable costs of a sheller were greater. It also displaced labour. Moreover, the by-products of husking were not raw materials for agro-industries, as conceived in the law, but instead were used in domestic productive activity as fuel (husk), binding material in construction (husk), cattle fodder (husk and bran), fertilizer (burnt husk) and payments in kind to labour (broken rice). The use of sheller technology for husking mills was unenforceable.

The illegal nature of the huller technology actually used stemmed from a tension between the West Bengal and central governments. While agriculture is a state responsibility, post-harvest processing is labelled as 'food', and food administration is the central government's responsibility. The brief attempt in 1967 by the Congress Party's Chief Minister in West Bengal, S.S. Ray, to protect local husking mills by issuing licences, was actually quashed by the Supreme Court. Ever since 1977, the Left Front Government had responded to this impossible situation by turning a blind eye towards husking mills, for instance, refusing even to attempt to levy commercial taxes on their operations. But as with the other unregulated elements in the markets for rice, this permitted and encouraged institutionalized bribery and harassment.

In 1982, our research in Birbhum district led us to predict that the development of the petty trading sub-system would be resisted by the rice mills, in alliance with the state, and indeed in Bardhaman district in 1990, it was alleged that rice mills were paying vigilance forces to harass illegal rice traders, who were technically ineligible for vigilance if operating without fixed premises, while the state allowed the storage laws for rice to be evaded by rice millers. Yet the resistance of the rice mills had been compromised not only by the informal accommodation with the state described above, but also because increases in production and the rapid rise in the gross marketed surplus had reduced the threat to mill supplies. The resistance of the state was reduced by the FCI's growing imports of rice from Punjab.

Nonetheless, as local production gathered pace, rice distributed in Bardhaman district under statutory and modified rationing declined from 66,500 tonnes in 1986–7 to 41,800 in 1989-90.[8] The Left Front Government appeared to be ready to accept the crucial role of illegal petty trade in provisioning provincial towns. This had an impact on trade flows, which underscored the lack of coherence in the increasingly informalized state regulations. For example, the increasing provisioning of Kolkata with rice from Punjab led to the diversion of grain flows from Katwa (in our study area) to north Bengal. Yet, petty trade exports out of Katwa were also constrained by the administrative barriers of check-posts monitoring commercial taxation. So, as a result of local interpretations of national and state regulation, and local accommodations between the state and the rice millers, Katwa tended to be glutted with rice, and yet its prices were un-integrated with those of regional rice markets.[9]

Oil mills were quite regularly scrutinized by the state because of the incentives to adulterate. The Food Department checked inventory, and controlled the supply of substitutes for mustard. Oil millers themselves had an interest in informing the Health Department if they found adulterated supplies in local markets, and did so. But another piece of disciplining regulation—a High Court Order requiring the technological upgrading of rotary mills—had been completely ignored.

As with other aspects of law, the Regulated Markets Act was operating according to neither its letter nor its spirit. In the two regulated markets in the places we studied, (UCO Bank, 1990) attempts were made to levy fees, but not on a percentage basis—'*ad valorem*', as the law requires—but *ad hoc*. Fees in one grain market varied from Rs 50 to Rs 250 per month and one per cent of the value of a load was extorted from all rice trucks passing through local check-posts. Price information was being collected but was not published as it ought to have been. There were no elections to governing committees (in one market, the committee consisted of MLAs and Food Department personnel), so committees were not democratic and participative as envisaged in the law. There was no inspection of weights and measures, no competitive bidding, and no open auction; there were no regulated payments by buyers to sellers and no dispute resolution (though there were disputes). 'All they do is extort an illegal fee and this is not the first [post-harvest] transaction!' (complained one rice 'retailer'). Yet with respect to commercial taxes, comminutions of the tax on oil from two per cent to one per cent, and on rice from one per cent to 0.5

per cent, were widely reported to have been negotiated between District Supply Officials and locally powerful trade association representatives.

Lastly co-operatives. These were not labour-managed firms, but state-bureaucratically managed. We encountered two marketing co-operatives which are offered here as case studies and object lessons. The first was a rice milling and marketing co-operative, which had ceased operations in 1988. The scale of operation required by modern rubber roll sheller technology was incompatible with the supply conditions in which it was forced to function. Its scale, capitalization and thus high break-even levels of capacity utilization needed higher total transport costs for raw materials and finished product than smaller-scale decentralized mills would have required. It worked to different regulations from those governing private trade. In particular it could only be supplied with paddy by village co-operatives and, as a result of their malfunctioning, supply was seriously inadequate.

The second co-operative was a potato cold store, established in 1984. It had technological problems of a different sort. By stipulation, it was constructed with an obsolescent defuser cooling system (working from the bottom up). Other things being equal, this was 150 per cent more costly than the bunker (top town) system widely adopted in the private sector, but the co-operative funding agency, NCDC, had been slow to sanction new technology for potato storage (while being quick to sanction inappropriate new technology for rice milling) (Harriss, 1976). As a result, the capacity utilization of the co-operative cold store was 30 per cent, while the break-even point was 80 per cent. Reasons for its mediocre performance also included a maintenance service provided by outside contract rather than by staff permanently on site (as happened in private firms). Sources of supply were restricted to 21 local co-operatives and to other co-operative members, which proved seriously inadequate, since co-operative members were not obliged to sell to a co-operative cold store. In practice, many were constrained to use their creditors' private cold stores.

The law also prevented the co-operative from trading on its own account, either to secure supplies by advance contracts, to store the potatoes of private traders, or to import at long distance. The penalties for co-operative employees for breaches of the law were punitive and staff did not have skills or institutional access to resources to transgress and trade privately. Consignments at the legal minimum size could not be refused, which increased the co-operative's transaction costs compared with those of private traders, and concessions on state-fixed rental prices could not be offered. Fixed transport rates had to be adhered to. Whereas private cold store owners bought up stored potatoes outright, co-operatives were restricted to providing credit on the basis of producers' receipts. External scrutiny of space reservations, temperature, and quality was systematic and regular rather than random and occasional, as with the private firms. It was alleged (by private traders as well as the co-operative management) that market prices could be manipulated by the powerful local syndicate of private traders in such a way that they were low when the co-operative cold store unloaded its stock onto local markets and then were raised afterwards. Under all these circumstances, it is perhaps not very surprising that management decision-making was also slower in this co-operative than in local private enterprises; a fact which was said to account for the serious delays in the supply of essential inputs such as sacks.

State regulation through co-operatives thus failed to discipline commercial capital in this region, while the failure of co-operatives was a cost to the state. The reasons for the latters' failure explain many of the breaches of regulative law by private trade. Inappropriate technologies represented defective decisions by funding agencies. More systematic vigilance by the State on state-marketing institutions than on private ones created variations in compliance which favoured the nexus of interests between the state and private trade from which these co-operatives seemed to be excluded. Further, private trade was perfectly capable of collusively sabotaging the operation of a co-operative. As a result, one co-operative manager expostulated: 'We were set up to eliminate the middleman, but the middleman eliminates us!'

To sum up: Regulation in practice is radically different from what the letter and spirit of the law implies. The state had most effective disciplinary power where the points of contact were few and concentrated (as with oil and potato) and with respect to public events rather than private scrutiny. Even for oil and potato, the details of operations and the social relations of marketing could not be regulated by the state. Where the system of markets was decentralized, as with rice, the state's parametric regulation was more weakly enforced. And where regulative law proposes to discipline the first and most decentralized transaction between traders and farmers (the first post-harvest exchange), it was not enforced at all. Regulative law was interpreted idiosyncratically by local administrations in a variety of rules which may well not have been legally binding. Market behaviour was moulded to some extent (often pre-emptively) by these local rules, and by the threat of sanctions, but it frequently flouted even these. It was not only the local agrarian structure that shaped the implementation of disciplinary law; the structure and the power relations of the local system of markets did so too. Laws may have important symbolic functions indicating desirable directions for social change. But in 1990 our field research showed that these laws were the basis of a diffused appropriation of bureaucratic and market rents, putting unavoidably in question the real intentions behind the policy agendas and procedures for the regulation of commercial capital by the Left Front Government and the central government.

Collective Action and the Social Regulation of Markets

While it is the state that is supposed to set the parameters of market order, Table 7.3 shows the institutional means whereby the potato, rice and oil markets were actually regulated.

The state played a negligible role in 'actually existing' market regulations. The Health Department regulated the adulteration of oil; local government severely rationed licences, and political institutions of the local government were drawn in to resolve disputes on transfers of property rights in cold stores. For the rest it can be seen that a multitude of institutions were involved. The system of social regulation was itself underdeveloped. Norms for marketing were not standardized—even in 1990 weights and measures and contractual forms could not be assumed. Conditions for marketing were not very secure—in terms either of property rights or moral hazard. Crime detection rarely involved the police but was carried out by a variety of civil society institutions which enjoyed—haphazardly and not legally—coercive powers and the authority to enforce penalties. The institutions of social regulation were either privately organized (where costly environmental externalities could be internalized—as with security, public hygiene, and crime detection) or institutionalized through collective action (for physical security and for contract observance, for example).

Appendix 7.2 also provides details of 27 institutions of civil society which had evolved rapidly around markets in the 1980s. They were established for three main reasons: to curb opportunistic behaviour by commercial firms and to create order in markets, to respond to organized labour (here the party political process that has generated competitive unionization had a multiplier effect on the organization

Table 7.3: Institutions for the Regulation of the System of Markets

	Cold Stores	Potato Wh	Oil Mills	Rice Mills	Husking Mills	P/P–R/R Trades
Licence	Local government	Local government	Local government	Local government/ FCI	Local government but rationed; many unlicensed	Local government but rationed; group membership/ unlicensed
Security	Physical fortification and own private security force	Market architecture organised by landlord/own paid labourers/ local collective action	Own private force/local collective action	Own private force	Local collective action	Market architecture local collective action
Public Hygiene	Privately paid sweepers	Market landlord/ ad hoc and occasional	Privately paid sweepers	Privately paid sweepers	Private sweepers/ farmers and traders	None
Weight and Measures	Kgs but sack-weight varies between 50–60 kgs	Calibrated by largest trader in local syndicate	—	Maunds and seers still used by some farmers	—	If at all by Bazaar committee

(contd.)

Table 7.3 (contd.)

Contract adherence/ dispute resolution	Political institutions of BDO/ syndicate	BDO/Bazaar committee/ regulated market committee/ officer/trade association/ mutual agreement	Bazaar management committee/ Brokers/ mutual agreement/ trade association	Largest trader in association/ mutual agreement	Mutual agreement	Bazaar committee/ town business association
Crime common type	Credit embezzlement	Credit default/ pilferage in transit	Adulteration/ repayment	Credit and repayment default	Theft of stored rice	Default on payment
Detection and punishment	Private agents	Trade association	Collective action/bazaar committee/ Health department	Private agents	–	Trade association

Source: Data from 1990 survey.

of commercial capital), and to relate to institutions inside the state, either for purposes of defence against regulation (e.g., rate-fixing, negotiations with enforcement agencies) or to compensate for inadequacies of regulation (e.g., physical security and the public health environment).

Their scope rapidly expanded and by 1990 it included:

- Reaping scale economies (as with the collective organization, by subscription, of security, and cleaning, sweeping and waste disposal). Political scale economies were reaped by groups over a certain size threshold in their representation to the state about issues such as regulation, about policy change, and in order to institutionalize 'rents'. ("We have a good hold on government", said the leader of one trade association).
- Collusive activity such as price and rate fixing, as in the case of the potato association (which appeared to be a 'lobby' but acted in practice as a collusive oligopoly), rice retailing and rice milling.
- Entry restriction, permitting competitive oligopolies (rice retailing and paddy agencies).
- Risk-spreading (e.g., interest-free group credit or group insurance for accident, calamity, loss, fraud or legal expenses.
- The reduction of transaction costs. This is an important function of these collectives. It took a number of forms. Information was diffused within the group. Some private regulation of transactions took place, for example, the calibration of weights and measures. Property rights were clarified and mechanisms for disputes over contracts were collectively enforced, with sanctions imposed on deviant behaviour. Groups were also developing mechanisms of protection against opportunistic behaviour and bad risks. The most obvious of these restricted entry to associations by using as selection criteria attributes about which information was cheap, such as being licensed. Uncertainty on related or derived markets was reduced by the collective negotiation of advantageous set rates (maxima for labour and transport; minima for processing rates), wherever possible fixing prices with other collective institutions. Conflicts of interest were institutionalized. These commercial relations were replacing old norms, often based on caste and 'faith', with new ones based on contract and commercial reputation.

- Lastly, these institutions of collective action were also social expressions of solidarity and, in defining themselves, also defined those who were excluded. This process of forming class-fractions was not only done through economic practice and regulation, and through political representation, but also through philanthropy, the provision of charitable relief, and other expressions of piety, and through social celebration.

The pathologies of state regulation also meant that 'groups of groups'—hierarchies of civil-cum-market society organizations—were emerging to reap political economies of scale. We observed a variety of institutions of collective action. They performed several roles, and these roles changed over time (for example, a group starting out to protect against theft evolved into one protecting against entry). The groups themselves were not all lawful, nor did their norms follow those stipulated by law. Collective institutions which failed did so for reasons of adverse selection (as when the costs of incorporating illegal husking mills destroyed trade associations) or because of opportunistic behaviour and co-variate risk (which destroyed one traders' credit association). But in the absence of strong enforceable state regulations, these groups were the institutions through which essential preconditions for the development of markets were created. They simultaneously restricted entry to markets and facilitated collusive behaviour, including with respect to labour.

Elsewhere in India we have found that these commercial 'guilds' deal with labour in one of two main ways. One is corporatist. Labour is formally involved in the membership only for their interests to be neutered; the labour sociologst Michael Burawoy has called this the 'enforcement of consent' (Burawoy, 1984). The other is exclusive. Labour is not permitted to join and is controlled through the sabotage of attempts to organize or negotiate (Basile and Harriss-White, 2000). Trade associations are able to act in this second way because agro-commercial labour is politically fragmented. Associations or guilds have been regarded as a fetter on the emergence and mobility of capital. But here, in the absence of enforceable state regulation, these organizations emerge with capitalism in order to stabilize and facilitate accumulation.

The state, then, must reckon with the existence of such groups when implementing reforms to regulatory policy. It was only the unlicensed and illegal components of these markets (most in need of collective action) which were unable to organize themselves (paddy/rice processors; illegal labour contractors, unlicensed husking millers etc.). They said, 'We are always in fear and cannot group'.

Conclusions 1: Problems for Policy

The three drivers of institutional change in markets—the dynamics of commercial accumulation, which made the system of markets ever more institutionally complex, the regulative activity of the state, which could discipline markets only in ways which aided and abetted concentration, and the development of collective action by merchants, which created market order at the cost of being arbitrary and exclusive—all have implications for the policy process.

As we noted at the beginning of this chapter, a practical question motivating the 1990 field research was to see if policies could be identified which might improve the operation of markets in which the mass of agricultural producers sell their crops. What became clear was that the system of food markets was instituted and regulated in complex ways and that the state was not necessarily the strongest party involved. To address the practical question about policy, instead of concluding with a conventional list of 'implications for policy' (in which 'policy' is no more than a set of desiderata, because the policy process has not actually been addressed), a list of claims was developed from the histories traders gave us of their engagement with the state. This list clearly demonstrates the unavoidable conflicts of interest at work inside commodity systems, conflicts which were not well mediated by existing policy:

- Potato cold store owners were operating under conditions of structural overcapacity, facing local stagnation of demand together with increases in supply from other regions of India. They pushed for mechanisms to increase demand (state-financed Research & Development to develop alternative uses for potatoes, rural distribution networks, and the liberalization of the international export trade in potatoes, which in 1990 was restricted to the co-operative sector).
- Co-operative cold stores needed to operate under the same rules and regulations as private cold stores.
- Potato wholesalers complained about the inadequacies of contract enforcement, and those excluded from the price-fixing ring complained about that.

- Rice millers resented the illegal competition from unlicensed trade and the squeeze on prices and profits that resulted from it.
- Millers also complained about the supply of electricity. ('Earlier the vigilance squads limited our use of electricity. Now because of load shedding, vigilance officers dare not show their faces here'.)
- The big merchant-processors faced challenges from labour unions (claims for wage rises, threats of withdrawal of labour) and wished to see union power reduced.
- In Katwa, the poor physical and telecom infrastructure was complained about because it restricted—and increased the costs of—information flows.
- The problems of oil millers covered almost every aspect of their operations, including insecurities of contract enforcement (adulteration), physical security (theft), and uncertainty on other related markets (spare parts, electricity, labour, and credit).
- Components of the commodity systems operating on a smaller scale had overlapping and different interests in policy reforms. Husking millers were hampered by licensing policy and consequent state harassment, and by two aspects of electricity supply: cuts and voltage fluctuations, both of which damaged machinery. Small paddy, paddy-rice, and rice traders wanted reforms in licensing, and reforms to their congested and filthy market sites. ('Look at the rats here!' exclaimed one). They lacked access to formal credit institutions. They wanted change to a credit policy which (whether by intention or neglect) forced them to borrow on private money 'markets'. As a result of the higher interest charges this implied, many small intermediaries were trapped in petty production, unable to employ wage labour ('The strain on my wife and children is very bad') and unable to reduce the seasonality of their operations by means of storage ('I cannot trade in the rainy season when it is impossible to travel').

There is also a set of policy-related aspects of markets which are not problematic because they had been solved using both 'voice' and 'exit' tactics. Potato cold-store owners did not complain about electricity, having their own generators, or about labour, having their own gangs on contract. Larger rice millers did not complain about defaults on payment or contract enforcement, having their own forces of intimidation, nor were many exercized about competition from the petty subsystem (because of the continual increase in production). Small traders did not complain about competition, even though the structural conditions for competition were intensifying continually in this subsystem. This was because some had created effective (coercive) institutions of protection and restriction. In other cases, traders conceived of marketing as a mechanism of social solidarity and security for the sharing of seasonal livelihoods among the poor.

Both large and small firms would benefit from state provisions of physical infrastructure and telecommunications, and from state enforcement of some of the institutional pre-conditions for market exchange. These include physical and contractual security and public hygiene. In 1990, far from being public goods, these were private, excludable and rivalrous. While powerful firms had an interest in de-regulated markets, small firms needed a state-regulated commercial environment and more inclusive access to credit. But the process of distributional politics by which their needs might be met was deliberately stunted by other interests in market politics.

Conclusions 2: The Role of the Left Front Government

For the longest-running democratically-elected communist government in the world, it is nothing short of astonishing that the West Bengal state regulated agricultural markets less coherently than most other states of India. The Left Front Government's political programme emphasized livelihood creation for its mass base (Ramachandran, 1997). It had energized petty trade through its project of agrarian reforms. Yet the Left Front Government had also set up, enforced—and refrained from reforming—considerable blocks to accumulation in petty trade. In Bardhaman district, these included:

- rationing licences to petty traders. This practice had two important effects. It put petty traders at the mercy of the state's coercive wing and it made them ineligible for formal credit and so also fed them to private money 'markets';
- the continual protection of local commercial magnates. This was carried out through legal regulative arrangements (though these were increasingly contested by smaller firms such as paddy agents, and were broken and by-passed by cold store owners and rice millers, the FCI and the Food Administration), and through subsidized formal sector credit, both for investments and for working capital.

With respect to trade finance, the Left Front Government—like the credit literature in general—has been concerned with credit for production. It did not ignore credit for trade, in fact it strictly prohibited lending for such purposes—yet it could not prevent state-regulated banks from financing the apex of rural commercial capital. It acknowledged 'lack of marketing facilities' as a constraint on demand for credit, while not acknowledging lack of credit as a constraint on marketing facilities. As a result, while the commercial elite was able to use credit to seek rents, small traders were starved of credit and/or stifled by interlocked trade contracts.

Among petty traders, only three formal sector loans were reported. They averaged Rs 3,000, were obtained on false pretences, and used for investment in trade. By contrast, the eight largest firms in the set studied declared—and we may assume they erred on the side of underestimation—investment borrowing from the West Bengal Finance Corporation, and from Nationalised and Co-operative Banks, of an average of Rs 88.9 lakhs per firm. The average borrowing of each of them was equal to 2,500 IRDP loans for the alleviation of poverty. The eight biggest firms declared borrowings equal to IRDP loans for 20,000 households below the poverty line. These financial transactions occurred outside the local political arena and were not visible from there.

By 1990, the Left Front Government was relying increasingly on an army of relatively petty traders which had emerged from its voting stronghold and was being locked into relations of trading and finance, and of state and non-state regulations, which were intrinsically costly for these traders and, arguably, for society as a whole. The Left Front Government's own interventions, designed to streamline state procurement of food for Calcutta and the coal belt, were in part responsible for this proliferation. Movement restrictions perpetuated the wide price margins that enabled livelihoods to be wrested from paddy-rice processing and small-scale trade. In other ways, petty accumulation was encouraged simply by turning a blind eye or selectively enforcing regulative law.

Over the 1980s, small-scale trade became significant in the distribution of staple food to provincial towns and cities, as well as their rural environs which could not rely on statutory forms of rationing. Yet, as a consequence of the illegality of this trade, accumulation in this sector was being constrained. The Left Front Government, whose rhetorical stance was to eradicate middlemen, was actually presiding over a multiplication of middlemen without precedence in the history of Bengal. It had effectively hobbled its own marketing co-operatives. Any further reforms to markets in West Bengal would have to deal with the new institutions of civil society through which markets were coming to be regulated, compensating for defective state regulations in a way which has not been observed elsewhere in India.[10] And any real 'eradication of the middleman', which was a live issue at the level of political discourse in Bardhaman district in 1990, would have involved the eradication of the local 'monopoly trading houses', that is, the destruction of the emerging commercial-cum-industrial bourgeoisie.

But so far from eradicating this class, the state's defective regulation and its incoherent interventions affecting the elements of agricultural markets which could threaten this elite, actively empowered it. In fact, as we saw in chapter 6 as well as here, the mix of state and social regulation—formal and informal conditions of exchange—which bore little relation in practice to the Acts and Laws which theoretically governed rural markets was showing signs of de-regulation long before the era of liberalization. This 'market freedom' was not the outcome of acts of political intention, but rested on the state's incapacity to enforce disciplinary regulation. It is the latter's detail which gives accumulation opportunities to capital. Hence, the informalized market freedom observed in 1990 was the result of discretionary, politically renegotiated rights, and obligations developed in the interstices of a formal structure of both regulation and state participation for which the Left Front Government was responsible, but which it did not implement.

Notes

1. See Jaffee, 1990, for a case that the technical characteristics of individual horticultural crops affected contractual institutions in Kenya; see Sarkar,1981; Raj et al., 1985; Nagaraj, 1985 and Bhaduri et al., 1986 for the impact of agrarian change on the way agrarian markets are instituted.
2. Harriss, 1982; see also Crow 1989, 2001 for Bangladesh and Chari, 2003, for parallels between agrarian contracts and contracts and relations of production in the textiles industry.
3. Since the research was done, the Rupee, at 40 to £ in 1990, has depreciated considerably to 56 per pound in 1997 and 80 in 2000, since when the exchange rate has been fairly stable.
4. At an exchange rate of 40 Rs per pound sterling, Rs 2,50,000 was 6,250 pounds.
5. See Harriss-White, 1996 for South India; Rutten, 1997 for West India.

6. See Hardgrove, 2002, for a history of Marwari speculation and gambling.
7. 'For Rs 4 a bag, you can buy stones removed from paddy and use them for re-adulteration', revealed a small trader.
8. From data provided by the District Supply Office, Bardhaman, 1990.
9. See the analysis of prices in Appendix 6.2.
10. This may of course be because such research is still rather thin on the ground outside the North West, Tamil Nadu, and West Bengal.

8 Liberalization and Institutional Development in the Rice Market System in the Early 21st Century

We aim to discover in this and the following chapter how the most dominant institutions for accumulation in the system of markets for rice, and the prominent institutions for livelihoods, have evolved in the 21st century—how they have coped with West Bengal's move from deficit to surplus, and with the destructive as well as constructive aspects of liberalization. In doing so we keep an eye on questions that arose in the two earlier studies. In particular, we predicted in 1982 that unless West Bengal's unusually wide distributive margins were reduced, the petty subsystem would continue to absorb entrants whose returns would be limited by the terms and conditions of their access to informal credit and by the costs of harassment. We argued that a reduction in these marketing margins would not happen while the state protected the local oligopoly of rice mills. In 1990, the prediction proved correct. But now that rice markets have begun to be deregulated, will the conditions for the proliferation of petty livelihoods—the wide margins—be threatened? Or will petty livelihoods be released from the constraints on accumulation, in particular their obstructed access to state-regulated credit? To explore these questions, we must try to disentangle the effects of deregulation from the possibly countervailing effects of growth.

This chapter covers the extremes of the systems of markets for rice. It was not possible to include potatoes and oil, as was done in 1990. Interested readers may consult a doctoral thesis by Jyotish Basu, based in part on field research in the late 1990s, on the potato markets and cold stores of Hooghly District (Basu, 2002). At about the same time too, Mitra and Sarkar examined rates of return to nearly 400 potato producers and the mechanics of potato bond markets in West Bengal.[1]

In 2002, we revisited the districts of Birbhum which we had studied in 1982—chapters 4 and 5—and Bardhaman which we had studied in 1990—chapters 6 and 7 (see note 18). The two districts have a mix of post-harvest processing technologies and scales of operation for rice and have proved to be good sites to observe institutional diversity as the rice markets develop. The last part of this chapter supplements our analysis of the impact of liberalization on these markets with some case material for Kolkata's retail markets, not visited in earlier rounds but studied in 2000 (Choudhury, 2001).

It was not possible, however, to collect the reams of price data necessary to analyse performance in the way we did for several years prior to 1990. Readers interested in the evaluation of price performance will find price data for potatoes from 1990–9 analysed in Jyotish Basu's thesis of 2002,[2] and paddy and rice prices series from north 24 Parganas district from 1987 to 1994 (with further insights from field work in1996) in the doctoral thesis of Sanjib Mukhopadhyay, 1998[3].

The chapter is organized as follows. Section 1 describes the expansion in production and exchange which took place in the 1990s. Section 2 describes the impact of this expansion on the elements of the marketing system, tracing the further increase of livelihoods at the smallest-scale of the system and growing concentration and asset accumulation at the top, as new technology was adopted more widely. We see the impact of this on the employed labour force. Section 3 briefly outlines the development of collective organization by traders during the period of expansion and deregulation and then follows the flow of rice to the retail markets of Kolkata. Finally we summarize the conclusions of this research, showing how in spite of deregulation and growth, a very large proportion of the rice market remains informal, criss-crossed by non-economic constraints on market organization and capital accumulation (especially those shaped by gender and caste) and vulnerable to predation by officials.

Production and Exchange

In the space of two decades, West Bengal more than doubled its rice production (Table 8.1), finally moving from deficit to surplus in 1992–3.[4] From 7.5 million tonnes of rice in 1980–1, output reached 10.4 million in 1990-1 and stood at 15.3 million tonnes in 2001–2. The new technology involves a massive increase in the inefficiency with which energy inputs are converted to edible calories, but it increases the productivity of labour and land. Even though output is still dependent on rainfall and supplies of irrigation water lifted by using electricity or diesel, and even though yield increases faltered after 1992 and stagnated after 1998, the sustained expansion of the area under paddy in the 'minor' *boro* season throughout the 1990s (yielding 37 per cent of total production by 2002) meant that the total growth rate

Table 8.1: Contribution of West Bengal to All India Production of Rice
(In Million Tonnes)

	1980–1	1990–1	1995–6	1999-00	2000-01	2001-02
West Bengal	7.5	10.4	11.9	13.8	12.4	15.3
All India	53.6	74.3	77.0	89.5	84.9	93.1
West Bengal to All India Production (Per Cent)	13.9	14.0	15.4	15.4	14.6	16.4

Source: Directorate of Agriculture, Government of West Bengal.

for the decade was 35 per cent. This performance is all the more remarkable when contrasted with the alarmingly mediocre all-India growth rates over the same period.

West Bengal is now the state with the highest production of rice in India; its share in national food grains production has risen from 14 per cent in 1980–1 to 16 per cent in 2002–3.[5] This very success has led to new political contention surrounding production, and new challenges to rates of return in agriculture (Rogaly and Rafique, 2003). Rural unrest has shifted from the grievances of tenants to those of the sons of landlords, attempting to wrest back by force land on which tenants now have legal security. Tenants have been offered a modicum of free land 'in perpetuity' in return for ceding back sharecropped land to a new generation of young landlords with 'attitude' (Dasgupta et al., 2002). New forms of *seasonal* sharecropping evade the law. The climatic and infrastructural conditions which resulted in a disastrous flood in West Bengal spared India as a whole from a major drought during the 1990s. So, partly as a result of a run of good rains, the scissors of costs and prices have slashed through producers' returns.[6] Paddy prices have slumped (Fig. 8.1). Returns per *bigha* in 2002 were down to Rs 3,000[7], while the costs of key inputs—fertilizers, agrochemicals and electricity for irrigation water (directly or indirectly the embodiment of thermal energy)—together with the costs of seed, labour and credit, soared (Ghosh and Harriss-White, 2002).

The impact on the marketed surplus is not known. Reliable state- or district-level evidence is not available. Existing published estimates of the marketed surplus vary from eight to 90 per cent of production. The lowest is from the Government of India's Department of Statistics and pertains to 'market arrivals'—deep code for sales at, or near the vicinity of, regulated agricultural markets. Given that most paddy sales

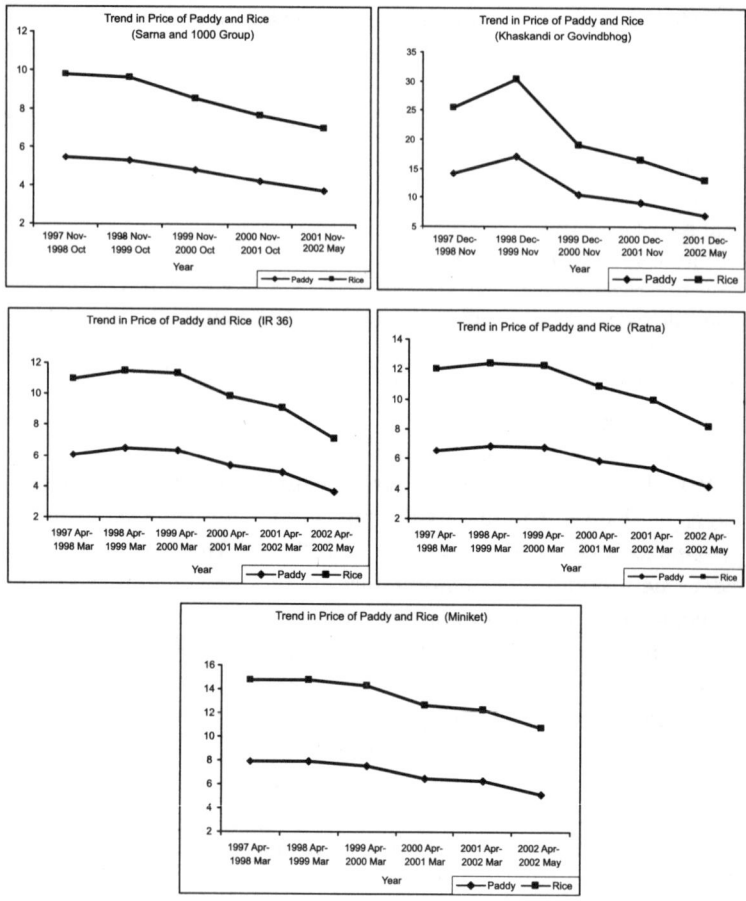

Fig. 8.1: Trends in Prices of Different Varieties during 1997–8 to 2001–2
Source: Field survey (P.K. Ghosh).

take place as far as possible from regulated markets, it is surprising that the estimate is so high. The highest estimate is from a piece of village level research (reported in Business Line, July 6th 2001). In between these extremes, the official data estimate West Bengal's marketed surplus as having declined from 16.4 per cent in 1983–4 to 15.5 per cent in 1999–2000, at a time when that for all-India has risen from 31 per cent to 42 per cent—the West Bengal estimates cannot be accepted with confidence.[8] Two other official sources make it in the region of 50-60 per cent, which we regard as more likely.[9]

The huge increase in production has affected exchange relations. In one of the rare repeated village-level studies, conducted on two sites in West Bengal in 1995–6 and in 2000–1, Vikas Rawal found formal production credit reduced from 24 per cent of loans to 7 per cent. Usurious moneylenders had completely disappeared, but had been replaced by land-owning traders (of fertilizers, pesticides, and agricultural products), whose share of total loans had increased from 25 per cent to 51 per cent, and by 'urban businessmen' (among whose number must surely feature rice millers), whose share had risen from 10 per cent to 31 per cent. By the 21st century, then, no less than four-fifths of all loans for agricultural production were tied to crop markets in these villages. In turn, some of these money advances consisted of the savings of salaried people who would not lend directly 'to avoid the disrespect associated with being a moneylender' (Rawal, 2005, p. 299—see also Table 10, p. 296). Sudipto Bhattacharyya's village-level research into tenancy and exchange also records the emergence of a new fraction of the rural elite with little land—often 'reverse tenants'[10]—but a dominant control over credit and the marketed surplus. In research on rural resource use in West Bengal carried out in the mid-late 1990s, Madan Ghosh also noted the disappearance of relationships of clientelage with professional moneylenders, but in his cases they were being replaced by a new class of scheduled caste and scheduled tribe, 'penny capitalists', lending horizontally 'at usurious interest rates' (1998, p. 222). He also recorded the emerging role of paddy traders as systems of mutual support rapidly atrophied. Between seven and 60 per cent of reported instances of interest-free consumption credit (varying by village) were from paddy traders, suggestive of increasing competition to secure supplies (Ghosh, 1998; pp. 214–16). Suman Sarkar and K. Chattopadhyay saw this production as being associated with an abandonment of periodic marketplace trade, together with a proliferation of itinerant moneylending traders operating increasingly collusive credit arrangements centred on the rice mills (Sarkar and Chattopadhyay, 1995).

From this kind of research, the dominant mechanism of surplus extraction appears to have been shifting from land rent to commercial exchange, the profits from which are fed back into trade and money advances. An increasing share of the state's marketable surplus is coming to consist of tiny consignments that result from the credit arrangements of petty producers. The fact is that the seasonality of production is losing its sharpness, so these small batches of paddy are increasingly released to the market system at a point in the agricultural calendar when processing is threatened by the monsoon.

Changes in the Elements of the System of Markets in Birbhum and Bardhaman Districts

Birbhum and Bardhaman districts form part of the non-Gangetic lowland region of West Bengal. Birbhum has had a more or less constant share (7–8 per cent) of West Bengal's rice output throughout the decades since 1980–1 (Table 8.2). In 2000–1, the district produced 815,000 tonnes of paddy in *aman* and 220,000 in *boro*. Bardhaman's share has been double that of Birbhum, but slid to 13 per cent of the state's total in 2000–1. In 2001–2, it produced 1,825,000 tonnes of paddy in *aman* and a million tonnes in *boro*. Over half of West Bengal's big rice mills (307 out of 562) are sited in Bardhaman district.

Over the last two decades, and particularly in recent years, the volume carried by the system has doubled.[11] Since 1990, the system has become strikingly more complex—Fig. 8.2 may be compared with Fig. 6.1. Table 8.3 provides as much evidence about firms as we could muster. It depicts the continued prominence of many different types of element in the market system. Using best estimates, Table 8.4 does the same for the scales of operation among the range of firms. The market margins within which they operate are summarized in Table 8.5.

When the Left Front Government was voted into power, price margins were twice as big in percentage terms as their 'equivalent' in South India. Table 8.5 shows that the price differences in central West Bengal, within which traders make their profits and livelihoods, expanded by nine per cent during the 1980s and remain as wide into the current period. There is no indication that price margins threaten the conditions for the proliferation of petty trade. The system has absorbed not only an increase in flows but also a large increase in the number of people making a livelihood from it.

Since the rice markets have been already described in this book at two stages of their development, the chapter will confine its discussion to those changes in the dominant and prominent elements which can be clearly attributed to growth. We argued earlier, however, that the state pervades the system and must also shape the response to growth, so that some aspects of growth cannot be separated from the turbulence of policy. We will indicate these where relevant, while changes to the

Table 8.2: District-wise Share of Production of Rice in West Bengal

(Per Cent)

State/Districts	1980–1	1985–6	1990–1	1993–4	1994–5	1995–6	1996–7	1997–8	1998–9	1999–00	2000–01	2001–02
West Bengal	100.0	100.0	100.0	100.0	100.0	100.0	100.0	100.0	100.0	100.0	100.0	100.0
Bardhaman	13.4	12.7	13.6	13.6	13.8	14.0	13.8	14.6	16.1	13.5	12.6	12.7
Birbhum	7.8	7.2	7.8	6.9	6.5	6.9	6.8	7.7	8.9	7.6	6.4	7.6
Bankura	7.9	8.5	8.1	7.5	8.0	8.9	8.2	9.0	7.0	7.2	8.0	8.0
Midnapore	16.8	18.2	14.7	17.3	18.7	17.6	18.7	17.4	15.4	17.6	20.8	17.8
Howrah	2.0	2.4	2.2	2.1	1.8	1.5	1.7	1.8	1.8	2.2	1.8	1.9
Hooghly	6.8	6.0	5.9	5.8	6.1	5.8	5.1	5.8	5.6	5.6	4.1	5.6
24 parganas (N)	6.0	5.4	6.2	6.2	5.6	5.6	5.4	5.2	6.5	6.0	5.2	5.6
24 parganas (S)	6.4	5.6	4.9	5.8	6.5	5.6	6.3	4.8	5.6	6.8	7.0	6.6
Nadia	3.8	4.7	6.7	6.2	5.7	6.1	5.6	5.6	6.3	5.9	5.2	6.3
Murshidabad	5.6	5.5	7.5	6.5	6.5	6.2	7.2	6.8	7.5	6.3	4.4	7.1
Uttar Dinajpur	6.5	6.6	7.4	7.1	6.9	6.8	4.0	3.7	4.4	4.1	5.1	6.4
Dakshin Dinajpur							3.4	3.3	3.5	3.1	3.8	
Malda	3.8	4.1	4.8	4.6	4.2	4.7	4.4	4.2	3.7	3.8	4.2	3.5
Jalpaiguri	3.9	3.3	2.4	2.7	2.2	2.6	2.2	2.3	2.1	2.8	3.1	2.7
Darjeeling	0.7	0.6	0.6	0.6	0.5	0.4	0.3	0.3	0.3	0.4	0.4	0.4
Cooch behar	3.7	3.6	3.8	3.5	2.8	3.2	3.2	2.8	2.8	3.2	4.2	3.1
Purulia	4.6	5.5	3.6	3.6	4.1	4.0	3.8	4.6	2.6	4.0	3.8	4.9

Source: Computed from the data given in Directorate of Agriculture, Government of West Bengal.
Note: Data for 1980–81 to 1995–96 and 2001–02 pertaining to the district Dinajpur have aggregated Uttar and Dakshin Dinajpur..

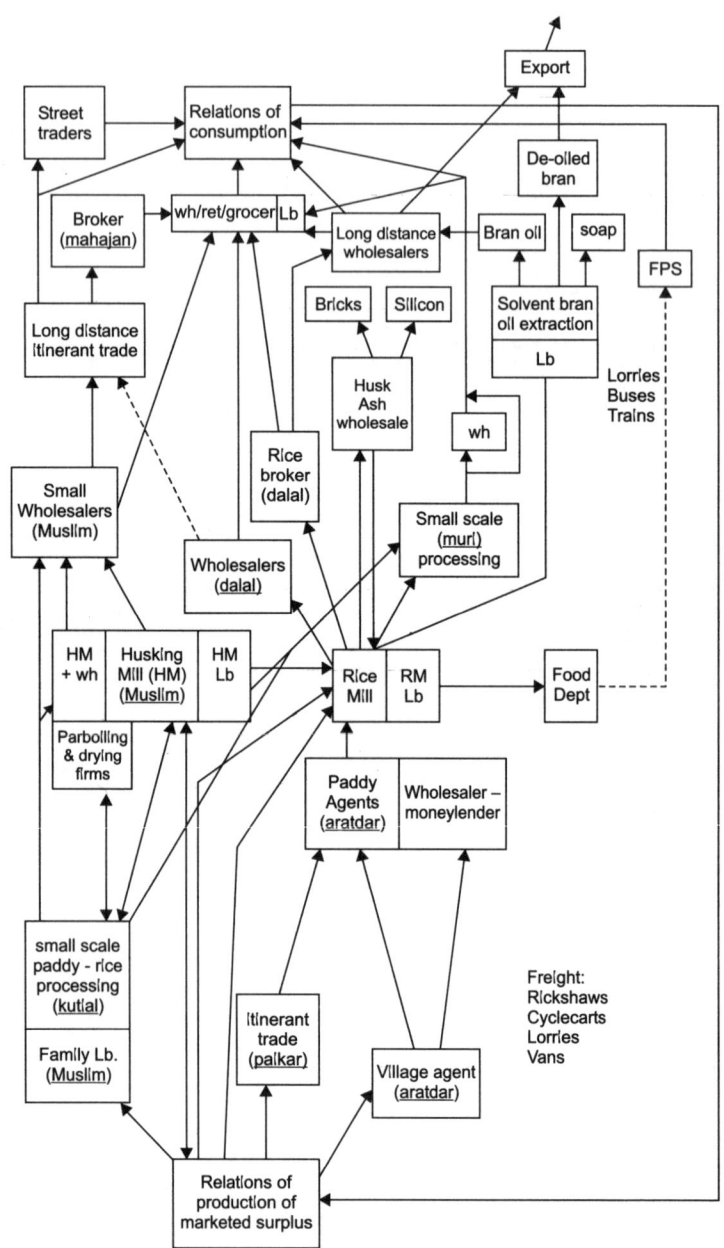

Note: Lb = wage labour

Fig. 8.2: Elements of the System of Rice Markets, 2002

Table 8.3: Firms in the System of Markets for Rice, 2002

	Birbhum Dt.	Bolpur + vicinity	Bardhaman Dt.	Burdwan + Katwa towns
Paddy sub-agents		200		
Paddy + aratdar		140		
Rice Mills	(60) 40	14	307	
Solvent bran oil extractors	2		1	
Rice brokers	20	1	>100	740
Wholesalers				
–with licence		150		
–without licence		25–50		30–40
Muri-makers		n.a.		
Husking Mill	2–3,000		3–4,000	50
Kutial		60	<15,000	300
Small local it. tr.		60		
wh/retailer				
–with licence		200		
–without licence		200		
Freight rickshaws		6000		
Cycle carts		2000		
Lorries		500		

Source: Author's and NCAER's field survey.

system that can be attributed directly to state policy will be the subject of Chapter 9.

Among the dominant elements, nothing has been destroyed. Husking mills have spread like wildfire. For West Bengal as a whole, the Chief Inspector of the Food and Civil Supplies Department for Bardhaman district estimated that their number has quadrupled from 9,000 in 1990 to 37,000 in 2002. In the set of 32 husking mills we surveyed in the two districts in 2002, 85 per cent had been set up in the 1990s. The 1990s also witnessed a 50 per cent increase in the number of rice mills: from 412 in 1990 to 562 in 2002 in West Bengal as a whole (Table 8.6). As ever, a proportion lay idle—estimated at 9 per cent in Bardhaman and 7 per cent in Birbhum.[12] The annual gross output of those that were not idle varied from 80 tonnes (Rs 6.1-6.7 lakhs) to 800 tonnes (Rs 61–7 lakhs) of rice per mill.

In the two districts, rice mills expanded in number from 305 in 1990 to 367 ten years later falling from being three quarters of West Bengal's total to 65 per cent. There is circumstantial evidence that while capital continues to be concentrated in rice mills, it may be in

Table 8.4: Indicative scales of operation—Birbhum District, 2002

Firm type	Av starting Capital Rs'000	Gross Output (rice equivalent) tonnes/yr	Approx net income (Rs)	Comments
Itinerant trader	n.a.	5–8	13,000	
Village agent	20	70–160	n.a.	
Paddy agent	35	3,500	300,000	Commission Rs 5/q paddy
Husking mill	175	100–550	25,000–100,000	
Rice Mill	17,500	6,000–8,000	1,185,000–2,005,000	
Small paddy-rice dealer	12	90	30,000	Net income Rs 53/q paddy
Puffed rice trader	n.a.	n.a.	30,000	
Rice commission Agent	n.a.	n.a.	n.a.	Commission Rs 50/q rice
Rice wholesaler	2–400	350	140,000	
Wholesaler-retailer-grocer	n.a.	3–450	1,200–180,000	Net income Rs 10–50/q rice
New itinerant rice traders	n.a.	35	48,000	
Freight cycle rickshaws	n.a.	n.a.	n.a.	

Source: Author's and NCAER's field survey.

the process of being de-centralized within this sub-system. In Bolpur for instance, out of 13 rice mills, one family has three mills, one has two and the rest own one each. Physical capacity per mill has expanded and gross output (no doubt underestimated for the poor year of 2002) varies between 2,250 and 8,000 tonnes of rice (valued at between Rs 2–7 crores).[13] Rice mills still depend critically on securing supplies in order to maintain high rates of capacity utilization. Moneylending to producers via a web of agents is still key to these supplies. One rice mill had lent out a total of Rs 81 lakhs. But millers have also started to deal directly with producers.[14]

In 1994, paddy agents won *de jure* recognition of the freedom they had wrested *de facto* in a process that started in the 1970s (Chapters 3, 4 and 6). From being tied to specific rice mills, they increased their long-distance reach as independent and dependent money-lenders and

Table 8.5: Price Margins in 2002, Birbhum District

Value chain	Rs/Quintal paddy	Rs/Quintal rice
Farm gate price Sorna variety	375–85 av. 380	575
Ditto IR 36 variety	500	757
Ditto Basmati variety	600	909
Paddy agent	385	583
Small husking mill trader sale price		650 plus bran 10.5 plus husk 34
Rice mill sale price		750–90
Rice wholesale sale price		750–90
Rice wholesale-cum-retail sales price		
Husking mill Sorna variety		650–80
Ditto rice mill Sorna variety		750 plus bran: 30 plus husk: 30

Note: For Sorna variety, the margin is from Rs 575 rice equivalent of paddy to Rs 750, that is 76 per cent, compared with 74 per cent in 1990 and 81 per cent in 1981. This is to be contrasted with 91 per cent in Coimbatore district in 1980 (from data in Harriss-White 1996, p. 217) and 92 per cent in N. Arcot district in 1973 (Harriss 1981a, p. 141). The margin is much wider in Birbhum.

Table 8.6 : Rice Mills in West Bengal

	1990	1995	1998	1999	2000	2001
Burdwan	250	270	–	–	300	307
Birbhum	55	–	–	–	–	60
West Bengal	412	477	532	541	553	562

Source: District Controller of Labour Office in West Bengal.

brokers. Paddy agents are also developing as wholesalers, and have started to store grain too.[15] The system of supply to the mills is therefore increasingly decentralized and complex. A larger number of agents hover around each mill and a new tier of village brokers, semi-attached to paddy agents, has emerged—dealing partly on their own credit and partly on agents' credit, and threatening paddy agents by sometimes negotiating boldly and directly with rice millers.

The new capital-biased technology depends on an assured supply of paddy and is therefore sourced at increasingly long distances. The transport of paddy and rice has generated a client-lorry industry. Bolpur has seen a massive investment in some 500 lorries. Lorry ownership is decentralized, however.

By-products continue to be commoditized and hold the key to the profitability of the rice mills. Income from their sale amounts to 86–93 per cent of the net returns to the rice mills sampled. Husk has been commercialized as a fuel for pre-milling processing (discussed below). Even husk ash has become commodified as a raw material now supplying two industries—low-tech brick kilns and the high-tech silicon industry. As for bran, it is the basis of an industrial transformation. During the 1990s, factories for bran oil extraction in the two districts doubled in number and expanded in capacity by a factor of at least 10. The first solvent extraction plant handled 30 tonnes per day (tpd). Now there are two more—with capacities of 100 and 200 tpd respectively. Operation on this scale calls for concentrated supplies from rice mills, and new specialist brokers have established themselves in order to bulk the bran.

Rice millers also sell via brokers at long distance. In Birbhum, the number of brokers has remained static, although Kolkata-based brokers have expanded their reach in this region. In contrast, the number of rice wholesalers (operating on verbal contracts and payment systems involving two- to three-week delays) has increased. During the 1990s, these long-distance wholesalers sometimes supplied exporters based in Kolkata. From 1996 onwards, rice was being exported from West Bengal to the Middle East, Sri Lanka, and Bhutan (see Appendix 8.1).

Turning to changes in the 'prominent' elements in these markets, it is possible to tell their direction, if not their precise magnitude. No elements have been destroyed. Large numbers of livelihoods have been created. New village sub-agents for paddy tie suppliers with loans in part borrowed from moneylenders, who borrow in turn from the independent paddy agents. Some of these credit relations are over long distances, with intermediaries sited in Katwa or Burdwan. Certain village agents are brazenly leap-frogging the paddy agents to reap a Rs 15 per quintal price advantage by negotiating directly with the mills.

The petty parboiling sector (whose practitioners are called *kutials*) is thought to have doubled after 1997, when an influx of pauperized handloom weaving families was absorbed (see Tables 8.7 and 8.8).[16] For an investment of Rs 11,000, an annual income of about Rs 30,000 could be obtained from parboiling, with a heavy reliance on family labour. New petty milling livelihoods have appeared in which paddy is turned directly (without parboiling) into raw rice. A new

Table 8.7: Petty Parboiling, 2002

Capital costs using family labour	Rs	Comments
Cement drying yard (720 square feet)	4,000	
Clay skin on drying yard	6,000	Annual replacement
Soaking tank (cement)	150	6–7 years
Aluminium vessel for parboiling	1,000	10 years
Husk fuel	Free good	
Total	11,150	

Note: This is a 3-day process involving soaking for 24 hours–boiling and drying for 48 hours.
Source: Author's field survey.

Table 8.8: Kutial business, 2002

Item	Rs
Paddy (60 kg bag @ Rs 230	
Rice (38 kgs @ Rs 6.5/kg)	247
Bran (2 kg @ Rs 3.5/kg)	7
Husk (20 kg @ Rs 1/kg)	20
Gross return	274
Costs	
Paddy	230
Milling charge	10
Cost of home-parboiling	1
Transport	<10
Gross margin	253
Net income	25–30
Net income per quintal of paddy	53

Source: Author's field survey, n=3.

miniaturized post-milling industry has also expanded to process puffed rice—muri—which finds favour as a Bengali fast food.

Rural wholesalers, grocers, and retailers are blurring their functions and developing wholesaling, no longer differentiated politically by licences. Generally they are self-employed, but a few have employees. The biggest such firm—a Marwari family business—had seven family members and three wage workers, recruited through personal reputation; it was openly reluctant to hire labourers from scheduled castes and tribes, or Muslims. Some wholesalers are growing rapidly and lend money to kutials to tie supplies. 'They have disproportionate power in judging quality and price fixing', according to one kutial. The highest quality rice from husking mills passes through their hands. New local itinerant traders in rice have squatted on land and created four primitive market-places in Bolpur. In 1995, there were estimated to be 25 such traders; by 2002 sixty were buying from kutials and selling rice around the villages and as far as the coal belt, pausing *en route* to transact with Bolpur's wholesalers/retailers. From rural Birbhum, an estimated 10 per cent of rice continues to be transported in the hands of a small army of women, to be retailed by itinerant female traders in Kolkata.[17]

A radical departure from former times, and proof that accumulation is happening at last, is that wage labour is emerging at a number of points in the sub-system. Terms and conditions vary according to local context (see Table 8.9).

The outcome is a highly differentiated structure of accumulation (Table 8.10) in which a mass of firms each handle on an average five tonnes per year, while a handful control 8,000 tonnes per year—a difference of 1:1,600. It is also a set of physical flows, in which it is impossible to distinguish changes due to growth from those due to policy.

Within West Bengal, paddy flows have become ever more complex: the ever greater distance at which paddy agents and money-lending millers fix contracts means criss-crossing currents streaming across

Table 8.9: Permanent Unskilled Labour within the Rice Market System (Rs/month, 2002): a labour market?

Type of firm	Monthly wage	Bonus for Durga Puja
Retail outlet	(i) Rs 500 plus food	Clothes
	(ii) Rs 700 plus occasional food (Rs 250)	One month's pay
Wholesale	Rs 1200	Rs 250-300
Rice Mill	(i) Rs 1200	Rs 300
	(ii) Rs 1200	Rs 1300
Husking Mill	Rs 1200	Rs 300
Paddy Agent	Rs 600 plus food	Clothes

Note 1. Agricultural Labour M and F : Rs 25 plus 2 kgs rice per day (Rs 6.5 × 2) = Rs 38 per day
2. Food = Rs 600 per month approx. Clothes = Rs 200 approx.
Source: Author's field survey.

Table 8.10: The economics of processing, 2002, Rs '000

Costs	Rice Mills		Rice Husking Mills				
	Bardhaman	Birbhum	Birbhum: Bolpur	Bardhaman: Katwa	Ba: Doludighi	Ba: Kalna	Ba: Nerodighi
	N = 10	N = 7	N = 3	N = 10	N = 5	N = 5	N = 8
Paddy	33,900	21,000	–	2,590	810	3,125	1,545
Electricity	94.5	1,406	36	83.5	76	69	44
Interest	331.4						
Taxes	134					30	
Telephone	31					1.5	
Maintenance	450			15.6	3.2	15.5	7.2
Overheads	207						
Social redistribution	40					6	
Transport	140			18.5	2.5		7.6
'Other'	310.5	1898		36.4	5.7	76.5	10
Labour	704.5	496		138.2	51.4	129	67
Bonus	52						
Total	36,051	24,800	36	2,850	938	3,814	1,681
Returns*							
Rice	36,180	24,215		2,960	867	3,500	1,336
Bran	1,667	909					
Broken Rice	159.5	120		26.8		37.5	
Husk	50				36	23	22
Custom Milling			86	77.3	142	87	
Total	38,056	25,214	92	3,039	1,046	3,981	1,756
Net income	2,005	1,185	57	149	106	174	75.2
Estd Capital Investment	9,500	9,500	149	472	290	530	330
Rate of Return (%)	21.1	12.5	38	31.6	36.5	32.6	23
Distributive share (wages/profits)	35			93	48	74	89
Imputed family labour	143	86	24	50.5	30	43.2	27
Net surplus	1,991	1,133	32	124.7	75.7	130.6	48
Surplus as % investment	21	12	22	26	26	26	15
Tonnes of rice milled	8,457	5,250	550	348	102	411	313

*Low estimates
Source: NCAER survey.

district and state borders to the rice mills in Birbhum and Bardhaman. Common rice is sent to Kolkata, the coal belt, North Bengal, Nadia, and Assam. The small percentage of superfine rice (including the *basmati* appreciated in export markets) is supplied to destinations all over India via brokers in Kolkata. Local demand still flows in separate spatial and social circuits. Products are increasingly differentiated, by quality, taste and price, into rice from husking mills, rice from rice mills, and muri. The monsoon shapes the main substitution possibility: sun drying is impossible under torrential rain; husking mills therefore stop operating and consumers are forced to buy rice mills' rice.

Bran from Bardhaman and Birbhum is transported as far as Andhra Pradesh to be transformed into edible oil—a new product—and soap. From the ports there de-oiled bran is exported for feed to Japan and the European Union (EU). In the early 21st century, premium beef in an organic butcher's shop, sold to the most discriminating palates of Western Europe, may well have been produced in part with a residue from the rice market system of rural West Bengal, which a generation ago was 'waste', thrown to village chickens.

Summing up

The system of firms, markets, and flows has accommodated a huge increase in the marketed surplus and in so doing has become even more highly differentiated and complex. West Bengal has an unusually large space for petty accumulation. Marketing margins that have done nothing but widen still draw in an abundance of what optimistic developmentalists will see as being 'micro enterprises'. Agricultural profits and rents are still important throughout the system except, paradoxically, at its apex. Investment in rice mills and bran oil is resourced from profits from commercial capitalist activity. Of new significance for livelihoods are the tiny capitals put together from savings from rural wage labour, and the businesses operating throughout the system entirely on money advances from millers, wholesalers and agents.

Changes in Dominant Institutions:
Capital and Technology in Rice Processing[18]

The NCAER survey of mills in 2002 covered three husking mills around the town of Bolpur in Birbhum district (where I additionally studied three), and 28 in Bardhaman district. (The latter were clustered in four different areas, Katwa, Doludighi, Kalna, and Nerodighi—see Map

3—with numbers ranging from three to 10 mills per cluster). The survey covered seven rice mills in Bolpur (where I also studied four), and 10 rice mills in Bardhaman. We therefore have information for a set of 55 mills. It is known, however, to be biased against the husking mills which have been the chief agents in the expansion of supplies. To make matters worse, the data for every one of these mills is partial in inconsistent ways.[19] Mills are complicated operations and with the best will in the world (which was not always there), the absence of written accounts made it difficult for owners to provide quantitative data. Estimates for the economics of operation of firms in the NCAER set of 48 mills are presented in Table 8.10. The consequences of the provision of partial information are evident. Some mills did not provide a breakdown of costs. Others provided cost breakdowns which were inconsistent with our accounting heads. Gross output was estimated in a range of ways. Profits, heavily dependent on by-products, were never directly divulged. We have attempted to make these results consistent, using reasonable assumptions and, in some cases, imputations. As with the overview of the system of markets, this account of the centres of power of the two principal sub-systems will focus on changes to these two sets of firms which are due to growth in supply over the decade of the 1990s.

Husking Mills: The Dominant Element among the Prominent Firms

About 75–85 per cent of paddy is milled in husking mills. The NCAER sample is even more biased to new mills than the estimated trends in their numbers suggest: 90 per cent of those studied had been established after 1990, many as second-generation investments by the sons of husking mill owners. The origin of their capital remains predominantly agricultural. A new mill costs between Rs 50,000 and Rs 5 lakhs—the average was Rs 2 lakhs. Entry is comparatively easy.

All that is now required is a Panchayat certificate with a Rs 10 stamp. Returns to investment are significantly higher than those of rice mills, though the cost of unwaged labour is not imputed in husking mills accounts. Most local consumers are said to prefer husking mill rice over rice mill rice because the lower polish makes it more tasty, so as in the early 1980s, it sill fetches a 10 per cent price premium. Returns to capital invested vary from 23 per cent to 38 per cent. The highest profits accrue to units combining custom-milling for the first time with milling on own account. This new practice started in Bardhaman in response to both growth and policy changes in the mid-nineties.

High capacity utilization also contributes to profitability. In custom mills, this is coming to depend on the number of small paddy-rice processors and traders using the mill. Most husking mills have a regular clientele, who are charged rates that vary so widely within the region —from Rs 8 to Rs 17 per quintal of paddy—that it does not suggest a competitive rental market. Some husking mill owners have invested in a set of small drying yards, sufficient for 6–10 quintal consignments. By renting out these yards to kutials, the latter are effectively attached to the mill and become parts of mini-conglomerates.

The major entry barrier remains electricity. Six husking mills in Bolpur region had been bankrupted, having lost business due to erratic electricity supplies and then having had power disconnected after failing to pay bills. The delays and 'speed money' that characterize relations with the Electricity Board have combined to persuade a younger generation to tap domestic electricity supplies. This then places capacity constraints on hullers, since their prime movers cannot exceed 25–30 HP. Other things being equal, the smaller the capacity of the huller, the higher the capacity utilization and higher the rate of return. Set against this, persistent load-shedding by the Electricity Board prevents high capacity utilization that would make 'modern' rice mill technology viable, so there has been little technological change. A few licensed husking mills with appropriate electricity voltages and regular clienteles of kutials have installed paddy cleaners and de-stoners—these being the cheapest and most flexible components of modernised rice mill technology.

The major by-product, bran, is still largely lost to the agro-industrial system in spite of its high market value; some 80 per cent of it is returned home with custom-milled rice or sold as cattle feed from the millers' own-account operations. 'Its protein content is too high for cattle', grumbled a rice miller about what he saw as an inefficient diversion from the solvent extraction plants. A new huller technology, developed at the CFTRI, Mysore, which yields bran with a 15 per cent oil content (capable of supplying the bran-oil factories), and which costs Rs 15,000, has not taken off - yet. It is likely to be hindered by the transport costs involved in centralizing bran supplies from the dispersed sites of small mills.

Husking mills have started to employ non-family labour (discussed in detail below). The relationship between total labour costs and profits/net returns to the owners—the distributive share—ranges between 48 per cent and 93 per cent. Although this is a very high ratio, due to the very small size of the workforce, the absolute return to the owner will in many cases not be much greater than the return to the one or two semi-skilled mechanics he employs.

Rice Mills: The Dominant Element

Over the two decades since 1980, it is likely that rice mills have increased their share of the much larger paddy market by about 10–15 per cent. In 2002, at least 25 per cent of paddy was processed through rice mills: millers reckoned it was 'half the marketed surplus'.[20] In Bardhaman district there was a 50 per cent increase in their number over the decade of the 1990s. In Birbhum district, where there was a 10 per cent net increase in the number of mills over the decade of the 1990s, there were 59 rice mills in 2001–2; 40 of which were working, 10 were 'in a poor state' running on one shift, and nine had fallen idle. Yet the appearance of decline is highly deceptive. The rice mills dominate long-distance, inter-regional trade. In Bolpur, we can see the contradictory trends at work: of the 19 mills operating in 1990, ten went out of business, but four new mills of much larger capacity had been set up. These 'dominant elements' are increasingly managed by college graduates from the owners' families. Entry barriers are not confined to education and kinship. Investment costs currently vary from Rs 70 lakhs to Rs 1.7 crores, and average one crore.[21] Another crore is needed for working capital. Gross output ranges from Rs 3 to 8 crores in Bardhaman and Rs 2 to 5 crores in Birbhum (Table 8.10). Rates of return vary. In Birbhum, where paddy is still largely sun-dried, returns average 12 per cent, while in Bardhaman, with husk-fired drying, they are 23 per cent. It is clear that expansionary forces are working alongside destructive forces. The NCAER sample of 17 mills was also biased towards new ones—66 per cent of them were set up after 1990. It is possible that we may have an account which underestimates the power of the destructive forces affecting the system of markets.

Expansionary Forces

Husk-fired drying technology, which enables rice mills to ignore the weather and protect against rain, will reduce the seasonality of operations. Such technology solves the 'boro harvest factor' when paddy streams into the mills under a threatening grey sky. At the same time, it solves the production problem for millers that 'labour holds the rice mills to ransom in the rainy season', when timeliness and vigilance is at a premium. It also overcomes the constraints of drying yard sizes, common in cases where milling capacity has exceeded the original layout of the factories and where adjacent land is unavailable or prohibitively expensive. These conditions increasingly constrain the operation of mills planted on the edges of growing towns.

All the rice mills have been converted to husk-fired parboiling, using majestic steam engines retired from a bygone era of the Indian Railways. The mechanical process reduces pre-milling processing from three to five days to 24 hours (and when combined with pressure parboiling technology invented in 1975, down to 12 hours), enabling the necessary pre-milling operations to keep up with the appetite of the rubber-roll sheller mill. These conditions also satisfy the need for the mill to work at ever higher levels of capacity utilization to cover the higher fixed costs involved in increasingly capital-intensive ancillary machinery. In this way by-products are also recycled (Table 8.11). Sun-drying paddy enables a mill to work between 250 and 300 days a year. Husk-fired drying allows a mill to operate continuously. It was introduced in 1993–4, before which less than 15 per cent of waste husk was recycled as fuel. Now much more is used. The standard steam exchange drier costs Rs 8 lakhs to install and processes up to 17 tonnes of paddy per day. For this it requires just over a tonne of husk. If less than four tonnes of paddy are milled per day, the rice miller has to buy husk. So husk has become a commodity, complete with specialist traders. The entrepreneurial frontier has been reached with a husk-fired gasifier from which electricity can be generated to avoid the increasing energy costs and disruptions that hobble the mills. A prototype of this machine has been built in Bolpur.

In the 1990s, no changes were made to rice milling technology *per se*. To the rubber-roll sheller, new to India in the late 1960s, all mills have now added the de-stoner (the necessity for which is sustained by

Table 8.11: Physical Outturn (% of paddy)

	Rice Mill	Price (Rs/kg)	Husking Mill	Price (Rs/kg)
Rice	62–64	8	63	6.5
Bran	6	5	3	3.5
Husk	25	1.2	34	1.0
Dirt/waste	3			

Source: Author's field survey, 2002.

Liberalization and Institutional Development

free-wheeling paddy agents and wholesalers who adulterate their supplies with stones),[22] the polisher, and the de-husker.

The mills are also mass-producing a commodity which involves a small act of vertical integration (Table 8.12). Puffing rice (muri) adds Rs 20 per quintal to the cost of production. A few rice mills can switch flexibly between rice and puffed rice, if puffed rice sells for about Rs 0.3 per kg more than ordinary rice.

The next technological frontier is automation. A quarter of the rice mills surveyed had computers and websites, but in 2002, these were not yet used for business.

The state acts as an expansionary force for these mills, having provided loans for technological upgrading at low interest rates (12–14 per cent) throughout the 1990s. Each mill is run on multiple bank accounts and can therefore access overdrafts on working capital, as well as raise investment finance, from a range of banks. The West Bengal Finance Corporation has continued to lend money for rice mill modernization, though Marwari millers also have their own private credit and finance institutions.

Destructive forces

What has happened to reduce shifts and render mills idle? One set of destructive forces arises from the life cycle of business families, the second-generation social problems which threaten the management of mills. Ageing patriarchs, quarrelling, partitioned, and litigious families are the stuff of legend and the stock-in-trade of films because

Table 8.12: Muri Rice Process

Day 1	
Wash rice 2–3 times	Pressure parboiling:
Soak 2–3 hours	Soak 15 minutes
Drain	Drain
Add salt *	Steam under 30 lbs pressure–max 30 min
Drain overnight –12 hours	Repeat
Day 2	
Spread rice to dry to 14% moisture–4 hours	
Feed into industrial puffing machine	
Or	
Sell rice to rice puffers	

Notes: * salt from saline aquifer in Rajasthan (50 gms per kg)
Source: Author's field survey, 2002.

they are so common. In practice, the more common threat to rice mills, however, is the continued expansion and development of scale in husking mills, based on multiple-battery huller technology combined with family labour. A third threat is policy affecting prices and therefore demand for rice, discussed later in Chapter 9. A fourth is the loss of security of output on contract to the state (about which complaints were made for two decades until the contracts were stopped —at which point the complaints amplified considerably). This affects capacity utilization and thus the profitability of upgraded technology (it is also discussed in the next chapter).

The distributive share averaged 35 per cent, and is increasingly adverse to labour as the capitalization of mills rises.[23] While family labour (5–20 per cent of the workforce) enjoys two thirds of the value added, in the form of the family's profit, up to one hundred workers per mill (80–95 per cent of all livelihoods in rice milling) make do with the remaining third in the form of wages that hover above and below the state's minimum wage. This labour has made no real gains in wages over the last quarter century.

Changes in Prominent Institutions: Labour Processes in Rice Processing

Most of the labour in these rice markets is self-employed. But we do not know the number of livelihoods generated, the caste and income strata, the proportion of household income such livelihoods generate, or the extent to which the markets complement other kinds of livelihood. Madan Ghosh's research into the incomes of poor rural households in seven localities throughout the state reveals up to 15 income sources, among which paddy processing contributes about 15 per cent among poor Muslim households in Bardhaman district, but little elsewhere. Rice mill labour, a third of which was female, contributes about 5 per cent of household income among poor scheduled tribal households in Birbhum. Two-thirds of it was earned by women (Ghosh, 1998; pp. 134–40). Almost all the pettiest livelihoods involve processing or transport as well as buying and selling. The division of labour inside the husking mills and rice mills is shown in Table 8.13, and wages in the 'market' for permanent unskilled labour in the rice mills and other firms making up the rice markets have been summarized in Table 8.9. The combination of family, permanent, casual male and female labour and contract labour is characteristic of the labour markets within the commodity market system.

Husking Mills

Husking mill work is physically demanding but intermittent. Limited skill is required, at most the capacity to repair motors and service hullers. If a mechanic is employed, he will be a permanent worker paid monthly at rates which hover around the poverty line for a household (Table 8.13). As output increases, owners introduce wage labour for the heavy work. The labour markets developing around husking mills have idiosyncrasies based on the social structure of the regions in which they are sited. They are shaped by the prior distributions of castes and religions—and their work-cultures—among the landless population. Payment is generally by piece rates and workers have as yet no security or work rights. In Katwa, all this labour is male and scheduled caste. In Doludighi, the wage work force is Muslim; in Kalna, scheduled caste husbands and wives work in pairs, and in Nerodighi, migrant scheduled tribal men and women from Jharkhand work in gangs on contract alongside local Muslim men.

Table 8.13: Labour In Rice Processing

	Family	Permanent	Casual	Comments
Numbers				
Rice Mill (largest–3 shifts)	12 (M)	21	100	
Rice Mill av (Birbhum)	2–4 (M)	8–12 (M)	20–50	90% F
Rice Mill av (Bardhaman)	2–4 (M)	4–8 (M)	6–10	0–30% F
Husking Mill	1 (+1) (M)	(1) (M)	3–6	up to 15 casual (rare)
Wages Rice Mill	(imputed: Rs 30k per year per person : v low est)	Mechanic: Rs 900 to Rs 3,500 per m	Rs 48–52/day Rs 45–50/day	(Birbhum) (Bardhaman)
Husking Mill	(imputed : Rs 18k per person per year)	Mechanic: Rs 1,200 plus 45 kg rice per m	Rs 1200–1500 plus 45 kgs rice/m	Piece rates: av Rs 45–50 /day
Poverty line (2000)				Rs 15,000 per hh per yr
Min. Wage (2002)				Rs 39 per day

Source: Author's field survey, 2002.

This part of the system cannot function without cycle-freight rickshaws. Table 8.3 shows that thousands of livelihoods are generated by the petty sub-system's demand for transport. In Bolpur, the rickshaw men are mostly SC/ST, although a quarter are estimated to be Muslim. Earnings are unreliable. A good day brings Rs 150, a bad one Rs 50. The average was Rs 75–100: at least double the minimum wage in 2002, which was Rs 39 a day.

Rice Mills

The labour process in rice mills described in chapters 4 and 6 is the most highly differentiated in the system of rice markets. The 1990s saw significant changes. For a start, the ratio of family to other kinds of labour *increased*; the displacement of wage workers reduced the total wage labour force by more than the tendency to professionalize tasks done by family labour added to it. Male family labour, organized under patriarchal authority, oversees buying, selling, credit, labour force management, and all investment-related decisions. Status within the family, rather than productivity, determines what individuals draw from the company. Technically, family members are 'residual claimants'. Over the quarter century through which we have watched these mills, the formal qualifications of family members have increased: by 2002 only one of 17 rice mill owners did not have a university degree.

Permanent labour occupies key positions in administration, accounts, stores, and security. It is 20 per cent of the total force in Birbhum and 35 per cent in Bardhaman. But the absolute numbers have dropped by 50 per cent in Bardhaman, a move reckoned to be a pre-emptive response to the threatened unionization of permanent labour. Though mechanics tend to be Muslim, 90–95 per cent of the remaining permanent labour is Caste Hindu. They are local in origin, recruited through kin and acquaintance, from among the contacts of existing permanent employees, and via tiers of patronage. Though not yet unionized, they are legally entitled to the provident fund (see below), paid leave, and a bonus at the time of Durga Puja. These entitlements come from just a subset of the 40 or so Labour Laws, which theoretically cover all paid labour; but in practice rarely cover any of it.

All rice mills are registered under the Factories Act. About 70 per cent of the labour force remains on casual contract. Under the Factories

Acts, some of this labour will appear in muster rolls, but much doesn't. 'Half of our labour is on the accounts", reported one miller. Those who are registered will have provident fund contributions paid. The provident fund is a scheme established in 1951 under which employers and employees contribute 12 per cent of pay (in a ratio of 30:70) to a deposit in the Provident Fund Organization which is withdrawn by the employee at retirement (See Singh, 2005 for full details). In theory a protective device, in practice it bristles with disincentives.[24] Employers are naturally unwilling to make contributions which add to their costs. Employees are also reluctant, not only because it reduces their current income but because if they change jobs, their PF deposits are hard to access and recover, and they are also—and especially—hard to redeem at 60 years of age. The concept of retirement is also not very relevant to a kind of work which people do until they drop. 'PF feels like a tax to us', one labourer said.

More significant to casual labour than their dubious entitlements under the Factories Acts is their organization in unions. Unions are registered with the state. Members are registered in union records. But unions have not been able to claim for their members the provisions in the state regulation of the labour process—minimum wages, standard terms and conditions, benefits, health and safety provisions, etc). Instead they negotiate contingent rights at work. They can and do prevent incremental lay-offs.

Employers also organize registered associations, one purpose of which is to respond corporately to unions in order to limit the rights of labour.[25] The accommodation between employers' associations and unions (of which there may be several in one factory) is one of continual politicized contestation. Employers have to deal with at least two major labour unions, attached to the CPI(M) and the RSP respectively. Employees have to deal with union officials who are not democratically elected, but are political appointees. 'Businessmen!' scoffed one mill owner about union officials. 'They aren't interested in the rice mill sector, rice mills or rice mill labour.' Occasionally, in the presence of officials from the Labour Commission, local rice mill owners and union representatives negotiate a modicum of rights specific to their jurisdiction. In Bolpur, casual labourers have rights to one day of unpaid leave after 6–7 days of continuous work. People 'loyal' to the mill, who manage to get work for more than 220 days a year, get a bonus of Rs 900 at the time of the Durga Puja festival. But the labour is laid off in the slack season. In Bardhaman, the unions have won more: the bonus is larger—Rs 975—and the entitlement threshold—150 days—is less restrictive. All categories of labour are entitled to five days' unpaid leave each month and 45 days' notice has to be given prior to lay-offs.

We cannot avoid the conclusion that the casual labour on whose toil rice mills have depended for decades is an 'institutional rigidity'. These men and women have a limited set of insecure rights which vary from region to region. Casual they are. They can be sacked at short notice and are paid by the day. Yet 'loyal' they have to be, or they forfeit the bonus. In turn, the owner of a mill that is in the doldrums regards them as lumpy and indivisible—not easy to lay off at the margin—for fear of threats by labour in future times when more of them might be needed again. Incremental change in the labour process involves entire shifts and all kinds of unskilled workers are needed to run a shift. The wider social status and reputation of employers rest in some small part on a political settlement in which they provide livelihoods and meagre bonuses to casual employees.

At the same time, 'formal' but casual rice mill labour is regulated through social institutions, which take different forms according to their regional history. In Bolpur, over 90 per cent of the casual labour consists of tribal Santals who have made long-term migrations from Bihar and Orissa.[26] They work in gangs of 8–15 on piece rates under contractors who skim 5 per cent. Living collectively, they provision themselves in groups.[27] These migrants are sometimes paid in rice. Evidently they are not expected to save money and have to exchange rice for money before they can buy any other commodity. They are therefore at the mercy of the traders who control such exchanges. In the rice mills visited in Bardhaman district, by contrast, the casual labour was local. Half were scheduled caste, and a further quarter was Muslim. They were paid gender-neutral daily wages, reckoned at between Rs 42 and Rs 53—anyway, above the minimum wage of Rs 39 and at parity with real wages in 1982.

Employers also use primitive technology to keep casual workers submissive. In this day and age there is no reason, apart from affirming the humiliating gulf of status, why men should head-load parboiled paddy in double gunny bags of 150 kgs,[28] or why women should have to bend double and stoop low in order to sweep up waste.

In the 1990s, the diffusion of husk-fired mechanical drying, discussed above, had a massive impact on the labour process in rice mills. It reduced the labour force to 20 per cent of that needed for sun-drying paddy. Table 8.14 has stylized the process of displacement of labour by capital for a standardized Rs 1 crore of gross output of rice. It is not a simple 'before and after' scenario, because threats to unionize permanent labour coincided with the process of technological change, as a result of which employers have been able to halve the number of permanent workers.[29] The burden of displacement was not borne by family labour, nor is it borne by male casual labour: it is female casual labour that is down—by an astonishing 98 per cent.[30] Where do these women go? From Madan Ghosh's account, women bring in between 25 and 35 per cent of the income in poor households (1998, pp. 134–40). They glean and gather, they work in brick kilns, domestic service, the care of livestock, construction sites (where wages are marginally higher than in agriculture), and petty rice processing; and if all else fails, they return to the paddy fields.

The displacement of labour by capital-intensive technology has not been due to a nosedive in demand for rice from the rice mills. It is not due to deregulation either (see chapter 9). It is due to the rigidity of drying yard capacity in relation to the increasing scale of capital-intensive milling, and to the cardinal need to keep capacity utilization high. It is also due to the de-linking of the harvest from the cycles of the monsoon, which means wet season processing. And by eradicating livelihoods for permanent male labour and casual female labour, it also makes their political organization difficult.

Self-organization in the System of Markets

The geographical spread of religions and castes, involving a great deal of migration to West Bengal and within the state, gives both of them

Table 8.14: Combined impact of Unions and Adoption of Mechanical Drying Livelihoods per Rs 1 crore (10m) of Gross Output (2002)

Type of labour	Before (Birbhum)	After (Bardhaman)	Change
Family (M)	1	1	None
Permanent (M)	4	2	−50%
Casual (M)	1.5	2	+33%
Casual (F)	12.4	0.3	−98%
Comments	3–5 day process	24 hour process	

Source: Author's field survey.

structuring roles in the system of markets. Muslims have entered husking milling and the small scale paddy-rice business in disproportionate numbers. In parts of Bardhaman district, OBC and SC migrants from Bangladesh have followed suit. These are all social groups which face social constraints on access to land-based livelihoods. In the rice mill sector in these districts, the old structural domination by Marwaris from Rajasthan and by Hindu migrants from East Bengal has only recently been challenged by the entry of general caste 'Bengali' *jotedars* (landlords).

The strongest structuring force, however, is patriarchy. The system is becoming increasingly male. Although female casual labourers are thought to receive daily wages and piece rates on par with men, female labour is disproportionately displaced. As family labourers, women toil unwaged at the domestic parboiling and drying of paddy—on top of their reproductive burden. The women of the families of rice millers will outsource much of their own labour-intensive domestic reproductive work to exploited female wage labour; but they themselves are deprived of much agency other than expressing or embodying the family's piety.

Collective activity helps to define the elements in the system: there are organizations serving the joint interests of paddy agents, of rice millers, husking millers, wholesaler/retailers (*Byabsai Samiti*), the neighbourhoods of shops, labour in mills, in the market town and freight rickshaw pullers. Some of these organizations already existed in 1990 and were described in chapter 7. Other, smaller, associations are new. The older organizations are not necessarily the most powerful. Many associations and unions mask conflicts of interest, the interests of workers in particular being neutralized when they are admitted into occupational associations (Basile and Harriss-White, 2000). Such is the clout of the rice mills that labourers are never admitted into the Rice Mill Associations. Such is the limited power of the labour unions that the businessmen who lead some of them can use them to pursue their private political interests. It was hinted by several informants that they might not even be above collusion with mill owners. Representatives of unions of wage workers organized by party politicians complained that wage negotiations are always controlled and fine-tuned by employers. And not all labour is unionized. 'Deregulation means the deregulation of labour unions too', declared one miller with an interest in informalizing his labour force.

Small intermediaries mobilize collectively in order to represent themselves to the state, fix wages and pursue private justice in cases of *Ravari* (robbery) theft and default. This collective representation to the state is both crude and subtle. Collective contributions as gifts are given to the Police and the Food Department officials. These 'gifts' crudely protect traders from threats to their security from the forces of law and order; they also subtly shape the negotiations through which—and the discretion with which—regulative law is implemented.

The Rice Mill Association towers at the apex. Formed in 1957, it pays off the Food Department, the Police and the Electricity Board. It has lobbied unsuccessfully to retain state entitlements which flowed from the rice mills' status as 'small-scale industry' (and which enabled mills to get access to subsidized credit for technological upgrading). It has lobbied successfully to decentralize the food administration (though this is a case of Mao Zedong's dictum, 'Success is failure', as will be seen in Chapter 9). It resolves labour disputes and fixes wages (thereby institutionalizing non-compliance with the Labour Laws). It determines the outer limits of the rights of casual labour—all matters that ought to be under the jurisdiction of the state. Lastly, it carries out well-publicized acts of distribution (flood relief), infrastructure (drinking water by roadsides and in schools, street lighting, hospital equipment, road construction and maintenance), and health care (eye camps). These substitute very inadequately for the lack of welfare and developmental activity on the part of the state and they constitute a broad field for the play of patronage. Rice mill owners are prominent members of elite society in the towns where they operate and through these organizations they express their economic status and consolidate influential local networks. They run the Rotary, the Red Cross, Youth and Sports Clubs, Caste associations and occupational associations. In Bolpur, rice mill owners were prominent and generous patrons of the Tagore Theatre, 'Gitanjali', inaugurated in 2000, which has incorporated distinctive architectural idioms from Rajasthan.

The Largest 'Industry': Kolkata's Rice Markets[31]

In 1991, Boudhayan Chattopadhyay wrote gloomily of the supply of food to Kolkata from districts including Birbhum and Bardhaman:

'So-called radical land reforms in West Bengal have hardly altered... the distribution of land ownership or marketed surplus...The thousands of unregistered husking machines—many more than the registered—provide the sinews of this unaccounted surplus rice output finding its way to the 'open' market, the rationed rice being inadequate and of poor quality. Smuggling of this rice into the urban rationed areas therefore becomes one of the largest 'industries' of West Bengal (Chattopadhyay, 1991a; pp. 374–5).

We look next at this largest 'industry' in 2000, three years after the abolition of the trading cordons which had made smuggling essential to the food supply of one of the world's hugest metropolises,[32] and one governed by the Left Front.

The flower touches her eyelids
A dewdrop brushes her lips
Lullaby Aunt wakes up before dawn
The morning star shines at the edge of the roof
The departing moon has stopped above the palm tree
Lullaby aunt begins the household chores.

A few dewdrops still gaze from blades of grass
Lullaby aunt gathers her bags of rice
And hastens to catch the train

Lullaby aunt has many mouths to feed
In her expanded and expectant family
But only a fistful of rupees

Where are the precious bags of rice?
Lullaby aunt is tense and fretful
The rail police again cause trouble

Come rain or shine
Lullaby aunt must trade her bags of rice
Can she afford to choose her time?

A millennium comes and a millennium goes
Lullaby aunt still carries her bags of rice
To markets in Lalgola and Bongaon.[33]

In 2000, Kolkata was a city of some 12.66 million people.[34] Their food supply has rested on a unique combination of state and market.

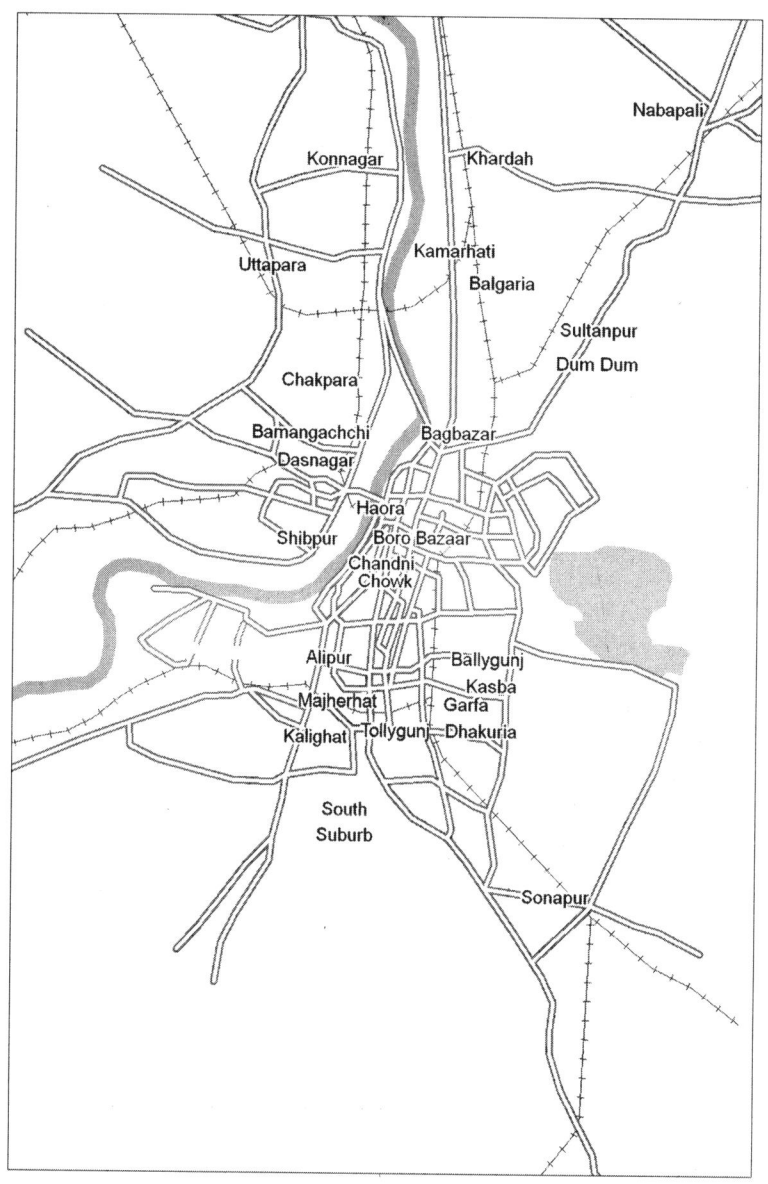

Source: Bodleian Library Map Collection, Oxford University.

Map 3: Kolkata/Calcutta

The state component is now a completely obsolete, but none the less still functioning, system of statutory rationing through wholesalers (agents to state-trading organizations) who in turn supply Fair Price Shops (see chapters 5 and 7). The other component consists of open market sales of rice by retail traders on whom the main impact of liberalization is that they are no longer actually smuggling.

The research reported here followed this trade into private marketplaces and municipal markets, and found it invading public space on pavements, footpaths and alongside railway tracks, and on routes through tenements and residential estates. The field work did not track down the big wholesalers, whose shadowy presence is part of the story of the next chapter. It drew its information from five sites in the south of the city : Lake Market, Alipur, Kasba, Dhakuria, and Garia (see Map 3) and from 50 of the many thousands of people gaining a living from this largest 'industry'.

It might be reasonably supposed that the demand for rice, a staple food, is constant and non-seasonal. This is not the case. The seasonality of consumption is not, however, connected with agricultural cycles in the ways which have been found to structure smaller urban economies (Harriss-White, 2003). In Kolkata it is the pulse of regular monthly salary payments, and less frequent religious festivals, which sends demand surging, and it is the time preceding the end of the month, and the days of strikes and phases of heavy rain, which stifle demand.

Table 8.15 shows that, not counting the large-scale wholesalers, Kolkata's rice market consists of five elements: female itinerant traders; the male *mahajans* (traders or money-lenders) who shadow their routes and dominate the women; street traders; traders operating from the eleven municipal markets; and wholesalers. Stylized economic facts about their businesses for the year 2000, obtained from roughly 10 firms of each type, are presented in this table. The range of scales of these firms is quite considerable: from 20 kgs to five tonnes per day, a difference of 1:25.

Kolkata's *lullaby aunts* are from the suburbs of the city or from rural districts such as South 24 Parganas, Birbhum and Bardhaman. They purchase rice from *haats* or kutials or are members of the families of kutials. They take consignments of 20–25 kgs by train to Kolkata, evading male ticket collectors. Informal collusive agreements with bus drivers in the end enable them to reach their destined neighbourhoods. There they walk from door to door on established routes through the residential middle or upper class neighbourhoods, where they can

Table 8.15: Kolkata's Rice Retail Markets, 2000

Firm type >	Itinerant Trader (F)	Itinerant Trader (mahajan)	Street trader	Marketplace trader	Wholesaler
Starting capital	negligible	negligible	Rs 1,000	Rs 10,000	'>30 years ago'...
Physical turnover (kgs/day	20–25	80–100	20–50	20–50 80–100 100–600	4000–5000
Approx physical turnover (tonnes) per year	5–7	38	1–12	12/29/115	< 1485
Approx gross output Rs/year	155,000	12,16,000	8000–3,00,000	3,00,000–40,25,000	4,45,50.000
Profit margin (min to max/kg)	Rs 0.5–2	Rs 0.8–1	Rs 0.8–1	Rs 0.3–1	Rs 0.8–1 (ret) Rs 0.2–0.4 (wh)
Approx net income: Rs/year Poverty line Rs 15,000 per hh	10,500	48,000	14,800	10,000–92,000	17,32,500

Source: Choudhury, 2001.

charge higher prices than in the city's marketplaces. From this business alone, however, they are most unlikely to make an income exceeding the official poverty line for a household (Rs 15,000 per year).

Mahajans, hailing from peripheral areas of Kolkata, act as itinerant brokers between wholesalers and petty retailers. They also lend money and may trade larger consignments on their own account. One estimate of an annual income is Rs 50,000. Four out of every five street-side traders are women. Their public sites bar them from storing their stock, so their livelihoods resemble those of the itinerant women retailers. Traders in the private markets have to be licensed by, and pay rent to, the owners. Internally differentiated and dependent on the mahajan, they may get incomes ranging from subsistence to around Rs 1 lakh. The local wholesaler is in a different league again, although wholesaling on a much greater scale than theirs is carried on in BoroBazaar.

Local wholesalers' supplies are brokered by *dalals* (brokers) who also take care of lorry transport. Based in Kolkata, they are networked to specific regions such as those we introduced earlier in this chapter. Wholesalers in the municipal markets have been regulated through licences and made to comply with storage laws. They are therefore visible to the state. Like many other states of India, which refused to tax staple food, the Left Front Government has been forced by the central government to charge a 2 per cent sales tax on this essential commodity, to be levied on all firms declaring sales in excess of Rs 2 lakhs.[35] There is therefore a certain amount of tax-avoiding development below this threshold, as well as the creative accounting thought to happen above it. Servicing all marketplaces and essential to the distribution system are the many gangs of male *koolis* who are paid on piece rates for loading and unloading the '*vans*' (alias freight rickshaws) which shift rice around the city.

The Left Front Government must have long ago decided to play a purely minimal role in establishing order in these markets, for they are socially regulated. The 1997 lifting of the trading cordon around Kolkata is thought to have removed many sites of extortion but reinforced the need for customary forms of regulation. With the exception of a few of the wholesaling firms, all of these thousands of livelihoods are single-person enterprises and are functional throughout. How is order being established and practised? We will look at the roles of patronage, identity, and self-organization.

The rice retail markets would not operate without high levels of trust, because throughout the multiple transfers of property rights, payment is delayed and often completed by instalments. Not every transaction in the entire system works this way, but payments delayed over 20–30 days are to be found. The system is called *baki*. The word translates as 'left-over' or 'remainder'. It works entirely without written record and is invisible to the state. It is the duty of the borrowers to phase their repayments. The lender is therefore exposed and vulnerable. Much time is spent in attempting to recover debts. Losses and failure to repay are a constant risk.[36] The necessary credibility for instalment payment is grounded in reputation, which is still a collective and ascribed phenomenon. We can do no better than quote from the work of Nandini Dasgupta who wrote an ethnography of petty trade in Kolkata and concludes: 'as in large trading or in any exchange activity, it is essential for petty traders to establish her or his credibility' (Dasgupta, 1992, pp. 166–7). In the petty retail markets, credibility refers to the period for which the petty trader has an intangible right to keep goods or delay payment. 'Since he has no collateral or in most cases not even an address, (social ties) acquire great significance ... in helping the trader establish his vertical linkages' (ibid).[37]

Dasgupta also shows the exploitative relations provoked by this need for credibility: 'With capital being the scarce commodity, most of the traders buy their goods on credit. The bulk of them buy from middlemen, large retailers or wholesalers generally referred to as the *mahajan*. The mahajan determines the rate and duration of the credit and directly affects the profit rate and the actual turnover of the petty trader. The relationship is dominated by the mahajan because of the petty trader's low bargaining power and credibility and it makes the petty trader totally dependent on the mahajan' (op. cit., p. 206). The mahajan can determine trading sites and impose severe sanctions for default on any baki arrangement (and ruin the defaulter's reputation). Dependence and clientelization may reduce decision-making power and rates of return, but they also reduce risk, increase inventory, and information availability and improve access to sites and credit, leading to modest forms of vertical integration. While both trust and power regulate the rice markets, their balance depends on combinations of financial, informational, geographical, and contractual independence. It is fundamentally indeterminate.

Likewise, the boundary between relations of patronage and those of coercion is ill-defined in conditions when the poor party, the 'client', has no alternative, and the patron's power is based on the structure of property rights. Nowhere is this more relevant than in the relations between rice traders and those empowered to enforce the laws—not only legal property rights, but also the laws regulating urban public space. The police harass rice traders for trespass by means of extortion that has been long institutionalized through the police raid. Bribes depend on the scale of trade. At the same time, political parties have installed themselves as patrons, competing for access to the market infrastructure and vying for votes based on this access. They establish sets of entitlements and structure the eligibility of poor traders to claim them. Political patrons, competing to ensure traders' immunity from police harassment, have wrought havoc with physical security as political gangs confront each other when competing to protect market places.[38] Markets can be violent places. In 2000, a trader had been assassinated in one marketplace in our study. Coercive relations of patronage add to costs as well as to insecurity. Our admittedly unsystematic evidence suggests that the impact of such costs may be felt disproportionately by the smaller traders. Examples of the cost of protection as a proportion of net income were 3 per cent for an itinerant trader, 8.3 for a street trader, as much as 8.8 per cent for a mahajan, but only 0.5 per cent for a wholesaler.

Over time, the economic content of other social institutions like caste, religion, gender and neighbourhood or place has become increasingly visible (Harriss-White, 2003). In the rice markets, the economic significance of gender is all too clear: women are the smallest traders, those unable to accumulate. Gender is also the basis for some defensive collective action, as are places of residence and of work, which will be described later. Residential neighbourhoods reflect a joint history of migration and occupational specialization, whether it is reproductive space for East Bengali wholesalers, or the basis of group travel into Kolkata for petty traders on trains and buses. Place also is the unit for the collective bribery of the state vigilance inspectorate. Religions regulate demand for rice through the ebb and flow of their festivals; the norms of divine authorities also regulate credit practices. For Bengali traders, all outstanding debts must be repaid on the eve of the Bengali New Year (which falls in mid-April)—*hal katha*, or 'clearing the book'. For the great Marwari wholesaling dynasties situated in parts of Kolkata, account books are cleared at *Diwali* in November.[39]

Caste also proved a sensitive subject which rice traders generally shrugged off as irrelevant.[40] But scheduled caste and tribal status are being used as barriers to entry to the power points of these markets, especially wholesaling. We know from Dasgupta's ethnography that caste-based links with other traders and mahajans improve an entrant's access to credit, just as they structure the access of established traders. Entrants are reported to be introduced to mahajans by friends, relatives or traders of the same caste group. Not only does caste establish economic links and so create artificial barriers to the entry of others, but it also helps the traders to affirm their own credibility (Dasgupta 1992; p. 295). For traders without caste links with the commercial sector, the process of establishing their credibility with mahajans is long and slow. As a result some low-caste traders have had to rely on and trust 'formalized' institutions such as the unions to facilitate and protect their entry. They even use union officials to approach commercial banks for loans.

In a socially-regulated market, traders band together to ensure reproduction of their sector in the face of police harassment and political manoeuvres. Security of property is even more essential than a clean site or one supplied with water. The most common groupings of traders were for the protection of sites against police raids. Through persistent activity, street traders develop 'Special Rights of Ownership' over public land,[41] and a place of illegal trade can become a marketplace. That process is continually being challenged and contested. Other examples of 'self-organizing' collective activity in Kolkata include: i) payments from groups of traders to the local police; ii) networks of informants to warn traders of possible police raids; iii) the organization of cleaning; iv) attempts by market traders to bypass the mahajan, deal directly with a wholesaler and collectively organize transport; v) the collective organization of travel and itinerant routes by women, said to be done 'for their physical security'; and vi) collective bribes to ticket collectors for free travel on buses and trains. Dasgupta also instances vii) mutual assistance to traders to recover goods from police custody in the wake of raids; and vii) group mediation to establish creditworthiness with the formal banking system. In the heart of metropolitan Kolkata, the seat of the Left Front Government, it is through socially regulated collective action rather than by state rules that most of the institutional conditions for retail transactions are supplied and market order is achieved.

The 'Residual' State Regulation of Kolkata's Retail Markets

In its regulation of agricultural markets, the Indian state is Janus-faced (chapters 2, 5, and 7). On the one hand, it regulates them to encourage private accumulation (as in the Regulated Agricultural Markets Acts). On the other, it *participates* in them, competing with private capital and even striving to replace private capital when it is believed to threaten productive accumulation (the assumption underlying the Essential Commodities Act) (Harriss, 1984; Harriss-White, 1995). It does not help resolve this confusion of roles that there are three states: central, state level, and that of the municipal corporation. It also does not help that the practice of the law is far removed from its letter, filtered as it is through local structures of economic and political power and social identity.

Even so, to see how the state's laws and institutions affect Kolkata's rice retail markets, we have to start by looking outside Kolkata. Rail and bus transport is heavily regulated both parametrically and participatively by the central railway authority and by state-owned transport companies. Petty traders collude to evade as much of the parametric regulation as they can with the intention of getting the state to transport their rice at minimum cost to themselves. Train compartments are separated into those for commercial use and those for passengers. This division is ignored and sacks compete with passengers. The humble ticket inspector, charged with the responsibility of regulating freight transport, is bribed to let this happen and to let traders travel free. Assuming that the bribe is less than the ticket cost, then either the rice retail price is lowered as a result, and open market consumers benefit from this unintentional state subsidy, or the rice retail price is unaffected and traders gain a small rent from it (which they may share with the ticket collector), or the rice retail price is lowered *and* the rent is distributed.

Inside Kolkata, the Government of India's Essential Commodities Act (ECA) operates in participative form of regulation to replace private retailing by a set of Fair Price Shops. Under the Food Control Order of 1967, the government of West Bengal requires rice retailers to be licensed. Unlicensed traders flout the laws of trespass. Until March 2002, licensed retailers also faced restrictions on the volumes traded and the stock held (Mooij, 1999a; p. 198; p. 201.). Two kinds of licence have been issued by the government of West Bengal's Food and Civil Supplies Department: 'B1', under which a maximum of 100 quintals may be stored, and 'B2', where the maximum is 500 quintals. These stocks are supposed to be inspected daily but the Enforcement branch of the Food Department has sufficient resources to inspect only about twice a year, and officials are widely alleged to be appeased with a bribe (estimated at Rs 8,000 per visit in 2002).

The Kolkata Municipal Corporation also regulates official markets in 'saturating' detail, with a mass of rules and regulations applied to transactions.[42] Each municipal market is run by a supervisor who concerns himself with public hygiene, provision of water, organization of storage and adjudication of disputes, and who makes sure the markets operate to a timetable (8 a.m. to 1 p.m. and 4 p.m. to 10 p.m.). The Corporation attempts to preserve the legal structure of rice markets run by the Municipality and from time to time evicts unlicensed traders as hazards to both traffic and planning. Operation Sunshine was one such episode in 2000, in which traders were forcibly relocated to the outskirts of the city, from where they soon swarmed back in.

This is the structure of regulation that provides the rents for the police and vigilance forces, the food supply to the metropolis, and a set of highly differentiated accumulation possibilities to the people gaining livelihoods from it.

Conclusions

Two decades of sustained growth in rice production enabled the top layer of capitalist accumulation—the rice mills—to expand their control over the food system by more than a third -, thus increasing their share from about 15 to 25 per cent of production. Their numbers have doubled, their capacity has greatly increased, and their capitalization has intensified. But what we also find is a deep diversity of technologies, forms of organization, and scales of operation which co-exist and flourish. And this diversity does not correspond to the diverse market sub-systems which were already in place by 1982, but is found within each of the sub-systems too.

Although our research cannot provide estimates of the numbers of firms in the system of rice markets, it does point to the direction of its development. The system is still creating large quantities of petty livelihoods. The conditions for their proliferation have not been threatened, for the marketing margins have become wider rather than narrower (Table 8.5). Crowding ought to increase competition, but competition is constrained by the acute dependence of petty traders on their sources of finance. The system of markets is not simply expanding: it is becoming ever more functionally intricate, a process we termed 'involution' in chapter 7. Labour markets are also developing throughout the system, as firms accumulate and graduate from self-employment (or from pure household production and trade) to small worker-capitalist firms and to 'family businesses'. At all stages and scales in the system of markets, producers, consumers and, traders (and their combinations) are controlled by money advances. Many are thinly disguised wage labourers, getting livelihoods at—or only just above—the poverty line on extremely insecure terms, and dependent on the contradictory stew of trust and power embodied in economic clientelage.

This dynamic, small-scale commercial capitalism redistributes the surplus value created in paddy production using wage labour, and the surplus product generated through petty production. Yet the rice markets themselves are also deeply interlocked with productive—processing—activity, so that secondary surplus appropriation in small conglomerate capitalist firms occurs alongside petty production and trade, and alongside surplus redistributed through pure buying and selling.

Among the commercial capitalist firms, we have seen two contrary accumulation dynamics. First, processes of concentration of capital (in the rice mills). Here, we have also observed a shift in the balance between family labour and wage labour, back towards family labour, as the net outcome of labour-displacing technology, responses to new threats to the structure of profits, and wages due to capital substitution. The mills have weather-proofed themselves; but in so doing they become ever more dependent on combinations of state policy and contractual arrangements assuring them supplies of paddy over ever-longer distances. These arrangements are essential for the constant and high capacity utilization needed to ensure positive rates of return from increasingly capital-intensive technology. When they fail, rice mills are faced with very powerful incentives to make profits by 'primitive' means - which we describe in Chapter 9. Second, processes of decentralization accompany processes of concentration. Ownership, which had been concentrating between 1980 and 1990, now appears to be dispersed among a larger set of agro-commercial capitalists. Some political constraints on accumulation have been lifted.

Yet this system of rice markets is increasingly differentiated. At both extremes are people whose lives have involved mobility and who often begin as outsiders to local society. At the pauperized end, itinerant traders, and street traders, moving regularly from the regions generating surplus, have incomes which, if unsupplemented, would leave their families below the poverty line.[43] At the elite extreme, the 'power points' remain in the hands of migrant mercantile dynasties of the sort described in chapters 6 and 7. In one not unusual example, accessible on the internet, the portofolio of a conglomerate includes rice mills, textiles, iron and steel distribution, property, and finance.[44] Accumulation still depends on a quantum of starting capital. The largest firms in the system began large.

Between the extremes, the intermediaries known as middlemen—wholesalers, brokers and commission agents—are on the march. Their relative power is increasing. They are needed because of the increasingly capitalized rice mills' insatiable demand for paddy. Agents reduce the supervision and transactions costs of co-ordinating supplies. They are now able to borrow independently from banks and to transport and store without constraint other than working capital. In this shifting context, rice mills may retaliate by deploying family labour to deal directly with producers and also by delaying repayments for paddy received through agents.

In this chapter, an attempt has been made to focus attention on changes due to growth rather than to policy; but, since the state is entangled in the system of markets, certain observations about the state are relevant to our conclusions here. During this long period of growth, the Left Front Government has acquiesced complicitously in flagrant breaches of regulative law. As we saw in chapter 5, when we considered the illegal status of most husking mills, this might be interpreted as resistance to the unimplementable laws of the central government, laws which are imposed from above and unadapted to local circumstances. But as we can see from the current status of Kolkata, retail and wholesale trade no longer has to transgress the laws that formerly cordoned off Kolkata and preserved it for statutory rationing, though it continues to transgress the laws concerning the use of public space. So, laws remain but their force is spent. This is hardly an organized defiant resistance by the Left Front; more the consequence of locally disorganized and disempowered state vigilance and of conflicts of interest within the state which are resolved through rents.

The fact that petty trade has never been given political or economic support, despite its large voting power and despite the CPI(M)'s declarations about alternative paths to those of capitalism and feudalism, makes nonsense of public choice theories which model policy as a commodity, voters as demand, and votes as currency. The 'currency' of votes has never been exchanged for a regulative environment which incentivizes livelihoods based on dispersed and small-scale accumulation. All that may have happened is that licensing has put paid to some of the grossest extortion.

In consequence, apparently unreformed laws become adapted to the local struggle over surplus. On the one hand, we see petty extortion of small traders by ticket inspectors, police and vigilance officials, where the inspectorates are the more powerful parties; and on the other, corrupt and fraudulent accommodations with rice mills where mills are more powerful than vigilance officials. While regulative laws and state institutions change, these relationships do not. For example, traders who are no longer breaking laws now declared obsolete are still forced to bribe check-post guards. Development is still driven pervasively by a wish to avoid regulation—for example, wholesaler–retailers staying small, or larger wholesaler–retailers declaring gross output as under Rs 200,000 to escape sales taxes on food grains, or street traders breaking the laws of trespass in Kolkata by trying to keep stock small enough to move rapidly when alerted to a raid. Even retailing is a micro-scale nexus of primitive forms of accumulation. In the next chapter we will see the vigour of these market arrangements, rife with rent-seeking, when faced with rapid liberalization.

Notes

1. Mitra and Sarkar, 2003. This study found exiguous nominal returns to all economic categories of producers, which turned negative as soon as labour was imputed at market rates. By contrast, returns to storage were 'exorbitantly high' (p. 4694). Rather than distress sales, they see the bond market involving speculation by well-informed traders as being principally responsible for the sharp discrepancy in returns.
2. Basu's analysis of price behaviour in Hooghly district and Kolkata concludes that while spatial markets are integrated and efficient, seasonal price fluctuations in the same markets increase over time even while the cold store technology which sharply reduces the perishability of the product has diffused widely. Further, these *spatially* integrated markets permit high returns to *storage over time*. The only conclusion possible is the one made: (2002, p. 225). *Storage activities have been by and large cornered by a group of traders*. Cold stores are found to have a significant influence on exchange relations and marketing behaviour. There are greater post harvest, and distress sales with growing distance from the cold stores. Credit from potato wholesalers (and cold store owners) is used to fine tune the timing and prices of producers' sales. The existence of technologies for cold storage enables farmers who are able to retain title to potato to receive higher prices than those in debt. But traders and store owners get higher returns than all types of producers.
3. Mukhopadhyay examines the local marketing system within 24 Parganas district. His most important conclusion is that there has been a sharp increase in the variability of seasonal arrivals such that there is increasingly less pattern to it. Supply data could not explain price fluctuations. However, the price relation between *kutials* (small paddy rice processors) and producers with marketed surplus was closely integrated and *that* segment of the local rice market was judged to work competitively. By contrast, the weekly price series of *kutials* was not well integrated with that for rice retailers. He concludes that at the stage of *retailing*, *rents* derived from market imperfections *are being reaped*. The field research also did not cover the organization and relations of credit and finance in an adequate way. Neglect of the political economy of the money trail is a severe deficiency in most recent field research and one being the more regretted because practically all studies of the politics of policy neglect this key element.

Liberalization and Institutional Development 255

4. This state-level surplus is fragile. In 1996–7, allowing for seed and normal levels of waste, the state fell back to an 18 per cent deficit (Government of West Bengal, 1999, p. 1).
5. IR36 ('Iyer 36') is the commonest rice variety but the range of varieties of rice has grown and even includes the production (sometimes for international export) of elite strains like *basmati*. The seasonal weighting of production is 63 per cent in amon, 7 per cent in aus and 29 per cent in boro (Government of West Bengal, 2000, p. 15).
6. By 2002-3, rice farmers in West Bengal earned 30 per cent less than in 1996–7 (Sharma, 2004). The decline in agricultural profits was argued by Sarkar, 2006, to account for the fact that cultivators, who were 38 per cent of the rural workforce in 1991 had declined to 25 per cent by 2001. Landless agricultural labourers, who were 39 per cent of the rural workforce in 1987 grew to being 50 per cent by 1999-2000 (Macroscan, 2003b).
7. For deflators with which to evaluate prices against those of earlier rounds, see the glossary before the preface.
8. Ministry of Agriculture, Bulleting of Food Statistics, several issues—see Chand, 2003).
9. Government of West Bengal, 2000; http://agmarknet.nic.in/rice_paddy-profile_copy.pdf.
10. Tenants with larger operational holding sizes than those of landlords. Bhattacharyya, 2003; 2005.
11. Because the quantities of rice needed for subsistence rise slowly, rates of increase in the marketed surplus exceed those in production. Petty producing households are even reported to be forsaking subsistence not for reasons of distress but by selling inferior high yielding rice in order to purchase higher quality and even processed puffed rice. There has also been a huge increase in the supplies of paddy from long-distance sources.
12. Raw data from FCI and Government of West Bengal, 1999, p. 4.
13. See the Glossary before the Preface for deflators for constant price comparison with earlier periods.
14. District Food and Supplies Officer, Bardhaman district, 2004, Pers Comm.
15. See pages 222 to 224 on the increasing dependence of rice mills on long-distance supplies brokered by agents due to the high capacity requirements of new pre-milling processing technology.
16. After the liberalization of the import of artificial fibres and the increase in demand for the products of an increasingly centralized textiles industry which relies to an ever greater extent on migrant labour to industrial districts, many rural livelihoods were displaced (Singh and Sapra, 2007).
17. This was the estimate of several rice millers and wholesalers.
18. Kaur, Ghosh, and Sudarshan, 2007.
19. See Appendix 1.1 for the general problems of field work on markets.
20. Government of West Bengal, 2000a, p. 2. There is no hard data. The calculation here is based on the marketed surplus having been about 40 per cent in the early 80s (Ghosh and Chowdhury, 1983) when rice mills cornered

15 per cent of total production; and the marketed surplus approaching 50 per cent now, with rice mills processing 25 per cent of production.
21. This variation is due to differences in the capital costs of combinations and permutations of pre-milling processing machinery, land prices, drying yard sizes etc. Bardhaman district is technologically ahead of Birbhum district for reasons discussed later on pages 231 to 234.
22. Adulteration becomes self fulfilling when rice millers routinise deductions for it.
23. The distributive share is the relationship between wages and the residual claim (or net returns). It has fallen by half from 65 per cent in 1982 (chapter 4).
24. Only 7 per cent of the labour force contributes, all-India. West Bengal had one of the worst rates of default on collection of Provident Fund for the year 2003–4 (Menon, 2005, pp. 6–7).
25. Some employers' associations deliberately co-opt workers so as to maintain class corporate control over them, but not Rice Mill Owners' Associations in West Bengal (Basile and Harriss-White, 2000).
26. Said by employers in 2002 to be for 8–10 years.
27. Migrants in agriculture are expected to save (Rogaly and Rafique, 2003).
28. This is far in excess of the ILO limit for human beings to carry.
29. However the displacement of permanent labour was not only due to political threats. Cooks, servants and security supervisors who were on permanent contract were no longer needed to service the casual labour force.
30. de Haan and Rogaly (1996) also trace the disproportionate anti-female bias in the decline of jobs in the jute industry in West Bengal.
31. This part of the story relies heavily on the field work of Sutapa Choudhury (2001) who studied markets in south Kolkata supplied mainly from the South of the state. There is no reason not to believe that the social relations of trade found in here are similar to those of retail markets supplied by petty trade from central Bengal.
32. A city described to me by a S. Indian bank employee working there as a 'great labour city where goods are cheap' in stark contrast to Madras (Chennai).
33. 'Lullaby Aunt', by Joy Goswami, about 1970, translated by Ashis Ranjan Choudhury; in Choudhury, 2001.
34. Estimated by the Population Division. United Nations on http://www.hsd.ait.ac.th.
35. The revenue crisis has also forced states like Tamil Nadu to introduce what is considered to be a regressive sales tax on this most essential of essential commodities.
36. This risk is assimilated in commercial costs.
37. Cases like this are also used by Jagganathan (1987) to exemplify what he calls 'intangible assets' which we take to refer to this 'functional' credibility.
38. Known as *goondas*, these threatening employees thread their way through Rohinton Mistry's novel: *A Fine Balance*.

39. Lachaier, 2000, shows that the regulation of business accounts still varies by region, by caste within region, and according to dates stipulated by astrological auspiciousness.
40. If drawn on the subject, traders justify its irrelevance with references to the long history of Communist Rule, together with the idea of 'equality' with which the CPI(M) is associated. It is also possible that the castes in trade benefit from this 'equality' and have never experienced caste barriers to entry.
41. This is a legal status.
42. For an example of which the reader may consult the label on any bottle of mineral water.
43. While most petty traders are from households with small plots of land, a significant fraction of the rice retailers studied by Choudhury (2001) were main breadwinners, often with dependent spouses and/or children together with provisioning obligations to more distant dependent kin.
44. http://wwwri3240.com/Dist/profilejugal.htm

9 State and Market, 1991–2002: De-Regulation, De-Participation, Re-Regulation, and Crisis

This chapter describes how the market for agricultural commodities in our study areas responded to the biggest external shock in its history—liberalization. Liberalization is a much-misunderstood phenomenon. In reality, it consists not of abolishing regulation so much as making complex rearrangements of state regulation. Moreover, apart from plantation agriculture, which accounts for only about three per cent of India's agricultural output, agricultural production is not directly regulated by the state in India; agricultural liberalization, or re-regulation, has primarily been concerned with the post-harvest processing and marketing system. Most of this re-regulation has occurred below the radar of most scholars, who have been almost exclusively interested in reforms of the regulative structures governing India's economic relations with the rest of the world, and the opening of domestic markets to international capital. We are mainly concerned, by contrast, with a continuous stream of less discussed internal, domestic reforms, which shifted control from the public sector to private capital, that also took place from 1993 onwards.

Indeed, the process began quite near the start of what is now called the 'era of liberalization'.[1] Initiated by the central government, the reforms were taken up actively by the Left Front Government in West Bengal, just as they were in other states. It was the Left Front which licensed all husking mills in 1994 and put an end to the dichotomy between licensed and illegal mills. It had also was the Left Front which repealed the power of rice millers to attach paddy agents in 1996, and gave *de jure* legitimacy to the *de facto* diversification and expansion of paddy brokerage. It was the Left Front which freed wholesale and retail ceilings on inventory in 1999 and de-licensed the wholesale and retail trade in March 2002. But despite vigorous local lobbying from various interests which successfully wrung concessions from the Left Front Government,[2] the process of repeal of regulative law which frames state trading and the Public Distribution System was driven by the central government. Its powers over markets were much more far-reaching than those of the states; and it was a necessary precondition for the inflow of international capital that there should be a domestic regulative market order that was sympathetic to it. Were a state to wish to resist (and after 15 years in office there was no evidence that the Left Front wished to resist), it would have had little authority to do so.

This chapter explores the sequence of reforms to the rice market and to the state interventions which operate alongside the market and mesh with it. It examines the impact of liberalization not only on the institutions of the market but also on the operation of the state. While small-scale production, trade, and unregulated labour markets expanded in a new wave of decentralised accumulation, the commercial elites preserved their power and profits by reaching ever further afield. While the procurement of price structures decreed by the central government led to increasing subsidies and an unprecedently mountainous buffer stock of grain—the opposite of what had apparently been intended— the centralization of state control introduced new complexities in co-ordination, while the widely-spread informal process of rent-seeking was hardly touched.

It then becomes possible to show how and why in the early 21st century both the market and the state ended up facing crises.

For a chapter devoted to seeing what liberalization involves, it is useful to have a typology for the political regulation of markets that is more nuanced than the concepts of 'liberalization' or 'reform', but of a higher order than the legal detail. The next section recapitulates the classification on which our analysis is based. Section 2 describes the main changes in regulation other than those involving the Public Distribution System (PDS), which is dealt with in Section 3. Section 4 describes the massive crisis of oversupply and the collapse in prices that resulted from liberalization, both domestically and in other countries. Section 5 returns to the central questions outlined above and looks at the overall impact of liberalization on the agricultural commodity markets of West Bengal.

Analysing Regulation and De-regulation

The state regulates markets to create the conditions for the orderly accumulation of capital. It must supply the general preconditions— the parameters—for the reproduction of capital, including such things as the creation, protection and validation of property rights, the identification of the unit of accumulation through licences, and the standardization of the units of transaction through weights and measures. It must pass laws and create disciplinary institutions to regulate what 'the market' may do in storage, processing, and transport, where it may operate, and how it may form prices, transfer property rights, and effect payments. It must make the rules with which market exchange is increasingly saturated, stipulations about the presentation of commodities and the precise context of transactions, the hours of sale, physical conditions of sale, the sales environment, quality, packaging and labelling.

In regulating conditions of exchange, a structure of rents is created alongside the structure of competition. For example, state regulation gives advantages to firms involved in long-distance trade, compared with the sort of socially-regulated firms we saw operating in Kolkata at the end of chapter 8; state regulation may thus enable rents to be reaped by the larger firms, or those enforcing the rules. Rent is likewise reaped by state officials who use discretionary authority corruptly to sell rationed public assets, and also to extort money from firms that are legally not entitled to trade. Parametric regulations raise the costs of trading in the interest of a desired structure and desired conduct— for example, stipulating that transactions are legal only when made in a specific place, which encourages the crowding of sellers and buyers, and leads to competitive price formation and spot transactions; all transactions that evade this rule generate rents. It is not inevitable that such rents have to be shared with enforcement officials, but officials are likely to demand that they are.

The politics associated with these kinds of state regulation will permeate the entire system of markets, and changes in regulative detail will therefore come as 'shocks' to the market system. Whether such perturbations are seen as originating outside the system, or are a consequence of its operation, is a somewhat arbitrary question, depending on how boundaries are defined for analytical purposes, since the system of markets is so deeply politicized. It is generally assumed that with modernization, the domain of regulation passes from social institutions to the state, from 'custom to contract', through a series of shocks and perturbations in which the state grows ever relatively stronger. Whether the recent experience of West Bengal tends to support this assumption may be doubted, because when the Government of India moves from state-led development towards a 'politics of de-regulation', is it the 'regulative' or 'participative' intervention that is actually being de-regulated and privatized? If a state-regulated market system, involving state participation in the market as well as state regulation of the markets, has been implemented according to neither the spirit nor the letter of the law, but instead has been transformed to serve as a local base for 'rents' and for accumulation—in such a case, does 'de-regulation' actually connote a regression to regulation by 'custom'? Or rather, is 'de-regulation' really a matter of shifts in the relative importance of various non-state market-making institutions, and non-market institutions? Indeed, are the power relations that already exist in the market sufficiently strong and 'path dependent' to prevent much of a shift at all?

The second general kind of politics of markets concerns the state's active *participation*. The Indian state is not exceptional in this respect. It buys, stores and sells, organizes processing, finances marketing and innovation, and owns and operates, or organizes transport. In so doing, the state alters the structure of capital bound up in the system of markets. It shapes technology and material flows, employs labour under terms and conditions which differ from, but which also affect, those of the firms in the market. And, with an in-built conflict of interest, it also regulates its own participation.

Participative intervention is the most directly and costly kind of regulation, so it is only undertaken if there are strong reasons and/or interests at stake. The aims of the Essential Commodities Act of 1955 were 'to provide for the control of production, distribution of and trade in certain essential commodities in the interest of the general public' because malpractices in trade could and should be prohibited and... a more equal distribution of essential commodities could and should be realized' (Mooij, 1996, pp. 198 and 201). From the earlier studies (chapters 3, 5, and 7) it is obvious that the practice of state participation is far from homogeneous, despite the 'universalist' discourse attached to it, and despite the all-Indian or state-wide organizations and instruments through which it is imposed.

When moves are made to de-regulate, it is likely to be state participation that is intended to be reduced or even ended by privatization; 'de-regulation' usually means a form of re-regulation in which participative intervention formally gives way to regulatory intervention. This will be much more unambiguously a shock to the system of markets than dismantling regulatory intervention. How much of this has happened? How has it been sequenced? How has it been resisted? What has been the impact of the withdrawal of state participation on regulative activity? Whose interests are served rhetorically, and whose served in practice, by de-regulation and 'de-participation'? What has been the impact on the rest of the system of markets? The causes and effects of individual components of de-regulation, de-participation and their sequencing are difficult to disentangle. Hence the outcome in 2002 was a complex process, in which growth as well as de-regulation and de-participation played a significant part.

De-regulation

During the 1990s and the early years of the 21st century, a key part of the structure of regulation—restrictions on licences—was removed, while some new parts were added (notably the unification of the structure of regulation of husking). Large parts were dismantled: movement restrictions (intra-, inter-state, and international), and rules concerning storage and the regulation of processing. In 1998, unmodified oil from rice bran was stated to be fit for human consumption. The details are summarized in Table 9.1.

Three elements in the regulative system, on the other hand, remained completely untouched. None of the structure of regulation of labour was altered, not because of the union's power of resistance, but rather because it did not need altering since so much of it remains un-enforced. The regulation of electricity connections by State Electricity Boards (SEBs) also remained unchanged and banks are still not allowed to lend for pure trade—yet throughout the last quarter century the nationalized banks' loans at concessional interest rates to 'Small Scale Industries' (SSIs) had allowed the rice mills to divert part of their own funds to pure trade.

Changes in Licensing Regulation: Plus ça Change

Several categories of licences have been abolished and entry barriers to most parts of the system lowered. Yet all firms still need licences—even if it is only a Municipal Trading Licence. Weights and measures are still inspected on the basis of licences. Licences also provide information for both local and central government taxes.[3] The system still leaves space for rents from licensing to be created and shared. Bribes are still considered necessary to get licences, as are bribes and fraud to avoid the obligations laid down in licences, and bribes to avoid penalties for breaches of residual regulative law. Liberalization has not put paid to corruption but has only decentralized it, as has been widely reported (Harriss-White, 1996; Khan, 2000).

State and Market 263

Table 9.1: Domestic Liberalization of Rice

De-regulation	
1993	Inter-state movement
1994	Husking mills delicensed
	Wholesale trade delicensed
	Exports (quantitative limits and minimum export price)
1996	Authorization to Rice Mills for licensing paddy agents repealed
1997	Rice Milling (Regulation) Act, 1958; Rice Milling Industry (Regulation and Licensing) Rules, 1959, repealed.
	Rice mills de-reserved as SSI.
1998	Bran oil de-regulated for human consumption
1999	Delicensing of Rice Mills: [Electricity Dept., Factories Act Regulation, Pollution (Dept. of the Environment); Border and Trade Licence (Municipality); Agricultural and Processed Food Products Export Development Authority.]
	Retail stock limit increased from 10 to 100q.
2002	De-licensing of wholesale/retail trade [Food Dept; Depts. of Commerce and of Industry; Small Scale Industry (SSI)].
	Licence still required in Electricity Department—Electricity; Department of Industry—Factory Act; Department of the Environment—Pollution; Municipality—Border and Trade Licenses; Department of Food and Supplies—Municipal Rice Permit; Permit for RM to custom mill; levy compliance release certification; Permit for purchase of paddy and sale of rice.
	License no longer required for Department of SSI; Department of Commerce (Agricultural and Processed Food Products Export Development and Authority Certification; Department of Commerce (Milling); Department of Industry.
2003	Repeal of WB Rice Mills (Control and Levy) Order of 2002.
De-participation	
1997	Food Department to replace FCI.
1999	West Bengal Rice and Paddy Levy Control Order introduced—50 per cent on RM.
	Husking mills brought under Levy Control Order—SMT fixed levy.

A second unexpected outcome is that most husking mills, which always operated illegally, have been *formalized* by de-regulation. Licensing has made them much more visible to the local state. If the Government of West Bengal still has difficulty in knowing how many there are, it is because it no longer has any urgent need for this information. The most obvious result is a new wave of husking mills, some of which are starting to install an appropriate subset of rice mill machines. From 1999, husking mill owners became eligible to use nationalized banks, and by 2002 in Birbhum district, about 40 per cent were estimated to have signed up for bank accounts. The huge increase in petty trade, and in the diversity of the niches the mills occupy, would have happened anyway; it was happening prior to liberalization, and still goes on without licences. The impact of licensing husking mills is that accumulation possibilities have been liberated.

Changes in the Regulation of Milling

The decades-old dichotomy between rice mills and husking mills is starting to blur. De-regulation enables some husking mills to mill rice on their own account—doubling net incomes (to an average of perhaps Rs 4,500 per month from a combined operation milling for custome and on their own account). Subject to the availability of power supplies, they can increase their scale, reduce their seasonality, and undercut the rice mills. With chains of hullers, two husking mills in Kalna have expanded to handle 700 and 1400 tonnes of rice respectively. Husking mill owners are starting to lend money for onward lending by itinerant paddy traders. Quantities and periodicities are said to be small, but it is in this way that a different layer of capital—husking mills—competes for supplies, using the same institutional techniques as the rice mills.[4] A few are starting to act as brokers. The revision of the criteria of eligibility to process rice under the Essential Commodities Act, so that husking mills become eligible, means that husking mills are also eligible to operate as paddy agents for procurement. The Food Department and Food Corporation of India (FCI) have yet to absorb the transactions cost implications of negotiating with up to 37,000 husking mills.[5]

Rice mills, now less enveloped in red tape, can now trade in rice, and it was reported that they have started to buy up rice from husking mills working on their own account, a move which will last only as long as the latter do not deal directly with long-distance rice wholesalers. Mills also seek to bypass paddy agents and to negotiate directly with farmers—but, as the Food Department also knows, this diffused marketable surplus is transactions-costly to bulk. Mills encourage groups of farmers to make cash sales and compensate for their bypassing of paddy agents with the Rs 15 per quintal of paddy that would otherwise have been given as a commission to brokers.

Paddy agents no longer depend so much on credit from the rice mills, so the numbers and scale of operations of a new kind of broker-cum-wholesaler have rapidly expanded. Paddy 'agents' are now in direct competition with rice mills for control over supplies, and have spawned a further tier of village paddy agents below them, struggling in turn for independence.

The delicensing of wholesale and retail trade means that all elements in the system can now stock grain. As a result, from 1997, there was a rapid increase in wholesale trade with unlimited storage and no costs of harassment. The only constraint on scale is that of formal credit. Banks still hold the key to accumulation. Only five per cent of local wholesaler-retailers have bank credit, and the nationalized banks still do not lend—at least directly—for pure trade, nor will they lend to petty traders. The decentralization of storage will be unproblematic until there is a drought, because only then will the problems involved in the co-ordination and monitoring of supplies become evident. There has been a proliferation of new kinds of firm with new activity-mixes in the rice markets: commission agents and itinerant traders. *Farias* and *beparis* (itinerant and village traders) can now process paddy (hence the new forms of attachment of paddy-rice processing to husking mills described in chapter 8). A new set of brokers negotiate rice sales to wholesalers; and new itinerant traders buy from kutials and sell to wholesaler-retailers.

Resistance: Procedural and Institutional Rigidity

The roll-back of the regulative state has certainly re-ordered the structure of rent, but it has also provoked resistance to the re-ordering. After three years of deregulation, new rice mills in Birbhum still had to register as SSIs, register for Commercial Taxes, and get Pollution Control certificates, Boiler Inspection Certificates, Food Department trading and milling certificates, and Government of India permits. Even after seven years of de-regulation, some rice mills still operate with the old system of attached paddy agents. Husking mills can be licensed but the Electricity Board enforces such lengthy queues that mills develop anyway, using domestic electricity supplies, and are *de facto* still uncertified. In other parts of the system, de-regulation has left structures of extortion intact: check-post guards continue to extort bribes even though intra- and inter- state movements restrictions were abolished in 1997. This behaviour has also been observed in S. India as well (Harriss-White, 1996). Although husking mills can bank with state banks, the latter do not lend to huskers for technological upgrading. Hence, vested interests gain from the slothful implementation of changes in policy.

Other structures also persist, with their own dynamics. The processing of muri (puffed rice) has diffused, unregulated, while Bolpur's primitive and dirty wholesale markets flourish in flagrant disregard of land use regulations in response to the needs of new itinerant traders, in the same way that the proliferation of street traders in Kolkata does. Labour markets remain heavily embedded in relations of locality, class, caste, and gender. There is little change in the economic opportunities for scheduled tribe people. In some localities, many Muslims have entered husking milling and the paddy-rice trading associated with it. The webs of *Aratdars* (commission agents), however, are still mainly Hindu. The 'power points' remain Marwari. While women are not completely excluded, they are confined to the pettiest—and still illegal—kinds of trade.

Summing-up: De-regulation as Re-regulation

Greater change has been unleashed in the rice markets than in agricultural production and the two sub-circuits of rice markets are increasingly intertwined. Novel niches have been created, and wage labour has been redistributed within the system of markets: away from rice mills. towards self-employment and small-scale work, which is at present decentralized, un-unionized and not regulated by the state. Throughout the system, the scales of operation and the level of capitalization have expanded. Investment in machinery—generating scale economies—is still protected by the state, but the state no longer provides circumstances (such as attached paddy-purchase agents) which will ensure a sufficient supply to run the mills at high capacity. This is a big change, but at the time of writing, it is too early to know its impact on rice mills. The business families running them are seizing exit options—investing in transport, construction, stone crushing, department stores, dairy businesses, and groceries as well as the professions (teaching, law, and financial consultancy). While this is nothing new (diversification reduces portfolio risks), the trend seems to have accelerated.

It was hypothesized that de-regulation would have little impact if the market system operated illegally or without regard for regulative law anyway. While much regulative law was in any case informally reconfigured for the purpose of accumulation, the system nonetheless did develop around it and had to take it into account. De-regulation, by allowing previously illegal sub-systems to operate, but now under licence, was in reality a process of re-regulation. Yet even this has not prevented a further huge rise in unlicensed petty trade, resulting from sustained agricultural growth.

With respect to labour, the regulative structure protecting labour remains intact but this has not prevented it from being further informalized. Increasing numbers of (petty) firms within the system have no effective work-related obligations, and their workers have no rights.

Are the rents which persist, such as those of the mills, of developmental benefit? According to Khan and Jomo (2000), rents are 'not unconducive to development if they maintain the social order necessary for growth'. In rural West Bengal, the social order that has presided over an era of agricultural growth has not changed the reality of widespread poverty, however it is measured. Reducing this poverty depends upon the countervailing power of new kinds of accumulation. Fostering widespread accumulation would require the re-regulation of a banking sector which at present is still protecting the rice mill oligopoly. The Government of India is behind the lack of change in rural banking rules which would support petty production and trade.

De-participation

While agriculture is a state-level responsibility, the central government is responsible for food. Although the Left Front Government plays an important part in the story of state de-participation, it is the Government of India (the political coalitions surrounding the BJP, the Congress and the economists advising them) rather than the Government of West Bengal that has taken the leading role in regard to food. And not only the Government of India, but the Bretton Woods financial institutions and their client think-tanks have also kept a particularly critical eye on two aspects of the Indian state's participative interventions in the food system.

One of these is the Public Distribution System (PDS) and its food subsidy. For several reasons, food subsidies are a 'favourite target in adjustment'.[6] First, public expenditure on food subsidies, alleged to be large, contributes to fiscal deficits. These, in turn, tend to pre-empt the satisfaction of interest obligations and the repayment of foreign loans (which most concern the Bretton Woods institutions) (Government of India, 1998–9.). Public expenditure on food subsidies is large partly because subsidized foodgrains are seen as a 'public good'—in the everyday sense of one about which there is a public consensus that it should be under public control. Food and rice are examples. Their distribution in remote areas, and the guarantee of national food security (including emergency relief), entail high costs, but these are seen as being appropriately borne by the state.[7] A second reason why food subsidies are a target in structural adjustment is that public expenditure on food distribution is said to be excessive, due to 'inefficiency'. But the efficiency of the PDS cannot easily be compared with that of private trade because of the public goods and services elements at the heart of the public distribution system. Madhura Swaminathan carefully investigated the relative efficiency of public and private distribution and formed the conclusion that the market does not always offer consumers a better deal than the FCI in terms of price in either rural or urban areas (Swaminathan, 1999; see also Choudhury, 2001; p. 23.).

A third 'Bretton Woods' critique relates to economic distortions due to corruption and fraud. As we have seen, corruption is not confined to participative intervention; and the case for liberalization as an attack on corruption has taken a general form (World Bank, 1997). Liberalization—'rolling back the state'—is supposed to remove the niches from which venal officials privatize public goods and services.[8] Firms wishing to cut red tape incur search costs to gain access to such goods and services—as well as the direct costs of bribery— and all these costs detract from investment in growth. The privately-appropriated returns are assumed to be consumed, or are laundered abroad—at any rate, they are losses to domestic investment and growth.[9]

Roy (1996) has estimated the latter as being some 20 times greater than the former.

Fraud can occur throughout the PDS and it takes the form of leakages in procurement, storage and distribution, and at the final local point of issue. Ahluwalia measured leakages by using NSS data on households' purchases from the PDS in 1986–7 and comparing it with data on FCI supplies. Over 36 per cent of the Government of India's PDS rice appeared to leak to the 'open' market. Further, only 25-30 per cent of the foodgrains supplied to the PDS reached the 40 per cent of the poorest population. If only a quarter of the food subsidy reached poor people, the question arose whether the PDS was reformable or whether it was best abandoned.[10]

The Food Subsidy and De-participation

Despite the formidable force of these arguments, it has not been easy to demolish food subsidies and the institutions through which they are delivered. This is because, however defectively, these institutions do deliver food. India has an electoral democracy, and food security is sensitive for votes. Far from being cut, the food subsidy has grown vastly during the first decade of the reforms. At Rs 2850 crores, all-India in 1991–2, the first year of the reforms, it grew to Rs 9200 crores by 1999–2000. In real terms it roughly doubled, and amounted to nearly one per cent of GDP.[11] In 2000–01, the Government of India was encouraged by the IMF to announce a 12 per cent reduction, but by 2002–3 the subsidy had ballooned still further to Rs 19,400 crores (Government of India, 2002; http://fciweb.nic.in.).

While the subsidy grew, the Public Distribution System was significantly altered. Congress took timid steps but under the BJP, with its strong all-India support from business (including the pervasive foodgrains markets and food business (Hansen and Jaffrelot, 1998)); the state has tried to deal a mortal blow to state participation in the markets. The turning-point was the year 2000. The following section outlines the way the all-India state withdrew from participation, and how this affected state institutions and the rice market system within West Bengal. Much of the information on state institutions comes from sources within the food administration and therefore must be taken on trust.

In the 1990s, de-participation in food provision took two directions. First the central food procurement agency, the FCI, was under pressure to privatise. This was planned incrementally. About 1200 of its smaller stores, under 10,000 tonnes capacity, were to be privatised, leaving a rump of 500. Second, there were changes in the structure of food prices and the rules of entitlement. On the one hand, in order to retain the political support of powerful farm lobbies in north-western India, the prices at which grain was purchased by state agencies were allowed to rise continuously in real terms. From 1990 to 1999 this rise averaged a massive 10.2 per cent per annum.

The subsidized issue price to consumers was also raised, but in a series of discontinuous stages. Between 1991 and 1994, the issue price rose by 86 per cent, at twice the rate of the index of wholesale prices.[12] Then, in 1997/8, under the BJP, people's access to PDS food was cut in two ways. First, a poverty line was introduced and ration cardholders were divided by income into households above and below it. The line was set at Rs 1,761 per household per month. Though plenty of households in rural India were eligible, few households in Kolkata were actually poor enough to be under this line; but in a 'mysterious way', the Left Front Government identified 'below the poverty line' (BPL) households in Kolkata as amounting to 32 per cent of the population.[13] Second, the prices at which the two categories gained access to the PDS were increasingly differentiated. Those 'above the poverty line' (APL) could access any amount of the PDS at an issue price which rose by 50 per cent to Rs 7 per kg, creeping ever closer to that of the 'open' market. The BPL category which needed PDS grain most, were subject to a quota of 10 kg per month—at a subsidized price of Rs 3 per kg. By 2000, the issue price for the APL category had reached Rs 11.30 and the difference between the issue price and prices in the 'open' market had almost disappeared. In 2000, the ration quota for the BPL category was doubled to 20 kg. But poor households were not allowed to purchase the quota in instalments and few could afford Rs 110 for the complete consignment. Then in 2001, this price shot up by 61 per cent to Rs 5.5 per kg. The erosion of the difference between the BPL and APL prices, at a time when consumer preference was more elastic to quality than price, left ration stock unsold and a growing pile of grains in stores. Meanwhile, the Government of India targeted 10 million BPL households with a 'take it or leave it' quota of 25 kgs to be lifted at Rs 3 per kg. In 2002 it was 35 kgs—ever more unaffordable. Uptake plummeted.

In the year 2000, under the destructive price policy through which a mountainous buffer of unsold stock built up, and uptake slackened, only 2 per cent of the stock was lifted. The highest quality grain was distributed first, leaving larger stocks of poorer quality grain and subsequently greater losses. Up to Rs 8,200 crores were needed to run the PDS and Rs 40,000 crores were locked up in stocks. Outright physical losses, estimated at Rs 10–20 crores at the national level, started to dwarf the subsidy (Swaminathan 1999, FCI sources, 2000).

The Buffer Stock and Exports

India's buffer stock of grain has long been set at a quantity[14] which will cover a major drought. When a drought occurs, it tends to last two years, so the buffer has been around 20–30 million tonnes. As a result of the PDS policies discussed above, buffer stocks grew out of control to reach 45 million tonnes in 2000 and 60 million tonnes in 2002. At that point, the Government of India incurred further expenditure to subsidize exports of grain. But, world prices being low (Rs 5 per kg for wheat compared with the Rs 5.75 per kg subsidized support price for wheat), it was reported by several different kinds of 'stakeholder' sources that private firms charged with exports had turned the flows back into India and reaped rents by selling this subsidized grain in the 'open' market.[15]

Decentralized Control

The decentralization of the control of food to state governments, which started in 1997, was a radical departure from the constitutional division of responsibilities. It had nothing to do with the process of decentralizing Government of India's development expenditure via the local *Panchayats* (Vyas, 2000; p. 4407). Panchayats are quite unequal to the task of identifying BPLs, controlling the logistics of food, and exerting vigilance.[16] In November 1997, West Bengal became the first state to pioneer the replacement of the FCI by its own agency. The Food Department became the state's monopoly agency for state trading and for the implementation of the central government's food policy. It was the first of several other states in the poverty belt which also made this move in 1997–99: UP, Rajasthan and Bihar. Why did West Bengal make the first move? Why did it take on the responsibility of managing the subsidy and establishment costs? This was a huge new commitment, especially in the absence of any reform in centre-state fiscal relations, which had become ever more centralised during the 1990s.[17]

Of course, pressure came from the Centre, itself under pressure to reduce the costs of procurement in marginal states (Government of West Bengal, 2002; pp. 18–21). But the main reason was that the Left Front Government, while actively participating in certain aspects of de-regulation, and forced to accept others, remained officially opposed to state de-participation in the food system. Throughout the 1990s, the CPI(M) was 'committed to maintaining supplies of foodgrains and other essential commodities at cheaper rates' and opposed the BJP government's continuous hikes in their prices as 'frustrating the very purpose of the PDS and causing hardship to the common people' (Budget speech of the Minister for Food and Civil Supplies, Kalimuddin Shams, Government of West Bengal, 2000–1).

There were several reasons for the later decision to take over the administration of the system as it then was. The first was fiscal. The Memorandum of Understanding (MOU) with the central government makes it clear that the Left Front Government expected to receive subsidies for procurement and distribution. The transport subsidy was as much as Rs 1,200,000 per 'rake' (train load of wagons of 2200 tonnes). A second reason for accepting local control was to regulate fraud. The Left Front Government had objected to being forced over many years to receive poor quality grain from the FCI (by virtue of the FCI's collusive relationship with rice millers and suppliers). As the enforcing agent, the local state had had little authority to pursue malpractices in and around the FCI, and reckoned it could work to a higher standard of enforcement, since the FCI's vigilance department had no powers of enforcement of its own. A third reason concerned efficiency. If the Food Department were to use the existing decentralized network of storage already built by private rice millers, it would reduce storage costs (by running them at high capacity) and reduce total transport costs (by stocking close to rural PDS consumers). Finally, the Left Front Government had been the object of energetic lobbying. The Rice Mill Lobby had also 'seized the day' and pressured the Left Front Government to take over procurement. Not only would this ensure the low-risk operating environment which had protected their oligopoly throughout the era of the Left Front, but also it would secure a steady river of state-controlled paddy and rice which could be made to leak an equally steady 2–3 per cent of rice.[18] This then fuelled a lucrative informal trade to Bangladesh. In short, decentralization was 'overdetermined'.

The Impact of De-participation

By the new century, the varied impacts of de-participation could be traced through changes in the roles of state institutions, from the central government and the FCI through the Government of West Bengal and its agencies down to the range of processing firms and sale outlets.

The Government of India: Strategic Control over West Bengal's Finance

The Government of India still bears the cost of the subsidy on transport and storage, funds for which are released by the Reserve Bank of India (RBI). The decisions on the timing of the release of these funds by the apex bank are absolutely essential to the operation of the PDS throughout India, and nowhere more so than in West Bengal. These are political decisions, urgently in need of research, but unfortunately outside the scope of this project, though their impact on West Bengal's Food Department is analysed below.[19]

State and Market

The Food Corporation of India: State-underwritten changes in staples

In West Bengal, as elsewhere, the FCI distributes PDS wheat (and sugar) as well as rice for the Government of India. It still procures some rice in West Bengal for other states, for plantations, and for military labour forces stationed in the state itself. Even in the era of liberalization, the FCI is continuing, by non-market means, to push the change in taste from rice to wheat, which was pioneered by the Ford Foundation in the 1960s, and the US wheat lobbies inside New Delhi's Agriculture Ministry[20] in the 1970s, and which ties West Bengal's market for staple food into a national market fuelled by wheat from Punjab and Haryana.

Within West Bengal, the coal belt and Kolkata are still administered under statutory rationing, a law, which, we saw earlier, is obsolete. The rest of West Bengal comes under the APL/BPL tiered and targeted PDS ('TPDS'). Kolkata needs 100,000 tonnes of grain a month (tpm) and the rest of West Bengal a further 120,000 tpm. But the state is remarkably unimportant to the national system of PDS procurement. Accounting for 15 per cent of total production, it uses just one per cent of India's PDS.[21] Self-sufficient in rice, but with demand and consumption dominated by a cosmopolitan city, West Bengal's de-regulation and de-participation has unleashed a market not only for rice but also for wheat—from UP, Punjab and Haryana. An estimated 6 m inhabitants of Kolkata hail from wheat-eating regions and middle-class Bengali consumers are developing a taste for *japatis* and bread. PDS wheat is attractive to these consumers. The procurement price is set according to a domestic political process and a well-established rate of return to the cost of production which is still the product of politically-administered input prices. Surplus wheat farmers in north-west India sell directly to procurement agents.

The appeasement of wheat farmers is a high political priority of central governments, of whatever political complexion. Kolkata is being supplied with increasing quantities of both open market and PDS wheat.[22] By 2000, nearly 60 per cent of the PDS took the form of wheat (Table 9.2). Even when world market wheat prices are below the domestic support price, the FCI has to purchase wheat from producers in Punjab and Haryana for political reasons. On the long route from the north west, pilferage gives rise to losses estimated at 1.3 to 2.6 per cent per month for rice and 0.5 to 1.4 per cent per month for wheat (Food Corporation of India, 2000; p. 6). Furthermore, FCI go-downs in the eastern zone, of which West Bengal is a major component, were ordered to accept unplanned consignments of PDS

Table 9.2 : Composition of State-controlled Supply

	Procurement of Foodgrains (Fig in M.T.)		
	Wheat	Rice	Total
1998-1999	12.7	11.8	24.50
1999-2000	14.1	19.1	33.20
2000-2001	16.3	19.1	35.40
2001-2002	20.6	21.2	41.80
2002-2003	19.0	14.48	33.48

Source: Data from FCI Eastern Zonal HQ, Kolkata.

grain moved from north-east states by order of the Government of India, which caused congestion, quality decline, and quantitative losses.[23]

The Government of West Bengal's Food Department

The Food Department took over procurement, from 1997; without heed to logistics, transactions costs or the lessons of the 1970s, it devised a system in which farmers were free to sell directly to the State Civil Supplies Corporation/ Food Department, and husking mills were given target procurement quotas, both of which proved to be unrealizable.[24] It also controlled the logistics of delivery of rice to the Fair Price Shops (FPS), from which rice is issued to consumers. Its first urgent need was for experienced personnel, so it accepted the transfer just mentioned, of some 3,000 employees from the West Bengal region of the FCI. Having but six stores of its own, the department was immediately dependent on the rice mills. As it—and they—foresaw, it did make savings on rent and transport over equivalent operations in West Bengal formerly run by the FCI. It also rented 23 go-downs from the FCI and established close co-ordination with it over a range of logistical activities. Increasingly, the monthly co-ordinating meetings were said to have become 'politicized'. Relationships with the rice mill sector also soured into antagonism. The Food Department delayed payments for rice milled on contract beyond the stipulated 72 hours. It did this because it was teetering on the edge of bankruptcy. Having borrowed Rs 120 crores in order to procure rice, it relied on the agreed transfers from the central government. These were not forthcoming because the Left Front Government apparently failed to satisfy the accounting procedures of the central government (that is, the Reserve

Bank of India) and thus forfeited its entitlement to compensation.[25] The central government then also ordered the Government of West Bengal to pay for the transport and PDS distribution of sugar, depleting resources available for the procurement, transport, and distribution of rice. From 2000 to 2004, the overdue payments to the Government of West Bengal tripled, from Rs 70 crores to Rs 200 crores.[26]

At the same time, the Food Department demanded higher quality standards than the FCI. But rice mills were widely reported to be entering into new relations of accommodation in order to protect the stream of rice syphoned off from the PDS as a 'leakage'.[27] Clearly it was not only in the sense of reducing the risks of operation that 'the levy kept the rice mills alive'.

Resistance: The FCI's labour force and its roles
To manage rice procurement and wheat distribution, even after the transfer of functions to the Food Department, the FCI still maintained a strong permanent establishment of employees in West Bengal on terms and conditions far superior to those of wage workers in the market system—in fact they had the best conditions of any paid labour in the rice system. It is worth looking at the structure of this relatively privileged and organized labour force, if only to illustrate how the organization of labour could not prevent the undermining of the FCI.

De-participation by the FCI has involved lay-offs as well as the reduction of the work-force by retirement and attrition. The FCI's all-India work-force was cut from 78,000 in 1980 to 66,000 in 2000 and was expected to reach 44,000 by 2005. The impact has been felt differentially by its three components. About a third of the FCI work-force is on permanent contract, with full rights under the Labour Laws. Another third is 'regular', contracted to work on a direct payment system (DPS) but with reduced rights; while the final third consists of daily casual 'contract' labour with no rights—or the right only to continuity of casual work. As if this were not complicated enough, each cadre of permanent employee (for depots, quality control, clerical, engineering, accounts and legal) has different terms and conditions. The representation of labour unions adds further complexity. The major union for permanent and semi-permanent/DPS labour is affiliated to the INTUC (associated with the Congress Party). It has haemorrhaged members to a break-away union, powerful in North India and owing allegiance to the National Democratic Alliance (NDA) which was in power in New Delhi from 1997 to 2004. The two unions owe allegiance to different political parties: CITU (Centre of Indian Trade Unions) to the CPI(M), and INTUC to Congress. Not only are the unions politically divided but the FCI Employees Union (CPI(M)) has been de-recognized at the all-India level.[28] And the recognized FCI Union represents at the most only 20 per cent of employees. One union is legitimate but unrecognized for purposes of negotiations, while the other is recognized but unrepresentative. In addition, both casual/contract and 'regular'/DPS labour, organized through the CITU, is in contention with permanent labour over the certification of overtime as well as with management over wages.

FCI workers have not taken the attack on their conditions of work lying down.[29] They have organized resistance to the direction of food policy and the labour force's de-legitimation and loss of rights. They have organized rallies and submitted memoranda to the Governor, the Chief Minister and Finance Minister in West Bengal, seeking them to pressurize the BJP coalition against the destruction of the PDS. They have also lobbied against Marwari rice wholesale merchants, accusing them of lowering open market prices in Kolkata by offloading FCI grain destined for export, and imploring them to desist. Thanks to achieving only very limited success—only 20 MPs supported their campaign—there was increased internal dissension. The 2,000 vacancies deliberately left unfilled in the permanent labour force affected efficiency. Casualization has caused higher grades to lose entitlements. But some 3,000 FCI employees in the state have been transferred to the West Bengal Food Department, which has guaranteed their job security. At one level, if this work-force is compared with that employed by private companies, it is secure and well-organized. Yet in the differentiated conditions of public sector work, two thirds of the labour force remains persistently deprived of work and social security rights. Worse, in the fractured politics of labour representation, the work force is unable to press its own interest or to defend the institution for which it works.

De-participation and Other Elements in the Food System
Rice mills
By 2000, not less than a hundred of the 324 operating rice mills were actively involved in litigation with the Food Department over charges of embezzlement of rice and stolen stock.[30] Yet not only did they continue to be protected by the state, they also continued to profit

from this protection. Rice mills had informally reduced their procurement obligations from a proportion to a fixed quantity (see chapter 7) and had upgraded their technology on the assumption that this arrangement would continue. Indeed, procurement targets for local rice mills (varying between 30 and 50 per cent of output over the period 1997–2001) confirmed this expectation.[31] However, the strained financial circumstances of the Food Department—in effect the involuntary de-participation of the state caused by the refusal of the Government of India/ Reserve Bank to transfer compensating funds—left these mills with idle capacity and backed-up stocks of low-grade paddy which had been destined for the PDS, causing a crisis of profitability.

Rice wholesalers
Sutapa Choudhury's field research on Kolkata's informal rice trade (see chapter 7) did not extend to the large rice wholesalers who shift the non-levy rice from the rice mills. Nor did the NCAER field project cover the wholesale-export houses. Nor, despite attempts, did our own field work in Birbhum in 2002 and Kolkata in 2000 succeed in reaching such firms or their associations. It is believed that rice wholesalers have benefited to a unique degree not only from the growth in the marketed surplus but also from both de-regulation and de-participation. In Kolkata, rice and wheat wholesaling is largely in the hands of migrant communities from Gujarat, Rajasthan, and Bihar. As with rice mills, they have been, and continue to be, poorly disciplined by the state. They have access to both private and nationalized banks, are agents for the state-subsidized exports widely alleged to have been illegally re-routed back into the domestic market when world market prices were depressed.

Fair Price Shops (FPS)
Ration shop dealers operate on a commission on sales. They therefore have the standard piece-rate incentive to maximize what they distribute. With adverse price conditions and lacklustre demand, and with stocks mounting up, the temptation to privatize and to 'leak' PDS rice into the open market has been irresistible. This rice joined the stream of re-routed exports, which both reduced 'open' retail market prices and raised these dealers' private returns above what they would have reaped had they not broken the rules.

Other sources of leakage

Faced with the mounting food grain mountain, the Government of India in 2000, under pressure from all sides, released more PDS grain into centrally-managed welfare schemes, such as the Midday Meal, Food for Work, and the *Annapurna Antyodan Yojana*. But, a proportion of these supplies also leaked into the retail markets, benefiting those who diverted them and adding to deflationary forces.

Summing up: The impact of de-participation

De-participation has been a separate political process from de-regulation. To date, it has neither had a major impact on improving efficiency nor has led to reductions in subsidies. It has had but a limited impact on fraud and leakages. Price controls in product markets create 'wedges' between issue prices, residual open market prices, and 'black' prices.[32] In new market niches, wholesalers and fair price shops can reap rents by buying at controlled prices and selling at open or black prices. De-participation has not had a significant long-term impact on stemming corruption. In 2000, credible sources reported that a possible reduction in corruption at the start of the Food Department's control was being sabotaged. De-participation had also intensified the casualization of labour employed by the state, and is a stark example of the erosion of labour rights.

De-participation by the Government of India was accompanied by participation by the state of West Bengal. Just as de-regulation has re-regulated the rice markets, formalized many elements, and resulted in new complexities, so also a form of de-participation requiring decentralization has increased the complexity of state participation, and its non-price-mediated co-ordination problems, chief among which are finance and logistics.

The central government's attack on its own parastatal, the FCI, was not the result of open political debate or a democratic decision, as the foundation of the FCI had been, (Harriss, 1984) but was the outcome of a manipulated crisis, that is, a crisis of prices. The final part of this chapter examines the local impact in West Bengal of a national crisis of participative regulation.

Crisis[33]

Over the turn of the millennium, prices for the paddy varieties (other than superfine) which make up most of the marketed surplus started to slump dramatically: from Rs 640 to Rs 790 a quintal in 1999 through

Rs 450 to Rs 550 in 2000–01 to a range of Rs 320 to Rs 515 over the post-harvest period in 2002. Even the price of superfine paddy collapsed from a post-harvest average of Rs 1,700 a quintal in 1999 to Rs 690 in the first six months of 2002, a drop of 60 per cent—see Appendix 9.1, Tables 1 and 2. In 2002, returns to rice production failed to cover costs.

It is not lightly that these events are labelled a crisis. The scholarly literature distinguishes three kinds of crisis. One results from instability and is inherent to the business cycles of capitalist over-accumulation. A second results from herd behaviour and pricked bubbles (e.g., the financial crises of East Asia, Argentina, and Mexico). A third is a destructive catastrophe in the real economy which undermines its fundamental organizing principles and out of which new elements emerge phoenix-like from what remains (e.g., Russia and Eastern Europe) (Bottomore et al., 1985). All are moments in which the elements and relations of a system may be more clearly seen. The crisis in West Bengal's food economy in 2002, however, appears to fit none of these definitions. It was clearly a crisis in markets, but instead of being due to their inherent instability, or of a failure on the part of the local state, it was due to policies of the central government. It was a crisis in the real economy but neither the local nor the central state showed any sign of collapse. West Bengal's crisis was also one of co-operative federalism, a relationship which had survived years of contention between the Left Front Government and hostile parties at the centre.

Many forces contrived to produce this paddy-rice price crisis. Several changes that affected farm wholesale prices resulted to a significant extent from changes in state regulation. One was that de-regulation allowed farm-gate prices to be influenced by prices in other states. Since the 1998-9 reforms to movement restrictions, grain can flow unimpeded between states. But states themselves had control over certain costs of production, could give limited subsidies to parts of the cost structure, and, therefore, could crucially affect returns to production and 'open market' competition. By 2002-3, significant state-level differences in the prices of fertilizers, pesticides, electricity, and transport had developed. As a result, un-milled paddy could and did flow in from Bihar at prices which were Rs 20 to Rs 30 lower per quintal than those in West Bengal. Furthermore, debt and distress sales in the nearby states of Jharkhand and Orissa meant that impoverished producers were parting with their paddy at prices as low as Rs 250 a quintal, paddy which then found its way to West Bengal. Last but not least, the late arrival of the 2002 boro season rain turned local rice yellow through dehydration, a factor which was reflected in price deductions for the quality of paddy produced in West Bengal.

The de-regulation of trade flows contributed to the crisis in 2002 in another way as well. In the 1990s, officially recorded rice exports from West Bengal varied between 20,000 and 100,000 tonnes. Rice from West Bengal had been exported or smuggled as far afield as Sri Lanka, Myanmar/Burma, Bhutan, Nepal, and Bangladesh. At the apogee in 1996-7, rice millers declared that as much as 20 per cent of the rice milled had been exported 'informally' to Bangladesh. By the end of the millennium, liberalization in south-east Asia had rapidly produced the predictable consequence of the 'fallacy of composition': a huge supply glut, exacerbated by 'participative intervention' by the states of other countries, which put paid to West Bengal's profitable informal exports. The Farraka Barrage agreement, which had regularized the allocation of water between India and Bangladesh, had led to an increase in domestic production in Bangladesh and, in order to sustain returns to producers there, Bangladesh in 2000 imposed a tax of 40 per cent on any rice imported from West Bengal. Vietnam had liberalized her exports and Thailand even provided export credits and subsidies. Myanmar turned from being an importer to exporting rice to Bangladesh (Gulati and Narayanan, 2002; Bandyopadhyay, 2003). In 2000, the world market price was lower than West Bengal's domestic price, so that this surplus state was importing rice, particularly high quality rice from Thailand.

Appendix 8.1 shows the unstructured pattern of imports and exports between the states of India from 1990 to 2000. West Bengal imported little paddy from neighbouring states; it exported little paddy, and mostly to Bihar. Rice exports from West Bengal within India were extremely unstable in quantity and direction, with destinations veering from Gujarat in the north to Kerala in the south. With the exception of Assam, exports to other states of the Indian Union also dried up over the 1990s. The largest and most constant flows were rice imports into West Bengal (especially after 1998-9 when movement restrictions were liberalized by the central government) from states where rice was produced under three special conditions : first, as a cash crop not consumed by the producers themselves—in Punjab, Haryana and UP; second, in regions where agricultural wages were even lower, as in Bihar and Madhya Pradesh; or third, where the agrarian structure still led to post-harvest sales at prices depressed by debt or other forms of coercion, as in Jharkhand and Orissa.

Another major factor affecting paddy wholesale prices was the way participative intervention was managed. De-participation meant that the Food Department rather than the FCI now procured paddy from farmers, presenting a new logistical challenge to the Food Department— getting it to the mills—and a new disciplinary challenge—controlling it once it reached the mills. The institutions acting as agents for state participation in the food system had been de-centralised. Even commission agents could now start processing paddy under the Essential Commodities Act. The Food Department subcontracted procurement from farmers to agricultural co-operatives. In 2002, the support price fixed by the central government was unprecedented in being above, not below, 'open' market prices. This was the first time the procurement price might have been a real support price. But until June 2002 when the Department was finally allowed the funds it needed, paddy producers in West Bengal wanting to sell to the Food Department at the announced price of Rs 685 a quintal (which rose to Rs 900 with transport and packing premia), faced an organization in paralysis; by then, most farmers had been forced to part with their grain. A classic case then unfolded, of the kind of perverse procurement practices that used to characterize the PDS in the 1970s (Harriss, 1984). In the past, when the procurement price was well below the market price, rice millers used every means at their disposal, from political patronage to the courts, to delay their compliance with procurement targets. (They would also hoist their open market sales to compensate for their procurement losses.) In 2002, the mediocre achievement of procurement targets (down to a state-wide average of 10 to 12 per cent of the procurement achieved in 2001[34]) was the result of a seriously delayed release of funds to the Food Department and a tight, politically-directed, lid on their quantity. Stores already full to capacity were yet another serious constraint on procurement.

Market forces and political forces also contributed to lower demand. Ten years without a major drought, and an embarrassment of riches inside Bangladesh—leading to efforts to block its border—thwarted the plans of West Bengal's rice millers. The lack of export outlets, and the reversal of flows described earlier, bottled up the surpluses within the state.

The Food Department did not purchase rice from producers generally but from the small set of rice millers who, until the 1990s, had defended their localized monopolies through webs of licensed money-lending and paddy-buying agents. In the first half of 2002, the above-market prices of the very small amount of rice that had been locally procured by the Food Department did not percolate back to producers because this rice was being procured from rice mills, not producers. The system of fair price shops, by then fed by a combination of Food Department rice and wheat procured by the FCI in other states (5.4 million tonnes of grain in total were procured in 2001–02), continued to sell grain according to the bifurcated issue price policy. Under this arrangement, the price-inelastic consumption preferences of APLs led them to boycott PDS rice and wheat, while the indivisible nature of the quota for BPLs caused a drop in the number of those buying it. Table 9.3 shows the start of this process of abandonment. By July, only 10 per cent of the planned quotas were being lifted by FPS retailers.[35] Stocks backed up in FCI and Food Department go-downs. To avoid an ever-increasing stock inventory, it was alleged that much of this highly subsidized rice was sold in the open market instead, enabling FPS retailers to reap rents.

The impact of this crisis of procurement rippled through the system of rice markets. The old, highly concentrated, state-backed system of rice mills and paddy agents had been constrained by the proliferation

Table 9.3: Quotas and Off-take of Rice and Wheat under the Targetted PDS in West Bengal, 1999–2000

Quarter of year	Rice				Wheat			
	quota '000 metric tonnes		% off take		quota '000 metric tonnes		% off take	
	BPL	APL	BPL	APL	BPL	APL	BPL	APL
1999 4th	21.5	15.2	92	50	21.9	38.1	91	74
2000* 1st	21.5	15.2	95	45	21.9	38.1	95	40
2nd	42.9	7.7	90	31	43.7	38.1	73	10

Note: APL = Above the Poverty Line (Rs 15,000/hh/year)
BPL = Below the Poverty Line
*APL Rice Rs 12.10/kg; wheat Rs 9/kg
BPL Rice: 20 kg/week @Rs 6.15/kg; wheat: Rs 4.7/kg
Source: Annexure C., Government of West Bengal, 2000

of intermediaries resulting from growth and de-regulation. In 2002, however, this commercial elite had the chance to demonstrate its economic power. Some producers were trapped by low returns into credit relations which put them, to all intents and purposes, in thrall to the rice millers and paddy traders who lent money before the harvest and expected repayment in kind. These were reversions to the exchange relations of an earlier era (see chapters 3 and 4). Traders were also tying down producers by paying them in instalments. Meanwhile bran oil factories, which are the key to the profitability of rice mills, found themselves searching ever further afield for un-rancid bran supplies, for to make profits they also had to run at high capacity.

Agricultural production was therefore caught in a destructive 'price scissors' effect. On the one hand, farm wholesale returns slumped to Rs 3,000 per *bigha* (roughly one-third of an acre). On the other hand, the reduction of subsidies on fertilizers, pesticides and electricity raised the costs of production to Rs 3,000–Rs 3,100 per bigha. The cost of labour had also been increasing by the year. These costs meant that for the main aman season, the value of total output was equal to or slightly less than the cost of production, while in the boro season, whose growth had been the massive success story in West Bengal's agricultural development, the additional cost of irrigation meant that producers faced heavy losses.

Many producers in West Bengal did not take this lying down. Refusing to sell at negative returns, those who had physical space and no urgent need for funds, stored their paddy at home and played a waiting game. But when local traders knew that a producer's physical capacity had been reached, they bought his unstorable paddy at prices that made losses for him. The Forward Bloc's Farmers' Association mobilized extensive political protests through Block Development Officers (BDOs) all over the state. Expressed at the local level, these messages were hard to coordinate, but BDOs relayed the demands to the Chief Minister. The *bandh* called by the opposition Trinamool Congress Party in June 2002 also featured the paddy price crisis on its agenda.

Perhaps as a result, the FCI was asked to resume control for a while to resolve the Food Department's funding crisis. In June 2002, the Reserve Bank of India finally sanctioned Rs 181 crores for West Bengal's Food Department to step up the purchase of paddy from farmers and even wholesalers.[36] But of this only Rs 50 crores were released to agricultural cooperatives. The funding of procurement was too little, too late—unable to support more than an estimated one per cent of production.

There is no doubt that the politically-protected oligopoly through which coarse rice has been supplied to West Bengal's consumers for decades was threatened as never before: not only by the atrophy of local procurement, but also by new forms of competition (from traders crowding onto the market).

This turn of events was at the expense of West Bengal's producers. They were fast becoming victims of state-level differences in the political regulation of agricultural costs—not just within India but also elsewhere in Asia—and of coercive relations of exchange involving even more victimized producers elsewhere in India.

Conclusions

We have now arrived back full circle to the questions posed at the start of this chapter. We asked: Is 'de-regulation' really a form of re-regulation in which participative intervention formally cedes to regulatory intervention? What has been its impact? Is de-regulation a matter of shifts in the relative importance of different non-state market-making institutions and non-market institutions? How 'liberating', how conducive to efficiency have the market-oriented changes been?

Although the sphere of markets and distribution has been more affected by changes in state regulation and participation than has the sphere of production, there has been less de-regulation and de-participation in practice than there has been on paper, or than was initially declared to be intended. Key aspects of the system of markets have not been touched at all: the regulation of labour, of credit, and of electricity.

Rather than de-regulating and de-participating, the state has really re-regulated and re-participated. Re-regulation has decentralized accumulation by reducing entry barriers, formalizing the activity of husking mills and paddy agents and increasing their capacity to accumulate. It has also decentralized storage, blurred the distinctions between husking mills and rice mills and between wholesalers and retailers and resulted in an expansion of hired labour at many new points in the system.

Since there has been little de-participation, there has been little corresponding re-regulation. No large stores were privatized in West Bengal. The FCI's labour force was slimmed by only 15 per cent over 20 years. A sizeable segment of its labour force in West Bengal has been re-deployed from the central to the local state, rather than laid off. On the other hand, other FCI labour has certainly been casualized, stripped of its rights and re-organized by contractors on the basis of their places of origin.

Re-participation has made the state system more complex. Two food bureaucracies, together with those of agricultural co-operatives, are now involved in the participative regulation of the food system, leading to increasingly complex coordination problems with their attendant transactions costs—problems not soluble by markets. Yet, while non-price-mediated co-ordination has become more elaborate, the finance of state trading remains in the control of the Reserve Bank, which is part of the state. Far removed from the action, the apex bank's decisions have knock-on effects on all of the elements which have to interact with the state. The state is not reducing the instability of markets or bearing its share of the costs and waste of the system of production and markets. On the contrary, as this discussion of West Bengal's agrarian crisis has shown, the state is responsible for those costs and that waste. As India's federal system becomes more competitive and less co-operative, the governments of both West Bengal and the Centre are responsible, but the greater share of responsibility lies with the Government of India.[37] This is to enter the unresolved argument about the extent to which West Bengal's development has been stymied by political antagonism from the succession of parties in power at the Centre.[38] Our evidence shows that centrally-regulated working capital has been crucial for the food system—as is food dependence on north-western India—over the entire period. The devil is definitely in the detail of the timing of working capital.

As the provisioning system develops, many questions arise. What are the developmental purposes of the new structure of rents? Whose strategic interests are protected? Not those of labour, except for labour in the guise of petty producers, transporters, and traders. So far, growth has meant little change in the social distribution of rents, despite the proliferation of petty trade. The new structure still protects the accumulation of the largest elements in the system: rice mills and the old and new mercantile firms, which have been the object of political hostility and scholarly criticism since before Independence. It is not simply that 'pre-de-regulation' interests remain powerful. It is rather that under liberalization the sort of politics that capital has always practised has become formally recognized at the level of discourse and law. The new structure has already encouraged the proliferation of purely mercantile firms. It is widely alleged that the state has colluded with large wholesalers in Kolkata who used fair means (cheap supplies from other states) and foul (the domestic recirculation of subsidized grain destined for export) to extract rent and raise private profits at the same time as they depressed retail prices. It is too early to predict the impact of the state's withdrawal of the preconditions it used to see as necessary for the rice mills to operate at high capacity, while simultaneously encouraging technological modernization which makes high capacity utilization ever more necessary. The state, in the form of its banks, does not yet encourage any challenge to the rice mills by extending to husking mills the investment finance needed to modernize their mill machinery.

Has there been change in the relative importance of non-market institutions? Our research did not show any decisive change in the balance between types of social regulation. Social regulation always co-exists with state regulation. There is no evidence that locality, religion, caste, and gender are playing *less* defining roles in social regulation in the early 2000s than they did in 1990. It is still next to impossible for a woman to occupy any niche in the system of markets where accumulation might be possible. It is still next to impossible for scheduled caste and scheduled tribal people to enter markets other than as labour or petty traders. Put another way, the system of markets does not liberate people who are economically disadvantaged by forms of ascription as well as by their class position. In this respect, we have yet to see that markets are the revolutionizing force assumed in liberal theory.

Clearly, measures of de-regulation and de-participation that were both uneven and partial, and ignorant of agrarian class and social structure and of the local system of markets, are to blame for prices that undercut the costs of production of the means of subsistence after 2002. It was not so much 'the market' that was to blame, as a serious coordination failure of central and local state governments and of other nation-states in south and south-east Asia, a failure due to the fallacy of composition at the heart of liberalization as a global strategy. Local states—and their international advisors—failed to anticipate the inevitable outcome.

The political process by which the regulatory needs of petty production and trade might be met has insufficient clout. West Bengal is not planning for the diversification of the petty producing rural system, either in agriculture itself or in the non-farm economy. In any case, much of the physical environment is not suitable for crops other than rice. Ultimately, it is collective action by state governments and the governments of neighbouring states that must coordinate the re-regulation of, and re-participation in, agricultural markets, so that they do not ruin home markets that have taken decades to create.

Notes

1. In fact, liberalization qua privatization had been ushered in rhetorically in the early 1980s under Rajiv Gandhi, but had suffered setbacks in implementation and was only consolidated after the crisis of reserves in 1991.
2. The 1996 release from attachment to rice mills of paddy agents was widely claimed (by rice millers and paddy agents alike) as a victory for the lobbying of District Magistrates by the Paddy Agents Association.
3. Local taxes include the profession tax in slabs from Rs 50–Rs 1000; and the property tax. Central government taxes include commercial taxes—if gross output exceeds Rs 200,000—and income tax if income exceeds Rs 50,000.
4. One example involved a 10–15 delay in repayment by an itinerant paddy trader, compensated for by a Rs 5–7 reduction per quintal in the price of paddy purchased by the husking miller.
5. In 2002, the Food Department released funds to procure rice through the larger number of producer co-operatives and husking mills. The timing was too late in the post-harvest season to have much of an impact (Government of West Bengal, 2003, p. 3).
6. Pinstrup-Andersen and Pandya-Lorcha, 1994, quoted in Swaminathan, 2000, p. 64.
7. See http://fcamin.nic.in/earthrelief for FCI's role in relief to victims of the Gujarat earthquake in 2001 and debates on the right to food. See Harriss, 1984, for early debates about state trading.
8. See contributors to Cassen, and Joshi, 1995, and see the general analysis in Pedersen, 2000. The Washington Consensus has always had significant intellectual support from many leading Indian development economists, who form part of what Ignacio Ramonet has called the 'planetary cosmocracy', which moves easily between institutions of national and global governance. In the case considered here, they move between Mumbai and New Delhi and Washington, and between the World Bank, the IMF, the International Food Policy Research Institute, and elite US universities.
9. Harriss-White, 1996; Ades and di Tella, 1996; Kannan Srinivasan, 2005.
10. Ahluwalia, 1993. See also FCI, 2000, p. 6 where losses in transit might be annualized at double those in storage. In theory, the system of delivery, vigilance, and inspection could be strengthened and coverage widened (Choudhury, 2001, pp. 22–4).
11. On a par with the proportion of European GDP allocated to the Common Agricultural Policy.

12. From Rs 3 to 5.25 (Swaminathan, 2000, p. 83). See alaso Government of West Bengal, 2000a.
13. FCI, 2000 (Employees' Union Appeal to the Prime Minister, FCI, New Delhi). The Food and Supplies Department, while concerned that ineligible households might be included falsely under the Poverty Line, reckoned that the figure for BPLs in Kolkata should be 45 per cent and argued that 70—100 per cent of the population of southern and tribal districts were below the Poverty Line—which in itself speaks volumes for other official statistics on the decline in the poverty head-count (Government of West Bengal, 2000b, pp. 5–6; Sen, 2002).
14. Representing a negative deviation from the trend of growth of two standard deviations.
15. See Government of West Bengal, 2000, p. 5 for the government's awareness of 'unscrupulous practices'.
16. Thorlind, 2000. Panchayats have had severe problems with democratic governance and have shown limited capacity to deal with other urgent development goals such as promoting education, health, co-operation, and womens' empowerment (Williams 1999; Rana et al., 2003). In West Bengal they were expected to monitor information on stocks and flows and to exert vigilance over them in practice (Govt of West Bengal, 2000, pp. 2–4).
17. Thakur, 1995, p. 77; Roy, 1999, p. 364. The Memorandum of Understanding between the Government of India, the Government of West Bengal and the FCI stated that in addition to procurement from rice mills, the 'state government shall hold with itself the stocks of rice thus procured and converted under proper scientific storage and shall distribute these stocks under Targeted Public Distribution System [sic: through the PDS] at the prices notified by the central government for BPL and APL families as per allocations made by the central government' and that 'the state government shall be paid, in respect of the foodgrains distributed under the TPDS, the differential between the economic cost and the Central Issue Price for BPL/APL families on a monthly basis'. Indeed great effort was invested in the detailed design of a distribution system with elaborate checks for quality and against malpractice and for high physical standards of infrastructure—from gunny bags to warehouses (Government of West Bengal, 1999, pp. 8–11, 30–43).
18. This results from the difference between the out-turn standards required by the Food Department and those to which the mills actually operated.
19. The implication of the ruling party or coalition's control of the finance of state trading is that states ruled by opposition parties or coalitions may face political interference in the administration of the public finance necessary for food security.
20. The Agriculture Ministry in New Delhi. See Anderson, Levy et al., 1981.
21. Contrast this with 32–33 per cent in Andhra Pradesh (p. 11 in Bandhyopadhyay, 2003).
22. The relative importance of 'open market' foodgrains sales had been increasing

not just in Kolkata but throughout the country. Whereas in 1985, publicly distributed food grains as a proportion of total net all-India availability were 12.7 per cent. By 1995, they had dropped by a quarter to 9.1 per cent (Swaminathan, 1996).
23. Reported in an open letter to Devendra Prasad Jadav, MP, Chair of the Standing Committee of Food, Civil Supplies and the Public Distribution System from the eastern zonal secretary of the FCI Employees Union, September 7th, 2000.
24. Government of West Bengal, 1999, p. 49; Government of West Bengal, 2003, p. 3.
25. *The Statesman*, 13 September, 2000. There were other problems. The RBI's credit limit varied according to the value of the stock sold rather than with the actual costs of procurement. Further, according to the Government of West Bengal, the price at which it was re-imbursed was less that the one at which the Government of India required FPS sales to take place. The costs of storage were only reimbursed up to six months and then only for grain stored in warehouses of the Central Warehousing Corporation or the state Warehouse Corporation (Government of West Bengal, 2000, p. 3).
26. *The Statesman*, 19 September 2004.
27. Mills could generate a few percentage points higher out-turn of rice from paddy than officially required and use it for their own devices.
28. The Government of India withdrew recognition after an error was committed by the Union in its symbols and logo.
29. Mooij, 1999.
30. Sources in the FCI. Source in the Rice Mill Lobby.
31. Government of West Bengal, 1999; p. 31; Government of West Bengal, 2003, p. 1.
32. Black markets still exist when subsidised exports are released domestically.
33. This section includes some re-worked material from Ghosh and Harriss-White, 2002.
34. 13 and 14 per cent of targets were procured in Birbhum and Bardhaman respectively (Kaur, Ghosh and Sudarshan, 2007).
35. From the *Daily Calendar*, 11 September 2000 (the CPI's Bengali newspaper).
36. Government of West Bengal, 2003. The Government of India repealed the B2 licence regulating grain wholesaling and legitimating non-compliance with the residual regulation under the West Bengal Rice Mills (Control and Levy) Order of 2002.
37. The characterizations of federalism are due to L Saez, 2002.
38. Mallick for instance provided evidence that in the late 70s and 80s West Bengal had received an average share of central budget transfers and financial flows to states (1993, Table 1.3, p. 3, p. 20). He argued that there had been no political discrimination. Our research is not comparative and also cannot show discrimination. But there is no doubt that decisions on PDS finance had an adverse impact throughout West Bengal's food system in 1997 to 2002.

10 Conclusions
Rural Commercial Capital, Market Systems, and the Left Front

This book has described the ongoing commodification of staple foods and the development of a system of markets in central West Bengal since 1977, when the Left Front Government—the longest serving elected Communist government anywhere in the world—came to power. The staple food markets of Birbhum and Bardhaman districts have been studied at three points in their development over the last quarter century: first, in a period of agricultural stagnation (Birbhum), second, in one of growth and diversification (Bardhaman) and third, after West Bengal had turned from being a state in a foodgrains' deficit to one producing in surplus, during an era of market de-regulation (both districts). The first part of this final chapter summarizes the findings. The second makes some points about the theory in terms of which these markets have been explored. Finally I suggest how an analysis that takes markets seriously puts the Left Front Government's long engagement with commercial capital in a different light from that cast by interpretations from which the true significance of markets is excluded.

The staple food markets of West Bengal, 1977–2002: a summary

Birbhum District in 1982 (Chapters 4 and 5)

Five years into the era of Left Front Government rule, in 1982, the system of rice markets in Birbhum was polarized into two circuits. One consisted of a large, crowded, and decentralized sub-system of petty trade and processing (through which most paddy passed), while the other was a much smaller set of comparatively centralized, large-scale rice mills, with closely state-regulated supplies and a North Indian reach. The large rice mills were owned and financed by the Bengali ex-zamindar and landed elite and the Marwari mercantile diaspora. In Bolpur town there were fewer than 20 mills in operation. Each member of the extensive family-firms owning one or more rice mills was conservatively estimated to have an income at least 130 times greater than that of the average producer on whose surpluses the mills depended. This difference was some 22 times greater than the average difference in income between merchant- and producer-households in northern Tamil Nadu about the same time. (Harriss, 1981 a).

In the edifice of commercial capital and livelihoods resting upon agricultural production, there were three strata: petty capital with annual returns to work of Rs 5–10,000; large capital with residual claims from milling, storage and trade, whose size was some 50–5 times larger, and between them a stratum of capital in which were clustered the husking mills (at the apex of the petty circuit) together with the wholesalers and commission agents linking the petty and the large-scale circuits. These intermediate-sized traders had annual incomes of around Rs 30,000.[1]

In the early 1980s, about half of West Bengal's rice mills were lying idle. But despite the indifferent performance of agricultural production, the market systems themselves were far from stagnant. Unusually large distributive margins preserved high rates of return and invited the entry of unlicensed petty firms. Small husking mills also proliferated without licences, displacing over a million women who had operated the dheki, a foot-operated pounding pestle. These decentralized firms diverted supplies of paddy from the rice mills and challenged their economic hegemony.

There was also a third process at work. Rice mills which were not idle had more than doubled their gross output in the first five years of the Left Front rule. At the same time, new mill technology (originally imported into India from Germany and Japan) (Harriss, 1976; Harriss-White, 2005a) was shaking up the system in a dramatic way. Under the protection of state-backed monopolies and state-subsidized finance, mechanization increased vertical integration inside the rice mills and destroyed another set of female livelihoods—those of wage workers in the mills. The interests of the state and the rice millers coincided, because the state needed centralized sites to minimize the transactions costs of procurement for the Public Distribution System (PDS), while the rice millers enjoyed a reduction of trading risks while they worked as agents on contract with the state, and were able to divert their own working capital (not to mention up to 3 per cent of rice out-turn in excess of state specifications) to private trade. They needed to operate at high-capacity utilization in order to reap economies of scale. While the role played in the weeding-out of mills by the second-generation management problems in the extended joint families which owned them was undoubtedly a contributing factor, this was of small consequence beside the concentration, increase in scale, and centralization of ownership of the large-scale fraction of the Marwari-owned milling industry in Birbhum district.

On both a large and a petty scale, the markets relied on micro-, local-level monopolies. Competition meant competitive attempts to avoid competing. For the rice mills, purchases and sales could now bypass physical market places and be made by phone with trusted contacts without face-to-face interactions. In the petty circuit, face-to-face interactions were still essential to transactions, markets had 'places' where traders excluded from access to formal bank credit met and transacted. Their credit needs and lending opportunities meant that spot contracts were the exception; and micro-level, tied, contracts were the rule.

So, a backward and almost stagnant agriculture did not prevent growth and change in agricultural markets. The role of agriculture in dynamizing the system took three forms. First, the agrarian structure generated a marketed surplus—estimated then at between 30 and 39 per cent of production, reflecting the polarized exchange relations with which it was produced. A stream of comparatively price-elastic supplies flowed from producers with holding power and storage capacity, but for most a flood of post-harvest sales (and of rural re-purchases) engulfed markets directly after harvest, at the lowest prices and under conditions which robbed the producers of any capacity to respond to higher prices later on. Money advances from agents and wholesalers set the terms of this involuntary involvement in the market. Second, profits and land rents generated the starting-capital for the market entry of all sizes of enterprises save the largest, which were most dependent on state loans and profits from other, socially networked forms of commercial activity. Third, agriculture was a seasonal shedder of surplus labour which had to be absorbed in petty trade and in wage work in the rice mills. Casual labour, invariably scheduled caste or scheduled tribe, some of which was migrant, made up 78 per cent of the work-force of rice mills. These workers were paid at, or below, the minimum wage, and obtained under 20 per cent of the total value added.

Women formed half of this wage labour force, and they also played a significant role in the family-based pre-milling processing of paddy in the petty commodity producing and trading circuit. The keys to accumulation were control over storage and credit—all in the hands of men. Those losing out in absolute terms—being displaced—were women wage workers; those losing out in relative terms, that is, working for returns they did not control were female family members working in petty rice-processing and trade. Those losing out as a sector were rural labourers, who were dependent on distorted residual open markets for basic grain and had no material base for a political alliance with the urban labour force which had access to rice at administered prices from Fair Price Shops.

In 1981–2, the principal shocks to the markets were coming from the state, through policies, ill-informed about the local culture of rice, imposed both by the state government in Kolkata (where agriculture is a state responsibility) and by the central government in New Delhi (which oversees both food and credit for rural development). While rice mills were encouraged to modernize, laws remained on the statute book which protected hand pounding and outlawed the most appropriate technology for small-scale rice surpluses—the huller mill, rented out and working 'for custom'.

The state's overwhelming need to cut the costs of procurement for the public distribution system, upon which the people of Kolkata and the industrial coal belt towns depended, had led to a pretty pass. The interests of the local agrarian society, those of the state, and the commercial elite were expressed through regulative laws which were re-interpreted so as to reinforce the power of the rice mills. Agro-commercial capital was focussed on resisting the implementation of disciplinary forms of regulation. What policy documents said was far less important than what policy implementation could be made to do on the ground.

Coercive state procurement, at prices below those of the market, resulted in compensating hoists to the prices of the non-procured residual rice supplies. Movement restrictions (imposed to prevent the haemorrhaging out of the state's control of rice needed for state procurement) constrained flows between surplus and deficit districts in ways which depressed prices in surplus districts and raised prices in deficit districts, to the detriment of those compelled to buy open market rice in deficit regions. Rural consumers in this position—small cultivators and agricultural labour—were in effect forced to subsidize the urban work-force. *Pace* Partha Chatterjee, this is *not* compelling evidence of organized class consciousness, via the Communist-paternalist control of 'prices of agricultural commodities in favour of both urban and rural consumers' (Chatterjee, 1997, p. 67).

The second type of perturbation to the system of rice markets came from finance. The biggest borrowers—owners of rice mills—were also the main lenders. The 'formal sector' funds (denied to petty traders) which the rice mills got from the state-regulated banks mingled with private finance to be lent onwards and downwards through distributaries of tied agents. Asymmetrical delays on payments for purchases and sales worked to the advantage of paddy agents and rice millers and aided their accumulation.

Bardhaman District in 1990 (Chapters 6 and 7)

Almost a decade later, after the growth rate had doubled for a sustained period and agriculture, still dominated by rice, had started to diversify, market systems for other staple foods—potato and oilseed—in this leading agricultural district of West Bengal were found to be instituted in ways similar to those of rice in Birbhum. They were complex, open systems, with differentiated structures, presided over by the same local agro-commercial bourgeoisie. Although agriculture in Bardhaman district was now generating a rapidly-rising marketed surplus, the high entry barriers, high degrees of capitalization, high asset-specificity, and extensive networks of private (Marwari) finance combined to allow this commercial capitalist class to pull in oilseed, potato, and rice not just locally but also from very long distances. Mustard seed, for instance, crucial in the Bengali diet, was coming by Marwari trade links from Rajasthan, and potatoes were being imported from Madhya Pradesh. At the base of the system, large numbers of petty firms pitted their unwaged family labour against the economies of scale enjoyed by the large family firms at the apex.

The system of markets does not, however, resemble the neat value chain of vertical markets stylized by economists who adopt uncritically the categories of the data collected by statistics departments. (Jha and Natarajan, 2002). It is marked by diversity in ownership forms, in its financial relations, in the social identities of merchants, and in the organization of labour. Firms cannot easily be compared. The market system is made up of firms which are individuated in ways which give them distinctive brands, and which give the system its plasticity. Judging from the analysis of open market prices (which are recorded in misleadingly neat layers for farm-gate, wholesale, and retail), all these markets were inefficient in the short term, and in ways which could not be interpreted without knowledge of each locality. It was not simply the inadequacies of infrastructure or information that caused the short-term deficiencies in price integration (the factors conventionally relied upon to explain inefficiency). The deficiencies resulted from crop- and place-specific features of the market structures, and from the way regulatory interventions were implemented.[2]

The 1990 study was not fine-grained enough to enable us to disentangle the effects on the rice markets of the Left Front Government's reforms in tenurial security from the effects of technical change in agriculture, or from those of a certain amount of state-regulated credit for agricultural production (though not for petty trade). All three kinds of intervention have been associated with growth in production in each of the three crops in question. During the 1980s, it was growth which had the major impact on the markets. Just as the Left Front Government's reforms to agricultural production are considered to have succeeded in consolidating forms of petty production and to have arrested historical trends towards polarization, (Webster, 1989) so the 1990 study confirms that the sustained expansion of the marketed surplus during the 1980s enabled the consolidation of the 'livelihood-intensive' petty trading circuit.

Petty-trading institutions developed via two routes. The first was involutionary, and involved an increasing internal intricacy in the existing small-scale circuit. Each stage in transport and pre-milling processing could and did become the basis of a different, specialized livelihood. The second was evolutionary: new institutional forms evolved from the earlier formal ones, in particular a proliferation of (supposedly registered) paddy agents who were shifting supplies to processing facilities, and an expansion in the reach of rice wholesale merchants based in Kolkata. But increasing supplies meant that elite rice and oil mills and potato cold stores were not challenged by these developments. They continued to straddle the key power points in the market system, capitalize their firms, increase their scale, and shed labour.

State intervention faced the contradictions between 'parametric' regulation, based on the assumption that markets operated effectively, and the active 'participative' regulation of markets which were assumed (or discovered) to operate so anti-socially that they had to be replaced. Under the first kind of disciplinary regulation came a draconian rationing of licences (which meant that firms operated illegally) and an unusually weak form of implementation of the state's Regulated Agricultural Markets Act, which all but reduced the Act to an arbitrary (and evadable)tax. Under the second kind of regulation, the difficult seasonal relationship between state-trading institutions and private commercial firms was informalized with the aim of creating incentives that would allow the state to keep control of post-harvest sales of the cheapest paddy and so minimize losses on sales to the Public Distribution System. The monopoly control of the paddy wholesale trade also started to unravel, while unrecorded rice also leaked into the wholesale rice markets. Thus, both of the sub-circuits and every kind of firm had a hand in smuggling rice across local, state, and even national borders. The state's own co-operatives (intended to threaten private agro-commercial capital) were regulated in such a way that they were hobbled. The state subsidized them, to no great developmental purpose.

The tension between market-driven politics and mass-democratic politics was clearly resolved in favour of capital. Both the Government of India and the Left Front Government gave liberal subsidies for labour-displacing technology at a stage when the labour-absorptive capacity of agriculture was not yet faltering. The eight largest firms in Bardhaman reported having received loans for labour-displacing processing technology equal in value to 20,000 IRDP loans for poverty eradication.[3] To make matters worse, even these anti-poverty loans were rarely destined for the labour displaced by technical change in rice mills; for this labour continued to be landless, female, and marginalized. The state-regulated banks also lubricated the markets with credit—rationed to the capitalist elite—which was lent onwards to secure supplies throughout the system. Although the state did not openly underwrite the risks of the commodification of staple foods, it acted in ways which reduced them.

By 1990, prior to 'liberalization', the Left Front Government had therefore effectively lost or abandoned what control it ever had of increasingly large parts of the system of markets. Illegal markets left large regulative spaces to be colonized by a variety of civil society institutions—notably business associations. They began to regulate markets by organizing the protection of property, public health environment of marketplaces, informal insurance, and access to credit. They were instrumental in supervizing market conduct, engaging in collective negotiations with labour, and making collective representations to the state. These informal regulative institutions brought—and still bring—order to markets, but at the cost of local idiosyncracy (which segments markets) and exclusivity (which denies access). The markets were also liberalizing well before the so-called era of liberalization. Rice was being imported to West Bengal from Bangladesh and Burma, and rice and potatoes being exported to Bangladesh. Rural West Bengal began relatively early to feel the first volatile currents of unstable international markets, that is, currents swollen by smuggling.

De-regulation and De-participation at the turn of the Millennium (Chapters 8 and 9)

The third study followed changes in the system of rice markets during the decline in growth rates and the upheavals of de-regulation and de-participation in the 1990s, and the first years of the new century. It focussed on the rice retail markets of Kolkata in 2000, the rural markets of both Birbhum and Bardhaman in 2002, and the role of the state throughout. It attempted to distinguish changes due to continued growth in the absolute size of the marketed surplus from those due to changes in policy.

Today, growth continues to supply resources for both petty production and trade centred on husking mills and the rice mill circuits. This is just as well, because the relation between agricultural growth and labour absorption is turning negative (Sen, 2002). With rice grown as a commercial crop and with marketed surplus in some rare villages reported to be as high as 90 per cent of production, by far the largest part of output (about 60–70 per cent[4]) still travels through the petty circuit via any one of a large set of specialized, niched trading services. Self-employment in markets is now being slowly opened to Scheduled Caste and Scheduled Tribal people. In the petty circuit, both technology and social relations are on a pathway characterized by complexity and super-exploitation. Not only is the technology of this circuit more primitive and much smaller in scale than that in the rice mill circuit, but the petty circuit also continues to use unpaid family labour. Labour organized in this way is also able to compete effectively with technologies using wage-labour and offering economies of scale.

It is also well beyond state control. In the rural depths and small towns of central West Bengal, new marketplaces have been established by a new wave of small itinerant traders, selling to wholesaler-retailers whose functions have become blurred. Tiny firms making puffed rice have also proliferated alongside firms transforming raw paddy into rice. The rural landscape is peppered with husking mills. Investment in these mills has been attractive to rich peasants, and also to some Muslims who have been unable to purchase land or who have been displaced from small-scale transport by the expansion in the number of lorries. The expansion in the number of husking mills is constrained by lack of access to electricity supplies, rather than by lack of either commodities or credit. Now many owners have access to bank loans. The husking mills are the site of a new kind of commercial accumulation: husking millers are working openly on their own account, installing appropriate components of modern rice mill technology, and constructing small parboiling facilities and miniature drying yards. These are rented out to processor-traders who tend to be tied by debt to the mill. Miniature commercial conglomerates are being created. But if the unpaid working female relatives of the stakeholders were to find paid work elsewhere, or to demand pay on a par with that of female rice mill labour, the men who run the petty circuit would find it much harder to compete against the rice mills' scale economies.

At the other end of the food system, in Kolkata, the city's food supply has depended for decades on a combination of state ration shops and petty retail trade, some of which is now supplied in the way it was before the long era of statutory rationing—that is, by Marwari rice wholesalers with substantial funds and reach, operating out of Boro Bazaar in the metropolis. Six different types of small firms are distinguishable in the rice retail sector. These markets are socially regulated through gender, kinship, caste, religion, trust, collective self management, and relations of patronage verging on extortion.

Despite the changes in market institutions, the structure of class interests dominating the markets has remained intact. Despite the halving of the growth rate in rice production during the 1990s, the large rice mills, while fewer in number, continue to be allowed to flourish. While the marketed surplus has risen in both absolute and relative terms, they may have increased their share of the local marketed surplus to around 40 per cent. These mills also assure their paddy supplies by fetching it from increasingly long distances. Supplies sufficient to ensure high rates of capacity utilization are more important as time goes on because of the next wave of labour-substituting technology which is diffusing throughout West Bengal, which 'weather-proofs' the mills. Husk-fired driers dispense with sunshine, so that the post-harvest season in which supplies have expanded most spectacularly—*boro*—coincides with the monsoon. Mills therefore need technologies to cope with rain when paddy needs to be dried, and these need high-capacity utilization to cover their ever-expanding fixed costs. So, increasingly complex flows of paddy help to season-proof their opera-tions. Without these, they could not compete with the petty circuit.

Over the decade in question, there is contradictory evidence for both concentration and decentralization. There has been concentration in scale and contraction in numbers of rice mills, and the adoption of technology such as mechanical drying, pressure parboiling, incremental additions to MRM technology (de-stoners, polishers and dehuskers), and vertical integration (rice-puffing machines). Further, there has been decentralization too, in that the structure of ownership of the rice mills appears to be more dispersed than 20 years before.[5] This is, however, likely to be a superficial third generation phenomenon, as business families split ownership for managerial and tax purposes. In conglomerate portfolios, such as that of the former Birbhum district governor of the Rotary International, which spans agricultural trade, rice milling, textiles, iron and steel distribution, with firms dispersed across northern India, the family portfolio as a whole may concentrate capital while the regional structure of mill ownership may move in the direction of decentralization.[6]

Meanwhile, real wages for casual rice mill labour have not risen over the quarter century covered by our work.

At the same time, the process of commodification of products grinds ineluctably on (Harriss-White, 2005b). Rice varieties are differentiated, and prepared dry rice products proliferate. The large-scale consignments of rice released by the rice mills have generated a downstream market in lorry transport, which co-exists for the time being with transport on rickshaw trolleys and bicycles. One by-product, husk, is now recycled as a fuel and markets have developed for surplus husk. A by-product of this by-product, burnt husk is also being commercialized as a raw material for the 'high tech' silicon industry and for 'low tech' brick kilns. Another by-product, bran, is the basis of an oil extracting industry, whose output has lately been declared fit for human consumption. And a by-product of this by-product, de-oiled bran cake, finds its way to Europe and elsewhere as commercial cattle feed. Even small stones, used as adulterants, have been commercialized for re-adulteration. Lastly, labour markets are developing at a number of new points in the system, in freight and haulage, husking mills, and newly decentralized wholesale firms.

The gains to organized labour have been local and small. Unionized workers are caught in a political pincer. Their interests are not championed by democratically-elected union representatives, while more capital-intensive technology is adopted to avoid employing them altogether.

Because of growth, the impact of destructive forces within the system has been confined to husk-fired driers. In substituting for sunshine, they threaten the most vulnerable livelihoods, those of casual female labourers, who are once again being displaced on a mass scale. The entire system of markets (which initially displaced the domestic dheki work of women) is becoming increasingly male.

This is a far remove from technology which maximizes the use of the kind of labour which is lowest cost and least militant.[7] Perhaps the employment of large quantities of low-caste female labour reduces the status of a merchant (many of the biggest of whom belong to the Marwari community, which promotes the domesticity of its women as part of its public identity, and as a normative aspect of capitalist modernity),[8] rather than enhancing it as an expression of patriarchy. Over this period, it is evident that the rights of people employed in markets are far less closely state-regulated than are rights to property. Most rice travels through a system of firms and markets where labour has never been politically mobilized at all, let alone enough to require reforms of the Labour Laws.[9]

State Regulation and De-regulation/Re-regulation

The research presented in this book has distinguished state regulation from active state trading or participation. Reforms can take the form of de-regulation or de-participation. Although the agenda of 'de-regulation' was driven throughout by the central government (both under the Congress and under the BJP-led National Democratic Alliance), the Government of West Bengal has played a complicitous role. It was the Left Front Government, in opposition to the Congress Party at the Centre, which in 1994 untied the paddy agents from their monopoly attachment to rice mills. It was the West Bengal state departments of electricity, industry, and commerce which by 2002 had liberated firms from many licensing and inspection requirements.[10] And the Left Front Government could not prevent a new wave of entirely unlicensed and unregulated trade and self-employment, invited in by the lifting of storage and movement restrictions.

Whether the role the state played in this was active and deliberate is a moot point, because some of the outcomes have been unexpected. One such outcome is that while the state made a serious attempt to

Conclusions

dismantle a key aspect of pervasive regulation (licensing), the informal sector, that is husking mills—a significant minority of which operated without any kind of registration or regulation—now have to be licensed by municipalities. This has entitled husking mill owners to gain access to the state-regulated banking system, but the husking mills remain in an ambiguous and tense disciplinary relationship to the electricity boards (because they may have been originally powered illegally by domestic power connections).

The structure of parametric regulation has been more successfully dismantled—in particular the rules governing storage and movement of grain. Even so, there is more continuity than might be thought at first sight since little de-regulation has been achieved with respect to the markets for labour, electricity or credit—however imperfectly this regulation has been enforced.

Most resistant to change—and left almost entirely intact—are the kind of laws which saturate markets—laws pertaining to sites, fees, weights, and measures, etc. One major change was to re-label unmodified bran oil as a human food. Yet the social reach even of this kind of saturating regulation is now being challenged by the emergence of primitive new marketplaces, with no state-made rules at all.

With respect to de-participation, since the state has long organized the distribution of food more directly than it has organized production, the most profound impact of de-regulation in the 1990s was felt in precisely that part of the system of markets in which the state directly participated. State-administered prices converged with those of the market. In the state trading institutions, the most privileged workers (with rights at work and rights to social security) were laid off, while jobs lost through natural attrition were not replaced. The balance of power lies with employers. Stores are to be privatized (though this is being resisted locally). Fine-tuning the subsidy on food by the device of 'targets' carried conditions which could not be met. This policy could not prevent—and was instead actually responsible for—an unprecedentedly large buffer stock from growing—and then deteriorating. And the subsidy ended up by doubling in real terms during the decade.

Here again there was a considerable amount of continuity, but some entirely new problems arose from the increased complexity of non-market forms of co-ordination. In 1997, decentralization of the management of the central government's fiscal deficit (and the off-loading of the Food Corporation of India's operations onto the West

Bengal Food Department)[11] quickly led to deadlock at the hands of the central Reserve Bank of India, which refused to accept Left Front Government's account of its expenditures. The ad hoc downsizing and systematic casualization of labour in the pay of the state, in order to reduce costs, affected efficiency in perverse ways (it ruined reporting structures and created low morale, unrest, and 'x-inefficiency'). To use 're-participation' of the Food Department as a means of addressing FCI's egregious leakages, fraud, and corruption may have had early successes, at least before new relations of accommodation had time to cement themselves. In any case in 2003, the FCI had to resume 'temporary' control over operations inside West Bengal to ease the blockage caused by the stalemate in finance between the local Food Department and the Reserve Bank of India.

In Kolkata, de-participation in retailing led to fair price shops being besieged by competing armies of illegal retailers on 'open' markets, most of them openly flouting the most elementary regulation, namely where markets can operate. The new retailing system is a case-study of rent-seeking on a micro-scale, for it rapidly led to harassment, raids, evictions, extortion, and party-politicized protection rackets.

And then in 2001–02, the agrarian economy was engulfed in a crisis entirely due to re-regulation. With movement restrictions completely lifted, paddy flowed in from states where production satisfied at least one of three conditions: greater subsidies on inputs (Madhya Pradesh); lower agricultural wages (Orissa); and/or oppressive agrarian structures and distress commercialization (Bihar). In West Bengal, local merchants took advantage of low prices elsewhere and reverted to the coercive exchange relations of a bygone era as local returns to production went negative.[12] The West Bengal Food Department, which for the first time found that its procurement prices were above market prices, had had no experience for 30 years in dealing directly with the mass of producers, and had no funds for procurement on the scale required.

Yet the regulative flux is deceptive. The bureaucratic design of regulation remains intact,[13] but departments dedicated to the regulation of agricultural markets have weak practical powers and are poorly resourced.[14] Not only is there more continuity than meets the eye, there is a great deal of inertia in the system. Scarce resources in the state allow nooks and crannies to persist, where mutually beneficial settlements are made (e.g., the informally-negotiated commuting of the levy extracted from rice mills from a proportion to a fixed quota).

Self-organization has continued to plug the egregious holes in the state's regulative capacity. Extortion is practised (e.g., by state vigilance forces on unlicensed traders and huskers) and rents are sought out and shared (e.g., between rice millers and the state agencies). Relations of petty extortion have persisted after the laws and institutions under which there were incentives for them have been abolished.

The result is a structure of accumulation which is actually more widely shared than would be the case were policies implemented according to the letter of the law. Many modes of accumulation co-exist within the system of rice markets—primary and secondary surplus appropriation, primitive accumulation, and redistribution through the market.[15]

Implications For Theory
Markets as Systems

In Chapter 2 we argued that when markets are studied, it is generally by economists, and the questions they ask generally concern efficiency. But reducing markets to contracts and prices, as mostly happens, assumes that markets' institutional complexity is irrelevant to efficiency. For what they are worth, all our attempts to measure price efficiency gave results showing short-term inefficiency. But in real life, there are no 'de-institutionalized' markets against which the relative efficiency of real markets can be measured. While industrial and institutional economics explore the competitive conditions of markets and certain stylized institutions, there is no reason why such approaches could not attempt to analyse post-harvest exchanges systemically. Yet this rarely happens (Ellis et al., 1991).

Value-chain analysis, on the other hand, has focussed on the transactions and transfers of rights over a commodity and on their governance. Value-chain scholars have been fascinated by the conditions under which property rights are internalized inside vertically integrated firms, and compared with those under which they are exchanged in markets. Within this literature, as with the new institutional economics, the competitive conditions are usually as neglected as the labour process.[16]

In these two approaches, 'the market' is conceived metaphorically as either a horizontal layer or a vertical ladder of buying and selling. In market systems I have studied in India, exchange from one firm to another is ordered neither horizontally nor vertically but in a variety of ways according to their activity profiles. These tend towards diversity and uniqueness. Further, existing approaches neglect the regulative role of social or 'cultural' institutions without which markets do not work (Crow's monumental study of rice markets in Bangladesh, for example, makes class central; it also allows for gender, but does not investigate it). And most 'residualize' the state.[17]

So to understand how agricultural markets work instead means conceiving them as systems. It also requires the inclusion of many factors which the orthodox frameworks for examining market institutions neglect, in particular: the labour process and its control; forms of social regulation through non-market institutions; market regulation and participation by the state and the incentives these offer; the full diversity of elements in the system; the structuring role of technology; the dynamic relationships between elements within markets; and the relationships between markets, and both production and consumption. The rest of this section discusses the general implications of the framework I have developed to incorporate these factors.

The central elements of the market system are firms. Their many forms of organization co-exist and persist. The relations between firms, and the physical transformations they perform do not map straightforwardly onto exchanges of property or many other transactions in which they are also engaged. Other contractual relationships and exchanges, notably credit, are necessary for the system to function at all. The dynamic relationships involved can be thought of in several ways. Most literally they are transactions and flows of resources accomplished by human and fossil forms of energy. They can also be conceived of in terms of the contradiction between capital and labour in the processes of subsistence and accumulation.

Social systems develop through political, economic and social agency, and through shocks. Inside a system of markets, the contestations involved take the form of 'competition to avoid competition' between individual units of capital, as well as conflicts between classes. In the development of the system, prices (the index of choice for both agricultural economists and those focussing on the value chain) certainly play an important role in creating the (seasonal) incentives for petty livelihoods and wage labour (in the case of West Bengal, for example, in enabling rice mills to exploit economies of scale using—and later displacing—wage labour). But, as the next section shows, they are only one factor among the many that determine the performance of these markets. And none of these relationships is confined within the system of commodity markets strictly defined.

Conclusions

External shocks to market systems can be environmental: weather, pests, and diseases directly affecting people or crops or livestock, or new or changing commodities affecting final consumption. Shocks can also take the form of new technology—since it is rare that technology is invented by agents within this system—and from politics. The intricacy and diversity of the elements and relations in a system of markets may serve to give it an institutional plasticity and robustness that allows it to contain the impact of such shocks.

What kinds of failure to deal with reality result from failing to see markets as systems? There seem to be at least three distortions. The most significant stems from the need researchers feel for analytical closure. Despite their institutional segmentation, social regulation, and entry barriers, market systems are open. Energy, commodities, capital, and labour are not confined within them. Leaving out these 'external' factors is fatal to market analysis.

The second kind of failure to deal with reality arises from the failure to include the state. The state can be seen as an integral part of the market system, or as an outcome of 'market politics'—the system's power relations; or as an institution capable of supplying external shocks to the market system. How should we distinguish dynamic forces and within-system perturbations from shocks from 'outside' it? How should we distinguish between shocks and crises? The analytical issues involved have not yet been adequately specified, let alone resolved.

Third, not conceiving of markets as systems enables institutions to be included in the analysis only as stylized 'constraints' on the exercise of subjective preferences. Yet as the next section also shows, social institutions pervade market systems; without them the system will not function. They may be conceived as forms of power which energize it, as elements of its organization, as relationships, as non-market institutions or even as external perturbations (since social authority exists outside as well as inside the market system, and changes in social power may happen for reasons unconnected with the economy).

What determines changes in the matrix of institutions—including identities—through which markets are socially regulated? Will competition itself, and the relative price changes which result from competition, produce such changes? The evidence presented here, while restricted to markets, casts doubt on competition's capacity to challenge the patriarchal gender relations under which agro-commercial capital has come to be almost exclusively male—or to dissolve the regulative power of community and religion. The tightly-knit Marwari banking system shows no sign of dissolving as a result of market liberalization. Quite the reverse. Nor do the barriers to entry to all but the meanest kinds of wage work and petty trade for scheduled caste and scheduled tribal category show any signs of weakening. The analytical power of social institutions, the explanation of change in such institutions—inside and outside markets—and their distinctive politics are far from being well grasped and need more systematic research.

Institutional Autonomy

The way in which production and circulation are embedded in each other has been presented as a model with particular relevance to conditions in West Bengal. But embeddedness is a general phenomenon, so a critic might concede this, yet still hold that production is always the ultimate determinant element in this relationship. To refute that argument, it is necessary to gauge empirically the extent to which production may be determining the ways markets are instituted. Land ownership, for example, may shape the way markets are structured and function in three ways. First, agrarian classes condition the quantities, timing and price responsiveness of the components of supplies to markets, and agrarian purchases from them. Second, the agrarian structure affects the modes of surplus extraction from agriculture, which will in turn shape the pattern of resource transfer from agriculture to other sectors of the economy—and hence the distribution of economic assets in the sector closest to agriculture—commerce. Third, land relations will mould the adoption of technologies which generate demands for labour or displace it. Together, land relations and technology dictate the phasing and the terms of the release of labour from agriculture, which must be absorbed as wage labour or self-employment by other sectors of the economy, the most proximate of which is local agricultural commerce.

But markets are clearly also institutionalized in ways that reflect 'capillary' forms of power, not dependent upon production. The markets studied here are structured through the wider social forces of caste status, ethnic solidarity, kinds of divine/religious authority, patriarchy, and ties based upon locality. With respect to caste, almost all of those who operate in these markets vehemently deny that caste is significant in them and say they have 'no idea' of the caste of their employees (in dramatic contrast to the strongly structuring role of caste in South India). It is very obvious, however, that the structuring role of caste varies with caste status. Being scheduled caste or tribe, for instance, is a massive barrier to entry into—and to accumulation from—all but the pettiest of trade for a third of the population of West Bengal. The state flinches from giving them trading licences, and banks do not give credit to scheduled caste borrowers. None own rice mills and very few own husking mills. The collective, corporatist, 'civil society' organizations through which markets are self-regulated, in rejecting scheduled castes, also reject the interests of labour, or at best they paternalistically seek to control labourers' interests. Caste and community are indispensible to market exchange because they are the institutions through which the collective preconditions for competition are most easily secured whenever the state fails to provide them. However, while the castes dominating trade are associated with rentier landlordism, with diasporic business networks and with migration from East Bengal, they are not reducible to these three factors. Over time, an increasing range of castes find livelihoods in markets, and markets are being cosmopolitanized. To conclude from this that market exchange dissolves caste or relegates it to the private domain, however, would be to ignore the co-existence of the relationships through which caste persists as an economic regulator—and may even intensify its role.

Ethnicity is generally treated as a territorial attribute, as in the northeast of India; alternatively it is also reduced to the issue of whether people are or are not members of scheduled tribes, to be grouped with scheduled castes and treated as 'backward sections'. Here, however, we have not been able to ignore Marwari ethnicity, long established as a social construct covering a range of migrant castes which have been in business for centuries and which operate through networks as well as through localities across most sectors of the economy. Rather than integrating 'backwards' into the ownership of land, their control over production is removed, through their control of credit, storage, and processing. The architecture of Marwari portfolios best embodies Chattopadhyay's conception of conglomerate capital set out in Chapter 2, though our field research yielded few insights into the processes through which he hypothesized it works. It persists as a major socially and economically distinctive stream of finance and accumulation in the rural economy.

Patriarchy also shapes markets in ways independent of the impact of production relations. With the exception of petty retailing, the system of markets is significantly more male-oriented than is agricultural production, and becoming increasingly more male—debarring a further 50 per cent of the population from entry to markets as anything but wage- or family-labour. Yet patriarchal power is also structured through class (Bardhan, 1993). While women are essential to petty production, where they work as unpaid family labour, they are increasingly being displaced from wage work in rice mills. By contrast, women in propertied families perform symbolic work. The women in patriarchal business families are carefully domesticated as part of the discipline of reproductive subordination through which business reputation and creditworthiness are constructed. Gender relations in markets illustrate the general point that the role of any non-market institution should not be treated in a reductionist way.

Locality is another powerful and complex social force which operates outside as well as inside the economy. Locality has been variously theorized as a discrete unit of information (Rudra, 1982b), a slice of regional agrarian structure (Rukmani, 1996), a collective moral and social unit (Lambert, 1996), a unit of (migrant) labour (Rogaly et al., 2002), a unit of regulation, a unit of language, and a concept which changes its significance and meaning at different scales of aggregation (Sengupta, 1998). In the markets described in this book, price behaviour and market structure have been found to be specific to locality. Information, together with a common—if restricted—language, is essential to market exchange; agrarian structure shapes the structure of assets, and the supplies of and demand for commodities and labour; moral communities are as necessary for the socialization of entrants to trade as they are for auto-regulation. So the way locality shapes local markets is significant, and in long-distance markets its functions must be performed by other agencies with, consequently, other effects. The precise meaning of locality as a regulator, and the balance of these meanings with those of other forms of social power discussed here, are obviously not things about which generalizations can be made, but that does not mean that they are not often causally significant. Region of origin may shape the way labour is organized in rice mills while the organization of finance through caste or community is a formidable entry barrier to gaining the heights of economic power, and gender sets up barriers throughout the market system.

The state is invoked by economists—though hardly ever seriously analysed—as a force whose bureaucratic rationalities can penetrate markets and dissolve archaic regulative practices.[18] Market exchange is also invoked by some economists as operating according to a rationality that must dissolve non-market social forms of regulation if market exchange is to be generalized. But if either of these things is happening in West Bengal, it is taking its time, while markets are developing rapidly. The development of both state- and market-rationality also appears to be consistent with their exact opposite—the reinforcement of social forms of regulation in the absence of state regulation. Both kinds of process co-exist, the balance being determined by local circumstances.

The general implications for political economy are, first, that production cannot be studied in isolation from markets, nor vice versa, without falling into more or less serious errors of analysis and explanation. Second, since neither markets, production nor the state can be understood without the non-market institutions that constitute culture and identity, political economy must pay attention to them too as essential elements of capitalist development.

Implications for Policy: Rural Commercial Capital and the Left Front Government

The Left Front Government's development policy agenda through the 1980s and 1990s has had serious implications for markets, if only by default. At the top of its agenda were reforms to the existing structure of agrarian production. It is well established that the break-down of 'law and order' which accompanied the CPI(M)'s earliest experience of power in the late 1960s de-radicalized it as much as did the decision to quash the Naxalite movement.[19] The move from radical to reformist productionism, however, not only lacked a programme equivalent to land reforms for the system of markets, but actually protected the market equivalent of the propertied elite in agriculture—the rice mill owners. The Left Front Government used every means to prevent petty trade from accumulating and to perpetuate striking 'market imperfections'. It reflected the general policy of directing credit to production, ignoring trade credit or confining it in ways which restricted it to elite firms. As a result, the numerically 'prominent' but pauperized segment of the system of markets was unable to use any consumption or investment power to dynamize the rural non-farm economy.

The policy for markets over which the Left Front Government presided was and still is made in both Kolkata and New Delhi. The word 'reformist', which has been applied to the Left Front Government's political project, (Kohli, 1987; Basu 2002), does not accurately describe its policy regime for agricultural markets. For much of the period covered by this book, it has been riddled with formal incoherence, which is only in very limited part due to differences between the evolving development projects of the Left Front Government and those of governments at the Centre. Instances of such difficulties do of course exist. For example, as we saw earlier in this chapter, the Left Front Government decided (but failed) to protect the dheki, yet when asked by the Centre to outlaw the husking mill, it failed to do so, so that husking mills duly replaced the dheki.

But incoherence also afflicts state polices made in West Bengal itself. First, the Left Front Government is committed to eliminating middlemen, yet it maintained and supported the rice mills' monopoly over the middlemen organizing the paddy trade. It practised a mass politics antagonistic to trade yet, with one of the most neglectfully implemented Regulated Agricultural Markets Act in India (making a mockery of the democratic, participative, and representative marketplace governance built into this law), it left the first post-harvest market transaction—that between producer and trader—completely unregulated in practice. Despite the law, the producer is *de facto* unprotected from the trader in the basic exchanges which determine the returns to agricultural production.

Second, the Left Front Government strictly forbade state-regulated credit for trading purposes, yet lavishly funded the commercial elite which needs some of these funds to lend for trade. This class is already amply financed from private sources and sends the state-regulated money it borrows cascading onwards unregulated, enabling money advances to be used—through interlocked contracts—for the indirect control of production and supplies at all points in the market system. Trade credit is now being freed up at the local regional level but it has historically been viewed as an incentive to speculation rather than a predisposing factor to market competition. In fact, it may, confusingly, perform both these functions.

Last but not least, the state has actively encouraged marketing structures and technological developments through which labour is continually being displaced. This is happening in a sector of the economy which might otherwise have the capacity to absorb the labour which will be shed from agricultural production in its next phase of development.

Many of the reforms which have unleashed a new wave of petty accumulation in West Bengal were made on the initiative and insistence of Congress or the BJP coalition at the Centre: for example, de-restrictions to the wholesale trade, de-regulation of inventory, and of the movement of grain. Important reforms which were in the Left Front Government's gift were—at least in some part—concessions to well-organized vested interests such as the paddy agents (freed from compulsory attachment to mills in 1994) and the rice mills, which backed the Left Front Government's take-over of trading from the FCI in 1997.

In practice, the Left Front Government has given consistent support to the agro-commercial capitalist class, dominated by ex-landlords and the Marwari diaspora. It addressed technical transformation by confining it to rice mills and continuing the protection of their oligopoly—a policy initiated by the Congress decades earlier. While individual rice mills qualify as 'Small Scale Industry' by national standards, locally they confront the average producer of the marketed surplus with a massive concentration of economic power. As petty production thrives on agriculture, it generates petty surpluses, while the scale of the ever more capitalized rice mills increases. Meanwhile, the Left Front Government cites the increasingly powerful rice mills as examples of a spectacular redistributivist project for 'Small Scale Industry'.[20]

There is a strong logic to the policy of 'betting on the strong', pursued by the central and state governments and the rice mills alike (even when they seem opposed in party-political terms). The PDS subsidies benefit the rice mill oligopoly in an indirect manner by giving rice millers contracts with state-trading agencies, as a result of which price risks and supply fluctuations are reduced. The transactions costs of PDS procurement are also reduced. The arrangement enables the rice mills to operate at the high capacity utilization they need to justify the installation of capital-biased technology, which also generates a high quality by-product—bran—which contributes significantly to their returns. PDS operations also enable the rice mill oligopoly to syphon off a small fraction of the milled rice out-turn to add informally to their profits. The Left Front Government has resisted the removal of subsidies anywhere in the system: it was only the Left Front Government's near-bankruptcy which halted operations of the subsidized PDS in 2002.

In his comparative study of regime types in India, Kohli (1987, p. 9 and p.95 ff.) argued that the Left Front Government had had the greatest developmental impact of all those he studied. The regulation of sharecroppers' tenurial security and shares under Operation Barga; the development of 'red' panchayats (politicized, participatory and decentralized local government); credit from co-operatives and from nationalized banks directed at smallholder production; and real increases in the wages of landless agricultural labour—all these represented a bundle of 'successful reforms aimed at altering the conditions of the poor...with significant long-term impact on the living conditions of the lower agrarian groups in West Bengal'.

There are two aspects to Kohli's argument. First, he concludes that the Left Front Government demonstrated the greatest autonomy of all the three regimes he studied. His explanation for this success emphasized the coherent nature of the leadership, the appropriate combination of centralized and decentralized organizational arrangements, the exclusion of propertied classes from participation in governance, and yet a pragmatism in facilitating a stable and non-threatening political atmosphere in which the propertied entrepreneurial classes could invest. Second, Kohli argues that the Left Front Government's agenda—evolving from a revolutionary to a reformist one—demonstrated a pragmatism according to which enemies are only those who are not productive, identified as absentee landlords, and big jotedars.

But Kohli's interpretation leaves the nature of the accommodation with the propertied classes unaddressed. His argument stresses the importance of Left Front Government's reforms in production relations for the government's electoral popularity. He neglects the nature of the sphere of circulation and of market exchange, where the classic Marxist position, which has been influential in justifying the case for state trading and other interventions in agricultural markets, is derived from Marx's argument that merchant's capital is unproductive but necessary.[21] West Bengal's Lead Bank, the financial agent of the Left Front Government, is by no means alone in developing this argument into a commitment to eradicating middlemen on the grounds of their being unproductive and unnecessary (UCO Bank, 1990). Whereas Ross Mallick pointed out that few interests were hurt by the Left Front Government's anti-capitalism, because few Bengalis were members of the big capitalist bourgeoisie, (Mallick, 1993; ch. 1) our analysis at a local level, where 'Bengalis' have been as important as marwaris and would indeed by hurt by an anti-capitalist politics, shows the Left Front Government's anti-capitalist stance has been at most rhetorical. It is fashionable to argue that discursive categories have real material consequences; but in West Bengal it has been so long apparent that the

Conclusions

former simply mask the latter that the interests served by such anti-capitalist rhetoric are obscure.

When it comes to markets, the Left Front Government is not at all autonomous, as Kohli believes. It is bound in tight relations of accommodation with a rural capitalist elite which does not support it electorally. Boudhayan Chattopadhyay saw the result as 'a sick but proliferating commercial tertiary capitalism unhinged from the requirements of production' (1991b, p. 376). The research presented here, however, has shown that the rural/small town version of such capitalism is not 'unhinged' from production but indirectly controls it. There is enough evidence from the rural Indian economy as a whole, most of which is outside the regulative ambit of the state, to show that this intermediate commercial capitalism is both pervasive and persistent (Harriss-White, 2003; Ch. 3). It is a form of capitalism in which those in receipt of money advances or advances in kind (or those forced in effect to deposit money with firms, through the latters' delay in making payments) are deprived of freedom to transact. Such arrangements mimic the subordination embodied in the labour contract. The credit relations through which commodity production is indirectly controlled have for decades been far more important than the arrangements that link landlords and sharecroppers (Rudra, 1982; Bhaduri, 1983; Sebastian, 2003).

The Left Front Government's lack of autonomy and its vulnerability to local market-driven politics raises serious questions about the intentions behind regulative policy. Has its marketing policy been clever? Has it intended to regulate the new small-scale commercial capital by suffocation and by barring it from access to credit? Are the markets which are so widely described by politicians, administrators, journalists, and bankers as 'unproductive', *meant* to be regulated by the diversion of formal credit to agriculture and industry, which are seen as 'productive' in classical Marxist terms? Or is this credit not meant to do any such thing, since in fact it does not suffocate agro-commercial capital, but nurtures it—by channelling formal credit unerringly to the apex power points of the marketing system? If so, it is strange, since until very recently it has harmed the livelihoods and the accumulation prospects of a crucial political constituency of the Left Front Government: that of petty production and trade in the food markets. This constituency has proliferated and become prominent in the rice markets both in numbers and in its command over the marketed surplus, despite rather than because of the Left Front Government policy. Is it deliberate to let markets develop by deliberate neglect or selective state abandonment, often moulded around defectively implemented state regulation? Or is it because petty trade is seen as 'illegal and nefarious', and research which shows how it has proliferated is simply dismissed?[22] Or is the problem of petty trade just very low among the Left Front Government's political priorities?[23]

When interviewed about the Left Front Government's failure to co-operativise agriculture, a prominent CPI(M) Central Committee member was reported by Robert Thorlind as suggesting this 'low priority' explanation. 'When the ministerial portfolios for the first Left Front Government were distributed in 1977,' he said, 'the two portfolios for co-operatives and agricultural marketing were mistakenly seen by the CPI(M) as not that important. These portfolios were therefore handed over to one of the smaller Left Front partners (the Forward Bloc) which... unfortunately did not have the vision or understanding for what really efficient pro-poor grass roots co-operatives could mean to promote more equal and participative socio-economic development' (Thorlind, 2000, pp.78–9). This revelation poses further questions. Why were producer co-operatives and agricultural markets conflated? How could a mistake made in 1977 remain unrectified for a quarter century? If taken at face value, it is at best a textbook illustration of path-dependent institutional inefficiency and of the lengths gone to by the CPI(M) to prevent instability in the alliances comprising its coalition.

The analysis and evidence advanced in this book show that this defence cannot be taken at face value. But, the politics of the appeasement of rural capital by the Forward Bloc, the appeasement of the Forward Bloc by the CPI(M), and the impact of the party's political allegiances of the elite in control of petty trade and processing have not been researched in detail by anyone, and are certainly beyond the scope of any study that could be undertaken by a foreign researcher.[24] In 2006, A. Sarkar argued that the very remarkable and enduring political stability of the Left Front Government—during what he describes as a period of decline in agricultural growth, industrial stagnation, and growth in employment below the all-Indian rate— was due to the explosion of the informal economy and the Left Front Government's role in either turning a blind eye to it, or acting as local protectors of it. Our argument here is different: that turning a blind eye was actually long-term neglect, and that this sector has been *not*

Conclusions

protected at all until extremely recently. If anything, it has been an arena of extortion. The electoral resilience of the Left Front Government is outside the scope of this book but must owe much to the 'plus' of powerful local organization and to the 'minus' of egregious lack of power bases or political projects for credible alternatives.[25]

The political programme of the Left Front Government has been preoccupied with inequality and insecurity in landed property, and poverty in production. This has led it to assign a high position on the reformist agenda for tenurial reforms and land rights, and for more widespread participation in local government. Such structural reforms required action against the interests of the landed-propertied classes—the issue which interests so many scholars and activists. Kohli's approach is a good example and he is in good company. His method stresses first the character of the regime, its broadness and its reliance on cadres; then the multi-pronged assault it has tried to make on poverty. It is not to deny the Left Front Government's achievements to point out that the argument proceeds by treating 'poverty' as a 'sector' and then wrenching it from the relations which cause and perpetuate it.[26] A set of interventions is then identified on *a priori* basis and seen as an explanation for changes in poverty. The subset of economic interventions examined by Kohli to provide explanations for the success of anti-poverty policy mainly concerns landed property, with many unexamined assumptions about the nature of the property relations being challenged.

The evidence of this book on the development of markets and commercial accumulation, and its method—examining the system of markets as institutions and as intertwining production and circulation—suggests a different explanation for the success of the agrarian reforms. In practice, the rural classes identified by Kohli as 'losers' (rentier landlords) had been losing interest in rural landed property anyway, by virtue of having diversified out of agriculture, while the other class fraction dominating markets, the marwaris, have not been much directly affected by land reforms. Their non-land wealth (as seen in the investment tables and diagrams for potato cold storage and rice milling in Appendix 4.2 and Appendix 7.1) is massive compared with the agricultural land component of their mercantile-financial-industrial portfolios. Inequality in land-holding has declined only slightly under the Left Front Government (Sengupta and Gazder, 1997). The fact that the structure of property rights has been so little transformed in the wake of Operation Barga (which reached its zenith in the early

1980s) is testament to the enduring power over the rural economy of commercial forces sited outside the arena of village politics, and operating in markets other than land. Once an appropriate HYV technology was available and well-water exploited, agro-commercial capital did not hinder agricultural growth because their profits, on a much larger scale than those of producers, are derived from it. This is not to argue that agrarian and market structures do not frame the social distribution of the gains from agricultural growth. That is exactly what they do. Petty producers and traders have not mobilized politically against apex capital, not only because this capital is protected by the politicized arrangements regulating the Public Distribution System, but also because petty producers and traders, even when harassed by state vigilance forces, can gain seasonal livelihoods out of the wide margins created by the accommodation between state and commercial capital.[27]

Commodity markets have been below the radar of most of the abundant scholarship on the political economy of agrarian change in West Bengal, save that of Visva Bharati. Had they been more studied, the significance of the Left Front Government's focus on rural production, which led it to neglect property relations in exchange and circulation—in practice, if not rhetorically—would have been appreciated. This political neglect has permitted the development of socially-regulated, as opposed to state-regulated, markets, and the perpetuation of an accommodation between the state and the agro-commercial power elite established under previous regimes.

In this, the Left Front Government is not at all exceptional.[28] It is only the political ideology in which its accommodation with the agro-commercial elite has been concealed that has been exceptional. 'We will implement our programmes not from Writers' Buildings (West Bengal Secretariat) alone but also from the fields and factories where our strength lies and with the help of the people', declared Chief Minister Jyoti Basu on his election in 1977.[29] The CPI(M) was 'completing a bourgeois democratic revolution... in which our administration is transparent and everything is taken to the people', explained West Bengal's then Attorney General in November 1991.[30] The problem is not so much the fact that the Left Front Government's revolution is a purely bourgeois one; it is that the Left Front Government lacks an economic-cum-political project for the petty-bourgeois class to which it has acted as midwife and which lives in the economic spaces between fields and factories. The Left Front Government has lacked a project for the actually existing factor endowments of the rural non-farm economy; or a project, as Datta puts it, for an entrepreneurial tradition that has its roots in the bazaar economy (Datta, 2002, p. 3/18)); or a plan to incorporate 'informal markets'; or even a vision for a worked-out 'people's capitalism' (the concept that Abhijit Banerjee and others drew from their reading of development in China, for lack of a critical analysis of West Bengal).[31]

Instead, in 2000, the Left Front Government followed the Communist Party line in China, Mozambique, and Vietnam. It employed McKinsey, the US management consultancy, to secure the involvement of some ten Indian and multi-national corporates to scale up West Bengal's commercial capitalism by many multiples. This is to be done through the contract-farming of poultry, shrimp, 'vision crops' in fruit and vegetables, and rice for export and for new supermarket retail outlets.[32] Rice is to be developed through new brands—'Bengal rice', or perhaps 'Darjeeling rice'. A few strategically-placed rice millers have lobbied to be the agents of these corporates.[33] The Left Front Government was asked by McKinsey, acting on behalf of its corporate clients, to organize pilot projects to collaborate with banks to release the credit needed for contract farming, to offer fiscal incentives, to build infrastructure, and to deliver an 'articulation' of the contract farming policy through its panchayats.[34] In this vision, which introduces a much larger-scale fraction of agri-business and reduces the current agro-commercial elite to the role of supplying-agents or contractors, petty, post-harvest production and trading is completely by-passed. For McKinsey, it simply does not exist.

But the kind of commercial capitalist development reported in this book strongly suggests that petty production and trade may be intrinsic to state-regulated capitalism, incorporated by it and an outcome of it. Activity outside the regulative ambit of the state—not just petty production and trade but also casualized labour in and around large registered firms (even the Food Corporation of India) —gives clear advantages to business and the state. The evidence in this book shows that market or environmental risks may be shifted onto independent out-workers, home-workers or unprotected wage labour. Costs may be reduced by avoiding overheads, abandoning or never meeting employers' obligations, undercutting legal wage floors, and replacing wage work by work regulated within families by patriarchal authority relations. New kinds of low-cost labour may be incorporated, or old forms of low-cost labour may be re-incorporated (e.g., rural, female and child labour, and migrant workers). The labour process is controlled by avoiding the creation of conditions where it might be organized in unions, through which it might grasp rights and exert some countervailing power. The state's regulative and welfare responsibilities towards labour can be shed and infrastructural responsibilities towards fractions of business and capital can be reduced. Petty production and trade is not a pre-capitalist relic. It is not confined to residual sectors. If it is transitional at all, the transition is long drawn-out.

In West Bengal until recently, petty commercial capital has not been encouraged to accumulate; it is quite the reverse. Now the dynamics of accumulation are extending the mass of petty trade, but unaccompanied by a development project for them. An unholy—and to date politically un-articulated—alliance between a mass of small peasant/petty traders, transporters, and processors on the one hand, and liberalizers at the Centre on the other, is providing a theoretically and politically uncomfortable challenge. This challenge exposes for all to see the local structure of agro-commercial capitalist interests which have been interlocked for decades with those of a government politically dedicated to opposing them.

Notes

1. See page (x) for price inflators and deflators.
2. Every scholar who has examined 'real markets' in Bengal cannot avoid drawing attention to their idiosyncrasies (Banerjee, 1995; Basu, 2002; Crow, 2001; Mukhopadhayay, 1998; Moitra and Das, 2004; Sarkar, 1979; Sarkar and Chatterjee, 1995).
3. Despite better targeted implementation than elsewhere in India (Saha and Swaminathan, 1994), West Bengal's IRDP loans were thinner on the ground than the all-India average (Ghosh, 1998).
4. *Business Line*, July 6th 2001.
5. District Food Controller, Pers Comm, 2004.
6. http://www.ri3240.com/Dist/profilejugal.htm
7. As hypothesised to be a prime mover of institutional change by North, 1989, p. 65.
8. Hardgrove, 2002.
9. Politically, this labour has been mobilized to support the cross-class peasant movement—the Krishak Sabha.
10. Ghosh and Harriss-White, 2002; Ghosh and Sudarshan, 2003, p. 6, pp. 29–31. It has even lost the capacity to aggregate data for the husking mill sector.
11. West Bengal was not alone in this and six other states were encouraged or forced to accept devolved control over their public distribution systems.

Conclusions

12. It was widely alleged by a range of stakeholders that subsidized rice exports for which the Bura Bazaar wholesalers acted as FCI agents were being illicitly re-routed back to Kolkata's retail markets, reinforcing the deflationary effect.
13. In West Bengal, as found earlier for Tamil Nadu, most departments have remits which some way or the other cover agricultural markets together with ad hoc rules at the procedural boundaries (Harriss, 1984; Harriss-White, 2004 a). Chibber, 2003, shows this is general.
14. See Harriss-White, 1995, for a general discussion; and 2004 b for a discussion of an analogous case in the sector of social security.
15. Much more detailed research than was possible for an outsider is necessary to determine the balance between them. It was not possible to research the political economy of the state's money trail, which we have seen affects accumulation possibilities in the petty sub-system, protects the oligopoly of rice mills, controls state procurement, and may well account for the perversities in the implementation of procurement which led to the crisis in 2002.
16. See Gibbon and Ponte, 2004; for the focus on governance.
17. Crow, 2001 is an exception.
18. Myrdal, 1968 after Weber. More often the state is seen as a mainly rent-seeking barrier to efficient markets. On the roles of bureaucratic rationality, rent-seeking and buy-offs see Khan, 2004.
19. Basu, 2002; p. 324–5. The Left Front's fingers were burnt after encouraging and supporting peasant organizations, seizures of land and struggles over the shares of share tenures which became politically destabilizing. See Mallick, 1993, ch. 1 for a critique of the Left Front Government for lacking a theory of the transition to socialism.
20. Interview with CPM Minister for Commerce and Industry , Bidyut Ganguly, quoted in *Frontline* July 11th, 1997, p. 123.
21. Merchant's capital, used for buying and selling commodities, is unproductive because by itself it does not change the physical nature of commodities. It is necessary because commodities must circulate in order to be consumed and a specialist mercantile function means that 'a smaller part of society's labour power and labour time is tied up in this unproductive function' than would be the case if there were no such mechanism to complete the process of production and consumption. Appendix 2.1 elaborates this argument and its consequences for policy; and see Marx, 1974, Vol.1, ch. 4.
22. Sarkar et al., 1992; p. 43.
23. See also the Reserve Bank of India, 1984, for more evidence of the wide neglect of markets as instituted phenomena.
24. See Hardgrove, 2002, for a powerful statement about the difficulty of researching an analogous topic, which forced her to approach it using historical evidence alone and which remains entirely unresearched for the current era.

25. Sarkar, 2006. Yet since Sarkar's explanation is an analytical residual, having eliminated others, the way the Left Front Government might 'protect' the informal economy would benefit from empirical research.
26. See Mallick, 1993, for a case that the anti-poverty project has been opportunistic and was bound to fail.
27. Sarkar's formulation that the Left Front Government's stability is due to the physical-political protection it provides to livelihoods in the non-farm economy (while being deduced without evidence and needing further research) is an indictment of the poverty of the political project for petty production and trade in the informal economy (Sarkar, 2006).
28. Harriss-White, 2003; Also, see the *Economic and Political Weekly's* Editorial 'Companies and Farming' 2002 July 13th in which Tamil Nadu's efforts to encourage corporates and contract farming, and the amendments needed to the Regulated Agricultural Markets Act to legalise contract farming and the transformation of 'wasteland', are critically discussed.
29. Quoted in Sankar, 1997; p. 123.
30. In a lecture in Nuffield College, Oxford.
31. Banerjee et al., 2002; see Bandhyopadhyay, 2001, p. 7/8; and Chatterjee, 1997, p. 67-68 on the limits to a paternalistic project for the small peasantry.
32. It had earlier commissioned other international management consultancy firms for advice on industry : Arthur D. Little and Price Waterhouse, as reported from an interview with the CPM Minister for Industry and Commerce, Bidyut Ganguly, *Frontline*, July 11th, 1997, p. 123.
33. They are not to be read as accepting a passive role as agents of industrial capital.
34. 'McKinsey move woos investors to West Bengal', *Business Line* Sept 14th, 2002; http://www.ciionline.org/Eastern/regional focus, 2003.

Appendix 1.1

Field Methodology

'Our agricultural markets in West Bengal have cancer, TB, cirrhosis of the liver, and ulcers. How can you begin to make sense of them?'
(A rice miller, Memari, 1990)

'Existing data and methods hide rather than reveal the nature of the market mechanism in its extractive role as distinct from its allocative role.'
(Boudhayan Chattopadhay, 1981)

In the absence of many other studies, this book, exploring the development of the system of markets, together with the principal institutions through which markets work in rural central West Bengal over the last quarter century, is based on first hand fieldwork

During this fieldwork, theoretical ideas have been constantly juxtaposed to actually existing 'real' markets and states. At the heart of the exploratory project throughout this entire period are three ideas: that post-harvest commodity circulation is a system of markets in continuous disequilibrium; that commodity exchange is central to class formation, and that institutional diversity is of foundational importance to these markets.

The elements of a system of circulation of staples are firms and their organization, technologies, sites, and commodities. The means of dynamizing the elements are, first, money (in the form of investment capital, finance, and as reflected in prices and profits and investments made) and, second, labour, both in its live 'organic' form and in its 'inorganic' form (technology, most specifically processing, storage, and transport technology). The diversity of the system of agricultural markets has been explored through the following attributes:

- the economic structures of the commodity systems;
- related markets, notably that for transport;
- the combinatorial complexity of trading activity;
- forms of property ownership;
- the organization of the labour process;
- physical flows; and
- price formation and behaviour.

The dynamics and relations between elements of the food system have been studied through:

- the history of ownership and control of assets (including land);
- age structure;
- the generation of trading capital;
- the costs, distribution, and control of information;
- the expression of power in exchange: contractual forms and the transfer of property rights;
- credit and finance;
- histories of expansion and of collapse; and
- the development of commercial portfolios.

The major disturbing elements were taken to be changes in production and in the regulation of the circulation of rice. In turn, this regulation is of two types. The first is political: state interventions in markets ; and the 'retaliatory' political action taken by managers of firms and by labour. The second is the play of social power and authority and the ways these are expressed in the economy: through gender relations, caste and religion, and the power of place and territory.

The regulation, de-regulation and re-regulation of rapidly developing markets can be understood by:

- comparing of the regulative agenda of the state with the actual experience of implementation; and
- analysing self-organization and the politics of collective action expressed in a range of business organizations and in labour unions.

Evidence for the social regulation of the market system was obtained partly by observation and partly by questions about:

- the history of the business family, its size and composition;
- the acquisition of skills, contact, information, and capital; and
- the roles of gender, caste/religion, migration history and the existence and meaning of features of elements, and relations that are specific to localities.

In Birbhum district in 1982, the data were obtained from interviews with 50 firms (see Tables 2.1 and 4.1). These firms were not randomly selected, for there was no population data. A snowball sample of rice mills was created, emanating from an initial contact with the President of the District Rice Millers Association. Other marketing intermediaries were sought out in local villages. Although I lived for three months in Santiniketan in early 1982, the interviewing fieldwork took two people 28 working days, in Bolpur and Ahmadpur towns and in Surul Layek Bazar, Sian, Iswarpur, Singhi and Bassapara villages, in the Bolpur and Sainthia blocks of Birbhum district (Map 2 page 51). These blocks cover 250 square miles (640 square kms). All these places were accessible by either train or bicycle from Santiniketan. Each firm was surveyed in as standard a manner as possible. No schedule was used and Dilip Chatterjee, the able field assistant who, like me, knew the questions by heart, played a key role in developing the interview technique which we used then and which was iterated 10 and 20 years later. The list of questions, answers to which were entered in a note book and then put on data sheets, is like that to be found at the end of this Appendix.

In Bardhaman in 1990, a survey of 60 commercial firms was undertaken once more with able field assistance from Pundarik Mukherjee during August and September 1990. The letter sent in advance to merchants, the fact-sheet describing the purpose of the project in a straightforward way in Bengali (which was freely given to anyone curious about the project), and the set of questions we used as a basis for the interviews are given at the end of the Appendix. In the absence of population data and knowing from previous field work that this lack of data combines with the complexity of markets to defeat attempts to obtain representative, stratified random samples, the three commodity markets in the second round—potato, rice, and mustard oil—were studied using social networks and spatial transects. The latter consists of those firms situated along a straight line drawn across the map of a settlement upon which all firms (identified through the inspection of every road) have been recorded (see Table 6.1 in Chapter 6).

Functional maps were made of the settlements as a guide to the likely trading populations and were continually modified in the light of information. Figure 6.1 shows how this fieldwork was restricted to certain points in the commodity systems. Ashok Rudra argued that greater operational complexity and variability of the larger firms make larger sampling fractions necessary (Rudra, 1989), and this is what we tried to put into practice. Information about state regulation and institutions of collective action came from the local Food Department, the Department of Statistics, the Zilla Shabatipati, and office bearers in trade associations picked up in our sample of firms. Petty trade and/or periodic marketplace trade had to be excluded due to lack of resources. We worked in, and within 10 miles of, three urban settlements in Bardhaman district: Memari, Katwa, and Gulsi. We walked and used cycle rickshaws, buses and trains to go about this region.

The field work in 2000–3 had to be carried out differently, since, for family reasons, I could myself no longer get to India to do field work for periods longer than 10 days. The fact that I could return to places where I am known certainly helped the work. In 2000, I carried out a reconnaissance for the second update. Working from Kolkata, I interviewed officials in the food bureaucracy, in the Food Corporation of India and its trades unions, in party politics, and in trade associations—a total of 18 'stakeholders'. At the same time, Sutapa Choudhury—with research assistance—carried out seven weeks of independent field research into rice retailing in Kolkata and interviewed 50 traders exemplifying five different kinds of retailing.

In a further week in 2002 with P.K. Ghosh, working in and around Bolpur in Birbhum district, a total of 16 firm-owners sited strategically throughout the entire market system agreed to talk to us. We got around using public transport and cycle rickshaws. P.K. Ghosh then went on to spend six more weeks independently researching a further set of 50 rice-processing firms in Birbhum and Bardhaman districts, as one of the four field components of a project on trade liberalization and the informal sector. He returned briefly to collect official data in 2003, and so did I, for final interviews with stakeholders in the food administration and in early 2004 to complete the updating of background material and to discuss the story with scholars.[1]

In 2002, yet again, there were no complete population lists from which a sample could be drawn. Ghosh interviewed 31 owners of small husking mills, 6 in Birbhum District and 25 in Barddhaman District. He found husking mills clustered idiosyncratically in distinctive small agro-cultural regions. He found 17 rice mill owners willing to be interviewed, 7 in Birbhum and 10 in Barddhaman. Ghosh's field experience was uneven, because of a high rate of refusal to respond to detailed questions on costs and gross output and also because the owners of rice mills were unwilling to devote time to these interviews. Firms ought to be accountable at the least to the Revenue Dept, the Labour Dept, the inspectorate for Environmental Protection and the

Electricity Board from which they take power. However, most of these firms experience the state as a rent-seeking institution and are reluctant to divulge facts which might make them vulnerable to penalties. The analysis relies heavily on a minority of respondents who were interested in the project, willing to give substantial time, and to discuss questions freely and in depth. From their testimony, which has been used as case studies, the incomplete costs of other firms could be carefully imputed.

The research questions have required a first-hand fieldwork characteristic of anthropology—but at a regional scale above the spatial and social scale at which anthropological field work is usually carried out. A collective project about field work on markets, commerce, and their regulation can be found in (ed) Harriss-White (1998). The periods of time I have spent in the field in West Bengal have been shorter than the 'total immersion' of over a year, which I have done twice in Tamil Nadu and the 8-month period spent in the field in Sri Lanka. However I have carried out profitable field studies of rice markets in Bangladesh over shorter time spans, like the ones for this research (Harriss, 1978a and b; Harriss-White, 1989). The approach used for fieldwork has not differed in any of these cases, only the scope of the work in terms of territorial space, the number of commodities studied, and the numbers and types of firms interviewed. There is no doubting the fact that the development of comparative experience elsewhere and over a period of decades is useful as an ice breaker and makes for profitable two-way comparative exchanges in interviews. It also reduces the start-up time between arrival and fieldwork (which, in the very first experience in Tamil Nadu in 1972, took three months but in the visits between 2000 and 2004 was immediate). In 1982 and 1990, the dedicatee of this book was highly instrumental in selecting my field assistants. Their industrious preparation also contributed to time in the field which was rarely idle. Prof Sengupta also dry-ran questionnaires prior to the pilot stage. He discussed the translation of technical terms from English into Bengali and back again—and vice versa with Bengali terms. I have not only been well briefed prior to field work, but also able to discuss my findings and provisional interpretations during fieldwork with local scholars and other knowledgeable people.

Being female and foreign has always been an advantage for me, since I am more likely to be accepted as independent from the state, although at some basic level, the very fact that I have been able to work in India tells the respondent that I am at least not regarded by customs and immigration as threatening. Being foreign, I have never been challenged when working in male-dominated space, or physically dirty space, and seem to have been regarded as an honorary male—one who is occasionally mocked for doing 'professor's work' which does not fit local preconceptions of what that work ought to be. West Bengal has an exceptionally male (political and public) culture. Being female has cut both ways. On the one hand a refusal to honour appointments with someone of inferior gender status has no political consequences to a local businessman. On the other hand, a foreign woman may have sensitive matters discussed with them without much consequence either. I have always worked with language assistance and set up my meetings in advance in as businesslike way as possible. Once initiated the interview has flowed through conversation—with a 'deep structure' in which sensitive questions are approached in many direct and indirect ways. It is argued that it is a gross form of ethnocentricity to assume that local people see their economic activity in the categories used by the researcher. While this may be broadly true, contested categories are often provocative of vivid discussion (for instance: the concept of an informal firm; the meaning of present market value; the depreciation of a mill, every component of which is replaceable; and the value assigned to family labour). Most concepts, however, were understood without confusion or challenge by respondents. We have also answered as many questions as asked, some personal and probably just as sensitive to us as the questions on costs, returns, loans, and disciplinary regulation are to traders.

Choudhury's experience of field work, as a British Bengali in Kolkata, differed from mine in several respects (Choudhury, 2001). She found that being foreign, female and Bengali, she was not expected to frequent marketplaces and once there, that traders were suspicious of her motives because of the many 'layers of illegality' involved in their work. She was even threatened. However, once she had been accompanied to the market by a well-known local politician, traders talked more freely. She was also plied with questions about personal matters and about the Bengali diaspora (Ibid).

Both Choudhury and I have found a simple style of living (in my case working out of small town commercial hotels[2])—and a local style of dressing—essential for this field work, if only because of the enormous range in the social background of people one may meet in the course of a single day. Both of us did not record interviews on tape, but took anonymized notes in local school notebooks. I have been very fortunate in being helped by motivated, street-wise, and scholarly local assistants who understood the purposes of the project, who were able to parry the questions of suspicious people, to deal with rumour, to work long and anti-social hours, to rise to the theatrical/performance demands of fieldwork, and to be at ease in not always very clean physical environments.

In the end, however, samples are discovered—rather than selected—in as orderly a way as possible. Interviews are rarely complete, so that the evidence is very rarely of a sort from which a confident statistical generalization may be made—least of all from the regions of central West Bengal to the state as a whole. It is, however, richly revealing of processes and relations.

In getting to grips with the process of commodity circulation, there have been costs, trade-offs, and errors of omission. As a result, this book cannot be a systematic inside account of the Left Front's food policy as it is decided and practised from day to day and decade to decade. I also could not follow the politics of state finance in any form, despite its crucial importance to regulation. Nor was it possible to observe centre-state relations. It is the view of state practice which gives incentives to, and which disciplines, food markets that is offered here.

Officially published data has been obtained from the libraries of the Agro-Economics Research Centre, Visva Bharathi, the Centre for Studies in the Social Sciences, Calcutta, and the Institute of Development Studies, Kolkata. The most important unpublished data for this study has been weekly price data copied out in the Dept. of Statistics, together with official flow and supply data from the Food Department and the District Office of the Regulated Markets Dept., Bardhaman district, various official documents from the FCI Employees Union, Kolkata, and lists of rice mills from the presidents of the two Districts' Rice Millers Association. All official statistics are collected in the first place through social processes and relationships. Their impact on official data has been well analysed by Adrian, 1998. Official data are not unusually incomplete and contain errors, both of which compromise their statistical analysis.

The methods used in the analysis of the price data are explained and justified in Palaskas and Harriss-White, 1993. I have also investigated the difference between the procedure and practice of regulation at various points in the system with the help of a range of interested stakeholders in politics, the food administration and the unions. In the end, as with field material, so it is with official data and with the accounts of officials that this story has been assembled using pieces of evidence of all sorts, evaluated, and then pieced together—as in a rather ill-fitting jig-saw puzzle, which, though still incomplete, reveals its content.

Questions Used in Interviews
Questions For Fieldwork, August–September 1990
Burdwan Dist., West Bengal

Section One: Land Reform, Technical Change, Anti-Poverty Policy, and their Effects on Markets
1.1. History:
   Family occupational history
   Caste
   Native Place
   Date of start of firm

   Reasons:
   Skill Acquisition/mobilization of labour/finding of contacts/licence/premises etc

   Starting Capital (SC): fixed; working
   Location of SC
   Sectoral Origin of SC

   Organization of ownership of firm:
   Changes/Reasons:
   Organization of family:
   Size and composition
   Changes/Reasons:

   Organization of family land:
   Size: wet/dry
   Changes/Reasons:

   Organization of family non-land businesses:
   Changes/Reasons

1.2. The Town and Region:
   At date of start: the types/numbers/size structures/and functions of firms and the flows of sampled commodity through the area

1.3. The firm:
   History of growth of firm:
   commodities/geography of flows/transport/sites of transactions/clientele-sellers and buyers/labour/finance/technical change (diversification/levelling/concentration)
   Now: origins/destinations/intermediaries/transport/byproducts
   Size now
   Assets/gross output (profiles per day , per season/storage
   Role of family and gender:
   Female and male family labour in firm
   Kinship-inheritance
   Close kin and occupations

1.4. Land reforms in the region—tenurial changes:
   Own land and impact
   Crops marketed/marketed surplus/number of intermediaries/dependence on other traders (information/transport/credit/storage/processing/other)/
   Credit relations
   Rents
   Physical infrastructure
   Locations of markets
   Changes over time:
   Historically
   Seasonally
   Geographically
   At times of crisis
   (concentration? if not why not?)
   Other changes in the area

2.0 'How marketing is organized': Diversity and Regulation: Rules of the Game

2.1 Functions/local labels and meanings
   In sampled commodity
   Buy/sell/broker/store/transport/process/finance trade/finance production/other

Reasons
Flexibility

2.2. Types of Contract/Transactions:
Proportion of sales/purchases large farmer/small farmer/landless peasant prices; spot/attached/closed negotation price dispersions
Forward/contracts (describe)   Weights/measures
Other   Payment systems
Linked contracts   Places/seasons
(credit/labour/paddy-rice transport/storage over season/other) velocities of storage (maximum/minimum/quantity/time)
kin/caste/other mediated and rigid trade

2.3 Uncertainty:
Losses and crises
Means of enforcement of contract
Disputes and Means of Resolution - costs
Crime: theft, adulteration, diffncs in weights and measures
Travel
Salaries of enforcement staff and costs (%)

2.4 Information:
Media
Prices and quantities
Places
Institutions/intermediaries
Changes over time of information base
Costs (bulletin/post and stat/telegrams/telephone/clerks/contacts/other)

Clients (question about a new client) costs
Other intermediaries (setting up contacts) costs
Clerks and employees

2.5 (Government) Regulation:
How are the following organized?:
Licensing
Price information
Place for transactions
Storage (location/quantities/time)

Contract
Technical change
Payment
Finance
Fee (for market/for transaction)
Security
Hygiene
Transport
Ancillary labour

3. Control over production, economic mobility and portfolio development: the relation between agriculture, trade and business

Turnover/gross output by profile
Assets
Development and the Merchants' Porfolio/pattern of investment over the lifetime of the firm;
Locations
Types/sectors (reasons/organization)
Savings (stocks/shares/human capital/education dowry etc)

Mobility
Land in last generation and now
Businesses in last generation and now

Own landholding, mode of operation, and decision making
Mode of operation and decision making on land of clients/advice

Finance-Borrowed (maximum/minimum/sources/terms and conditions/seasons and places)

Finance-Lent (maximum totally/minimum totally/maximum to individual/minimum to individual/variety of terms and conditions (traders/agents/large farmer and small farmer archetypes) no. of large farmer/no. of small farmer/means of repayment/interest rates/losses/default and outstanding/terms and conditions)

Ties with marketing and the ensuring of supplies of commodities and credit

Labour in firm
permanent
casual male maximum/minimum/rates/jobs/dispersion of contracts/type of payment/bonding/perks
female ditto
child ditto

4.0 New Crops and Marketing Problems:
Last 10 years:
Changes in cropping patterns
Needs of crops for marketing
Technical problems/decentralization/processing, transport , perishability
Information (price/place/intermediaries/orgn of subordinate markets/spatial flows)
Technology
Finance
Exchange relations (entry and structures, dependence and flexibility of transactions)
Dependence of intermediaries upon each other

5. Policy:
Lobbies
Associations/date of start
History (TUs/labour/state controls/auto-regulation/crime etc)
Other associations

Politics:
Parties (finance/election funding/affiliation and action through parties/policies towards trade)

Other Activity (Temple/Lions/Red Cross/Rotary/Panchayat/Co-operative/School and hospital governing board etc.)

Contact with State:
Price and procurement (state trading etc)
Storage
Processing
Co-operation
Licensing

Commercial taxation
Finance of trade
Finance of production
Small scale industry, IRDP etc

Biggest problems with marketing and solutions:

Net profit (rough estimate)
Per unit (specify unit and minimum/maximum)
Per year: under Rs 5,000
5,000–10,000
10,000–20,000
20,000–50,000
Over 50,000

Notes

1. The team formed for the project on trade liberalization was drawn from the National Council of Applied Economic Research in New Delhi and Queen Elizabeth House, Oxford University. The project used insights from field work in the design of a CGE model disaggregated for the formal and informal economy, All-India (Adam and Harriss-White, 2007). From this model, the impact of reforms undertaken during the 1990s was simulated. The field projects problematized informality and elicited information on the impact of trade liberalization, which enabled a comparison of the two approaches to understanding liberalization. Formal and informal rice processing firms were studied in Punjab as well as West Bengal. (Kaur, Ghosh and Sudarshan, 2007). Garments were also compared in Delhi and Tiruppur (Singh and Sapra, 2007).
2. The International Guest House at the Ramakrishna Mission, Gol Park, was a base for working in Kolkata.

Appendix 2.1

Marx's Merchant's Capital and its Influence in India

For Marx, merchant's capital or 'circulation capital' is the oldest form of capital, predating capitalism. It is money used in a specialized sphere of circulation in which commodities are bought and sold and which is distinct from that of production. Marx argues that there are no activities on the part of merchant's capital in the sphere of circulation which can increase the use value of the commodities which it buys and sells, because the act of buying and selling on markets does not change the physical nature of the commodity. In terms of use value, then, merchant's capital is therefore unproductive—even though it is clearly necessary to the process of social reproduction. It follows that its social value is confined to the fact that 'a smaller part of society's labour power and labour time is tied up in this unproductive function' than would be the case were there to be no such a mechanism for the facilitation of the turnover of capital (Marx, 1970; vol. 1, ch. 4). Without merchant's capital, the mass of surplus value produced by industrial—and agricultural—capital would be (greatly) less efficiently produced. Merchant's capital is a drain on surplus value but it facilitates the turnover of capital (See Fine and Saad-Filho, 2003; ch. 11). Marx has been criticised for having an inadequate theory of the transition to capitalism (See Bottomore, 1985 for a sympathetic treatment, and Hodgson, 2001 for an unsympathetic treatment). However, he can be read as arguing that merchant's capital plays a fundamental role in this transition. This argument is significant because it introduces the idea that merchant's capital itself embodies contradictory relationships with respect to production.

For Marx, the role of merchant's capital is *essentially ambivalent* and has both progressive aspects (conducive to the establishment of (industrial) capital) and retrogressive aspects (blocking this process). He is clear about its ambivalent roles: first, '(t)he development of commerce and merchant capital gives rise everywhere to a tendency towards the production of exchange values, increases its volume, multiplies it, makes it cosmopolitan, and develops money into world money. Commerce therefore has a more or less dissolving influence on the producing organisation which it finds at hand, and whose different forms are mainly carried on with a view to use value.' (Marx, 1974, vol. 3; ch. 20). For Marx, another progressive aspect of the role of merchant's capital is to enable the concentration of capital to be invested in production. This is a process which is 'logically' prior to the development of capitalist production because production takes place in time and investment capital is necessary for plant, raw material, and wages before production is able to happen.

Yet at the same time, merchant's capital cannot avoid having a retrogressive role because—as Lenin, writing about the development of capitalism in Russia, explained—it is unable to avoid being dependent on pre-capitalist labour processes to generate the production it devours. Furthermore, insofar as merchant's capital re-invests resources got from buying cheap and selling dear into markets and speculation, it clearly does not re-invest in the expansion of production. 'The independent development of merchant's capital is inversely proportional to the degree of development of capitalist production' (Marx, 1974; vol. 3; ch. 20; p. 329). It is productive investment rather than merchant's capital which revolutionizes capital. It 'is an obstacle to the real capitalist mode of production' (ibid.)

So, the way Marx argues about the balance of contradictory effects is to privilege production relations: '(t)o what extent it (commerce) brings about the dissolution of the old mode of production depends upon its solidity and internal structure, and whether this process of dissolution will lead, in other words, what new mode of production will replace the old, does not depend on commerce, but on the character of the old mode itself' (Marx, op. cit., ch. 20). Productive industrial capital is also privileged in Marx's historical prediction that the development of capitalism would force merchant's capital to be progressively subordinated to the role of a passive 'wing of industrial capital' (ibid).

Despite the specificity of Marx's model of 19th century British capitalism, his concept has been influential in India in part because, as the quotations used here reveal, Marx tended to elide the abstract concept of merchant's capital with the concrete one of commerce.

First, Marx's formulation of merchant's capital as being unproductive but necessary found resonance in many of the colonial inter-war investigations into wide marketing margins (price differences between producers and consumers which reflected, as these reports revealed, the exploitation of impoverished producers by strikingly wealthier traders and commission agents). Their culmination was surely the *All India Rural Credit Survey* carried out after Independence in 1951, which concluded that the root problem of agrarian backwardness was the 'colonial-cum-commercial-cum urban domination over the rural economy'...to such a degree that...'private trade can be tolerated only if the government does not have viable alternatives' (Chattopadhyay, 1969; pp. 221–2). Not only was merchant's capital seen as unproductive but, contrary to Marx's theorizing, it was also *not necessary*, at least not in the form of the mercantile firm. From this sprang many state interventions—not only in West Bengal but throughout India—aimed at 'eliminating middlemen' and at by-passing merchant's capital altogether.[1]

Second, Marx's conclusion that the independent development of merchant's capital is inversely proportional to industrial capitalist development seemed able to explain backward forms of production in agriculture as well as industry, and found fertile ground in empirical conditions in West Bengal. 'The merchant's ability to dominate the commodity market through stocking and price manipulation implies a deduction from the returns of producers, the real income of wage, and labour-income earners as well as from consumers.' (Chattopadhyay, 1969; p. 234). Locked together with land rent and interest-bearing capital, it was able to delay or block the process of agrarian transformation (Bhaduri, 1983).

Third, debates in peasant studies have grappled with the concrete form of merchant's capital—Marx's 'commerce'—initially stylized as money used for buying and selling in combination with money advances for production. These debates engage with the question whether the indirect control of small-scale production by moneylending from merchants does or does not proletarianize producers who are dependent on such relations for their reproduction (Banaji, 1977; 2003). Disguised proletarianization may be an unfamiliar way of describing the commercial relations which preserve small scale production (petty commodity, small scale producer or family forms). They were strongly expected to be eradicated. 'Their position is absolutely hopeless as long as capitalism holds sway...capitalist large-scale production is absolutely sure to run over their impotent antiquated system of small production as a train runs over a pushcart' wrote Engels (in *The Peasant Question in France and Germany*, p. 472). Yet these are remarkably persistent forms of production throughout agrarian societies. Now they are being relabelled as 'micro enterprise' by many development agencies in the 21st century and presented as worthy aspirations and objectives of the ironically fashionable 'pro-poor development'.[2]

Fourth, Marx's formulation of circulation as an independent sphere—though one which is progressively stripped of independence with the development of capitalism in production—and of merchant's capital as having an unavoidably ambivalent role carries strong implications for a developmental state faced with a backward agricultural sector. Both agrarian transformation and the disempowerment of agricultural merchant's capital must be effected through changing production, an argument giving legitimacy both to land reforms and to the new technology of the Green Revolution (Rogaly et al., 1999). It is only very recently, and in dramatic contrast, that 'merchant capital' is actually credited with financing and directing productive investment in agriculture in West Bengal in the post land reform period ' in a context in which an adequate supply of formal credit was not forthcoming' (Rawal, 2005, p. 300).

While merchants' capital is a necessary theoretical concept, Marx can hardly be blamed for failing to anticipate or to theorize the development of the composite forms of capital that have proved to be so persistent in India's economy, as elsewhere (Banaji, 2003; Subrahmanyam, 1990; 1994). As Jairus Banaji observes: ' (I)t is logically absurd to imagine a history of capital using a notion of commerce that was developed by Marx for the kind of capitalist economy that evolved only in the 19th century. In practice that is largely what has happened...there is a methodological impasse at work here, a staggering confusion of history and of logic' (2003). The actually existing counterpart to merchant's capital—commercial capital—is not an autonomous independent force floating above production relations and about to be subordinated to industrial capital. It is deeply rooted in production, and indirectly controls production. Even though the incidence of distress commerce is now low (and this in itself is a developmental achievement), the mass of agricultural producers are involved in markets from which they cannot possibly withdraw under any circumstances, barring a crisis of destitution.

The mechanisms of control are money advances and the state's protection of the rice mill oligopoly, which includes the state's support for their role as net contributors to the cascade of rural credit, and net recipients of the stream of marketed surplus destined for rural-urban trade. Conversely, commercial capital is closely involved with productive activity. Trade cannot take place without processing ('an interruption of the process of circulation for productive purposes'), transport (' the use value of things is materialized in their consumption and their consumption may require a change of location') or storage (productively preventing deterioration in the way Marx allowed for the repair of factory machinery). The way production and circulation are intertwined is not exceptional but general to West Bengal.

Until the 21st century, the impact, both of the ways in which production and circulation are mutually embedded, and of the way the state accommodated the interests of the agro-commercial elite, set strong constraints on any challenge from any other class or class fraction. And when it comes, the challenge is from above, with the blessings of the state, rather than from below, with support from labour.

Notes

1. See Harriss, 1984, for a history of state interventions in trading, warehousing, transport, and their finance.
2. Otero and Rhyne, 1994; and see the critique of micro-credit in Ramachandran and Swaminathan, 2005.

Appendix 4.1

The Processing of Rice

Pre- and Post-Milling Processing in the Domestic Sector—1982

After the processes of harvest and threshing, paddy is stored, it is imbued with qualities of sacredness, and is also used as a medium of exchange like a currency. When required, paddy is removed in lots, cleaned and parboiled. Parboiling takes place in batches—8 kgs for domestic preparation and consumption, and 30 kgs per mud pot for petty trade. The process is identical: cold water is put in a mud pot, paddy is added and brought to the boil over 20 minutes then allowed to simmer for 10 minutes. After this, paddy is steeped in water for 24 hours, then the process of boiling is repeated. The fuel for boiling is usually husk leaves or cowdung cakes. After parboiling, the paddy is dried. For this, a drying floor of earth is weeded, smeared with soft mud and then with cowdung water to bind it. This is left to dry. In a petty trading household, the drying yard will be repaired in this way once every three days. Then paddy is spread thinly and dried. Care is taken to dry the paddy over 2 days in two periods of four hours in order to minimize the sun-cracking that causes broken rice on milling. The process of drying is the capacity constraint in a petty trading household. A batch actually takes three half-days of continual work, or two batches can be dried in five days, or one batch per two days on a continual process using domestic labour. Women work in pairs on this pre-milling processing.

After husking, rice, bran, brokens, and husk are separated by winnowing with a *kula*—a bamboo basket—either by women at the husking mills, who are paid in kind by the customers, or more usually by domestic female labour.

Small traders, especially Muslims among whom womenfolk are not permitted to work outside the home, depend on unpaid female labour for this petty commodity production. In a very small number of cases, *adivasi* (tribal) or harijan women are employed for this work at Rs 6 per day. If we impute these market rates to the labour costs of pre- and post-milling processing and add the husking charge, then the cost of Rs 11 per quintal of paddy equals that of the rice mills. The sub-system of petty trade through husking mills relies on labour being valued at rates below those of the market, or not valued at all, in a process of petty commodity production and trade in obedience to the laws of capitalist production.

The *dheki* is still used in most rural families, and dhekis are still made. Their current cost is Rs 50–60. They are, however almost completely displaced, now used but for a few hours per month in order to grind winter rice to flour for rice preparations and in order to dehusk pulses. Labour for this purpose is almost completely domestic. The wage, for those very few women employed part time on the dheki is Rs 6 per day, below the minimum wage rate then of Rs 7.

Technology and Technical Change in Commercial Rice Processing—1982

'(B)igger rice mills are driving out single hullers and will replace hand pounding if hand pounding is not protected' (Government of India, 1955, App. III, p. 57). The Government of India has been proved wrong on both counts.

Here we examine phenomena found elsewhere in India (Harriss-White, 1996). These are the co-existence of a range of processing storage and transport technologies and the politics of technological change.

In Birbhum district in 1981–2, four processing technologies operated side by side. Table 1 shows details of these technologies for the years 1954 and 1981–2 (when the Government of India survey revealed the same characteristics).

The number of 'single hullers' (husking mills) now vastly exceeds that of the rice mills, and it was the expansion of the husking machines from about the time of the report which led to the decline of the dheki. While in the 1950s the cost of milling by husking machine was already 40% of that of the dheki, the cost of milling in rice mills (though 65% of the dheki milling costs) was already greater than that of the husking machine. The same relative cost structure was found in 1981–2. For the dheki, this was because of increase in the labour cost whereas for rice mills it resulted from the increasing costs of components of the machine technology that gave greater cost advantage to the husking mill. The process of drying was the major capacity constraint in a petty trading household.

Technological Change in Husking mills

The technology of the husking mill has diffused despite legislation

Table 1: Rice Processing Technologies in West Bengal—1982

	No.	Total rice output '000 tonnes	No. employed (total)	No. employed per '000 tonnes	Per cent recovery	Cost Rs/q[1] paddy	Daily output per mill (paddy)
1954							
Dheki	n.i.	3300	12,00,000	163	70	Rs 3.37	65 kgs
Husking mill (unmodernized)	500	600	10,000[4]	60	67	Rs 1.35	1,500 kgs
Rice mill	403	800	30,884	27	67	Rs 2.2	15,000 kgs
1981-2							
Dheki	n.i.	n.i.	n.i.	163	70	Rs 18.6 [2]	65 kgs
Husking mill (modernized)	15,000	n.i.	60,000	77	63.5	Rs 5.5	4,000 kgs
Rice mill	300 Working + 400 idle	n.i.	47,220	32	64	Rs 11.2 kgs	18,400

Source: Government of India, 1955, *Report of the Rice Milling Committee*, p.132 and own survey, 1982.

Notes: (1) Milling cost is cost of milling and parboiling. 1954 data was originally expressed in annas per *maund* (37 kg).
(2) This is comprised of wage labour at Rs.6/day for two women who pound 65 kgs of paddy plus Rs 3.6 per quintal for parboiling.
(3) Assuming days of 8 hours.
(4) This is 20 people per husking mill while our data gives 4 employees per mill.
n.i.: no information

against it throughout South and South-east India. Elsewhere (Harriss, 1976: Harriss and Kelly, 1982) it has been shown that the arguments used to justify such legislation are based upon a misunderstanding of cultural aspects of rice processing and that the technical, engineering justification was never satisfactorily proven for *Indica* rice varieties. However, the Left Front Government ordered husking mills to modernize, to install rubber roll shellers and polishers before 1981 on pain of losing licences. There are no incentives for such a change, so the regulation was experienced as disciplinary regulation and was unimplementable and unenforceable. For a start, licences are not a constraint to operation. It was estimated by the District Husking Mill Owners' Association that the cost of sheller-milling would increase from about Rs 2 to Rs 8.9 per quintal because of the much higher level of capitalization and the higher fixed cost element.

The machinery would be more economically vulnerable to vagaries of electricity supply. There would be no increase in rice out-turn unless paddy quality was improved. There is no incentive in the higher-priced by-product—bran with a high oil content—because of the need to export rapidly to the solvent extraction plants what would be extremely small daily consignments of bran. Besides, there is the technical problem that if such machinery is not run continuously (as is the case with husking mills), then bran will clog the rice polishing machinery, even rendering them dangerous. Bran would have to be relinquished by producers who presently use it as cattle feed. They would then be dependent upon markets controlled by a very few large firms for de-oiled bran cake or for commercial cattle feed at prices double that of locally sold husk and bran. Finally, the brokens from rice huskers, a greater proportion than produced by rubber roll shellers, are not 'lost', as alleged by official reports, but instead are ground to powder for rice preparations or are separated and sold.

Technological Change in Rice Mills

In 1981–2, rice mills were divided into two groups: (1) those operating at 40 per cent or higher capacity utilization, and (2) those operating at 20–27 per cent of capacity. The majority of mills comprising group (2) will have fixed cost elements double to those of mills in group (1).

Although only nine of the total 55 mills in Birbhum district lay idle, the figure for West Bengal as a whole is much larger—400 out of 700 were not in working order. We should expect to see considerable economies of scale, yet we found a scatter of costs for a given level of capacity and no clear signs of economies of scale that were all too visible in husking mills. The distinguishing characteristics of rice mills were their lack of viability, the lack of relation between capacity utilization and costs, polarization in capacity utilization in those mills that run, and high milling costs, double those of the husking machines using domestic labour, and approaching those of the dheki. These paradoxical features can be explained with reference to the modernization of technology and state intervention.

The rice mills of Bolpur and Sainthia blocks are most unusual in regions of India where rice is predominantly a subsistence crop.

Without exception, they contain machinery unknown in India until it was imported (using foreign aid). At that time, in the mid-1960s, only a decade after a legislation was passed to protect hand and foot pounding, the capital costs of such equipment was thought to rule out private ownership. Yet the modern rice mills in Birbhum district are all in private hands. The new mills were installed under the aegis of the National Cooperative Development Corporation and the Food Corporation of India.

The 'modern' technology consists of elevated godowns, paddy cleaners, aspirators, bucket elevators to raise paddy to hoppers capable of storing 1–2 days' supply of paddy for parboiling, a number (varying from 4 to 12) of steel parboiling vats of individual capacities varying from 2.5 to 5.5 tonnes, and a usually smaller number (2 to 4) of usually smaller capacity (2 to 2.5 tonnes) vats for pressure parboiling. The parboiling process consists of soaking paddy in the hot water in the vats for six to eight hours, followed by draining the water, and steaming the paddy once for 40 minutes. Under pressurized conditions, this steaming can be reduced to 20 minutes. By evening the entire process of parboiling is finished. Paddy is taken in trolleys to drying yards, and kept overnight, in heaps protected by huge conical bamboo hats. Drying takes place the following day over six to eight hours. The modern parboiling process renders the rice hard enough to withstand any sun-cracking on the drying yard. During the monsoon months of May to August, drying is done in the morning before the afternoon rains. Two mornings may be necessary for full drying. Alternatively paddy, parboiled and dried in the months preceding the monsoon, can be stored to tide the mill through the rainy period.

One of the ten rice mills had an electrically operated batch drier of a 123-tonne capacity powered by a 30 h.p. electric motor (and diesel electricity generator). Twelve tonnes could be dried within eight hours (10 hours including loading and unloading). A night batch is just as feasible as daytime operation. However, lack of sunshine is a problem only for the *boro* crop and boro is still a small proportion of total paddy production. The main reason for introducing a drier was to displace (female) labourers. Even though female labour is unorganized and employed on casual contracts, their numbers went from 50 to 4. We discuss this paradox later.

The unmodernized process of bulk parboiling still exists, in tandem with the modern one, in three mills of our sample. The product produced with the older technology is locally prized and gets a price premium. In this processing system, paddy was soaked in cold water in cement tanks for 48 hours, being steamed in much smaller vats. The process of drying required at least two days, for the same reason of vulnerability to sun-cracking as in the domestic system, and during the monsoon, it could take up to 4 half-days, raising labour costs and physical risks and constituting a capacity constraint on milling. Such was this constraint that many modernized mills closed down completely during the rains.

The modern process of milling includes at least three rubber roll shellers of larger capacity (2–3 tonnes). The paddy is shaken and cleaned before passing through the shellers. After the penultimate sheller pass, the remaining unmilled paddy (5 to 10 per cent) is separated, and unmilled paddy goes through a final machine. Husk from the shellers is sent to a husk disintegrater from which it is taken to stock as fuel for the mill's boiler. One of the ten mills used two tonnes per hour under runner disc shellers and stone mills revolving horizontally. This was the first technological upgrade from the huller. Maintenance costs per machine for the under-runner disc sheller are Rs 1,500 per year (for the emery rough linings), while those of rubber rollers for the newer type of sheller came to Rs 50,000 per year, roughly Rs 1 per quintal of paddy milled. Disc shellers, however, produce 2–3 per cent of saleable bran, as opposed to 2 to 4 per cent of bran per quintal of paddy produced by rubber shellers. Rice, still covered with bran then travels through between 2 to 4 cone polishers (of 30" to 50" diameters), where it is flung out by centrifugal force through wire meshes which retain the layer of bran. Rice can be polished to a variable degree. Highly polished rice will have had removed much of the nutritive layer into which vitamins and oils from bran had been absorbed. Bran and pulverized particles of rice and debris then go to a bran-husk separating machine. Husk goes to the boiler. Bran, as we know, is sold. The prime movers of these modernized mills are still for the main part, steam engines fired by husk. It is steam from boilers made in the early decades of the twentieth century that parboils the paddy. The benefits of free husk as fuel for steam engines are offset by the high costs of lubricating oil- 10 litres (Rs 110) per day. So now, modern mills driven by husk-fired steam engines have to be supplemented by 30 h.p. electric motors (usually run by diesel generators to avoid load shedding from the public electricity system). One mill still relying on the Electricity Board was considerably hampered by power cuts. One-third of all operating mills run entirely on electricity privately generated by 100 h.p. motors and diesel generators.

The unmodernized milling technology consisted of batteries of the largest capacity hullers. These would be set at calibrations to dehusk, debran, and then to polish the rice as it passes through the units of this battery. The process of milling was actually faster than with the 'modern' system, but there were more brokens, and the bran was of lower quality. Furthermore, because weather affected other parts of the processing system, the mills were forced to lie in seasonal idleness.

While the older technology took between three and six days to complete the processing of a batch, 'modern' technology can complete processing within 36 hours and milling no longer has to be a seasonal activity. This has been an important factor encouraging modernization. The large differences between paddy and rice prices in the immediate post-harvest period can be better exploited by modern technology.

Modernized technology is also quite flexible. The level of capitalization may vary considerably from mill to mill. Experiments with combinations of equipment have created winners and losers as the mill system transforms. In 1974, modernization cost between Rs 1.2 lakhs and Rs 6 lakhs, depending on the number and capacity of machines, and on whether they were purchased new or second-hand. This may help to explain the lack of relation between capacity and costs which was observed earlier. It is the high fixed cost component in the rice mills which hoists the average costs of production to double those of husking machines and domestic parboiling.

Modernization has generally occurred in two stages: firstly milling and later parboiling. While in the mid-60s full modernization required about Rs 0.5 lakhs, by the early 80's it was expected to be Rs 5 to 6 lakhs. In the 10 mills sampled, a total of Rs 32 lakhs had been invested in the modernization of technology during the period 1969 to 1979.

Some of the distinctive characteristics of West Bengal's rice mills are now evident, but we have not yet adequately accounted for the relatively huge capitalization in private hands. A number of factors are involved. First, the speeding up of production time was one reason to modernize: rapidly moving gaps in prices (of a sort most official data mask by averaging), could then be manipulated. Not only could local post-harvest price fluctuations be exploited but long-distance spatial price fluctuations for paddy could also come into play as a source of profit. Paddy harvested early in West Bengal could be moved as rice over long distances to regions where the harvest was yet to occur, again at large profit.

Another reason, as we saw earlier, was and is the profitability of the high-quality bran. Processed bran from Bengal's rice has a low free-fatty acid content. We have seen that it can fetch Rs 10–11 per quintal of rice. However, for bran to realize these prices, it is necessary for a solvent oil extraction plant to be easily accessible. Here the investment of a single highly entrepreneurial rice miller provided an incentive to other local millers to modernize their mills. The firm was not only the first rice mill to modernize (in 1965). It had also constructed the first bran oil solvent extraction plant, in 1962. Though the number of such plants have risen, this particular family still retains control of the bran-oil industry in West Bengal. This first, risky, innovative modernization was financed privately. State finance had actually been refused. This entrepenurial miller provided the conditions that were both necessary and sufficient for innovation by other mills.

A third reason for modernization was to reduce labour costs and avoid the problems of organizing unskilled labour when their conditions of work were of great concern to unions organized by political parties, and to the state's vigilance forces monitoring the provisions for labour of the Factories Act.

A fourth reason for modernization was the existence of a specialized and large market in West Bengal for muri—puffed rice—(which until recently has constituted half the demand for non-levy rice from rice mills). As we saw earlier, puffed rice is easily carried around. Supplemented with salt, chillie, dried lentils, and tucked in the fold of a sari or in a pocket, it is the 'snack' used commonly to nourish field labourers and anyone on a journey.

The fifth reason was the existence of not less than three types of protection from the State. One was the existence of liberal financial resources for the upgrading of this 'Small Scale Industry' (SSI) by the West Bengal Finance Corporation and by the nationalized banks. No cases of the sort of tardy repayment on overdues on loans that bedevils state lending were reported by rice millers, while there were several cases of repayment in a period earlier than stipulated. The second was the existence of a state-backed incentive in the form of the 15 per cent subsidy equivalent to a gift of Rs 75,000 on a loan of Rs 500,000.

But the third type of protection is quite extraordinary and actually gives the circulation of rice in West Bengal its particular institutional character. This was the legislation, put through in 1967, which gave rice mills monopolistic control over the wholesaling of paddy. It ensured the supplies necessary to run these mills at the high levels of capacity utilization that their high capitalization required. In states such as Tamil Nadu where this law does not exist, there is an even continuum of kinds and scales of firms from custom mills with no parboiling facilities and no paddy purchase through small mills with both activities to rice mills and merchanting businesses of various sizes. In West Bengal there is none of this. One single piece of law sufficed to perpetuate a polarization of structure in milling. Marketed surplus is dominated by large mills. In return the state benefited from: (a) profitable investments in 'Small Scale Industry' and (b) a small number of geographically centralized points at which it could tap the system of circulation of rice for the Public Distribution System (PDS). Less state scrutiny and vigilance was necessary, thus reducing (in theory) the transactions costs of the local PDS.[1]

Idle Mills

We have now explained that modernization could take place ostensibly in private hands while—by virtue of parametric regulation—actual control was vested indirectly in the state. We have still not explained polarization in capacity utilization and the financial crisis that forced many mills to remain idle. Some of the reasons are likely to affect the process of adaptation of any imported technology. Others reflect a confused and even contradictory political environment.

Firstly, there are logistical problems with modernized technology. In the early 1980s, only three companies manufactured modern technology (Dandekar with German collaboration in Bombay, Binny-Satake in Madras, and Kisen Engineering, the only wholly Indian firm, in Punjab), while a fourth, Damodar-Kiowa, had already closed down. Dandekar had local monopoly on machinery in West Bengal. Its headquarters and skilled maintenance people need to be consulted in Calcutta whenever a non-routine breakdown occurs. The costs of the inevitable delays will vary according to the season, but are highest immediately after harvest.

Other technical problems included the quality of rubber rolls. The types available were good while imported in the early 1970s, and poor while import substitution was developed. Now they are improving. The current cost of a pair varies from Rs 600 (with a life of 70 to 80 tonnes of paddy) to Rs 1,200 (with a life of 150 tonnes).

Few rolls are upto mill to specifications (200 tonnes). Polishers have also been inappropriate for bran which has been parboiled, as opposed to raw bran. Machines have been persistently clogged. One 3 tonne per hour capacity polisher exploded. The modern parboiling process produces an extremely hard rice which requires 25 per cent more time to cook for final consumption and for this reason—paradoxically—fetches Rs 2-5 quintal less on the market.[2]

A further set of problems are created by the markets for rice. For instance, the demand for muri, which had justified the installation of pressure parboiling equipment, and was said to have declined ' for reasons unknown' during the late seventies. There was over-investment in capacity in the solvent oil extraction industry. West Bengal had an installed capacity of 64,000 tonnes of bran oil but produced just 800 tonnes in 1980 and 2,000 in 1981, a capacity utilization of three per cent, at which it is uneconomic to run highly capitalized factories. The bran industry faced a crisis and this in turn affected the profitability of rice milling. By 1982 it had now become clear that plants with installed capacities of 100 tonnes per day were unable to acquire supplies of un-rancid bran. By contrast, the earliest bran plant installed is still the most profitable and is probably the smallest. Its capacity has been raised in stages from 1 to 25 tonnes per day. It is located in the centre of gravity of bran supply and it also has a bran stabilizer to inactivate lipase.

The most intractable problems have been produced by the very same structure of state and central policies and institutions which have encouraged the finance of modernization. High capacity utilization and high profits depend on free long-distance trading. To the extent that this trade is circumscribed by restrictions on the movement of either paddy or rice, not simply in West Bengal but also to and from other states, local rice mills are left vulnerable. To the extent that congestion in the Food Corporation of India godowns (where the levy rice is stored) acts as a capacity constraint on local mills, their vulnerability is intensified. To the extent that storage laws, state government regulations, and institutional finance formally discourage long-term stocking, again the mills are at a disadvantage.

Polarization of capacity utilization in modernized mills therefore results from varying abilities to solve all these problems. It is lack of finance that reduces milling firms to idleness. The most crucial problem is access to 'non-institutional' finance in order to store over long periods.

Few of the mills lying idle in Birbhum had been modernized. The reasons for lack of modernization and lack of access to subsidized finance lie substantially with the joint ownership structure in the second generation of the families which built the original mills. Multiple shares in mills, the syphoning off of milling profits into other investments, and taking on of partners with financial resources have all worked to prevent easy decisions over modernization, especially the collateral of Rs 1 to 2 lakhs necessary to qualify for a bank loan of Rs 5 lakhs. Thus, it was that the hold of the first generation of big rice mills to a certain extent passed out of the hands of the Bengali landed elite who had originally bought them into the hands of more tightly organized Marwari business families, who were able to modernize them.

Table 2: Equipment Costs for Domestic Pre-milling Processing, 1982

Equipment	No.	Capacity	Cost/item (Rs)	Duration (years)	Cost for one year (Rs)
Mud pots	4	60 kg.	15	2	30
Aluminium handi (pot)	3	15 kg.	50	2	75
Baskets	4		3	1	12
Winnowing baskets	4		3	1	12
70 gunny bags	70		4	1	280
Palm leaf mats	75		6	1	450
Husk—own plus	60 bags/month		0.5-2.5/bag		1,080
Stoves—made with own labour					
Transport—bicycle or bullock cart used for other purposes					
Labour—domestic					
Total					1,939

Source: Data from 1982 survey

Table 3: Husking Mills Charges and Profits Per Quintal of Paddy (Rs)

1981	Ahmadpur	Surul	Nayek Bazar	Bolpur	Sian	Total
N	4	5	3	3	2	17
Av. charge	3.9	2.4	2.7	2.8	2	2.9
Max. charges as per cent of min. charge	114	110	120	120	—	200
Average costs						1.9
Average profit from husking						Rs 1.2

Yet despite the fact that half of West Bengal's rice mills appear to be in a state of seedy decline, seemingly threatened by husking mills, and the latter's subsystem of petty trade, there is no convincing evidence of a secular decline in the turnover of *active* rice mills. Most working mills have doubled their turnover from the volume milled at their start. Supply constraints in 1982 were as much the result of drought and plant disease, exacerbated by a very high levy and by illegal paddy trade to rice mills outside Birbhum as they were of by competition from husking mills. Further, modernization led to an increase in the technical capacity of rice mills by an average of 47 per cent, from 0.5–1.8 averaging 1.25 tonnes per hour in the huller system, and by 1.8–3 averaging 2.3 tonnes per hour in the modernized system. Modernization has also increased the active milling season from four to six months to 10 to 12 months. Ownership is strikingly concentrated, 10 millers own 21 mills, almost all of which are modernized. In the face of this evidence and the unreliability of official statistics on rice milling, it can equally well be concluded that the industry is experiencing concentration, not decline.

Notes

1. Another reason was said to be an out-turn of rice from paddy of a few percentage points more than in the huller. This did not prove operationally possible. The nutritional argument for the modern parboiling technology (see Harriss and Kelly, 1982) is invalidated when rice is highly polished, which is the case for all 'free-market' rice.
2. This process is used to mill levy rice because it reduces the costs of production and is not penalized in price by the FCI's food technologists who test the quality of levy rice. It is the general public, who depends upon ration shops for both rice and kerosene, who pay the costs in cooking time of pressure-parboiled rice.

Appendix 4.2

The Process of Accumulation, 1982

Table 1: Entry Costs 1950–82 (Land, Buildings, Machinery Equipment and Initial Working Capital) Current '000 Rs.

	1950s		1960s		1970s		1980s	
	min	max	min	max	min	max	min	max
Paddy Agents	–	–	2	5	2	21	5	27
Husking Mills	6	11	4	17	6	19	15	28
Rice Brokers	–	–	1	1	1	21	–	–
Rice Whitesales	–	–	3	21	5	23	–	–
Rice Mills	60	90	60	160	150	300	–	–

Source: Author's survey, 1982.

Table 2: Investment Portfolios of Firms in the Marketing of Rice, Bolpur and Sainthia blocks, Birbhum district, 1981

		Rice mills	Rice wholesale	Rice broker	Paddy agent	Husking mill
	N	10	4	4	13	17
Cases of investment	*Agriculture*					
	purchase of land	3			2	
	fishponds	2				3
	ag. machinery				3	2
	sericulture					1
	Total agri. investments	5	–	–	5	6
Over and above own rice mills	*Agricultural processing*					
	rice mill	11				
	husking mill	1			1	2
	mustard oil mill	8	1		1	3
	dal mill	3				
	flour mill	1	1	1	1	3
	bran oil mill	3				
	bran stabilising unit	1				
	bakery	1				
	coconut hair oil	1	1		1	
	share in co-op. cold storage (potatoes)	3				
	Total no. of investments	3	3	1	4	8
	Rice firms					
	rice wholesale				2	
	rice brokerage			1		
	paddy agency		2			2
	rice ration shop		1		2	
	paddy trader/rice retail			1	8	
	rice bran trade		3	1	1	1
	Total no. of investments		6	4	13	3
	Wholesale trade: agric.					
	bread		1			
	grocery		1	1	1	1
	potato	2	1		1	
	wheat		2	1	3	
	molasses	2	1	1		
	pulses	2		1	1	
	mustard seed			1	1	
	mustard oil			1	1	
	coconut oil			1	1	
	Total no. of investments	6	6	7	9	1

Table 2 (contd.)

Other wholesale trade						
jute	2					
cloth	2	1				
coal			1	1		
medicines	1		1		1	
automobiles	1					
TV/electronic goods	1					
Total no. of investments	7	1	2	1	1	
Productive 'industry'	Apart from mill lorries					
transport lorries	2			1		
transport buses	1				2	
constructive contracting	2				1	
coal mine	1					
coal briquette factory					1	
brick making					1	
welding					1	
icecream factory				1		
board tea	1					
cinema				1		
Total no. of investments	7			3	6	
Other						
finance company/	3	n.i.	n.i.	n.i.	3	
moneylending	2	3	3	4	4	
property for rent						
education	n.i.	n.i.	n.i.	n.i.	4	
dowry	n.i.	n.i.	n.i.	n.i.	2	
Total no. of investments	5	3	3	4	13	

n.i. = no information
Source: Author's survey, 1982.

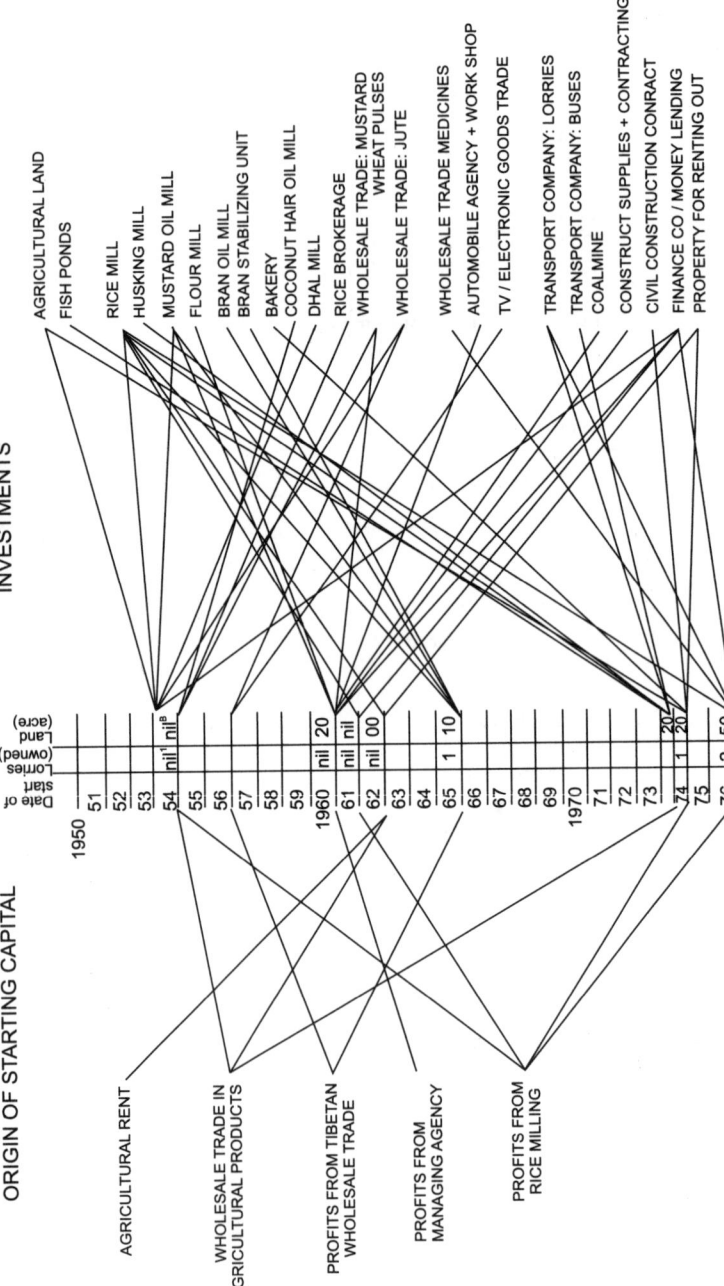

Appendix 4.2: Fig. 1: Investment Portfolios of 10 Rice Milling Families in Bolpur & Sainthia Blocks

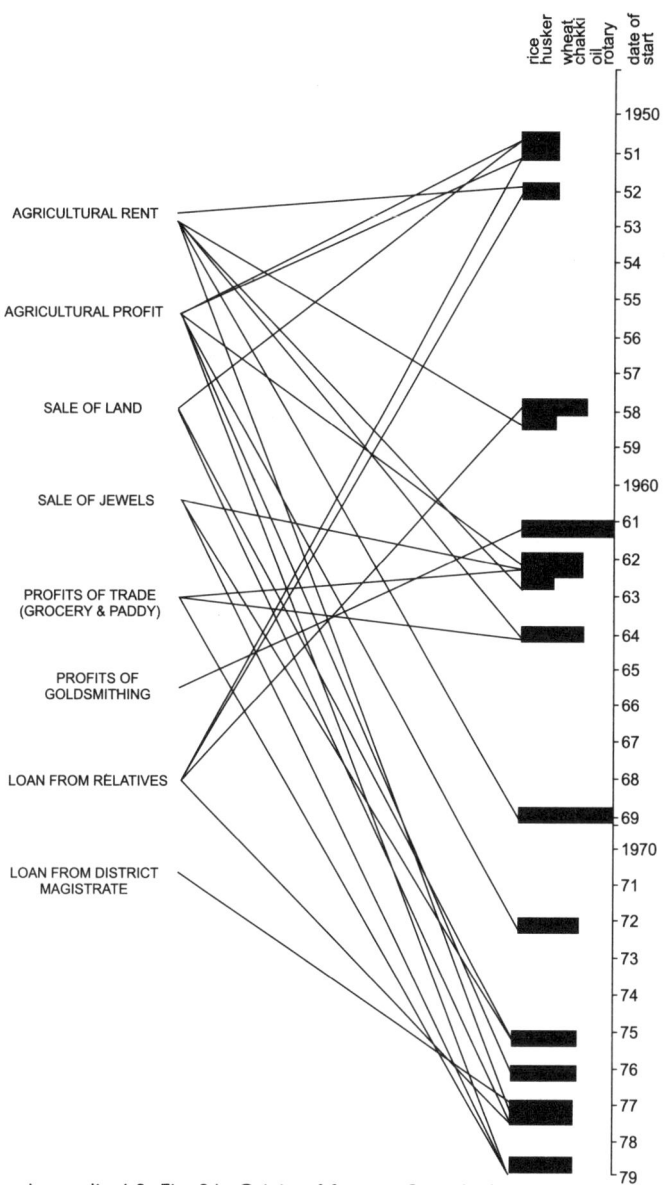

Appendix 4.2: Fig. 2A: Origin of Starting Capital of 17 Husking Mills, Bolpur and Sainthia Blocks, Birbhum District

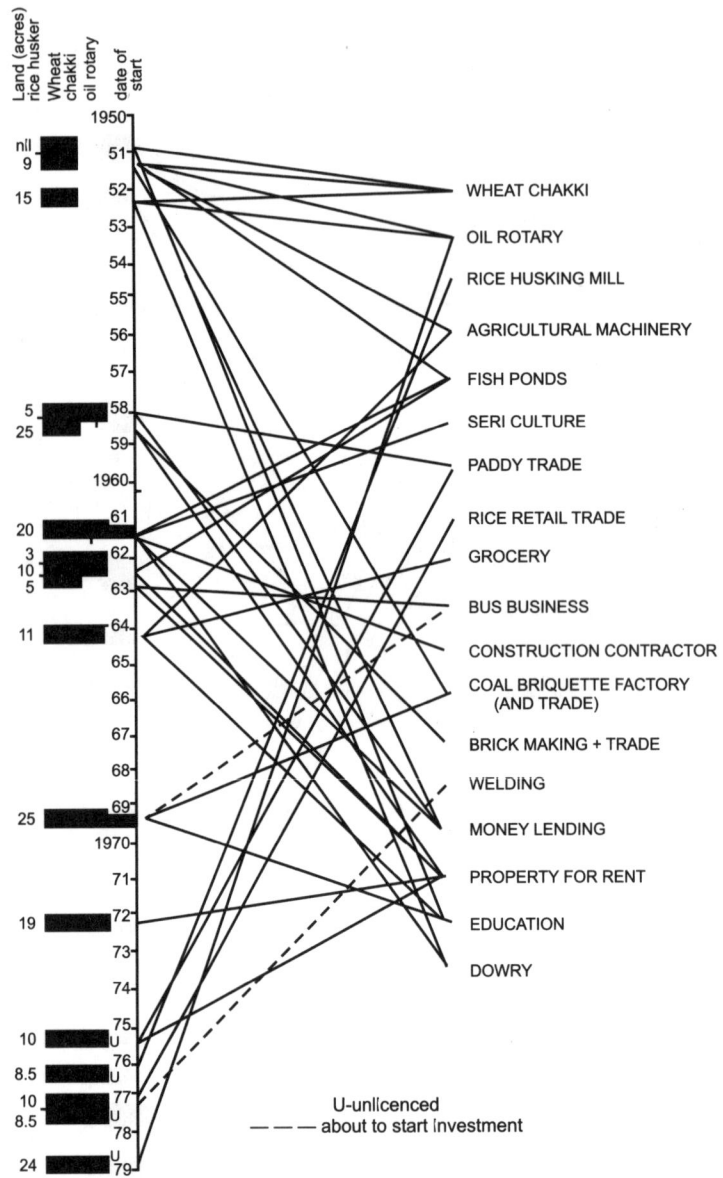

Appendix 4.2: Fig. 2B: Investment Portfolios of 17 Husking Mills, Bolpur and Sainthia Blocks, Birbhum District

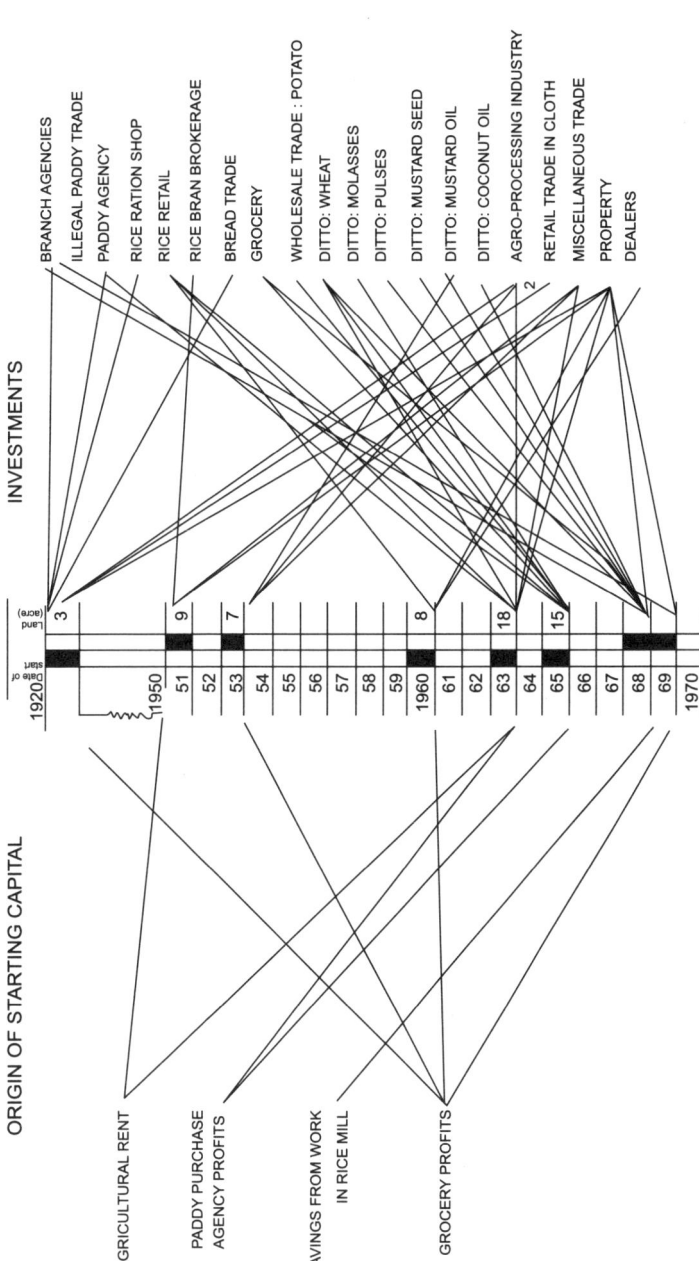

Appendix 4.2: Fig. 3: Investment Portfolios of 8 Rice Wholesalers and Brokers in Bolpur and Sainthia Blocks

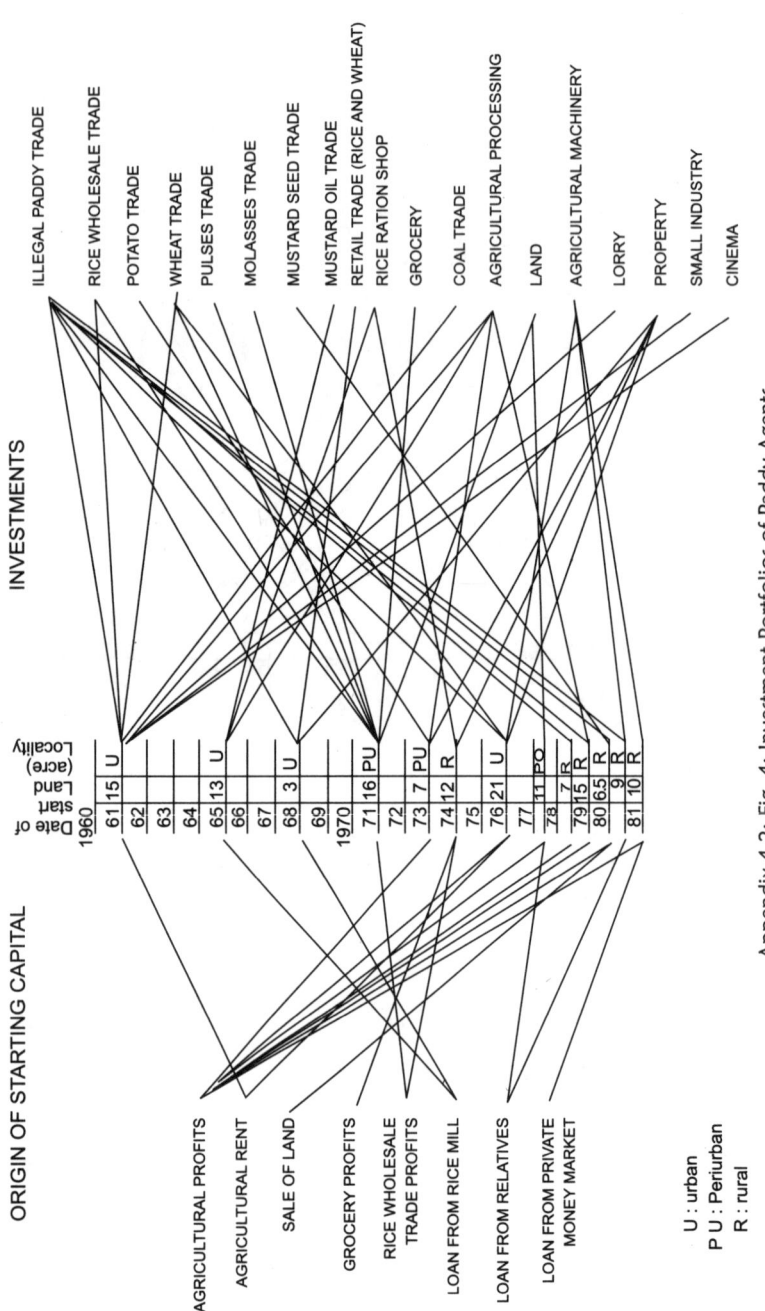

Appendix 4.2: Fig. 4: Investment Portfolios of Paddy Agents

Appendix 4.3

Price Behaviour – 1977 to 1980

Table 1: Average Prices, Birbhum district (Rs./Qtl)

		Bolpur	Sainthia	Nalhati	Suri	Price Difference
Paddy	1977	109	110	105	109	5
	1978	89	89	85	92	7
	1979	116	112	103	119	16
	1980	125	125	129	124	4
	1981	135	128	136	133	8
Rice wholesalers	1977	191	198	106	192	15
	1978	167	164	170	162	8
	1979	211	207	209	209	4
	1980	222	227	224	226	5
	1981	236	240	237	237	4
Rice retail	1977	197	209	192	–	17
	1978	172	167	175	–	8
	1979	220	217	213	216	7
	1980	230	236	233	233	6
	1981	245	250	249	248	5

N.B. These averages smooth out the variations by which merchants obtain profits.
Source: Month-end wholesale price data—Dept. of Agricultural Marketing, Suri

Table 2: Seasonal Fluctuations in Price, Birbhum District (Rs./Qtl)

		Bolpur		Sainthia		Nalhati		Suri	
		highest prices % of lowest price	absolute difference between highest and lowest price						
		(1)	(2)	(1)	(2)	(1)	(2)	(1)	(2)
Paddy	1977	150	40	154	43	156	43	166	50
	1978	121	17	114	12	131	30	144	35
	1979	137	35	140	30	124	28	140	40
	1980	130	31	129	30	148	48	138	38
	1981*	147	51	130	32	139	45	130	40
Rice wholesale	1977	155	80	146	61	147	100	152	75
	1978	135	48	127	39	130	45	123	33
	1979	138	67	135	63	151	90	133	60
	1980	131	52	123	45	125	42	115	30
	1981	142	80	128	60	133	69	131	63
Rice retail	1977	153	70	148	75	161	100	-	-
	1978	131	45	123	35	130	45	-	-
	1979	139	70	132	60	150	90	114	60
	1980	131	60	122	45	126	55	114	30
	1981	140	80	127	60	123	60	138	80
Bran	1981	166	80						

Notes: *Swings in villages near Bolpur were 168–178 per cent in 1980-81; the absolute price difference was Rs 65 for paddy.
Source: As for Table 1.

Table 3: Annual Average Gross Margin for Rice Retailing, Birbhum district (Rs./Qtl)

	Bolpur	Sainthia	Nalhati	Suri
1977	6	11	—	—
1978	5	3	5	—
1979	9	10	4	7
1980	8	9	9	7
1981	9	10	11	11

Table 4: Levy Percentages and Prices, Birbhum district

Year	Percentage	Price Rs./q	
		Paddy	Rice
1978–79	50%; and 20% on imports	89	160
1979–80	November 1979 50% or a contracted quota May 1980 15%	99	173
1980–81	November 1980 55% May 1981 40%	109	180
1981–82	November 1981 60%	119	193

Appendix 6.1

Details of the Official Price Data

West Bengal's data on agricultural prices are rarely put to analytical use. Detailed, local level data were unavailable in Calcutta and had to be obtained in situ. The data used here consists of daily spot prices for weekly intervals copied from the Regulated Markets price registers in Katwa's Regulated Market Office, the Memari Panchayat Office and from the Directorate of Agricultural Marketing in Burdwan for the period November 1988 to August 1990.

Price data are divulged by 'reliable informants' on a regular basis to minimize measurement error. The very few omitted data were interpolated from neighbouring observations. Data for three staple agricultural commodities were copied—rice, potato, and edible oil. Rice and oil are far from homogeneous commodities, so selectivity was necessary.

The rice price pertains to two varieties: *Kalma*, a fine variety and a coarse or 'common' high-yielding variety. The data have three forms—wholesale paddy, wholesale and retail rice. The transformation of paddy to rice in the cases of both varieties involves parboiling—soaking and steaming the grain in its husk—prior to sun drying, double milling, and polishing the kernel.

Potato prices are for their wholesale and retail forms. From January until May, wholesale potatoes are fresh from the first harvest, but from June to November, these prices refer to potatoes preserved in cold storage, a process involving grading and bagging, controlled refrigeration at 36 degrees Fahrenheit, and controlled reclimatization afterwards.

Oil prices are for mustard oil and for the mustard seed from which it is derived in a process of grinding, expulsion, and filtration.

By-product prices (for rice bran and brokens, potato cut pieces, and mustard oil cake) are not available at all, or not consistently enough to be used here. Prices for by-products reflect at the very least the substitution relationships with other commodities with varying supply patterns. Their prices substantially affect the profitability of agro-processing and of trading in the main product, but their impact on the main product price perturbations is unfortunately outside the scope of the present study.

Table 1: Price Behaviour, Bardhaman district (Rs/q)

Commodity[1]	1988 Mean	1988 Co-eff of Var[2]	1989 Mean	1989 Co-eff of Var	1990 Mean	1990 Co-eff of Var
PKFB	224.77		235.53		240.63	
PKFK	217.12	5.6	226.15	6.9	244.35	4.7
PKFM	225.0	3.8	237.22	4.7	246.58	4.5
PHCB	214.12	8.9	214.17	5.1	224.55	4.8
PHCK	220.5	7.4	218.48	8.4	228.90	5.5
RWKFB	416.88	5.6	436.08	6.9	447.38	4.7
RWKFK	387.92	4.8	411.95	6.9	429.88	5.3
RWKFM	408.67	5.8	425.33	8.8	448.38	3.9
RRKFB	423.00		443.08		456.75	
RRKFK	398.45		421.85		440.13	
RRKFM	428.33		446.67		476.25	
RWCB	365.00	8.2	369.67	4.7	346.48	6.2
RRWCK	322.63		346.48		350.50	
PWB	142.75	31.6	164.58	25.4	155.65	21.5
PWK	142.37	31.5	164.62	26.7	140.33	27.3
PWM	140.00	32.6	159.48	27.7	141.40	28.1
PRB	174.22		199.15		185.75	
PRK	147.35		178.68		171.50	
MWSB	885.00		766.47		903.55	
MWSK	810.00	11.6	729.97	10.0	890.75	10.0
MOWB	2323.82	9.8	2041.12	5.1	2556.28	13.0
MOWK	2226.67	4.3	2016.67	6.8	2412.75	12.3

Notes: 1. Key to commodity abbreviations:
Product : quality/ type : place
Left side of abbreviations
P – paddy
PK – Kalma paddy
PH – HYV paddy;
F – fine; C – coarse
R – rice; RW – rice wholesale; RR – rice retail; K and H as above
PW – potato wholesale; PR – potato retail
MS – mustard seed; MO – mustard oil
Right side of abbreviations
B – Burdwan; K – Katwa; M – Memari
2. Not all were calculated.

Table 2: Price Variations (%)

	Within a day	According to quality
Potato CS	3–10	5–10
Wholesale	0–1	5–10
Rice Mill Markets	0–6	<25 (paddy)
Husking Mill Markets	–	–
P/P–R/R trade	0–6	<20 (rice)
Oil Seed	5–7	<5 (seed)
Oil	2–4	<10 (oil)

Appendix 6.2

Price Integration Models and Results – 1988–1990

1) $\Delta LPKFK_t = 0.003 + 0.049 \Delta LPKFK_{t-1} - 0.088 \Delta LPKFK_{t-2}$
   $(0.001)\ \ (0.074)\ \ \ \ \ \ \ \ \ \ \ \ \ \ (0.069)$
   $ + 0.315 \Delta LPKFB_t + 0.030 \Delta LPKFB_{t-1} - 0.096 \Delta LPKFB_{t-2}$
   $\ \ \ (0.067)\ \ \ \ \ \ \ \ \ \ \ \ (0.072)\ \ \ \ \ \ \ \ \ \ \ \ (0.069)$
   $ - 0.192 Z_{t-1} + 1.060 D_{89.3,4Apr}$
   $\ \ \ (0.055)\ \ \ \ \ \ (0.155)$

   $R^2 = 0.357$ \quad s.e. $= 0.027$ \quad D.W. $= 1.93$
   LM(7,157) $= 1.28$ \ ARCH(7,150) $= 0.92$ \ CHOW TEST(25,139) $= 0.36$

2) $\Delta LPKFM_t = 0.002 + 0.035 \Delta LPKFM_{t-1} - 0.101 \Delta LPKFM_{t-2}$
   $(0.001)\ \ (0.078)\ \ \ \ \ \ \ \ \ \ \ \ \ \ (0.078)$
   $ + 0.126 \Delta LPKFB_t - 0.011 \Delta LPKFB_{t-1} + 0.020 \Delta LPKFB_{t-2}$
   $\ \ \ (0.050)\ \ \ \ \ \ \ \ \ \ \ \ (0.050)\ \ \ \ \ \ \ \ \ \ \ \ (0.049)$
   $ - 0.107 Z_{t-1} + 1.121 D_{89.2Dec}$
   $\ \ \ (0.048)\ \ \ \ \ \ (0.197)$

   $R^2 = 0.219$ \quad s.e. $= 0.019$ \quad D.W. $= 1.84$
   LM(7,157) $= 1.46$ \ ARCH(7,150) $= 0.89$ \ CHOW TEST(25,139) $= 0.70$

3) $\Delta LPKFK_t = 0.003 + 0.010 \Delta LPKFK_{t-1} - 0.083 \Delta LPKFK_{t-2}$
   $(0.002)\ \ (0.073)\ \ \ \ \ \ \ \ \ \ \ \ \ \ (0.068)$
   $ + 0.092 \Delta LRWKFB_t + 0.129 \Delta LRWKFB_{t-1} + 0.090 \Delta RWKFB_{t-2}$
   $\ \ \ (0.064)\ \ \ \ \ \ \ \ \ \ \ \ \ \ (0.061)\ \ \ \ \ \ \ \ \ \ \ \ \ \ (0.066)$
   $ - 0.137 Z_{t-1} + 1.071 D_{89.3,4Apr}$
   $\ \ \ (0.048)\ \ \ \ \ \ (0.162)$

   $R^2 = 0.317$ \quad s.e. $= 0.028$ \quad D.W. $= 1.95$
   LM(7,157) $= 1.37$ \ ARCH(7,150) $= 1.10$ \ CHOW TEST(25,139) $= 0.27$

4) $\Delta LPKFM_t = 0.002 + 0.051 \Delta LPKFM_{t-1} - 0.123 \Delta LPKFM_{t-2}$
   $(0.001)\ \ (0.076)\ \ \ \ \ \ \ \ \ \ \ \ \ \ (0.075)$
   $ + 0.084 \Delta LRWKFB_t + 0.002 \Delta LRWKFB_{t-1} + 0.029 \Delta LRWKFB_{t-2}$
   $\ \ \ (0.045)\ \ \ \ \ \ \ \ \ \ \ \ \ \ (0.043)\ \ \ \ \ \ \ \ \ \ \ \ \ \ (0.043)$
   $ - 0.090 Z_{t-1} + 0.967 D_{89.2Dec}$
   $\ \ \ (0.043)\ \ \ \ \ \ (0.194)$

   $R^2 = 0.295$ \quad s.e. $= 0.020$ \quad D.W. $= 1.89$
   LM(7,157) $= 0.95$ \ ARCH(7,150) $= 0.66$ \ CHOW TEST(25,139) $= 0.55$

5) $\Delta \text{LPKFK}_t = 0.001 + 0.003\Delta \text{LPKFK}_{t-1} - 0.088\Delta \text{LPKFK}_{t-2}$
     $\quad\quad\quad\quad (0.002)\quad (0.073)\quad\quad\quad (0.067)$

   $\quad\quad\quad\quad + 0.098\Delta \text{LRRKFB}_t + 0.166\Delta \text{LRRKFB}_{t-1} + 0.084\Delta \text{LRRKFB}_{t-2}$
   $\quad\quad\quad\quad\quad (0.061)\quad\quad\quad (0.059)\quad\quad\quad\quad (0.064)$

   $\quad\quad\quad\quad - 0.138 Z_{t-1} + 1.057 D_{89.3,4\text{Apr}}$
   $\quad\quad\quad\quad\quad (0.047)\quad\quad (0.161)$

$R^2 = 0.334 \quad\quad\quad \text{s.e.} = 0.028 \quad\quad\quad \text{D.W.} = 1.92$
$\text{LM}(7,157) = 1.12 \quad \text{ARCH}(7,150) = 1.30 \quad \text{CHOW TEST}(25,139) = 0.27$

6) $\Delta \text{LPKFM}_t = 0.002 + 0.059\Delta \text{LPKFM}_{t-1} - 0.122\Delta \text{LPKFM}_{t-2}$
   $\quad\quad\quad\quad (0.001)\quad (0.076)\quad\quad\quad (0.077)$

   $\quad\quad\quad\quad + 0.117\Delta \text{LRRKFB}_t + 0.015\Delta \text{LRRKFB}_{t-1} + 0.028\Delta \text{LRRKFB}_{t-2}$
   $\quad\quad\quad\quad\quad (0.044)\quad\quad\quad (0.042)\quad\quad\quad\quad (0.044)$

   $\quad\quad\quad\quad - 0.108 Z_{t-1} + 0.937 D_{89.2\text{Dec}}$
   $\quad\quad\quad\quad\quad (0.039)\quad\quad (0.193)$

$R^2 = 0.226 \quad\quad\quad \text{s.e.} = 0.019 \quad\quad\quad \text{D.W.} = 1.91$
$\text{LM}(7,157) = 0.91 \quad \text{ARCH}(7,150) = 0.65 \quad \text{CHOW TEST}(25,139) = 0.58$

7) $\Delta \text{LRWKFK}_t = 0.001 + 0.053\Delta \text{LRWKFK}_{t-1} + 0.040\Delta \text{LRWKFK}_{t-2}$
   $\quad\quad\quad\quad\quad (0.001)\quad (0.067)\quad\quad\quad (0.066)$

   $\quad\quad\quad\quad + 0.079\Delta \text{LRWKFB}_t - 0.010\Delta \text{LRWKFB}_{t-1} + 0.076\Delta \text{LRWKFB}_{t-2}$
   $\quad\quad\quad\quad\quad (0.050)\quad\quad\quad (0.051)\quad\quad\quad\quad (0.053)$

   $\quad\quad\quad\quad - 0.174 Z_{t-1} + 1.022 D_{89.3\text{Dec},2\text{Jan}} + 1.012 D_{90.4\text{Jun}}$
   $\quad\quad\quad\quad\quad (0.042)\quad\quad (0.178)\quad\quad\quad\quad (0.247)$

$R^2 = 0.335 \quad\quad\quad \text{s.e.} = 0.023 \quad\quad\quad \text{D.W.} = 2.11$
$\text{LM}(7,156) = 1.05 \quad \text{ARCH}(7,149) = 0.62 \quad \text{CHOW TEST}(25,138) = 0.73$

8) $\Delta \text{LRWKFM}_t = 0.003 + 0.140\Delta \text{LRWKFM}_{t-1} - 0.011\Delta \text{LRWKFM}_{t-2}$
   $\quad\quad\quad\quad\quad (0.001)\quad (0.068)\quad\quad\quad (0.070)$

   $\quad\quad\quad\quad + 0.035\Delta \text{LRWKFB}_t - 0.078\Delta \text{LRWKFB}_{t-1} - 0.010\Delta \text{LRWKFB}_{t-2}$
   $\quad\quad\quad\quad\quad (0.061)\quad\quad\quad (0.053)\quad\quad\quad\quad (0.058)$

   $\quad\quad\quad\quad - 0.092 Z_{t-1} + 1.038 D_{89.2\text{Nov}}$
   $\quad\quad\quad\quad\quad (0.029)\quad\quad (0.126)$

$R^2 = 0.339 \quad\quad\quad \text{s.e.} = 0.026 \quad\quad\quad \text{D.W.} = 2.06$
$\text{LM}(7,157) = 1.31 \quad \text{ARCH}(7,150) = 0.38 \quad \text{CHOW TEST}(25,139) = 0.24$

9) $\Delta \text{LRWKFK}_t = 0.001 + 0.039\Delta \text{LRWKFK}_{t-1} + 0.039\Delta \text{LRWKFK}_{t-2}$
   $\quad\quad\quad\quad\quad (0.001)\quad (0.067)\quad\quad\quad (0.066)$

   $\quad\quad\quad\quad + 0.071\Delta \text{LRWKFB}_t - 0.010\Delta \text{LRRKFB}_{t-1} + 0.087\Delta \text{LRRKFB}_{t-2}$
   $\quad\quad\quad\quad\quad (0.048)\quad\quad\quad (0.050)\quad\quad\quad\quad (0.051)$

$$- 0.171 Z_{t-1} + 1.057 D_{89.3Dec,2Jan} + 1.004 D_{89.4Jun}$$
$$(0.041) \qquad (0.179) \qquad (0.246)$$

$R^2 = 0.339$ s.e. = 0.023 D.W. = 2.08
LM(7,156) = 0.95 ARCH(7,149) = 0.55 CHOW TEST(25,138) = 0.34

10) $\Delta LRWKFM_t = 0.003 + 0.137 \Delta LRWKFM_{t-1} + 0.007 \Delta LRWKFM_{t-2}$
$\qquad\qquad (0.001) \quad (0.067) \qquad\qquad (0.068)$

$\qquad\qquad + 0.054 \Delta LRRKFB_t - 0.086 \Delta LRRKFB_{t-1} + 0.031 \Delta LRRKFB_{t-2}$
$\qquad\qquad\quad (0.057) \qquad\qquad (0.052) \qquad\qquad (0.056)$

$\qquad\qquad - 0.106 Z_{t-1} + 1.061 D_{89.2Nov}$
$\qquad\qquad\quad (0.038) \qquad (0.129)$

$R^2 = 0.347$ s.e. = 0.025 D.W. = 2.04
LM(7,157) = 1.46 ARCH(7,150) = 0.36 CHOW TEST(25,139) = 0.25

11) $\Delta LRRKFK_t = 0.001 + 0.138 \Delta LRRKFK_{t-1} - 0.052 \Delta LRRKFK_{t-2}$
$\qquad\qquad (0.001) \quad (0.051) \qquad\qquad (0.067)$

$\qquad\qquad + 0.082 \Delta LRRKFB_t - 0.036 \Delta LRRKFB_{t-1} + 0.009 \Delta LRRKFB_{t-2}$
$\qquad\qquad\quad (0.046) \qquad\qquad (0.047) \qquad\qquad (0.049)$

$\qquad\qquad - 0.162 Z_{t-1} + 1.046 D_{89.3Dec} + 0.952 D_{90.4Jun}$
$\qquad\qquad\quad (0.042) \qquad (0.180) \qquad\quad (0.236)$

$R^2 = 0.334$ s.e. = 0.022 D.W. = 2.10
LM(7,156) = 1.15 ARCH(7,149) = 0.69 CHOW TEST(25,138) = 0.57

12) $\Delta LRRKFM_t = 0.003 + 0.119 \Delta LRRKFM_{t-1} - 0.015 \Delta LRRKFM_{t-2}$
$\qquad\qquad (0.002) \; (0.068) \qquad\qquad (0.071)$

$\qquad\qquad + 0.126 \Delta LRRKFB_t - 0.065 \Delta LRRKFB_{t-1} + 0.061 \Delta LRRKFB_{t-2}$
$\qquad\qquad\quad (0.062) \qquad\qquad (0.056) \qquad\qquad (0.060)$

$\qquad\qquad + 0.126 Z_{t-1} + 1.100 D_{89.2Nov}$
$\qquad\qquad\quad (0.040) \qquad (0.134)$

$R^2 = 0.333$ s.e. = 0.028 D.W. = 2.01
LM(7,157) = 0.89 ARCH(7,150) = 0.03 CHOW TEST(25,139) = 0.63

13) $\Delta LPHCK_t = 0.004 - 0.006 \Delta LPHCK_{t-1} - 0.029 \Delta LPHCK_{t-2}$
$\qquad\qquad (0.002) \quad (0.059) \qquad\qquad (0.068)$

$\qquad\qquad + 0.049 \Delta LPHCB_t - 0.039 \Delta LPHCB_{t-1} + 0.122 \Delta LPHCB_{t-2}$
$\qquad\qquad\quad (0.062) \qquad\qquad (0.062) \qquad\qquad (0.062)$

$\qquad\qquad - 0.121 Z_{t-1} + 1.024 D_{88.2Oct} + 1.026 D_{88.2Nov}$
$\qquad\qquad\quad (0.062) \qquad (0.302) \qquad\quad (0.156)$

$R^2 = 0.302$ s.e. = 0.032 D.W. = 2.07
LM(7,156) = 0.53 ARCH(7,149) = 1.11 CHOW TEST(25,138) = 0.61

14) $\Delta LPHCK_t = 0.004 + 0.020\Delta LPHCK_{t-1} - 0.039\Delta LPHCK_{t-2}$
   $(0.002)\quad (0.070)\quad\quad\quad (0.071)$
   $ + 0.094\Delta LRWHCB_t - 0.079\Delta LRWHCB_{t-1} + 0.099\Delta LRWHCB_{t-2}$
   $\ \ (0.082)\quad\quad\quad (0.078)\quad\quad\quad\ \ (0.079)$
   $ - 0.118 Z_{t-1} + 1.076 D_{88.2Oct} + 1.056 D_{88.2Nov}$
   $\ \ (0.035)\quad\ \ (0.308)\quad\quad\ \ (0.167)$

$R^2 = 0.287482$ \quad s.e. = 0.03326 \quad\quad D.W. = 2.10
LM(7,156) = 0.35 \ ARCH(7,149) = 0.96 \ CHOW TEST(25,138) = 0.61

15) $\Delta LRWHCK_t = 0.002 + 0.076\Delta LRWHCK_{t-1} + 0.055\Delta LRWHCK_{t-2}$
   $(0.002)\quad (0.070)\quad\quad\quad (0.070)$
   $ + 0.049\Delta LRWHCB_t + 0.055\Delta LRWHCB_{t-1} + 0.109\Delta LRWHCB_{t-2}$
   $\ \ (0.076)\quad\quad\quad (0.075)\quad\quad\quad\ \ (0.075)$
   $ - 0.112 Z_{t-1} + 0.735 D_{88.2.3Apr} + 1.009 D_{88.1,4Nov}$
   $\ \ (0.033)\quad\ \ (0.144)\quad\quad\quad (0.199)$

$R^2 = 0.282$ \quad s.e. = 0.032 \quad D.W. = 2.04
LM(7,156) = 0.67 \ ARCH(7,149) = 0.46 \ CHOW TEST(25,138) = 0.53

Potatoes

1) $\Delta LPWK_t = 0.001 - 0.041\Delta LPWK_{t-1} - 0.055\Delta LPWK_{t-2} + 0.359\Delta LPWB_t$
   $(0.001)\quad (0.077)\quad\quad\quad (0.072)\quad\quad\quad (0.054)$
   $ + 0.197\Delta LPWB_{t-1} + 0.118\Delta LPWB_{t-2} - 0.102 Z_{t-1}$
   $\ \ (0.068)\quad\quad\quad (0.061)\quad\quad\quad\ \ (0.054)$
   $ + 0.734 D_{88.2Apr} + 0.817 D 87.12 + 0.901 D_{90.1Apr}$
   $\ \ (0.207)\quad\quad\quad (0.318)\quad\quad\quad (0.391)$

$R^2 = 0.398$ \quad\quad s.e. = 0.067 \quad\quad D.W. = 2.03
LM(7,156) = 0.39 \ ARCH(7,149) = 2.02 \ CHOW TEST(25,138) = 0.30

2) $\Delta LPWB_t = -0.002 - 0.042\Delta LPWB_{t-1} + 0.012\Delta LPWB_{t-2}$
   $\ \ (0.005)\quad\ \ (0.063)\quad\quad\quad (0.068)$
   $ + 0.466\Delta LPWM_t + 0.148\Delta LPWM_{t-1} + 0.148\Delta LPWM_{t-2}$
   $\ \ (0.069)\quad\quad\quad (0.078)\quad\quad\quad\ \ (0.079)$
   $ - 0.216 Z_{t-1} + 1.069 D_{81.3,4Nov} + 1.133 D_{89.1,2Dec}$
   $\ \ (0.052)\quad\ \ (0.247)\quad\quad\quad (0.124)$

$R^2 = 0.630$ \quad\quad s.e. = 0.064 \quad\quad D.W. = 1.97
LM(7,156) = 1.17 \ ARCH(7,149) = 1.07 \ CHOW TEST(25,138) = 0.35

3) $\Delta LPWK_t = -0.001 - 0.102\Delta LPWK_{t-1} - 0.101\Delta LPWK_{t-2}$
   $\ \ (0.001)\quad\ \ (0.078)\quad\quad\quad (0.067)$

$$+ 0.487\Delta\text{LPWM}_t + 0.133\Delta\text{LPWM}_{t-1} + 0.182\Delta\text{LPWM}_{t-2}$$
$$(0.058) \qquad\qquad (0.087) \qquad\qquad (0.086)$$
$$- 0.391 Z_{t-1} + 1.190 D_{89.4\text{Dec},2\text{Jan}}$$
$$(0.076) \qquad\quad (0.215)$$

$R^2 = 0.569$ \qquad s.e. = 0.057 \qquad D.W. = 2.00
LM(7,156) = 1.89 ARCH(7,149) = 1.96 CHOW TEST(25,138) = 0.35

4) $\Delta\text{LPRB}_t = + 0.003 - 0.136\Delta\text{LPRB}_{t-1} - 0.088\Delta\text{LPRB}_{t-2}$
$\qquad\qquad\quad (0.005) \quad (0.068) \qquad\qquad (0.061)$

$$+ 0.338\Delta\text{LPWM}_t + 0.151\Delta\text{LPWM}_{t-1} + 0.071\Delta\text{LPWM}_{t-2}$$
$$(0.072) \qquad\qquad (0.089) \qquad\qquad (0.084)$$
$$- 0.167 Z_{t-1} + 0.883 D_{88.1,2\text{Dec}} + 0.803 D_{89.1,2\text{Jan}}$$
$$(0.052) \qquad (0.243) \qquad\qquad (0.233)$$
$$+ 0.838 D_{89.1,2\text{Mar}}$$
$$(0.112)$$

$R^2 = 0.538$ \qquad s.e. = 0.070 \qquad D.W. = 2.02
LM(7,155) = 1.56 ARCH(7,148) = 1.41 CHOW TEST(25,137) = 0.25

5) $\Delta\text{LPRK}_t = 0.002 - 0.062\Delta\text{LPRK}_{t-1} - 0.079\Delta\text{LPRK}_{t-2} + 0.273\Delta\text{LPWM}_t$
$\qquad\qquad\quad (0.001) \quad (0.069) \qquad\qquad (0.064) \qquad\qquad (0.079)$

$$+ 0.232\Delta\text{LPWM}_{t-1} + 0.091\Delta\text{LPWM}_{t-2} - 0.213 Z_{t-1}$$
$$(0.093) \qquad\qquad (0.016) \qquad\qquad (0.043)$$
$$+ 1.434 D_{89.2\text{Jan}} + 1.040 D_{90.4\text{Jan}} + 1.076 D_{90.1\text{Apr}}$$
$$(0.382) \qquad\quad (0.285) \qquad\quad (0.473)$$

$R^2 = 0.435$ \qquad s.e. = 0.076 \qquad D.W. = 1.86
LM(7,156) = 2.00 ARCH(7,149) = 2.02 CHOW TEST(25,139) = 0.05

6) $\Delta\text{LPRB}_t = 0.003 - 0.055\Delta\text{LPRB}_{t-1} - 0.017\Delta\text{LPRB}_{t-2} + 0.343\Delta\text{LPRK}_t$
$\qquad\qquad\quad (0.003) \quad (0.075) \qquad\qquad (0.068) \qquad\qquad (0.061)$

$$+ 0.092\Delta\text{LPRK}_{t-1} + 0.118\Delta\text{LPRK}_{t-2} - 0.221 Z_{t-1}$$
$$(0.065) \qquad\qquad (0.064) \qquad\qquad (0.060)$$
$$+ 0.980 D_{89.1,2\text{Jan}} + 0.830 D_{89.1,2\text{Mar}}$$
$$(0.251) \qquad\qquad (0.122)$$

$R^2 = 0.468$ \qquad s.e. = 0.075 \qquad D.W. = 2.00
LM(7,156) = 1.82 ARCH(7,149) = 1.13 CHOW TEST(25,138) = 0.38

Mustard

1) $\Delta\text{LMSWK}_t = - 0.001 + 0.261\Delta\text{LMSWK}_{t-1} - 0.144\Delta\text{LMSWB}_{t-1}$
$\qquad\qquad\qquad (0.001) \quad (0.065) \qquad\qquad (0.064)$

$$+ 0.303\Delta\text{LMSWB}_{t-1} - 0.082Z_{t-1} + 1.170D_{81.10}$$
$$(0.065) \qquad (0.028) \qquad (0.300)$$
$$+ 0.827D_{89.1\text{Jan}}$$
$$(0.194)$$

$R^2 = 0.362$ \qquad s.e. = 0.030 \qquad D.W. = 2.02
LM(7,156) = 0.34 \qquad ARCH(7,149) = 2.12 \qquad CHOW TEST(25,138) = 0.77

2) $\Delta\text{LMSWB}_t = -0.001 + 0.256\Delta\text{LMSWB}_{t-1} + 0.204\Delta\text{LMOWB}_t$
$$(0.001) \qquad (0.064) \qquad (0.073)$$
$$- 0.130\Delta\text{LMOWB}_{t-1} - 0.197Z_{t-1} + 0.981D_{81.1,2\text{Dec}}$$
$$(0.074) \qquad (0.035) \qquad (0.147)$$
$$+ 1.058D_{87.1\text{Jan}}$$
$$(0.129)$$

$R^2 = 0.499$ \qquad s.e. = 0.027 \qquad D.W. = 1.95
LM(7,158) = 0.69 \qquad ARCH(7,151) = 0.35 \qquad CHOW TEST(25,140) = 0.25

3) $\Delta\text{LMSWK}_t = -0.001 + 0.199\Delta\text{LMSWK}_{t-1} + 0.149\Delta\text{LMOWB}_t$
$$(0.001) \qquad (0.074) \qquad (0.086)$$
$$+ 0.067\Delta\text{LMOWB}_{t-1} - 0.093Z_{t-1} + 1.004D_{88.4\text{Nov}}$$
$$(0.085) \qquad (0.033) \qquad (0.328)$$
$$+ 0.849D_{89.1\text{Jan}}$$
$$(0.211)$$

$R^2 = 0.237$ \qquad s.e. = 0.033 \qquad D.W. = 2.10
LM(7,158) = 0.74 \qquad ARCH(7,151) = 1.68 \qquad CHOW TEST(25,138) = 0.56

4) $\Delta\text{LMOWK}_t = 0.001 + 0.006\Delta\text{LMOWK}_t + 0.126\Delta\text{LMOWB}_t$
$$(0.001) \qquad (0.069) \qquad (0.055)$$
$$+ 0.095\Delta\text{LMOWB}_{t-1} - 0.121Z_{t-1} + 0.939D_{90.1\text{Jul}}$$
$$(0.059) \qquad (0.037) \qquad (0.151)$$

$R^2 = 0.288$ \qquad s.e. = 0.022 \qquad D.W. = 2.09
LM(7,159) = 0.41 \qquad ARCH(7,152) = 0.52 \qquad CHOW TEST(25,139) = 1.42

Source: T.B. Palaskas and B. Harriss–White, 1993.
See Appendix 6.1, Table 1, notes, for the key to the abbreviations.

Appendix 7.1

Investment Portfolios in Bardhaman and Birbhum – 1990 – Estimates

Table 1: Potato Wholesale and Cold Storage (Current prices, Rs)

	1960	1962	1968	1970	1975	1977	1979	1982	1984	1988	1989
Sources of trading capital											
Agricultural rent		300,000									
Agricultural profit		300,000	60,000		5,000		100,000				
Agricultural trade	50,000	300,000	60,000	10,000	40,000	60,000	100,000			10,000	
Agricultural trade and processing		80,000					400,000		500,000		10,000
Non-agricultural trade					40,000						
Non-agricultural industry											
Inherited gold						10,000					
State finance	50,000	80,000	60,000				300,000	10,000	500,000		
Estimated present value of investments											
Land/water		1,000,000					1,000,000		800,000		
Agricultural trade	1,000,000	1,000,000	200,000	40,000	20,000	1,000,000	1,000,000	100,000	800,000		10,000
Agricultural trade and processing	1,000,000	1,000,000	200,000			1,000,000	1,000,000		800,000		
Non-agricultural trade				40,000	60,000	1,000,000	1,000,000		800,000		
Non-agricultural industry	1,000,000										
Property	1,000,000				60,000	1,000,000	1,000,000		800,000	30,000	
Transport		1,000,000			60,000	1,000,000					
Finance											
State finance			200,000								

Source: Author's survey.

Table 2: Mustard oil (Current prices, Rs) – 1990 – Estimates

	1960	1965	1969	1970	1972	1980	1984	1985	1987	1989
Sources of trading capital										
Agricultural profit						50,000	40,000			
Agricultural rent (land reform compensation)		80,000								
Agricultural trade		80,000	30,000		50,000			30,000	50,000	
Agricultural trade and processing				35,000		200,000	100,000			
Non-agricultural trade										500,000
Non-agricultural industry						200,000				
Private loan										
Caste finance										
State finance										500,000
Urban property rents	30,000									
Estimated present value of investments										
Land/water						80,000				
Agricultural trade			400,000	300,000	150,000	800,000			200,000	800,000
Agricultural trade and processing			400,000	300,000		880,000	200,000	40,000		
Non-agricultural trade							200,000			
Non-agricultural industry							100,000			
Property	5,000,000	900,000				800,000	100,000			
Transport		900,000	400,000				100,000			
Finance										
State finance										

Source: Author's survey.

Table 3: Rice milling and husking (Current prices, Rs) – 1990 – Estimates

	1950	1958	1960	1961	1962	1965	1966	1970	1973	1976	1980	1983	1987	1989
Sources of trading capital														
Agricultural profit				10,000				10,000	10,000			10,000	10,000	
Agricultural rent			5,000		5,000		10,000							
Ag. (dowry)			5,000											
Agricultural trade	10,000	5,000				5,000	5,000	10,000	5,000	300,000				200,000
Agricultural trade and processing						5,000	5,000							
Non-agricultural trade														
Non-agricultural industry														
Caste finance	10,000	50,000								300,000	500,000			200,000
State finance				10,000						300,000			10,000	10,000
Estimated present value of investments														
Land/water			20,000		10,000							10,000	10,000	
Agricultural trade				100,000		10,000								200,000
Agricultural trade and processing	600,000	610,000		600,000	10,000	10,000				3,000,000	900,000			220,000
Non-agricultural trade										3,000,000				
Non-agricultural industry	600,000							20,000		3,000,000				
Property	600,000	600,000				10,000			10,000					
Transport		600,000			10,000	10,000	100,000							
Finance	600,000	600,000							10,000	3,000,000				
State finance											900,000			

Source: Author's survey.

Table 4: Paddy and Rice trading (Wh/Ret/CA) (Current prices, Rs) – 1990 – Estimates

	1950	1960	1961	1966	1970	1975	1978	1979	1982	1983	1984	1986	1987
Sources of trading capital													
Agricultural profit	5,000												
Agricultural rent		40,000					10,000				40,000		
Employment in ag. trade									5,000			5,000	
Agricultural trade		5,000	5,000		5,000					5,000		10,000	
Agricultural trade & processing				5,000		5,000							
Non-agricultural trade													
Non-agricultural industry							10,000						
Private loan								5,000					20,000
Caste finance													20,000
State finance											40,000		
"Black"			5,000										
Estimated present value of investments													
Land/water	100,000	40,000	70,000										
Agricultural trade							80,000	50,000	80,000	50,000	490,000		
Agricultural trade and processing	100,000			80,000	20,000			200,000					
Non-agricultural trade										200,000			
Non-agricultural industry												100,000	
Property			70,000							50,000			
Transport			70,000										
Finance			70,000										
State finance													

Source: Author's survey.

Appendix 7.2

Collective Action in Markets

Potato
1. Memari Potato Syndicate—1988—about 50 members
   Active officers 6
   Functions:
   - i) price setting
   - ii) contract adherence
   - iii) dispute resolution
2. West Bengal Cold Stores Owners' Association—275 members
   Functions:
   - i) negotiate rents with government
   - ii) collude over and negotiate trade policy
   - iii) lobby MLAs and Ministers on reservations for categories of producers, on export policy

Oil
3. Katwa Oil Millers' Association—35 members
   Functions:
   - i) set minimum crushing rate
   - ii) 'regulate' prices
   - iii) lobby state for electricity power supply, better conditions for maintenance of machines, and against sales tax
4. Gulsi Oil Mills Association—1984—20 members
   Functions:
   - i) fix rates
5. Burdwan District Oil Millers' Association—1972
   Functions:
   - i) defence of oil price increases
   - ii) fix wages of labour

Rice
6. Memari Rice Retailers' Association (Chal Bazaar Samiti)—1973—about 50 members —5-6 officers
   Functions:
   - i) restrict entry
   - ii) fix commissions

iii) calibrate weights and measures
iv) rotate guarding
v) resolve disputes
vi) recompense for losses/accident/calamity among members via subscriptions
vii) mutual credit
viii) resistance to state regulation
7. Memari Husking Mill Association (defunct)
no longer able to fix rates
unable to bear costs of litigation and campaigning to protect unlicenced members
8. Katwa Husking Mill Association—1986 (defunct)
same reasons as Memari above
9. Katwa Association of Rice Retail Traders —1983 —32 members (serving over 100 because of 'group membership' of licences)
Functions:
   i) dispute resolution/curbing of antisocial behaviour
   ii) fix minimum commissions
   iii) fix rates for weighing and measuring
   iv) organize security on subscription
   v) mutual interest-free credit
   vi) compensation on defaulted payments by subscription
   vii) management of relations with labour gang
   viii) accommodation of police
   ix) resistance to state regulation, sales taxes, licence fees
   x) lobby against storage rules
10. Gulsi Paddy Agents' Association—1990—130 members
Functions:
   i) dispute resolution
   ii) prevention of competition from unlicenced agents
   iii) resistance to regulation and fees from the state
11. Burdwan District Rice Mill Owners' Association—1972—170 members—6 active officers
Functions:
   i) negotiations with organised labour about rates and working conditions
   ii) representations to government on quotas and transport rates
   iii) lobbying State Food Minister, District Food Controller, District Magistrate
   iv) relief and philanthropy

v) 'fixing open market paddy price when necessary'
12. Burdwan District Husking Mill Association —1982
    Functions:
       i) resistance to state on closure of unlicenced mills
       ii) collective protest and campaigning (e.g. collective default on electricity bills if charges rise)
       iii) defence of victims of arbitrary action by state through subsriptions of money for income and court expenses
13. Solvent Oil Extractors' Association—1965—representing industrialists and government
    Functions:
       i) meets in Bombay to develop industry
       ii) regulation of international export of bran oil cake

Neighbourhood

14. Bazaar Street Committee (memari) —1975—45 members—2 active officials —variety of trades
    Function:
       i) resolution of disputes and 'abuse by strangers'
       ii) security via monthly subscription to pay watchmen
15. Bazaar Committee (Katwa)—1976—250 members—12 active officials
    Functions:
       i) security organized by subscription
16. Vegetable Market Committee—40 members
    Functions:
       i) constitutive group for Businessmen's Association (see below)
       ii) dispute resolution
       iii) security (by subscription)
       iv) resistance to 'spying by Municipality'

Locality

17. Memari Chamber of Commerce
18. Memari Credit Samiti (defunct)—membership of small paddy/rice traders
    Functions:
       i) collective supply of production credit to farmers
    Failed because implicit tying of credit contract with grain supplies was not adhered to by farmers

19. Gulsi Coolies' Association
    Functions:
    i) fix minimum rates and perks with traders
20. Katwa Truck Owners' Association—100 members
    Functions:
    i) fix minimum rates
21. Katwa Rickshaw Pullers' Association
    Functions:
    i) fix minimum rates
22. Gulsi Traders' Committee—1987—300 members
    Functions:
    i) dispute resolution
    ii) restrictions on entry
    iii) lobby state for credit
23. Katwa Town Businessmens' Association (Mahakumar Byabasayee Samiti)—1983—500 members (representing 1,500 because of group membership on licences)
    Functions:
    i) intermediation with state
    ii) information diffusion about a wide range of commodity markets
    iii) organization of protest (trade bandhs)
    iv) religious—subscriptions for pujas
24. Katwa Marwari Association—about 50 members
    Functions:
    i) 'caste solidarity'
25. Burdwan Agricultural Co-operative Society —offices dominated by large private merchants
    Functions :
    i) credit and marketing

State

26. Bengal Chamber of Commerce
27. Association of Small Scale Industrialists

Appendix 8.1

Exports and Imports: West Bengal and Other States of India (Year ending 31st March)

a. Exports

(In MT)

States	Rice in the Husk							Rice not in the Husk						
	1990	1995	1996	1997	1998	1999	2000	1990	1995	1996	1997	1998	1999	2000
Assam	–	–	–	–	–	–	205	17471	7597	25022	38766	19764	5710	13462
Bihar	–	231	–	–	2595	–	–	261	–	–	2659	–	–	2083
Orissa	–	–	–	–	–	–	–	–	–	–	–	–	–	–
Uttar Pradesh	–	–	–	–	–	28	–	200	4588	–	–	418	–	–
Punjab	–	–	–	–	–	–	25	–	–	–	–	–	–	–
Madhya Pradesh	–	22	–	–	–	–	–	24	–	–	–	–	–	–
Maharashtra	–	–	–	–	–	–	–	–	–	3496	–	–	–	–
Tamil Nadu	45	–	–	–	–	–	–	256	–	–	–	–	–	–
Andhra Pradesh	–	–	–	–	–	–	–	–	–	1833	63	–	–	–
Kerala	–	–	–	22	–	–	–	–	6346	5086	8132	–	–	–
Gujarat	–	–	–	–	–	–	–	–	10191	58249	–	–	–	–
Karnataka	–	–	–	–	–	–	–	–	–	–	–	–	–	–
Jammu & Kashmir	–	–	–	–	–	–	–	–	2288	–	–	–	–	–
Himachal Pradesh	–	–	–	–	–	–	–	–	–	–	–	–	–	–
Orther States & Territories	1	–	–	–	–	1675	368	47	342	528	3071	18	–	–
Total	46	253	–	22	2595	1703	598	18259	71352	94214	52691	20200	5710	15545

Source: 'Interstate Movements/Flows of Goods by Rail, River and Air', Directorate General of Commercial Intelligence and Statistics, Kolkata.

Appendix 8.1 (contd.)

b. Imports

(In MT)

States	Rice in the Husk							Rice not in the Husk					
	1990	1995	1996	1997	1998	1999	2000	1990	1995	1996	1997	1998	1999	2000
Assam	–	–	–	–	–	–	–	25	–	–	–	–	5710	–
Bihar	45	–	1661	30	–	–	–	2106	7323	1661	831	–	–	113
Orissa	–	1664	554	–	–	–	–	382	56540	57155	–	–	–	–
Uttar Pradesh	48	24	45	–	–	–	–	21	12805	17768	–	2332	–	–
Punjab	–	–	–	–	–	–	–	611	200	4387	–	–	–	–
Madhya Pradesh	67	–	–	–	–	15546	–	25416	8166	48791	49291	–	–	–
Maharashtra	–	–	–	–	–	–	–	28	–	25692	5054	27	–	–
Tamil Nadu	–	–	–	–	–	–	–	–	–	–	–	–	–	–
Andhra Pradesh	151	5	5	–	–	–	–	4417	452	2900	161	–	–	–
Kerala	–	–	–	–	–	–	–	9	–	–	–	–	–	–
Gujarat	708	–	–	–	–	–	–	–	–	–	–	–	–	–
Karnataka	17	–	–	–	–	–	–	–	–	–	–	–	–	–
Jammu & Kashmir	–	–	–	–	–	–	–	–	–	–	–	–	–	–
Himachal Pradesh	–	–	–	–	–	–	–	–	–	–	–	–	–	–
Other States & Territories	–	24	–	–	–	–	–	494	7539	72	–	11701	–	–
Total	**1036**	**1717**	**2265**	**30**	**–**	**15546**	**–**	**33509**	**93025**	**158425**	**55336**	**14060**	**5710**	**113**

Source: 'Interstate Movements/Flows of Goods by Rail, River and Air', Directorate General of Commercial Intelligence and Statistics, Kolkata.

Appendix 9.1
Price Collapse

Table 1: Absolute Prices of Paddy and Rice in Rupees – 1997 to 2002

	Paddy (60 kg bag)			Paddy (100 kg)			Rice (100 kg)		
	Min	Max	Average	Min	Max	Average	Min	Max	Average
Aman Season									
Sarna + 1000 group									
1997 Nov - 1998 Oct	300	350	325	500	580	540	900	1050	975
1998 Nov - 1999 Oct	300	340	320	500	560	530	900	1025	963
1999 Nov - 2000 Oct	280	300	290	460	500	480	825	875	850
2000 Nov - 2001 Oct	240	270	255	400	450	425	720	810	765
2001 Nov - 2002 May	225	250	238	375	417	396	680	725	703
Govindobhog (Superfine)									
1997 Dec - 1998 Nov	800	900	850	1333	1500	1417	2400	2700	2550
1998 Dec - 1999 Nov	950	1100	1025	1583	1833	1708	2800	3250	3025
1999 Dec - 2000 Nov	600	650	625	1000	1083	1042	1800	2000	1900
2000 Dec - 2001 Nov	500	600	550	833	1000	917	1500	1800	1650
2001 Dec - 2002 May	380	450	415	633	750	692	1200	1400	1300
Boro Season									
IR 36									
1997 Apr - 1998 Mar	325	400	363	542	667	604	1000	1200	1100
1998 Apr - 1999 Mar	350	425	388	583	708	646	1050	1250	1150
1999 Apr - 2000 Mar	340	420	380	567	700	633	1025	1250	1138
2000 Apr - 2001 Mar	300	350	325	500	583	542	925	1050	988
2001 Apr - 2002 Mar	270	320	295	450	533	492	850	975	913
2002 Apr - 2002 May	210	230	220	350	383	367	700	725	713
Ratna									
1997 Apr - 1998 Mar	360	430	395	600	717	658	1100	1300	1200
1998 Apr - 1999 Mar	375	450	413	625	750	688	1150	1325	1238
1999 Apr - 2000 Mar	360	450	405	600	750	675	1125	1325	1225
2000 Apr - 2001 Mar	325	380	353	542	633	588	1025	1150	1088
2001 Apr - 2002 Mar	300	350	325	500	583	542	950	1050	1000
2002 Apr - 2002 May	240	260	250	400	433	417	800	850	825
Miniket									
1997 Apr - 1998 Mar	425	525	475	708	875	792	1350	1600	1475
1998 Apr - 1999 Mar	425	525	475	708	875	792	1350	1600	1475
1999 Apr - 2000 Mar	400	500	450	667	833	750	1300	1550	1425
2000 Apr - 2001 Mar	330	450	390	550	750	650	1100	1425	1263
2001 Apr - 2002 Mar	325	425	375	542	708	625	1100	1350	1225

Sources: Figures are as quoted by Farmers, Traders and Millers
Variety-wise total production unobtainable. Cultivation of Sarna is high in Rainy (Aman) season and IR36 in Winter (Boro) season

	Sowing time	Harvesting time
Aman Paddy	Mid July–Mid Aug	last Oct–Mid Dec
Boro Paddy	Jan-Feb	Apr-May

Appendices

Table 2: Price Collapse: Percentage Change in Price of Paddy and Rice, 1997 to 2002

	Paddy (100 kg) Average	Rice (100 kg) Average		Percentage Change Paddy	Rice
Aman Paddy	(Actual price in Rupees)		**Aman Paddy**		
Sarna + 1000 group			Sarna + 1000 group		
1997 Nov–1998 Oct	540	975	1997–98 to 1998–99	−1.9	−1.3
1998 Nov–1999 Oct	530	963	1998–99 to 1999–00	−9.4	−11.7
1999 Nov–2000 Oct	480	850	1999–00 to 2000–01	−11.5	−10.0
2000 Nov–2001 Oct	425	765	2000–01 to 2001–02	−6.9	−8.2
2001 Nov–2002 May	396	703	**1997–98 to 2001–02**	**−26.7**	**−27.9**
Govindobhog					
1997 Dec–1998 Nov	1417	2550	1997–98 to 1998–99	20.6	18.6
1998 Dec–1999 Nov	1708	3025	1998–99 to 1999–00	−39.0	−37.2
1999 Dec–2000 Nov	1042	1900	1999–00 to 2000–01	−12.0	−13.2
2000 Dec–2001 Nov	917	1650	2000–01 to 2001–02	−24.5	−21.2
2001 Dec–2002 May	692	1300	**1997–98 to 2001–02**	**−51.2**	**−49.0**
Boro Paddy					
IR 36					
1997 Apr–1998 Mar	604	1100	1997–98 to 1998–99	6.9	4.5
1998 Apr–1999 Mar	646	1150	1998–99 to 1999–00	−1.9	−1.1
1999 Apr–2000 Mar	633	1138	1999–00 to 2000–01	−14.5	−13.2
2000 Apr–2001 Mar	542	988	2000–01 to 2001–02	−9.2	−7.6
2001 Apr–2002 Mar	492	913	**1997–98 to 2001–02**	**−25.4**	**−21.9**
2002 Apr–2002 May	367	713	**2001–02 to 2002**	**−39.3**	**−35.2**
Ratna					
1997 Apr–1998 Mar	658	1200	1997–98 to 1998–99	4.4	3.1
1998 Apr–1999 Mar	688	1238	1998–99 to 1999–00	−1.8	−1.0
1999 Apr–2000 Mar	675	1225	1999–00 to 2000–01	−13.0	−11.2
2000 Apr–2001 Mar	588	1088	2000–01 to 2001–02	−7.8	−8.0
2001 Apr–2002 Mar	542	1000	**1997–98 to 2001–02**	**−23.1**	**−17.5**
2002 Apr–2002 May	417	825	**2001–02 to 2002**	**−36.7**	**−31.3**
Miniket					
1997 Apr–1998 Mar	792	1475	1997–98 to 1998–99	0.0	0.0
1998 Apr–1999 Mar	792	1475	1998–99 to 1999–00	−5.3	−3.4
1999 Apr–2000 Mar	750	1425	1999–00 to 2000–01	−13.3	−11.4
2000 Apr–2001 Mar	650	1263	2000–01 to 2001–02	−3.8	−3.0
2001 Apr–2002 Mar	625	1225	**1997–98 to 2001–02**	**−17.3**	**−12.2**
2002 Apr–2002 May	517	1075	**2001–02 to 2002**	**−34.7**	**−27.1**

Appendix 10.1

Political Parties in West Bengal (% seat shares)

	1978			(82)	1983			(87)	1993			(96)	2003			(01)
	ZP	GP	PS	LA*	ZP	GP	PS	LA	ZP	GP	PS	LA	ZP	GP	PS	LA
CPI (M)	77	61	67	50	68	54	60	47	81	58	67	43	77	58	67	44
RSP	5	4	4	–	3	3	3	–	2	2	3	–	3	3	3	–
FB	7	3	4	–	4	2	2	–	3	2	2	–	4	3	2	–
INC	10	29	22	45	22	32	30	49	11	27	23	48	9	13	12)	49
AITC													2	13	9)	
BJP													0.2	3	2	4

Notes: * Left Front
ZP = Zilla Parishad Elections
GP = Gram Panchayat
PS = Panchayat Samiti
LA = Legislative Assembly

Source: CPI(M) West Bengal State Committee; from data in Sarkar, 2006, p. 347

Glossary

adivasi	Tribal person—believed to be from the descendents of the earliest settlers
aman	main, rainfed (monsoon) cultivation season—July to November
aratdar	commission agent
aus	minor dry cultivation season—June to September
baki	instalment payment system
baniya	hindu trading caste
basa	home and base of commercial operation (for Marwari business)
bigha	a third of an acre
boro	dry cultivation season—mid January to May ('summer')
crore	10 million
dadan	an unwritten contract linking debt and crop sales on a range of terms and conditions
dalal	broker
dalit	low caste, oppressed person—generally from SC/ST
dheki	foot operated pestle mill
durga puja	religious festival in October at which bonuses are given to wage labour
faria	itinerant trader
hat/haat	periodic marketplace
jotedar	landlord
krishani	tenure using (1/3) sharecropping labourer
kula	bamboo basket
kutial	small-scale paddy/rice processor (firm or person)
lakh	100,000 : 1,00,000
mahajan	rich farmer/moneylender
marwari	name given to business castes originally from Marwar in Rajasthan
maund	volumetric measurement for rice (mound) approx 37 kgs
mistry	master; leader of work gang
morai	domestic rice store

mouja	village revenue unit
muri	puffed rice
paikar	itinerant rural trader
vaisya	trader
vanaspati	a refined vegetable oil
zamindar	rent farmer
zilla shabatipati	district political leader

Bibliography

Adam, C. and B. Harriss-White, 2007, 'From Monet to Mondrian: Characterizing Informal Economic Activity in Field Research and Simulation Models', in Harriss-White and Sinha (eds), *Trade Liberalization and India's Informal Economy*, Oxford University Press, New Delhi.

Ades A. and R. di Tella, 1996, 'The Causes and Consequences of Corruption', in Harriss-White and White, (eds), pp. 6–11.

Adrian, L., 1998, 'Large data bases—"not worth the paper they are written on"'?, in Harriss-White (ed), pp. 191–217.

Agrawal, K.P., V. Puhazhendi and K. Satyasai, 1997, 'Gearing Rural Credit for the 21st Century', *Economic and Political Weekly*, Vol. 42, No. 32, pp. 2712–28.

Agro-Economics Research Centre, 1969, *Economics of Potato Cultivation in West Bengal, 1967–8*, Visva Bharati, Santiniketan.

Ahluwalia, D., 1993, 'Public Distribution of Food in India: Coverage, Targeting and Leakages', *Food Policy*, Vol. 18, No. 1, pp. 33–54.

Akerlof, G, 1984, 'The economics of caste and of the Rat Race and other Woeful Tales', in Akerlof, *An Economic Theorist's Book of Tales: Essays that Entertain the Consequences of New Assumptions in Economic Theory*, Cambridge University Press, Cambridge, pp. 3–44.

Andersen, R., P. Brass, E. Levy, and B. Morrison, 1981, *Science, Politics and the Agricultural Revolution in Asia* Boulder, Westview.

Appadurai, A., 1988, 'Introduction: Commodities and the Politics of Value' in Appadurai (ed), *The Social Life of Things: Commodities in Cultural Perspective*, Cambridge University Press, Cambridge, pp. 3–63.

Athreya, V., G. Djurfeldt, and S. Lindberg, 1987, *Barriers Broken: Production Relations and Agrarian Change in Tamil Nadu*, Sage, London.

Attorney General, Government of West Bengal, 1991, Lecture at Nuffield College, Oxford.

Bain, J.S., 1959, *Industrial Organization*, Wiley, New York.

Banaji, J., 1977, 'Capitalist Domination and the Small Peasantry: Deccan Districts in the late 19th Century', *Economic and Political Weekly*, Vol. 12, 33–4, pp. 1375–1404.

Banaji, J., 2003, 'Islam, the Mediterranean and the Rise of Capitalism', Paper to the Conference on Theory as History: Ernest Mandel's Historical Analysis of World Capitalism, Transnational Institute, Amsterdam, http://sacw.net/left/AmsterdamJB.pdf.

Bandhyopadhyay, D., 2001, 'West Bengal: Recipe for Industrial Revival', *Economic and Political Weekly*, 29 December.

Bandhyopadhyay, D., 2003, 'Land Reforms and Agriculture: The West Bengal Experience', *Economic and Political Weekly*, 1 March, pp. 879–84.

Banerjee, A., P.J. Gertler, and M. Ghatak, 2002, 'Empowerment and Efficiency: The Economics of Tenancy Reform in West Bengal', *Journal of Political Economy*, 110.2.

Banerjee, A., P. Bardhan, K. Basu, M. Datta Chaudhury, M. Ghatak, A.S. Guha, M. Majumdar, D. Mookherjee, and D. Ray, 2002, 'Strategy for Economic Reform in West Bengal', *Economic and Political Weekly*, 12 October.

Banerjee, D., 1995, 'Market and Non-Market Configurations in Rural West Bengal: Local Organisations and Silk Weaving', *Economic and Political Weekly*, Vol. 30, No. 47, November 25, pp. M–135–142.

Banerjee, D., 1996, *'Rural Informal Credit Institutions in South Asia: An Unresolved Agrarian Question'*, Occasional Paper No. 155, Centre for Studies in Social Sciences, Calcutta, May.

Banerjee, D., 1996, *'Market and Exchange: Frontier and the Hinterland'*, Centre for Studies in Social Sciences, Calcutta.

Banerjee, N,. 2004, *'National Security in North East India'*, Paper to the workshop on 'Ethnicity, Democracy and Conflict in S. Asia', CERI, Paris.

Banerjee, H.K.S., and Kundu, 2001, 'Agriculture in West Bengal: An Analysis of Recent Trends', *Artha Beekshan*, Vol. 10, No. 1, June, pp. 21–32.

Bardhan, K. 1993, 'Social Classes and Gender in India: The Structure of the Differences in the Condition of Women' in Clark (ed), *Gender and Political Economy: Explorations of South Asian Systems* Oxford University Press, New Delhi.

Bardhan, P., 1989 a, 'The New Institutional Economics and Development Theory: A Brief Critical Assessment', *World Development*, Vol. 17, Issue 9, 1389–95.

Bardhan, P., (ed), 1989b, *Conversations Between Economists And Anthropologists*, Oxford University Press, New Delhi.

Basile E., and B. Harriss-White, 2000, 'Corporatist Capitalism, Civil Society and the Politics of Accumulation in Small Town India', *Working Paper*

38, Queen Elizabeth House, Oxford, http://www.qeh.ox.ac.uk/research/wpadtion.html?jor_id=44.

Basu, A. 2002, 'Parliamentary Communism as Historical Phenomenon: the CPI(M) on West Bengal', in Hasan (ed), *Parties and Party Politics in India*, Oxford University Press, New Delhi, pp. 317–50.

Basu, J., 2002, 'Marketing Efficiency and Marketing Channels: A Study of the Potato Market in Rural West Bengal', PhD Thesis, Vidyasagar University.

Basu, K., 1985, 'Markets, Power and Social Norms', *Economic and Political Weekly*, XXI, 43, pp. 1893–6.

Bates, R., 1981, *Markets and States in Tropical Africa*, University of California Press, Berkeley.

Bates, R., 1990, *Beyond The Miracle of The Market*, Cambridge University Press. London.

Bernstein, H., 1990, 'Agricultural Modernization in the Era of Structural Adjustment', Development Policy and Practice Working Paper 16, Open University, Milton Keynes.

Bernstein, H., et al., (eds.), 1990, *The Food Question*, Earthscan, London.

Beteille, A., 1996, 'Caste in Contemporary India' in Fuller (ed), *Caste Today*, Oxford University Press, New Delhi.

Bhaduri, A. 1983, *The Economic Structure of Backward Agriculture*, Academic Press, London.

Bhaduri, A., et al., 1986, 'Forced Commerce and Agrarian Growth', *World Development* 14, 2, pp. 267–72.

Bhalla, G.S., and G. Singh, 1997, 'Recent Developments in Indian Agriculture: A State Level Analysis', *Economic and Political Weekly* 13.

Bharadwaj, 1974, *Production Conditions in Indian Agriculture*, Cambridge University Press, Cambridge.

Bharadwaj, 1985, 'A View on Commercialization in Indian Agriculture and the Development of Capitalism', *Journal of Peasant Studies*, 13, pp. 82–9.

Bharadwaj, 1989, *On the Formation of the Labour Market in Rural Asia*, International Labour Office, Geneva.

Bhattacharjee, J.P. et al., 1958, *Sahajapur, West Bengal: Socio-Economic Study of a Village, Studies in Rural Change*, Agro-Economic Research Centre In Eastern India, Santiniketan.

Bhattacharya, S., N.K. Roy, and A. Roy, 1981, *The Economics of Mustard Cultivation in West Bengal*, Agro-Economics Research Centre, Visva Bharati, Santinketan.

Bhattacharyya D., 1999, 'Politics of Middleness: The Changing Character of the Communist Party of India (Marxist) in Rural West Bengal (1977–90)', in Rogaly, Harriss-White and Bose (eds), *Sonar Bangla: Agricultural Growth and Agrarian Change in West Bengal and Bangladesh*, Sage, New Delhi.

Bhattacharyya, S., 2000, *Participatory Rural Transformation, Agrarian Change in West Bengal*, Seminar Paper, Queen Elizabeth House, Oxford.

Bhattacharyya, S., 2001, 'Capitalist Development, Peasant Differentiation and the State: Survey Findings from West Bengal', Journal of Peasant Studies, Vol. 28, No. 4, pp. 95–126.

Bhattacharyya, S., 2003, 'Agrarian Reform, Growth and Development: Recent Debates on Rural Transformation in West Bengal, *Mainstream*, XLI, 34, pp. 21–30.

Bhattacharyya, S., 2005, 'Interest Rates, Collateral and (de) Interlinkage: a Micro Study of Rural Credit in West Bengal, *Cambridge Journal of Economics* 29,1, pp. 1–24.

Bhaumik, S.K., and Rahmin, A., 1999, 'Interlinked Credit Transactions in Rural West Bengal', *Indian Journal Agricultural Economics*, Vol. 5, No. 2, pp. 169–84.

Biswas, S, 2000, 'Death of the Bhadralok', *Outlook*, September 4.

Blaikie, P.M., J. Cameron, and D. Seddon, 1981, *Nepal In Crisis*, Oxford University Press, London.

Bose, S., 1987, *Agrarian Bengal: Economy, Social Structure and Politics, 1919–47*, Orient Longman, New Delhi.

Bottomore, T., L. Harris, V. Kiernan, and R. Miliband, 1985, *A Dictionary of Marxist Thought*, Blackwell, London.

Boyce, J., 1987, *Agrarian Impasse in Bengal: Agricultural Growth in Bangladesh and West Bengal, 1949–86*, Oxford University Press, London.

Brus, W., 1972, *The Market in a Socialist Economy*, Routledge, London.

Bryceson, D., 1993, *Liberalizing Tanzania's Food Trade*, Heinemann, Portsmouth.

Burawoy, M., 1985, *The Politics of Production: Factory Regimes Under Capitalism and Socialism*, London: Verso.

Byres, T.J., 1983, (ed), *Sharecropping and Sharecroppers*, Frank Cass, London.

Byres, T. J., 1999, *The Indian Economy: Major Debates since Independence*, Oxford University Press, New Delhi.

Caille A., 1994, 'D'une Economie Politique qui aurait pu etre' in Caille et al. (eds), *Pour une Autre Economie*, Revue du Mouvement Anti-utilitariste dans les Sciences Sociales (MAUSS), Eds La Decouverte, Paris.

Bibliography

Caille, A., B. Guerrien, and A. Insel, (eds), 1994, *Pour une Autre Economie, Revue du Mouvement Anti-utilitariste dans les Sciences Sociales* (MAUSS), Eds La Decouverte, Paris.

Cassen R. and V. Joshi, (eds), 1995, *India: The Future of Economic Reforms*, Pauls Press, New Delhi.

Chand, R., 2003, 'Reorienting State Intervention in Foodgrains Markets in India to improve Food Security, Regional Equity and Efficiency', Institute of Economic Growth, Delhi University. www.gdnet.org?pdf2/gdn_library/awards_medals/2003/r_m/Market_state/chand_papers.pdf

Chandrasekhar, C.P., 1993, 'Agrarian Change and Occupational Diversification: Non-agricultural Employment and Rural Development in West Bengal', *Journal of Peasant Studies* 20, 2.

Chang, H-J., 2003, 'The market, the state and institutions in economic development' in Chang (ed), *Frontiers of Development Economics*, Anthem, London, pp. 41–61.

Chari, S., 2003, '*Fraternal Capital: Peasant-workers, Self-made Men and Globalization in Provincial India*', Stanford University Press, Palo Alto.

Chatterjee, K.S., and S. Sarkar, 1995, 'Agriculture Market Characteristics and Agricultural Development: Lessons from West Bengal', Paper presented at the Workshop on Agricultural Growth and Agrarian Structure in Contemporary West Bengal and Bangladesh, Centre for Studies in Social Sciences, Calcutta, 9–12 January.

Chatterjee, P. 1997. *The Present History of West Bengal: Essays in Political Criticism*, Oxford University Press, Delhi.

Chattopadhyay, B., 1969, 'Marx and India's Crisis' in P.C. Joshi, (ed), *Homage To Karl Marx*, People's Publishing House, Delhi.

Chattopadhyay, B., 1981, 'An Approach to The Research Design for the Study of Market Circuits in Eastern India', CRESSIDA, Calcutta, mimeo.

Chattopadhyay, B., 1991a, '*Food Systems and the Human Environment in Eastern India*', Vol. 1: *Food Insecurity and the Social Environment*, K.P. Bagchi, Calcutta.

Chattopadhyay, B., 1991b, '*Food Systems and the Human Environment in Eastern India*', Vol. 2: *Food Insecurity, Climate Variability and Community Perceptions*, K.P. Bagchi, Calcutta.

Chattopadhyay, B., and P. Spitz, 1987, *Food Systems and Society in Eastern India*, UNRISD, Geneva.

Chattopadhyay M., C. Neogi, and S. Maity, 1993, 'Growth and Instability in Crop Production in Eastern India', *Asian Economic Review* 35, pp. 69–94.

Chaudhuri, K.N., 1979, 'Markets and Traders in India during the 17th and 18th centuries' in Chaudhuri K.N. and C.J. Dewey, (eds.), *Economy and Society: Essays in Indian Economic and Social History*, Oxford University Press, Delhi, pp. 143–62.

Chibber, V., 2003, *'Locked in Place: State-Building and Late Industrialization in India'*. Princeton, N.J: Princeton University Press.

Choudhury, S., 2001, 'The Public Distribution System and Informal Traders: A Study of Rice Markets in Calcutta', M. Phil. Thesis in Development Studies, Queen Elizabeth House, Oxford University.

Chowdury, S. K., and A. Sen, 1981, *The Economics of Potato Production and Marketing in West Bengal*, Agro-Economics Research Centre, Visva Bharati, Santinketan.

Chowdhury V.K., et al., 2000, 'Groundwater Arsenic Contamination in Bangladesh and West Bengal', *Environmental Health Perspectives*, 108, 5.

CIRAD, 1990, *Economies Et Filieres En Regions Chaudes: Formation Des Prix Et Echanges Agricoles*, CIRAD, Montpellier.

Clark, A., (ed) 1993, *Gender and Political Economy: Explorations of South Asian Systems* Oxford University Press, New Delhi.

Clay, E., and B. Schaffer, (eds.), 1984, *Room For Manoeuvre*, Heinemann, London.

Colatei, D., and B. Harriss-White, 2004, 'Social Stratification and Rural Households', in Harriss-White and Janakarajan (eds), *Rural India facing the 21ˢᵗ Century*, Anthem, London.

Crow B., 2001, *Markets, Class and Rural Change in Bangladesh*, Palgrave, London.

Cummings, R.W. Jr., 1967, *Pricing Efficiency In The Indian Wheat Market*, Impex, New Delhi.

Dasgupta, B., 1995, *'West Bengal's Agriculture Since 1997'*, Paper presented at the Workshop on Agricultural Growth and Agrarian Change in West Bengal and Bangladesh, Centre for Studies in Social Sciences, Calcutta, Calcutta, 9–12, January.

Dasgupta, B., et al., 2002, 'Bleeding Bengal: Trinamul Terror: Report of a Field Visit by Nine MPs,' Left Front, West Bengal, Calcutta.

Dasgupta, N., 1992, *Petty trading in the Third World*, Avebury, London.

Datta, S., 2002, 'Urbanisation and Development of Small Rural Enterprise', *Economic and Political Weekly*, 27 July.

Datta Roy, S., 2002, 'Agricultural Growth in West Bengal in the 1980s', *Economic and Political Weekly*, 14 September.

Desai, M., S.H. Rudolph, and A. Rudra, (eds), 1984, *Agrarian Power and Agricultural Productivity in South Asia*, Oxford University Press, Delhi.

Dey, L.B., 1879, *Bengal Peasant Life*, Book Society of India Ltd., Calcutta.
District 3240, 'District Governor 1994–95: Jugal Kishore Somani', www.ri3240.com/Dist/profilejugal.htm, accessed on 25/01/2004
Djurfeldt, G., and S. Lindberg, 1974, *Behind Poverty: The Social Formation of a Tamil Village*, Scand. Institute for Asian Studies Series, No. 22, Curzon, London.
Dobbin, Christine, 1996, *Asian Entrepreneurial Minorities*, London: Curzon.
Drèze, J., and A. Sen, (eds), 1997 *Indian Development: Selected Regional Perspectives*, Oxford University Press, New Delhi.
Dutta, S., 1997, *Family Business in India*, Sage, New Delhi.
Ellis, F. et al., 1991, *Indonesia Rice Marketing Study, 1989–91*, Bulog, Jakarta.
Elson, D., 1989, 'Market Socialism or Socialization of the Market?' *New Left Review*, 172.
Engels, F., 2001, *The Peasant Question in France and Germany*, Elecbook Classics, London.
Evers, H.D., 1994, 'The Traders' Dilemma: A theory of the Social Transformation of Markets and Survey in Evers and Schrader (eds), pp. 1–10.
Evers, H.D., and H. Schrader, (eds.), 1994, *The Moral Economy of Trade; Ethnicity and Developing Markets*, Routledge, London.
Farruk, M.O., 1972, 'Structure and Performance of the Rice Marketing System in East Pakistan', Cornell International Agricultural Development, Bulletin 23, Cornell University Ithaca, New York.
Fine B., 2002, *Social Capital versus Social Theory: Political Economy and Social Science at the Turn of the Millennium*, Routledge, London.
Fine B. and A. Saad-Filho 2003, *Marx's Capital*, Revised 4th edition, Pluto Press, London.
Folbre N., 1995, *Who pays for the Kids? Gender and the Structures of Constraint*, Routledge, London.
Food Corporation of India, 2000, 'Eastern Zone at a Glance', FCI Zonal Office [East], Calcutta.
Fox, R., 1969, *From Zamindar to Ballot Box—Community Change in a North Indian Market Town*, Cornell University Press, Ithaca.
Fukuyama, F., 1995, *Trust: The Social Virtues and the Creation of Prosperity*, Penguin, London.
Fuller C., (ed), 1996, *Caste Today*, Oxford University Press, New Delhi.
Garcia, R., 1981, 'A Conceptual Framework for the Analysis of Case Studies', in 'Food Systems and Society', CRESSIDA *Transactions*, Vol. 1, No. 1, pp. 1–18.

Garcia, R., 1984, *Food Systems And Society: A Conceptual And Methodological Challenge*, UNRISD, Geneva.

Gazder, H., and S. Sengupta, 1999, 'Agricultural growth and Recent trends in Wellbeing in Rural West Bengal', Ch 3 in Rogaly, Harriss-White and Bose, (eds), *Sonar Bangla: Agricultural Growth and Agrarian Change in West Bengal and Bangladesh*, Sage, New Delhi.

Geertz, C., 1970, *Agricultural Involution: The Processes of Ecological Change in Indonesia*, University of California Press, Berkeley.

Ghosh, A, and Dutt, K., 1977, *Development of Capitalist Relations in Agriculture (A Case Study of West Bengal, 1793–1971)*, People's Publishing House, New Delhi.

Ghosh, B., and S.K. Mukhopadhyay, 1988, 'Gender Differences in Impact of Technological Changes in Rice-Based Farming Systems in India', in Poals, S.V., Schmink, M., and Spring, A. (eds) *Gender Issues in Farming System*, Boulder, Westview Press.

Ghosh, J., 2002, 'Rural Employment Trends from the Census', *Macroscan* 11 April, http://www.macroscan.org

Ghosh, M., and S. K. Chowdury, 1983, *Marketing of Paddy and Rice in West Bengal*, Agro-Economics Research Centre, Visva Bharati, Santinketan.

Ghosh, M., 1995, 'A Profile of Two Villages in West Bengal', Paper presented at the Workshop on Agricultural Growth and Agrarian Change in Contemporary West Bengal and Bangladesh, Centre for Studies in Social Sciences, Calcutta, January, 9–12.

Ghosh, M., 1998, 'Natural and Social Resource Use and the Poor in Rural West Bengal', IDRC/Visva Bharati.

Ghosh, P.K., and B. Harriss-White, 2002, 'A Crisis in the Rice Economy', *Frontline* 19, 19, 14 September.

Ghosh, P.K., and R. Sudarshan, 2003, 'Trade Liberalisation and the Rice Processing Industry in West Bengal', NCAER, New Delhi.

Gibbon, P., and S. Ponte, 2004, 'Quality Standards, Conventions and the Governance of Global Value Chains', www2.qeh.ox.ac.uk/pdf/qehconf/gibbon.pdf

Gilbert, E.H., 1969, 'Marketing of Staple Foods in Northern Nigeria: A Study of Staple Food Marketing Systems Serving Kano City', PhD Thesis, Ahmadu Bello University, Zaria, Nigeria.

Goldsmith, A., 1985, 'The private sector and rural development: Can agribusiness help the small farmers?' *World Development* 13, 10–11, 1125–38.

Government of India, 1954, *Report on the Marketing of Rice in India*, Ministry of Food and Agriculture, New Delhi.

Bibliography

Government of India, 1955. *Report of the Rice Milling Committee*, Ministry of Food and Agriculture, New Delhi.

Government of India, 1960. *Report on an Enquiry into the Pace and Pattern of Market Arrival of Foodgrains (Season 1958-9)*, Directorate of Economics and Statistics: Ministry of Food and Agriculture, New Delhi.

Government of India, 1961, *Rice Economy of India*, Directorate of Economics and Statistics, New Delhi.

Government of India, 1999, *Economic Survey, 1998-99*, New Delhi.

Government of India, 2001, *Economic Survey, 2000-01*, New Delhi.

Government of West Bengal, (Board of Revenue and Directorate of Agriculture Socio-Economic and Evaluation Branch), 1975. *World Agricultural Census 1970-71*, West Bengal State Agricultural Information Unit, Calcutta.

Government of West Bengal (Board of Revenue and Directorate of Agriculture Socio-Economic and Evaluation Branch), 1979, *Agricultural Census 1976-77*, West Bengal State Agricultural Information Unit, Calcutta.

Government of West Bengal, 1952, *First Five Year Plan*. Calcutta.

Government of West Bengal, 1989, *Economic Review 1988-9*, Calcutta.

Government of West Bengal, 1993, *Economic Review: 1992-3*, Calcutta.

Government of West Bengal, 1996, *Economic Review: 1995-6*, Statistical Appendix, Calcutta.

Government of West Bengal, 1999, 'Decentralised Procurement: A Brief Report, 1997-8', Directorate of District Distribution, Procurement and Supply, Food and Supplies Department, Kolkata.

Government of West Bengal, 2000a, 'Targeted Public Distribution System in West Bengal', Directorate of District Distribution, Procurement and Supply, Food and Supplies Department, Kolkata.

Government of West Bengal, 2000b, 'Decentralised Procurement: A Brief Report, 1999-2000', Directorate of District Distribution, Procurement and Supply, Food and Supplies Department, Kolkata.

Government of West Bengal, 2002, *Economic Review; 2001-02*, Kolkata.

Government of West Bengal, 2003, 'A Handbook of District Distribution, Procurement and Supply: Burdwan District', District Food and Supply Office, Burdwan.

Granovetter, M., 1985, 'Economic Action and Social Structure: The Problem of Embeddedness', *American Journal of Sociology* 91, pp. 481-510.

Green D. and I Shapiro, 1994, *Pathologies of Rational Choice*, Yale University Press, New Haven.

Gulati, A and Narayanan, S., 2002. 'Rice Trade Liberalization and Poverty', *Economic and Political Weekly*, 28 December, pp. 5237–43.

Gupta, J., 2002, 'Woman Second in the Agenda', *Economic and Political Weekly*, May.

Hardgrove, A., 2002, *Community and Public Culture—The Marwaris in Calcutta, 1897–1997*, New York: Columbia University Press.

de Haan, A., and B. Rogaly, 1996, 'Eastward Ho! Migration and Leapfrogging in Eastern India', in Rodgers et al., (eds), *An Institutional Approach to Labour and Development*, Frank Cass, London.

Hansen, T.B. and C. Jaffrelot (eds), 1998, *The BJP and the Compulsions of Politics in India* Oxford University Press, New Delhi.

Harriss, B., 1976, 'Paddy-Rice Processing in South Asia. A Review of the Case for Modernisation', *Tropical Science*.

Harriss, B., 1977. 'Besieging the Free Market: The Effects of the Paddy-Rice Levy', in B.H. Farmer, (ed), *Green Revolution*, pp. 268–73, Macmillan, London.

Harriss, B., 1978a, 'Rice Processing Projects in Bangladesh: An Appraisal of a Decade of Proposals', *Bangladesh Journal of Agricultural Economics*, 1, 2, 24–52.

Harriss, B., 1978b, 'Post Harvest Rice Processing Systems in Rural Bangladesh: Technology, Economics and Employment' *Bangladesh Journal of Agricultural Economics* 2, 1, 23, 50.

Harriss, B., 1979, 'There is Method in my Madness, or is it Vice Versa? Measuring Agricultural Market Performance', *Food Research Institute Studies*, Stanford, Vol. XVII, No. 2, pp. 197–218.

Harriss, B., 1981a, *Transitional Trade and Rural Development*, Vikas, New Delhi.

Harriss, B., 1981b, 'Inaction, Interaction and Action: Regulated Agricultural Markets In Tamil Nadu', *Social Scientist*, 100, pp. 96–137.

Harriss, B., 1982, 'Food Systems and Society: The System of Circulation of Rice in West Bengal', CRESSIDA *Transactions* 2, 1–2, 158–250.

Harriss, B., 1984, *State and Market: The Political Economy of Exchange in a Dry Region of South India*, Concept Publishing Company, New Delhi.

Harriss, B., 1989, 'The Organized Power of Grain Merchants in the Dhaka Region of Bangladesh' *Economic and Political Weekly*, Rev Ag. XXIV, 12, A 39–A44.

Harriss, B., 1990, 'Agricultural Exchange, Markets and Marketing Policy in India', in Indian Society of Agricultural Economics, *Agricultural Development Policy: Adjustments and Reorientation*, Oxford IBH. Pub Co., New Delhi, pp. 275–95.

Harriss, B., 1991, *Masters of The Countryside*, Report to the Overseas Development Administration, Queen Elizabeth House, Oxford.

Harriss, B., 1992, 'Talking to Traders about Trade', in J. Hoddinott and S. Devereux, (eds.), *Fieldwork in Africa and Asia*, Harvester Wheatsheaf, London. pp. 122–33.

Harriss, B., et al., 1984, *Exchange Relations and Poverty in Dryland Agriculture*, Concept, New Delhi.

Harriss B., and C. Kelly, 1982, 'Policy for Rice and Oil Processing in South Asia', *Bulletin of the Institute of Development Studies*, 13:3, pp. 32–44.

Harriss, J., 1982, 'Making out on Limited Resources in West Bengal, or Whatever Happened to Semi-Feudalism?', *CRESSIDA Transactions*, Vol. 2, 1–2, pp. 16–76.

Harriss, J., 1992, 'Does the 'Depressor' Still Work? Agrarian Structure and Development in India: A Review of Evidence and Argument', *The Journal of Peasant Studies*, Vol. 29, No. 2, January, pp. 189–227.

Harriss, J., 1993, 'What is happening in West Bengal? Agrarian Reform, Growth and Distribution', *Economic and Political Weekly* XXVIII, 24, pp. 1237–47.

Harriss-White, B., 1993, 'Collective Politics in Foodgrains Markets in South Asia' *Bulletin, Institute of Development Studies* 24, 3.

Harriss-White, B., 1995, 'Order, Order....Agro-commercial Microstructures and the State: the Experience of Regulation' in Stein and Subrahmanyam (eds), *Institutions and Economic Change in South Asia*, Oxford University Press, New Delhi.

Harriss-White, B., 1996, *A Political Economy of Agricultural Markets in South India: Masters of the Countryside*, Sage, New Delhi and London.

Harriss-White, B., (ed) 1998. *Agricultural Markets from Theory to Practice*, Macmillan, Basingstoke.

Harriss-White, B., 1999, 'Agricultural growth and the Structure and Relations of Agricultual Markets in West Bengal, in Rogaly, Harriss-White and Bose, (eds), *Sonar Bangla: Agricultural Growth and Agrarian Change in West Bengal and Bangladesh*, Sage, New Delhi.

Harriss-White, B., 2003, *India Working: Essays in Economy and Society*, Cambridge University Press, Cambridge.

Harriss-White, B., 2004a, 'Policy and the Agricultural Development Agenda', Ch. 2–1 in Harriss-White and Janakarajan (eds), *Rural India facing the 21st Century*, Anthem, London.

Harriss-White, B., 2004b, 'Socially Inclusive Social Security: Social Assistance in the Villages', Ch. 3–7 in Harriss-White and Janakarajan, (eds), *Rural India facing the 21st Century*, Anthem, London.

Harriss-White, B., 2004c, 'Food, Nutrition and the State in Northern Tamil Nadu', Ch. 3–5 in Harriss-White and Janakarajan, (eds), Rural India facing the 21st Century, Anthem, London.
Harriss-White, B., 2005a, India's Market Society, Three Essays Press, New Delhi.
Harriss-White, B., 2005b, 'Commercialisation, Commodification and Gender Relations in Post-Harvest Systems for Rice in South Asia', Economic and Political Weekly, Vol. XL No. 25, 18 June, pp. 1530–42.
Harriss-White, B., and N. Gooptu, 2000, 'Mapping India's World of Unorganised Labour' Socialist Register, Vol. 37, pp. 89–118.
Harriss-White, B. and S. Janakarajan (eds), 2004, Rural India facing the 21st Century, Anthem, London.
Harriss-White, B., and A. Sinha (eds.), 2007, Trade Liberalisation and India's Informal Economy. Oxford University Press, New Delhi.
Harriss-White, B. and G. White, 1996, 'Corruption, Liberalisation and Democracy' in Harriss-White and White, (eds), Liberalisation and the New Corruption: Bulletin, Institute of Development Studies, 27, 2.
Hasan Z., (ed), 2002, Parties and Party Politics in India, Oxford University Press, New Delhi.
Hazlehurst, L., 1966, Entrepreneurship and the Merchant Castes in a Punjab City Duke University Monograph No. 1, Commonwealth Studies Center.
Hill, Douglas., 2003, 'Politics and Chronic Poverty: The Experience of Bankura District, West Bengal', Paper to the Conference on 'Staying Poor: Chronic Poverty and Development Policy', Inst for Development Policy and Management, Manchester University.
Hodgson, G., 2001, Why Economics forgot History Routledge, London.
Huws, U., 2003, The Making of a Cybertariat Merlin, London.
Illori, C., 1968, An Economic Study of the Production and Distribution of Staple Foodcrops in Western Nigeria, Ph.D. Thesis, Stanford University.
International Bank for Reconstruction and Development (IBRD [World Bank]), 1981. Accelerated Development in Sub-Saharan Africa, Washington, DC.
Jaffee, S., 1990, Alternative Marketing Institutions for Agricultural Exports in Sub Saharan Africa with Special Reference to Kenyan Horticulture, D.Phil.Thesis, Oxford University.
Jagganathan, 1987, Informal Markets in Developing Countries, Oxford University Press, New York.

Janakarajan, S., 1986, 'Aspects of Market Interrelationships in a Changing Agrarian Economy: A Case Study from Tamil Nadu', PhD Thesis, University of Madras.

Janakarajan, S., 1993. 'Triadic Exchange Relations: An Illustration from South India', Bulletin, Institute of Development Studies 24, 3, pp. 75–82.

Janakarajan, S., 2004, 'Populism and Electricity in Rural Tamil Nadu', Ch. 2–3 in Harriss-White and Janakarajan, (eds), Rural India facing the 21st Century, Anthem, London.

Jasdanwalla, Z.Y., 1966, Marketing Efficiency in Indian Agriculture, Allied, Bombay.

Jessop, B., 1982, The Capitalist State, Blackwell, Oxford.

Jha, R., and H.K. Nagarajan, 2002, 'Noisy Vertical Markets', Economic and Political Weekly, December 21, pp. 5135–41.

Jones, W.O., 1972, Marketing Staple Foodcrops in Tropical Africa, Cornell University Press, Ithaca.

Kaur, R., P.K. Ghosh, and R.M. Sudarshan, 2007, 'Trade Liberalization and Informality in the Rice Processing Industry', in Harriss-White and Sinha (eds), Trade Liberalization and India's Informal Economy, Oxford University Press, New Delhi, pp. 128–232.

Kaviraj, S., 1990, 'On State, Society, and Discourse in India', IDS Bulletin, 21:4, pp. 10–15.

Khan M., 2000, 'Rent Seeking as Process', pp. 70–144 in Khan and Jomo, Rents, Rent-seeking and Economic Development: Theory and Evidence in Asia, Cambridge University Press, Cambridge.

Khan, M., 2004. 'State Failure in Developing Countries and Institutional Reform Strategies', in Stein (ed), Annual World Bank Conference on Development Economics – Europe – 2003, Washington, IBRD.

Khan, M., and K.S. Jomo, 2000. Rents, Rent-seeking and Economic Development: Theory and Evidence in Asia, Cambridge University Press, Cambridge.

Kohli, A., 1987, The State and Poverty in India: The Politics of Reform, Cambridge University Press, London.

Kurien, C.T., 1977, 'Abstract Generalisations', Economic and Political Weekly 10, pp. 428–30.

Lachaier, Pierre, 2000, 'Le Culte de la Déesse de la Fortune Laksmi chez les Marchands Lohana', Bullentin de L'École Française D'Extrême-Orient, Vol. 87, pp. 787–808.

Laidlaw J., 1995, Riches and Renunciation: Religon, Economy and Society among the Jains Clarendon, Oxford.

Lal, D., 1988, The Hindu Equilibrium, Vol 1: Cultural stability and Economic stagnation, 1500 BC to 1980, Clarendon, Oxford.

Lambert H., 1996. 'Caste, Gender and Locality in Rural Rajasthan', in Fuller (ed), pp. 92–124.

Landy, F., 1997. 'Fertilisers, Structural Adjustment and Food Policy', *Pondy Papers in Social Sciences*, 25, French Institute, Pondicherry.

Larsen M.N. 2004, 'Governing Post-liberalized Markets: National Market Co-ordination and the Global Cotton Chain', PhD. Thesis, University of Copenhagen.

Lawson, T., 1997, *Economics and Reality*, Routledge, London.

Leiten, G.K., 1990, 'De-peasantisation Discontinued: Land Reforms in West Bengal *Economic and Political Weekly*, 25, 40, pp. 2265–71.

Lele, U., 1971. *Foodgrains Marketing in India: Public Policy and Private Performance*, Cornell University Press, Ithaca, New York.

Lele, U., P. Fishtein, and M. Gbetibuono, 1990, 'Planning for Food Security in Africa: Lessons and Policy Implications', *MADIA Discussion Paper*, 13, International Bank for Reconstruction and Development (World Bank), Washington DC.

Lipton, M., 1989, 'The Fear of Trade: Equity Considerations in the Analysis of Marketing in ICRISAT', *Agricultural Markets in the Semi-Arid Tropics*, International Centre for Research in the Semi-Arid Tropics (ICRISAT), Hyderabad.

Mackintosh, M., 1990, 'Abstract Markets and Real Needs', in H. Bernstein et al., (eds.), *The Food Question*, Earthscan, London, pp. 43–53.

Macroscan, 2003a, 'Per Capita Income Growth of States', *Macroscan*, http://www.macroscan.org

Macroscan, 2003b, 'Employment Trends in India' *Macroscan*, http://www.macroscan.org 22 April.

Majid, N., 1994, 'Contractual Arrangements in Pakistani Agriculture: A Study of Share tenure in Sindh', D.Phil. thesis, University of Oxford.

Mallick, R., 1993, *Development Policy of a Communist Government*, Cambridge University Press, Cambridge.

Mamdani, M., 1990, 'State Formation and State Processes', paper for the Codesria network on "Social Movements, Social Transformation and the Struggle for Democracy in Africa", Department of Political Science, Makerere University, Tunis.

Mamdani, M., 1990, 'The Social Basis of Constitutionalism in Africa', *Journal of Modern African Studies*, 28:3, pp. 359–74.

Marion, B., et al., 1986, *The Organisation and Performance of the US Food System*, DC Heath and Co., Lexington, Massachusettes.

Marx K., 1974, *Capital*, Lawrence and Wishart, London.

Marx, K. ((ed), D. McLellan), 1971, *Grundrisse*, London: Harper.
McClelland, D. C., 1995, *Human Motivation*. Cambridge University Press, Cambridge.
Mendelsohn, O., 1993, 'The Transformation of Power in rural India' *Modern Asian Studies* 27, 4, pp. 805–42.
Menon, S., 2005, 'Indian Provident Fund: A Systematic Denial', Labour File, Issue No. 60, October.
Minot, N., 1986, *Contract Farming and its Impact on Small Farmers in Less Developed Countries*, Michigan State University, Dept. of Agricultural Economics.
Mitra, S., and A. Sarkar, 2003, 'Relative Profitability from Production and Trade: A study of Selected Potato Markets in West Bengal', *Economic and Political Weekly*, 1 November, pp. 4694–99.
Moitra, B. and Das, P.K., 2004, 'Groundwater Markets in West Bengal, India: Emergence, Evolution and Market Structure'. South Asian Network of Research Institutes, V Programme http://saneinetwork.net/pdf/sanei_V/Groundwater%20Markets%20in%20West%20Bengal,%20India-%20Kolkata.pdf
Mooij, J., 1991, 'Socio-Legal Observations About Rice Procurement in a South Indian District', mimeo, Agricultural University, Wageningen and Institute for Social and Economic Change, Bangalore.
Mooij, J., 1996, *Food Policy and Politics: The Public Distribution System in Karnataka and Kerala, South India*, Ph.D Thesis, University of Amsterdam.
Mooij, J, 1999a, 'Dilemmas in Food Policy', *Economic and Political Weekly*, 25 December.
Mooij, J., 1999b, *Food Politics and Policy in India: the Public Distribution System in South India*, Oxford University Press, New Delhi.
Moustier, P., 2001, *Developpement Durable de l'Agriculture Urbaine en Afrique Francophone*, CIRAD_FLHOR, Paris.
Mukhapadhyay, S.C., 2000, 'CPI (M) In West Bengal', *Economic and Political Weekly*, 10–16 June.
Mukarji, N., and M.K. Sanyal, 1995. 'Growth and Institutional Change in West Bengal Agriculture, 1901–88', paper presented to the Workshop on Agricultural Growth and Agrarian Change in Contemporary West Bengal and Bangladesh', Centre for Studies in Social Sciences, Calcutta, 9–12 January.
Mukherjee, P., 1965, 'Growth of Bolpur Town in the District of Birbhum', in *Birbhum District Census Handbook*, 1961, Census Operation, West Bengal, Calcutta, pp. 126–36.

Mukherjee, P., 1966, Productivity and Profitability of the Rice Milling Industry in Birbhum, Khadi Gramodyog, December.

Mukherjee, S., 1981, 'Some Aspects of Commercialization of Agriculture in Eastern India 1891-1938', paper for Seminar on Commercialization of Indian Agriculture, mimeo, Centre for Development Studies, Trivandrum.

Mukherji, B., and S. Mukhopadhyay, 1995, 'Impact of Institutional Change in a Small Farm Economy: Case of Rural West Bengal', Economic and Political Weekly, 26 August, pp. 2134–7.

Mukhopadhayay, D., and N. Sarkar, 2001, 'Has There been an Acceleration in the Growth of Agriculture in West Bengal? A Fresh Look Using Modern Time Series Techniques', Sankhya: The Indian Journal of Statistics, Vol. 63, Series B., Part 1, pp. 89–107.

Mukhopadhyay, S.K., 1994, 'Differentiated Impact of Modern Rice Technology across Production Environments', Indian Statistical Institute, Calcutta.

Mukhopadhyay, S., 1998, 'Marketing of Paddy and Rice in West Bengal: with particular reference to 24 Parganas (North)', Unpublished PhD. Thesis, Calcutta University.

Myrdal G., 1968, Asian Drama: An Inquiry into the Poverty of Nations, Penguin Books, Clinton, Mass.

Nadkarni, 1980, Marketable Surplus and Market Dependence in a Millet Region, Allied Publishers, New Delhi.

Nagaraj, K., 1985, 'Marketing Structure for Paddy and Arecanut in South Kanara: A Comparison of Markets in a Backward District' in Raj et al., (eds), Essays on the Commercialisation of Indian Agriculture, Oxford University Press, Bombay.

Nash, M., 1987, 'Peasant Markets and Indian Peasant Economics' in T. Shanin (ed), Peasants and Peasant Societies, 2nd ed., Blackwell, Oxford.

NCAER, 2004, East India Human Development Report, NCAER, New Delhi.

North, D.C., and J. Wallis, 1987, 'Measuring the Transaction Sector in the American Economy, 1870–1970' in S.L. Engerman and R.E. Gallman, (eds.), Long-Term Factors In American Economic Growth, Chicago University Press, Chicago.

North, D.C., 1989, 'Institutions and Economic Growth: An Historical Introduction', World Development 17, 9, pp. 1319–32.

Olsen, W. K., 1991, '"Distress Sales" and Exchange Relations in a Rural Area of Rayalaseema, Andhra Pradesh', D. Phil. Thesis, Oxford University.

Olsen, W. K., 1996, Rural Indian Social Relations: A Case Study in Andhra Pradesh, Oxford University Press, New Delhi.

Von Oppen, M., et al., 1983, 'Impact of Market Access on Agricultural Productivity in India', in ICRISAT, *Agricultural Markets in the Semi-Arid Tropics*, International Centre for Research in the Semi-Arid Tropics (ICRISAT), Hyderabad.

Otero, M., and E. Rhyne, 1994, *The New World of Micro-Enterprise Finance: Building Healthy Institutions for the Poor*, Intermediate Technology Publications, London.

Pache Huber, V., 2002, *Noces et Négoces: Dynamiques associatives d'une Caste de Commerçants Hindous*. Neuchâtel: Éditions de L'Institut d'Ethnologie/ Paris, Maison des Sciences de l'Homme.

Palaskas, T.B., and B. Harriss-White, 1993, 'Testing Market Integration: A New Method with Case Material From West Bengal', *Journal of Development Studies*, 30:1, pp. 1–57.

Palaskas, T.B., and B. Harriss-White, 1997, 'The Evolution of Wholesale Price Behaviour in Tamil Nadu, 1973–93', *Journal of International Development*, 9, 1, pp. 101–115.

Panini, M.N., 1996, 'The Political Economy of Caste', in Srinivas (ed), *Caste: Its Twentieth Century Avatar* Viking, Delhi.

Patnaik, P., 2001, 'The Left Front and West Bengal Developments', *People's Democracy*, Vol. XXV, No. 20, http://pd.cpim.org/2001/may20/may20_eco.htm, accessed on 14.03.2004.

Patnaik, U., 1981, 'The Process of Commercialization under Colonial Conditions', paper for Seminar on Commercialization of Indian Agriculture, Centre for Development Studies, Trivandrum.

Pedersen J., 2000, 'Explaining Economic Liberalisation in India: State-society perspectives' *World Development*, 28, 2, pp. 265–82.

Perelman, M., 2000, *The Invention of Capitalism: Classical Political Economy and the Secret History of Primitive Accumulation*, Durham, NC; Duke University Press, London.

Poals, S.V., M. Schmink, and A. Spring, [eds] 1988, *Gender Issues in Farming Systems*, Boulder, Westview Press.

Pujo, L., 1997, 'Towards a Methodology for the Analysis of the Embeddedness of Markets in Social Institutions: Application to Gender and the Market for Local Rice in Eastern Guinea', D. Phil Thesis, Oxford University.

Raj, K.N., N. Bhattacharya, S. Guha, and S. Padhi, (eds), 1985, *Essays on the Commercialisation of Indian Agriculture*, Oxford University Press, Bombay.

Ram, M.M., and V.R. Murthy, (eds.), 1980, 'Proceedings of a Workshop on Nutrition Education' (UNICEF, ICAR), National Institute of Nutrition, Hyderabad.

Ram, S.A., 1982, 'Household Type in Rural Area - a Case Study of 26 villages in Bolpur Block, Paper to seminar on Society and Economy in Rural India', mimeo, Palli Charcha Kendra, Sriniketan.
Ramachandran, V.K., 1997, 'Achievements in the Countryside', *Frontline*, 11 July, p. 124.
Ramachandran, V.K., and M. Swaminathan, 2005, 'Introduction', Ramachandran and Swaminathan (eds), *Financial Liberalization and Rural Credit in India*, Tulika, New Delhi, pp. xxi–xiii.
Ramachandran, V.K., and M. Swaminathan, (eds), 2002, *Agrarian Studies: Essays on Agrarian relations in Less-Developed Countries*, Tulika, New Delhi.
Rana K., S. Das, A. Sengupta, and A. Rafique, 2003, 'State of Primary Education in West Bengal', *Economic and Political Weekly*, 31 May.
Rawal, V., 2002, 'Institutional Credit and Credit Markets in Rural West Bengal: A Note on Trends in the 1980s and the 1990s', presented at the Workshop on Financial Liberalization and Rural Banking in India, Indian Statistical Institute, 8–9 March, 2002.
Rawal, V., 2005, 'Banking and Credit Relations in Rural West Bengal', in Ramachandran and Swaminathan, (eds), *Financial Liberalization and Rural Credit in India*, Tulika, New Delhi, pp. 279–325.
Rawal, V., and M. Swaminathan, 1998, 'Changing Trajectories; Agricultural Growth in West Bengal, 1950 to 1996', *Economic and Political Weekly*, 3 October, pp. 2595–602.
Ray, D., 1958, 'Food Administration in East India, 1939–54', Agro-Economic Research Centre, Visva Bharati, Santinketan.
Ray, Tapas, 1997. 'Left Landmark: Twenty years in power', *Frontline*, 11 July, p. 122.
Reserve Bank of India/NABARD, 1984, *Agricultural productivity in India: Report of the Committee on Agricultural Productivity in Eastern India*, Bombay
Robinson, J., 1962, *Economic Philosophy*, Penguin Books, London.
Rodgers, G., K. Foti, and L. Lauridsen, (eds), 1996, *An Institutional Approach to Labour and Development*, Frank Cass, London.
Rogaly, B., 2003, 'Who Goes? Who Stays Back? Seasonal Migration and Staying Put Among Rural Manual Workers in Eastern India', *Journal of International Development*, Vol. 15, pp. 623–32.
Rogaly, B., et al., 2002, 'Seasonal Migration and Welfare/Illfare in Eastern India: A Social Analysis', *Journal of Development Studies*, Vol. 38, No. 5, pp. 89–114.
Rogaly, B., Barbara Harriss-White, and S. Bose, 1995, 'Sonar Bangla: Agricultural Growth and Agrarian Change in West Bengal and

Bangladesh', *Economic and Political Weekly*, Vol. xxx, No. 29, 22 July, pp. 1862–8.

Rogaly, B., Barbara Harriss-White, and S. Bose, (eds.), 1999, 'Introduction: Agricultural Growth and Agrarian Change in West Bengal and Bangladesh', Ch. 1 in Rogaly, Harriss-White and Bose, (eds), *Sonar Bangla: Agricultural Growth and Agrarian Change in West Bengal and Bangladesh*, Sage, New Delhi.

Rogaly, B., and A. Rafique, 2003, 'Struggling to Save Cash: Seasonal Migration and Vulnerability in West Bengal, India', *Development and Change*, Vol. 34, No. 4, pp. 659–81.

Rogaly, B., et al., 2001. 'Seasonal Migration, Social Change and Migrants' Rights: Lessons from West Bengal', *Economic and Political Weekly*, 8 December, pp. 4547–59. Vol. 36, No. 49.

Roy, R., 1996 'State Failure: Political-Fiscal Implications of the Black Economy' *Bulletin, Institute of Development Studies*, Vol. 27, No. 2. pp. 22–31.

Roy, R., 1999, 'Riches amid Sterility: debates on Indian fiscal policy' in Byres, (ed).

Roy, T., 2002, 'Economic History and Modern India—Redifining the Link', *Journal of Economic Perspectives*, Vol. 16, No. 3, pp. 109–30.

Rudra, A., 1984, 'Local Power and Farm Level Decision Making' in Desai, Rudolph and Rudra, (eds), *Agrarian Power and Agricultural Productivity in South Asia*, Oxford University Press, Delhi.

Rudra, A., 1982, '*Indian Agricultural Economics: Myths and Realities* Allied Publishers, New Delhi.

Rudra, A., 1989, 'Field Survey Methods', in Bardhan, (ed), (1989b),

Rudra, A., and P. K. Bardhan, 1983, *Agrarian Relations in West Bengal: Results of Two Surveys*, Somaiya, Bombay.

Rukmani, R., 1996, 'Factors underlying the High Dispersal of Towns in Tamil Nadu' *Review of Development and Change* 1, 1 pp. 133–45.

Rutten, M., 1997, *Farms and Factories: Social Profile of Large Farmers and Rural Industrialists in West India* Oxford University Press, New Delhi.

Ruud, A., 1999, 'From Untouchable to Communist: Wealth, power and Status among Supporters of the Communist Party (Marxist) in Rural West Bengal', in Rogaly, Harriss-White and Bose, (eds), *Sonar Bangla: Agricultural Growth and Agrarian Change in West Bengal and Bangladesh*, Sage, New Delhi.

Saez, L., 2002, *Federalism without a Centre: The Impact of Political and economic reform on India's Federal System*, Sage, New Delhi.

Saha, N.C., 2003, The Marwari Community in East India: A Historical Survey Focusing on North Bengal, Decent Books, New Delhi.

Saha A., and M. Swaminathan, 1994, 'Agricultural Growth in West Bengal in the 1980s—a Disaggregation by Districts and Crops' Economic and Political Weekly, 26 March, pp. A.2–11.

Sarap, K., 1987, 'Transactions in Rural Credit Markets in Western Orissa, India', Journal of Peasant Studies 15,1, pp. 83–107.

Sarap, K., 1991, Interlinked Agrarian Markets in Rural India, Institute of Economic Growth, Sage, New Delhi.

Sankar, R.V., 1997, 'A Lasting Contribution', Frontline, 11 July, p. 123.

Sarkar, A., 2006, 'Political Economy of West Bengal: A Puzzle and a Hypothesis', Economic and Political Weekly, 28 January, pp. 341–8.

Sarkar, D., R.R. Pattnaik, and K.S. Chatterjee, 1992, 'Study of Emerging Problems of Agricultural Marketing with a Special Focus on Processing and Input Supplies (West Bengal)', Agro-Economic Research Centre, Visva Bharati, Santiniketan.

Sarkar, S., 1979, 'Marketing of Foodgrains and Patterns of Exploitation', Department of Economics, Occasional Paper No. 1, Visva Bharati, Santiniketan.

Sarkar, S., 1981, 'Marketing of Foodgrains: An Analysis of Village Survey Data in West Bengal and Bihar', Economic and Political Weekly, Vol. 16, No. 39, pp. A.103–A.108.

Sarkar, S., and K.S. Chattopadhyay, 1995, 'Agrarian Market Characteristics and Agricultural Development: Lessons from West Bengal's Case', Paper presented at the workshop on Agricultural Growth and Agrarian Change in West Bengal and Bangladesh', Centre for Studies in Social Sciences, Calcutta, Calcutta, 9–12 January.

Schaffer, B., 1984, 'Towards Responsibility: Public Policy in Theory and Practice', in E. Clay and B. Schaffer, (eds.), Room For Manoeuvre, Heinemann, London.

Sebastian, G., 2003, 'Reining in the Lesser Lords: 'Social Structures of Accumulation' in India's Informal Economy' Indian Journal of Labour Economics 46, 2, pp. 305–19.

Sen, A., and N. Bandyopadhyay, 1975, 'Problems of Public Distribution in West Bengal', mimeo, Centre for Studies in Social Sciences, Calcutta.

Sen, A., and N. Bandyopadhyay, 1978a, 'A Note on Procurement, Distribution and Vulnerable Sections in West Bengal', mimeo, CSSS, Calcutta.

Sen, A., and N. Bandyopadhyay, 1978b, 'State Food Accounts in West Bengal: Production and Availability', mimeo, CSSS, Calcutta.

Sen, A.K., 1981, *Poverty and Famines: An Essay in Entitlement and Deprivation*, Clarendon, Oxford.

Sen, A.K., 1990, 'Gender and Co-operative Conflicts', in Tinker, (ed), *Persistent Inequalities: Women and World Development*, Oxford University Press, New York, pp. 123–49.

Sen, A.K., 1993, 'Markets and Freedoms: Achievements and Limitations of the Market Mechanism in Promoting Individual Freedoms', *Oxford Economic Papers* 45, pp. 519–41.

Sen, Abhijit, 2002, 'Agriculture, Employment and Poverty: Recent Trends in Rural India' in V.K. Ramachandran and M. Swaminathan, (eds), *Agrarian Studies: Essays on Agrarian Relations in Less-Developed Countries*, Tulika, New Delhi.

Sen, A. and R. Sengupta, 1995, 'Recent Growth in Agricultural Output in Eastern India with special reference to the case of West Bengal', Paper to the Workshop on Agricultual Growth and Agrarian Change in West Bengal and Bangladesh, Centre for the Study of Social Sciences Calcutta, Calcutta.

Sen, C., 1985, 'Commercialization, Class Relations and Agricultural Performance in UP: A Note on Bhaduri's Hypothesis', in K.N. Raj, et al., (eds.), *Essays on the Commercialization of Indian Agriculture*, Oxford University Press, Bombay. pp. 319–31.

Sengupta, A., 1998, 'Embedded or stuck? The Study of the Indian State, its Embeddedness in Local Institutions and State Capacity', M. Phil. Thesis in Development Studies, Queen Elizabeth House, Oxford.

Sengupta, S., 1981, 'West Bengal Land Reforms and the Agrarian Scene', *Economic and Political Weekly*, June, Volume XVI, No. 25–26, pp. A.69–A.75.

Sengupta, S., 1989, 'West Bengal Rural Scene: A Review', Agro-Economics Research Centre, Visva Bharati, Santiniketan.

Sengupta, S., and M. Ghosh, 1978, 'State Intervention in the Vulnerable Food Economy of India and the Problem of the Rural Poor', mimeo, CSSS, Calcutta.

Sengupta, S., and S. Gazdar, 1997, 'Agricultural Policy and Rural Development in West Bengal' in Dreze and Sen, (eds).

Shariff, A. [ed], 2004. *Eastern India Human Development Report*, NCAER/Oxford University Press, New Delhi.

Sharma, A., 2004, 'Budget 2004–5: Farmers are the new Untouchables' *Macroscan* 7 December, http://www.macroscan.org.

Shetty, S.L., 2005, 'Regional, Sectoral and Functional Distribution of Bank Credit' in Ramachandran and Swaminathan, (eds), *Financial Liberalization and Rural Credit in India*, Tulika, New Delhi, pp. 50–109.

Singh, G., 2000, *Ethnic Conflict in India: A Case Study of Punjab*, Palgrave, London.

Singh, P., 2005, 'Provident Fund as Social Security' *Labour File* 3,3, pp. 26–8.

Singh, N., and M.K. Sapra, 2007, 'Liberalisation in Trade and Finance: India's Garment Sector, in Harriss-White and Sinha (eds).

Spoor M., 1991, 'The State and Domestic Agricultural Markets in developing Countries: The Case of Nicaragua', PhD Thesis, University of Amsterdam.

Srinivas, M.N., (ed), 1996, *Caste: Its Twentieth Century Avatar* Viking, Delhi.

Srinivasan, K., 2005, 'Capital Flight recycling in India', *Tax Justice Focus* 1, 4 httpo://www.taxjustice.net.

Stein, N. (ed), 2004, *Annual World Bank Conference on Development Economics – Europe – 2003*, Washington, IBRD.

Stern, B., and S. Subrahmanyam, (eds), 1995, *Institutions and Economic Change in South Asia*, Oxford University Press, New Delhi.

Stiglitz, J., 1986, 'The New Development Economics', *World Development*, 14, pp. 257–265.

Subbarao, K., 1978, *Rice Marketing Systems and Compulsory Levies in Andhra Pradesh: A Study of Public Intervention in Foodgrain Marketing*, Allied Publishers, New Delhi.

Subrahmanyam, S., 1990, *The Political Economy of Commerce: Southern India 1500–1650*, Cambridge University Press, Cambridge.

Subrahmanyam, S., 1994, *Money and the Market in India: 1100-1700*, Oxford University Press, New Delhi.

Swaminathan, M., 1996, 'Structural Adjustment, Food Security and the System of Public Distribution of Food', *Economic and Political Weekly*, Vol. 31.

Swaminathan, M., 1999, 'Understanding the Costs of the Food Corporation of India', Indira Gandhi Institute of Development Research, Mumbai.

Swaminathan, M., 2000, *Weakening Welfare*, Leftword Books, New Delhi.

Taknet, D.K., 1986, *Industrial Entrepreneurship of Shekhawati Marwaris*, EDI Press, Jaipur.

Thakur, R., 1995, *The Government and Politics of India*, Macmillan, Basingstoke.

Timberg T., 1978, *The Marwaris: From Traders to Industrialists*, Vikas, New Delhi.

Bibliography

Tinker, I., (ed), 1990, *Persistent Inequalities: Women and World Development*, Oxford University Press, New York.

Thorlind, R., 2000, *Development, Decentralization and Democracy: Exploring Social Capital and Politicisation in the Bengal Region*, Nordic Institute of Asian Studies, Copenhagen.

UCO Bank, 1989, *Annual Credit Plan 1989–90*, Burdwan District (W. Bengal), Calcutta.

UCO Bank, 1990, *Annual Credit Plan 1990–91*, Burdwan District (W. Bengal), Calcutta.

Van Ufford, P.Q., 1999, Trade and Traders: The Making of the Cattle Market in Benin, PhD Thesis, University of Amsterdam.

Vaidyanathan, A., 1986, 'Labour use in Rural India: A Study of Spatial and Temporal Variations' *economic and Political Weekly* 21.52, Review of Agriculture, 27 December.

Vaidyanathan, A., 1992, 'Poverty and Economy: The Regional Dimension', in B. Harriss, S. Guhan, and R. H. Cassen, (eds), *Poverty in India: Research and Policy*, Oxford University Press, Bombay.

Vakulabharanam, V., 2005, 'Growth and Distribution in a South Indian Peasant Economy during the Era of Economic Liberalization' *Journal of Development Studies* 41, 6, pp. 971–97.

Vidal, D., 2003, 'Markets' *Oxford-India Companion to Sociology and Social Anthropology*, Oxford University Press, Delhi, pp. 1342–60.

Vyas, V.S., 2000, 'Ensuring Food security: The State, Market and Civil Society' *Economic and Political Weekly*, 35, 50, 9 December, pp. 4402–7.

Wanmali, S., and C. Ramasamy, 1994, *Developing Rural Infrastructure for Poor People* ICAR, New Delhi, and IFPRI, Washington.

Webster, N., 1989, '*Agrarian Relations in Burdwan District, West Bengal*', Working Paper, 89.2, Centre for Development Research, Copenhagen.

Webster, N., 1999, 'Institutions, Actors and Strategies in West Bengal's Rural Development—a Study on Irrigation', in Rogaly, Harriss-White and Bose, (eds), *Sonar Bangla: Agricultural Growth and Agrarian Change in West Bengal and Bangladesh*, Sage, New Delhi..

White, G., 1991, 'Towards a Political Analysis of Markets', *Bulletin Institute of Development Studies*, 24, 3.

White, G., (ed), 1989, *Developmental States in East Asia*, Macmillan, London.

Williams, G., 1999, 'Assessing Poverty and Poverty Alleviation: Evidence from West Bengal', *Transactions of the Institute of British Geographers*, NS24, pp. 193–212.

Williams, G., 1999, 'Panchayati Raj and the Changing Micro-politics of West Bengal' Ch. 8 in Rogaly, Harriss-White and Bose, (eds).

Williamson, O. E., 1985, *The Economic Institutions of Capitalism*, Free Press, New York.

World Bank, 1997, *The State in a changing World: World Development Report*, IBRD, Washington.

Unpublished Documents

Letter to Shri Debendra Prasad Jadav M.P., Chair, Standing Committee of Food, Civil Supplies and the Public Distribution System, from the East Zonal Secretary, FCI Employees Union, 7 September, 2000.

Memo to Mr. Jawahar Sircar, Principal Secretary, Commerce and Industry, May 2002, High Power Committee, Agribusiness.

WBIDS-McKinsey 'Memo to Minister-in-Charge, Department of Agriculture, Government of West Bengal', 6 May, 2002. Project on Attracting Investment in West Bengal Agribusiness Sector.

Newspaper and Internet Sources

The Hindu: Business Line 2001. 'Plea to modernise Rice Hulling Units' 16 June.

The Hindu, Business Line 2001. 'West Bengal Task Force for Rice-bran Oil Development' 6 July.

The Hindu Business Line 2002, 'McKinsey move woos investors to Bengal', 14 September, www.thehindubusinessline.com/bline/2002/09/14/2002091401930300.htm

The Hindu, Business Line 2003, Food and Fertiliser Subsidy', 3 April.

Confederation of Indian Industries, "*Changing Face of West Bengal*", http://216.239.59.104/search?q=cache:3NpwAMZgynEJ:www.ciionline.org/Eastern/regionalfocus/817/images/Changing%2520face%2520of%2520West%2520Bengal.pdf+mckinsey+west+bengal&hl=en

http://www.ri3240.com/Dist/profilejugal.htm

http://feamm.nic.in/earthrelief

http://fciweb.nic.in

http:www.ciionline.org/Eastem/regionalfocus,2003.

Index

Subject Index

accumulation 31, 32, 39, 81, 133, 183, 207, 226, 267, 292, 303, 307
  capitalist 251
  commercial 2, 315–18
  dynamics 189
  and market system 188, 213, 303–6
  primary/ primitive 22–3
  process of 351, 58, 371–72
  relationship of, in rice markets 84–118
agricultural commodity market(s) 11–13, 33, 38, 39, 316
  autonomy of 40
  in Bardhaman district 186
  commercial capitalism in 2
  and development 20
  diversity of system 321
  dominant institutions in 25–6
  and failure of agriculture in West Bengal 1ff
  state's incentives to 33
    See also commerce, firms, rice wholesalers, trade
Agricultural Costs and Prices Commission 129
agricultural labourer, households, house plots allocated to 6
  landless 20
  wages of 8, 14n
  real wages of 7–8
Agricultural Markets Regulation and Enforcement Act 34
agriculture(al)/ agrarian, backwardness 5, 336
  caste/ class 39, 118, 226, 306
  commodities 26–7
  credit 8, 86, 217
  crisis, in West Bengal 278–85
  development 1–11, 61–66, 213–18, 283, 290–303
  economy of West Bengal 1–11, 116, 302, 316–18
  failure of 1ff
  growth 3–11, 6, 42n, 214–18, 316

  poor/ poverty 2, 11 see Poverty
  price data 358–60, 362–64
  production 1, 119, 141
  commercial capitalism and 102–4
  and markets in Bardhaman district 61–70
  reforms 2, 187, 315
  relations 42n
  rent, as capital 84, 85, 228
  research 16n
  role of, in market system 292
  stagnation 1, 38, 53, 120
  state protection of 33
  structure 63–4, 69, 280–1, 306
    in Bardhaman district 63–4, 186
    in Birbhum district 56–59
    changes in 186–7
    in post-land reform period 66
  structural characteristics of, in West Bengal 21
  technology, new 2, 214–18
  and trade, and business 331
  transformation 38
    and agricultural achievements 4–11, 290–303
  underdevelopment 4
agro-commerce, costs and returns to 94–9, 189–92, 227, 228–34
agro-commercial borrowing, and lending 177–8
  See banks, credit
agro-commercial capital 13, 41, 142, 290–303
  and agricultural growth 316
  and Left Front 3, 18, 209–11, 246, 283–4, 309–18
agro-commercial elite 12
  philanthropy of 241
  privileges of 2–3
agro-commercial firms 103, 109
agro-commercial portfolios 105, 352–58, 370–74
  conglomerate property 22, 307

Agro-Economics Research Centre xviii, 64
agro-processing 1, 54, 59
  plants, in Memari 67
    see also husking mills, rice mills, technology
Ajoy river 52, 62, 67
Alcohol 127
All Bengal Association 138
All Bengal Rice Millers' Association 139, 140
aman (monsoon) season 5, 6
  paddy cultivation in 47, 218
Annapurna Antyodan Yojana 278
anti-poverty, loans 296
  policies, effects on markets 328
  'anti-poverty policy' 11, 311–13
Aratdars (commission agents) 266
assets, control over 169–71, 182
  ownership of, in Bardhaman district 169–71
    by commercial firms 191
    see also agro commercial portfolios
ash, use of 74, 224, 299
Association of Small Scale Industries 378
aus season 6, 8

baki system 246
Baniyas 118, 307
banks, 'bonds' for credit from 175, 254n
  loans from 87, 178, 179, 210
Bardhaman District Co-operative Central Bank 180
bargadars (sharecroppers) 6, 71n
Bengal Chamber of Commerce 378
Bengal Famine 71n   see famine
Bengal Rice Millers' Association, Marwaris in 31
Bengali elite, landed 118
'Bengali' *jotedars* 240
Bharat Chamber of Commerce 139–40
Bharatiya Janata Party 269, 271, 276
  elite merchants' support to 181
Birbhum District Husking Mill Owners' Association 138
Birbhum District Paddy Agents' Association 138
Birbhum District Rice Millers' Association 138, 139
Birbhum District Rice Wholesalers' Association 138
Birla, industrial companies of 43n

black market, in rice 80, 126
boro crop 15n
Boro Bazar 298
boro season 6, 8, 214, 283
  paddy in 218
Brahmins 110
  in rice trade 155
bran 122n, 299, 342, 346
  income from sale of 96
  industry, problems faced by 348
  oil 74, 228, 230, 283, 299
  price of 92
  processing technology 142
  transportation of 228
  use in industry 224
  yields 230
Bretton Woods institutions 267
  critique of 268
bribe/bribery 38, 97, 130, 139, 253, 262
  see corruption
British Raj, and Marwaris' business in Calcutta 30
brokers/ brokerage service 75, 78, 99–102, 175, 220, 222, 224
  see also dalal, intermediary, middleman
buffer stock, and exports 270–1
Burdwan Agricultural Co-operative Society 378
Burdwan District Husking Mill Association 377
Burdwan District Oil Millers' Association 375
Burdwan District Rice Mill Owners' Association 276–7
bureaucratic rent 36
bureaucracy, and agro-commercial capital and 195
  food merchants collusion with 38
business class/family 27
  ownership of mills by 2
  see also agro-commerce, family Marwari
by-products, of rice 232
  income from sale of 224
  prices 363
Byabsai Samiti 240

Calcutta High Court 138
canal irrigation 5, 10, 47
capacity utilization 222, 230
  polarization of 348

Index

capital, accumulation 32, 84, 94099, 99–107, 189–92, 227, 228–34, 352–58, 370–74
  formation and investments 5
  in informal economy 316–18
  individual, growth of 99–102
  origin of, in rice markets 84–5, 189–91
  for rice mill, expansion 120
    processing 228–34
    for starting 101, 118
caste 13, 107, 110–11, 155–60, 238, 248, 297, 306–07
  barriers in Katwa 167
  and rice trade in Bardhaman district 155
  and social exclusion 110–11
Centre of Indian Trade Unions (CITU) 276
Central Warehouse Corporation 135
Centre of Indian Trade Unions 159
cereal production 48
  in Bardhaman district 48
  in Birbhum district 48
  see also grain, paddy, rice, wheat
CFTRI, Mysore 230
circulation, system of, for rice 23–4, 40, 81, 303–09
class, and exchange relations 20–3, 226, 313, 315
  fraction 206
  interests, structure in markets 298
  see also agriculture, agro-commerce, capital, elites, labour, rice mill owners
cold storage firms 172
  state finance to 189
  see also co-operatives, potatoes, Marwari
'collective action' 13, 168, 207, 214, 239–41, 287, 324
  in oil 375
  in potato 375
  in rice 375
  and social regulation of markets 188, 202–7
  see also guilds, self organisation
collective organizations, of traders 214
collusive oligopolies, in marketing system 58
commercial enterprise/firm 252
  polarization of 52–3
  see also agro-commerce, family
commercial finance/ capital 86–9, 99–106, 290, 317, 318, 337
  and agricultural production 102–4

  intermediate 313
Commercial Taxes Department, inspection by 194
commodity, associations 137
  exchange, and class formation 321
  flows, in Bardhaman district 160–3
  types of 56
  system, components of 208
  traders, role of 47
  see also agricultural commodities, collective action, power relations
commodification 218–28, 299
Communist Party xvi
  government 3
  see also Forward Bloc, Left Front
Communist Party of India –M 140, 257n, 309, 314
  and labour unions 237, 275
Congress Party 269, 300, 311
  government 10, 52
    land reform under 6
  on wholesale paddy trade 131–2
contractual behaviour, and economic power 175–7
contracts, for agricultural commodities 21, 23
  in market institutions 26
  payment system as power relations 85–6
co-operatives 26, 137, 154, 200–1
  cold stores 179, 200–1, 207
  crop loans 179–80
  regulation of 296
  trading and processing 194
cooperative banks, and agricultural credit 7, 88, 179–81
corruption 23, 268
  see also bribe, bureaucratic rent, extortion, fraud
credit, for agricultural production 4, 7, 10, 187, 217, 304
  to asset-powerful firms 179
  from co-operatives and nationalized banks 312
  and debt 174
  informal 180
  to producers 176–7
  state-regulated 195
  subsidized 135
    see also banks, baki, dadon, moneylending

culture/ cultural 31-2, 306-9
  societies, merchants' membership in 136

dadon loan 87, 88, 142
dalals (brokers) 246
  see also brokers
dalit 111
  see also scheduled castes
Damodar river 62
Department of Agricultural Marketing 35
Department of Co-operation 35
decentralization 4, 6, 9, 271-72, 299
de-participation 259, 267-9, 284, 297-300
  impact of 272-6, 278
  see also regulation
de-regulation, of trade firms 13, 259-67, 280, 284, 297-300
  impact of, on market system 266
  see also regulation
dheki processing 300, 342
  employment in 116, 139, 143
  failure of government protection to 310
  use of 340
diasporic trading communities, in West Bengal 29
distress/forced commerce 21, 42n, 56, 63, 69, 217
District Husking Mill Owners' Association 341
district 40, 47-70, 146, 218, 290-303
distributive share 116-18, 227, 234
dominant institutions 26-7, 228-34
drought 5, 52, 56, 270

East India Human Development Report 14n
economic mobility 331
education 2, 111, 236
  illiteracy 14n
electricity, to husking mills 230
  regulations 262
  in rural areas 36
  to wells 47
Electricity Board 138, 197, 230
elites 32, 39, 63, 315, 322
employment, guarantee 35
  in rice markets 107
  see also dheki processing, labour, underemployment
entry barriers, costs, in rice markets 109, 110 230, 231, 294, 307, 308, 351

to trade 167, 168, 205
Essential Commodities Act 1955 249, 250, 261, 264, 281
ethnicity 13, 31-2, 183, 307
European Union 228
exchange rates x
exchange relations 63, 64
  barter and 75
  class and 20-3
exploitation, of labour 116-18
  see also labour, migrants, markets
exports, buffer stock and 270-1
  of rice from West Bengal and other states 280, 379
extortion 303, 315
  see also corruption

Factories Act 112, 115, 151, 236-7
  registration of mills under 132
'fair price shops' (FPS) 35, 244, 250, 277, 282
  and Food Departments 274
  and illegal retailers 302
family 26, 27
  investments 102
  labour 26, 155, 236, 252
    firms 158
    male 111
  size 104
family business 27, 44n, 154
  diasporas, relevance of 28-31
  see also agro-commerce, joint family
famine, of 1943 61, 71n
  in South Asia 2
farm family livelihoods 102-7
Farraka Barrage agreement 280
female *see* women, labour
fertilizers 47
  decontrol of 10
  demand and supply of 5
  distribution networks 7
field methodology 40-1, 321-33
  questionnaire 328-33
finance, and credit 177-81
  government 210
  to potato cold-store owners and wholesalers 178
  to rice mills and trading 178
  see also banks, credit
firms, family-owned 154, 158

Index

diversity in organizations 154–5
forms of organization 304
funds for 85
'prominent' 75
trading 26, 160
types of 75–7
  see also agro-commerce, family, markets, trade
Five Year Plan, First 59
floods, in West Bengal 215
food, economy, crisis in 278–84
  distribution by government 267–8
  history of West Bengal's 47ff
  policy 46n
  public distribution of 3, 35–38, 367–78
  security 269
  subsidies, and de-participation 269–70
  expenditure on 267
  system, de-participation in 276–8
  elements of 322
  participative regulations 285
Food and Civil Supplies Department 250
Food Control Order, 1967 194, 250
Food Corporation of India (FCI) 11, 35, 48, 129, 130, 131, 264, 269, 271, 272, 278, 302, 324, 343
  de-participation by 275
  distribution of rice and wheat by 273–4
  godowns, congested 348
  labour force in 275–6, 284–5
  payment for rice purchases 85
  unions 275, 276
Food Department 35, 99, 139, 154, 199, 250, 264, 272, 275, 302
  rice procurement by 274, 281, 282
  state trading by 271
Food for Work 278
food merchants, collusion with state bureaucracy 38, 274–5
Ford Foundation 273
Forward Bloc 314
  Farmers' Association of 283
fraud 23, 268
  see also corruption
Ganges river 48
gender, division in labour 110–16, 119, 147–53, 155–60, 234–41, 242–51
  relations, in markets 308
  role of 32, 107, 170
  segregation 159

Government of India, control over West Bengal's finance 272–4
Grain, markets 20
  Output 5
  See also cereals, paddy, rice, wheat
gram panchayat 6, 7
Green Revolution 5, 70n, 337
  See also high yielding variety rice
groundwater, exploitation of 62
'guilds', commercial and labour 206
  see also collective action
Gujarati Banias 29
  migration to rural West Bengal by 52
  see also baniya, Marwari
Gulsi Coolies' Association 378
Gulsi Oil Mills Association 375
Gulsi Paddy Agents' Association 376
Gulsi Traders' Committee 378

haats, rural 79, 121n
hal katha 248
hand pounding, of rice, organized 59, 60
  see also dheki
Health Department 202
high yielding variety (HYV) rice 5, 7, 8, 47
  multiple cropping of 62
  programme 61–2
  see also agriculture, Green Revolution
Hindi Prachar Samiti 136
Hindu caste, permanent labour 236
  migrants, from East Bengal 240
  see also caste
hoarding 172, 173
  see storage
huller mill technology 59, 198
  see husking mill
human development, ranking of West Bengal 2, 14n
husk 299
  ash 74, 224, 299
  -fired drying technology 231
    impact on casual labour 238–9
  price of 92
  use as fuel 74
husking licenses 132, 139
husking machines 74
  diffusion of 53–4
Husking Mill Owners' Association 139
  unlicensed 139
husking millers 208

investments by 105, 191
lobby 138
husking mills 64, 71n, 78, 136, 143, 189, 229, 324, 350
  access to state-regulated banking system 301
  dominant elements among 229–31
  expansion of 221, 298
  investment portfolio of 356
  labour in 230–1
  licensing/ formalization of 258, 263–4
  in Memari town 67
  modernization of 133, 134
  owners of 81
  profits/returns from 97–8, 230, 349
  prominent elements in 26–7, 234–39
  starting capital for 355
  state regulation on 132–4
  technology change in 340–2
  turnover in 101
  unlicensed 77, 133, 139
  wage labour in 235–6
  see also huller

imports, of grains, between states of India 47, 280, 380
income, from agricultural production 102
  from husking 98
  from land 124n
  and livelihoods in Birbhum district 103
  in Muslim households 234
  from rice brokerage 104
  of rural population 47, 102
  from trade 97–100, 102–4, 190, 227
indebtedness 21
  see also credit
Indian National Trade Union Congress (INTUC) 275, 276
industrial organization, and 'market structure' 23, 303
infant mortality rate 14n
informal economy 316–18
information, control, costs and flow of 173–5
  technology 89–90
institution/ institutional, autonomy 19–33, 146, 306–9
  change/ diversity 32–3, 70, 75–83, 154–63, 175–81 159, 188, 218–41, 260, 303–09, 321

destructive forces in 233–4
complexity in 19.38, 76, 154–69, 218, 220 dominance in 25–8, 218–34
non-market institutions 39, 286, 306–9
prominence in 25–8, 234–41
rigidity, procedural and 265–6
Integrated Area Development Programme (IADP) 70n
Integrated Rural Development Programme (IRDP) 7, 11
  loans 197
Intensive Agricultural District Programme 61
inter-regional trade movements, restrictions on 38, 61, 65, 134, 135, 279, 280, 293
  lifting of 80, 300, 302
  see also trade
intermediaries 53, 57, 63, 67, 174, 176, 178, 186, 224, 241
  powers of 252
  see also brokers, agro-commerce, markets, trade
International Monetary Fund (IMF) 269
investment(s) 60, 189–91, 352–58, 370–74
  in agriculture 106
  in agro-processing and storage 68
  by husking millers 105, 191
  by oil traders 191
  portfolios 104–7
    in Bardhaman and Birbhum Districts 371
    of cold store firms 191
    of firms marketing in rice 352–3
    of husking mills 356
    of rice milling families in Bolpur and Sainthia blocks 354
    of rice wholesalers and brokers 357
  public 10
  in rice mills 191, 228
  in rice processing 55
irrigation water 214
  private 8

Jain religion 29
joint families 154
  property rights of 34
  see also family

Katwa Bazar Committee 377
Katwa Husking Mill Association (defunct) 376

Index

Katwa Oil Millers' Association 375
Katwa Marwari Association 378
Katwa Rikshaw Pullers' Association 378
Katwa Town Businessmen's Association 378
Katwa Truck Owners' Association 378
Kayasths 29
Kisan Sabha 16n
Kolkata Municipal Corporation, regulation by 250
krishani rental terms 124n
kulak-traders 57
'*kutials*' business 152, 171, 197, 224–6

labour 60–1, 107–18, 147–54, 155–60, 229–31, 234, 41
 from Bihar 158
 'casual' labour, in rice mills 113, 115, 118, 153, 158, 182, 237–8
  social regulation of 116
  wages of 299 coolie 114–5
 contract 158
 costs 346
 demand for 9
 displacing processing technology 296
 displacement of 59, 239
 exploitation of 118
 permanent labour force 112, 113
  in Birbhum district 112
 organized 299
 from Orissa 158
 permanent labour 236
  unskilled 226, 234
 process 318
  in Bardhaman district 155–60
  in Birbhum district 108–10
  social structure and, in rice markets 107–11
 productivity 146
 regulations 262
  in rice/ husking mills 234–9, 292, 308
  processing mills in Sainthia block 113
 surplus extraction from 107
 unions 208, 237
 unpaid domestic 144
 unskilled labour 238
  conditions of 115
  piece rate for 107, 113–15 wages for 116, 158–9, 234
  see also distributive share, family, migrant, minimum wage, wages

Labour Commission 237
labour market 9, 251, 299
 in Memari and Gulsi 69, 158
 relations 108–10, 155–60, 266
land, ceilings 6
 control over, in Bardhaman district 171–2
 distribution , reforms and 6
 fertility 47
 holdings 63
  fragmentation of 4
  inequality in 6, 315
 investments in, ceiling on 106
 ownership 102
 registration 7
 relations 141, 306
 see also agriculture
land reforms 6, 14n, 15n, 38, 39, 172, 328
 and land distribution 6
 in 1980s 3, 4
 opposition to 32
 tenancy reforms 128
 see also Opepration Barga
Lead Bank 312
Left Front Government 2, 3, 23, 61, 80, 81, 131, 139, 185, 198, 202, 218, 246, 253, 290ff, 341
 agrarian reforms under 187
 Centre and 279
 on de-participation 267, 271
 development policy of 309
 intervention by 135, 210
 land reforms under 172
 market control, relaxation of 65
 merchants as benefactors of 181
 on panchayats 7
 policy on agricultural markets 4
 politics 41
 price behaviour under 92, 94
 reforms under 12, 258, 295, 311, 312
 regulative policy of 313
 role of 209–11
 rural commercial capital and 4, 309–18
 subsidized loans from 128
 see also agro-commerce, communist party, forward bloc
levy/ levies 37, 92, 99, 129, 130
 compulsory 48
 evasion of 123n, 131
 impact of 135

loss on 122–3nn
percentage and prices in Birbhum district 361
returns to 96–7
on wholesalers 138
liberalization 3, 11, 41, 258, 268, 285, 287n
and institutional development in rice market system 213ff
protective structure of 267
see also reforms
licenses/ licensing, de-regulation of, 289n
policy 134–5, 250, 295, 300, 301
regulations, changes in 262–4
retailers 250
trading 52
loans, from market 88
interests charged on 88
subsidized, from government 128
see also credit
locality, as social regulator 308
see also neighbourhood
losses 192

'*Mahajans*' 187, 244, 247
borrowings by 178
moneylending by 245
market(s)/ marketed, and accumulation 20
and agrarian structure 13, 39
analyzing 19ff
in Bardhaman district 182
in Birbhum district 182
complexity in 19–38, 76, 154–69, 218, 220
concept of 19, 303
conditions 63
-driven politics 121, 296
efficiency 164–69, 359–61, 363–70
entry 84, 109–10, 167–8, 205, 230–1, 294, 307, 308
'imperfection' 309
institutions 23–5
dynamics of, in Bardhaman district 185ff
liberalization of 65
losses and risks in 192
margins (relatively wide in WB) 12, 223, 291
'open market', competition from 279
grains sales in 288n organized 329
participative regulation of 36, 261, 295

politics in Bardhaman district 185ff
for potatoes 65–6
problems of 332
and production 40
reductionism 19
regulation 39, 41, 168–9, 202
for rice 64–5, 72, 348
state's relationship with 33–8, 258ff
'structure' 23, 141, 303–6
surplus 54, 186, 215–17, 228, 298, 347
impact of 215–16
and 'livelihood-intensive' petty trading 295
as system 23, 290ff, 303–6
elements of, in Bardhaman district 218–28
in Birbhum district 218–28
in 24 Parganas district 254n
shocks of 25, 305
structure in Bardhaman district 156–7
see also agricultural market, regulation
market towns 66–70, 226
Marwari business families, in West Bengal 29, 105, 118
in agro-industrial processing 30, 68
in *Bura* bazaar in Calcutta 30
capitalists 49
and Congress 30
credit by 66
diaspora 290
as distinctive economic 'other' 29, 31
domination of 240
economic power of 186, 266
ethnicity 183
identity 28
in Katwa owning firms 170
market power of 120
mercantile and money-lending by 56
migration from, East Bengal 31
from Rajasthan 109
millers 143
money /brokerage by 30, 87
in mustard trade 151
in rice trade 155
role in West Bengal's rural economy 31
Shekawati marwari 28, 29
trade in rural areas by 30
in wholesale rice trade 120
McKinsey 317
Memari Bazar Street Committee 377

Index

Memari Chamber of Commerce 377
Memari Credit Samiti 377
Memari Husking Mill Association (defunct) 376
Memari Potato Syndicate 375
Memari Rice Retailers Association 375–6
mercantile, diaspora 43n, 290n
    family 107, 108–9
    firms, political activity of 136–41
    see also agro commerce, Marwari
merchant capital 19, 319n
    Marx's, and influence in India 334–8
    role of 334–5
merchant(s), control over land in Bardhaman district 171–2
    -moneylender class 56
    organizations of 136–7
Midday Meal 278
middlemen, eradication of 3, 210, 211, 312
    see also agro commerce, broker, dalal, intermediary
migrant labourers 109–10, 119, 158–9, 239
    from Bihar 116
    in Birbhum district 109
    from East Bengal 105
    from Orissa 116
    from Rajasthan 109
    from Uttar Pradesh 116
    social constraints on 240
    wages for 116
migrant mercantile dynasties, 'power points' with 252
    see also Marwari
minimum wage 4, 115, 187
    at district level 7
modernization, of mills 64, 350
    lack of, in Birbhum 349
    lobby against 139
    problems with 347–8
    see also technology
money, access to 29
    market 87
    see also bank, baki, credit, dadon
moneylenders, landlords-cum- 5
    see also moneylending
moneylending 87, 106, 222
    destructive role in agriculture 22
    by *Mahajans* 245
    and price behaviour 56–9
    by traders 22, 217

    see also credit
'monopoly trading houses' 211, 292
movement restrictions *see* inter-regional trade movements
municipal markets, regulation on 250
    see also market towns
muri (puffed rice) 233
    demand for 348
    market for 346
    processing of 266
Muslim labour, as casual labour 238
    in Doludighi 235
    in husking mills 266
    see also religion
Muslim households, income of, in Bardhaman district 234
mustard, production 62–3
    in Bardhaman district 62, 146
    see also oil(seed)
mustard oil, by-products of 151
    commercialization of 166
    labour in 151
    markets 41
    in Bardhaman district 147, 151
    price behaviour 164
    production of 62–3, 176
    trading capital and investments 372
    see also oil(seed)

National Cooperative Development Corporation (NCDC) 35, 194, 343
'National Democratic Alliance' government 3, 275
Naxalite movement 309
NCAER survey, of mills 228–9
neighbourhood, and occupational specialization 248
    see also locality
non-market institutions 39, 286, 306–9
    and diversity 25–8, 306
nutrition 2, 3, 127

oil, price data on 362
    see also mustard
oil mills 59, 173, 174
    in Gulsi 170
    investments in 191
    problems of 208
    regulations on 194, 199
    and wholesalers, contracts between 176

see also mustard
oilseed production 9
  in Bardhaman district 294
  see also mustard
Operation Barga 4, 6, 63, 128, 187, 311, 315
  See also land reform
Operation Sunshine 2000 250

paddy 70n, 72–3
  from Andhra Pradesh 79
  area under 47
  by-products of 81
  commodification of 81
  hoarding of 130
  prices, determining of 89–93, 140, 144, 165–7, 174
    and rice price crisis 279
    of different varieties 278–9
    wholesale 281
  and rice trade under government control 52
  storage of 92, 132
  support price for 281
  surplus 81
  trade/traders, illegal, to rice mills 350
    monopoly on 135
    role of 217
  trading capital and investments in 374
  from Uttar Pradesh 79
  wholesale trade 131, 136, 296, 347
paddy agents 75, 79, 81, 84, 91, 101, 102, 112, 161, 187, 196, 222–3, 264–5, 240, 300
  borrowing by 86, 88
  centralized arrangements for 85–6
  'illegal trade' by 99
  investment portfolios of 358
  portfolios of 105
  profit rates of 99
  wealth of 103–4
  see also rice
Padma river 48
panchayats 4, 6, 7, 271, 288n, 314
  in Birbhum district 131
  effectiveness of 9
  grain procurement by 35
  as purchasing agents for FCI 131
  role of, in agricultural growth 7

'parametric' disciplining institutions 34–5, 36, 259–61
'parametric' regulatory interventions 36, 46n, 259–61
parboiling 339
  husk-fired 232
  sector 224–5
  technology in 343
  see also paddy, processing, rice
Parsees 29
'participative' intervention 34–7, 261–2
partnership firms 154
patriarchy 240
  in business families 28
  gender relations 305
  and markets 307–8
  role of 32
  see also gender
patronage 36, 241, 247
peasants, middle 20
  small 20, 34
  see also class, land
Permanent Settlement 49
pesticide, distribution networks 7
petty trade/ traders, in rice market 12, 13, 53, 77, 78–9, 84, 85, 105, 119, 177, 196, 197, 199, 210, 253, 264, 317, 318, 350
  in Bardhaman district 186–7
  in Birbhum district 290
  in Gulsi 69
  institutions, development of 295
  in Kolkata 246, 298
  license to 209
  problems of 314
philanthropy 136–7, 241
Planning Commission, on urban minimum needs 124n
Policy – *see* agriculture, agro commerce, collective action, communist party, congress, co-operatives, credit, electricity, fair price shops, FCI, labour, land, Left Front, Liberalization, modernization, movement restrictions, price, processing, PDS, reforms, regulation, state, storage, tax, technology, United Front and index references to departments of government and parastatal corporations.

Index

political parties, power of 181–2
population, in Birbhum and Bardhaman districts 49
  in Burdwan town 69
potato, cold store cooperatives 200–1
  in cold stores 148, 150–1, 170, 175, 207, 371
    in Bardhaman and Hooghly districts 65
    regulations on 195–6
  cultivation/production 9, 62
  export from Bardhaman district 161
  HYV 'Jyoti' variety of 62
  markets for 41, 65–6
    in Bardhaman district 147, 148–51, 166, 294
    regulations on 195
  prices 164–7, 362
  production 175
    in Bardhaman district 62, 146
  trade, regulations on 192, 194
  wholesalers/ firms 189, 207, 254n, 371
  wholesaling and cold stores in Memari and Katwa towns 170
poverty 2, 104, 315
  rural 5
poverty line 10
  'above poverty line' (APL), population 270, 273, 282, 288n
  'below poverty line' (BPL) population 269, 270, 273, 283, 288n
  population living below 4, 14n
  see also anti-poverty policy
power relations 85–6, 146ff, 169–82
price(s) 20, 56, 89–96, 164–69, 278–80
  behaviour in Bardhaman district 164–9, 363
    in Birbhum district 89–94, 359, 360
    and market structure 308
  collapse of, of rice and paddy 381–4
  control by State 61, 278
  deflators xi
  distortions 129
  fluctuations in agricultural markets 21
  formation 23, 89, 164–9, 175–7
  inflators xi
  integration model 164–9, 365–70
  margins (relatively wide in WB) 223, 291
  performance in Bardhaman district 146ff
  policy 37, 270, 282

role of 304
  structures, in open markets 37
  see also retail, wholesale
private banking, access to 29
  see also credit
processing, chowbacha 116
  costs for pre-milling 349
  economies of 227
  industries 53
  pre- and post-, in domestic sector 339–40
  see also technology
procurement, performance 37–8
  prices 164
  and trading by state 2, 3
  see also public distribution system
production, and consumption 20
  control over 331
  credit 6
  exchange 214–18
  incentives 3
  and markets 19
  mode of 32
  relations, circulation and 40, 335
  technology, transformation in 47
profits, in oil mills 189–90
  of potato wholesalers 189–90
  in rice trade 95–7, 189–90, 227, 245
  growth and investments 191–2
  see also distributive share, income, losses
'prominent' institutions 26–7, 234–39
property rights 33, 34, 315
protectionism, in United States 11
Provident Fund, for employees 237
public distribution system (PDS) 34, 35, 37, 48, 58, 61, 99, 258, 259, 267, 268, 269, 291, 311, 316, 347
  access to 269, 270
  compulsory sale of rice to 129
  procurement for 281, 293
  reach of 268
  see also targeted PDS
puffed rice see muri
Punjabi Hindus 29

rainfall 47, 48, 214
rain-fed agriculture 8
Rajasthani Marwaris, migration to rural West Bengal 52
  see also Marwaris

Ramakrishna Mission xiii–xv, 136
ration shops 79, 298
  in Bolpur 78
  see fair price shops, public distribution system
rationing, in Kolkata 253, 273
reforms, in agrarian structure/ production 2, 6, 41
  domestic 258
  see also Left Front Government, liberalization
Regulated Agricultural Markets Act 295, 310
regulation/regulatory, de-regulation 202–7, 258, 259–67, 271–2
  incentives 34
  parametric regulation 34–5, 36, 259–61
  participative regulation 34–7, 261–2, 295
  re-regulation 258, 284
  state in rice markets 35–7, 126, 194, 322
  see also de-participation, de-regulation, markets, social regulation
Regulated Market Act 194, 199, 249
religion/religious 234, 248
  minorities 29
  see also Hindu, Jain, Muslim
rent/rental, collectors 56
  creation 260
  '-seeking' 36
  tenure 4
  see also land
Republican Socialist Party, and labour in 237
Reserve Bank of India, funding by 272, 283, 285, 289n, 302
resource, access to 7
  flows by state 33
  see also accumulation, agro-commercial portfolios, credit, moneylending, private banking
retail firms/trade 78, 136, 149, 241–51, 301
  delicencing of 258265
  in Birbhum district 134–5
  prices 93–4
rice, and barter exchange 141
  'bowl' districts 10, 49
  by-products of 74, 75, 92, 120, 152
  as cash crop 280
  coarse 92
  custom-milled 74
  demand for, in Kolkata 244
  exports from West Bengal 224
  hoarding of 130
  import of 65, 198, 199
    from Bangladesh and Burma 56, 297
  long-distance trade in 49, 55, 80
  parboiled 70n, 152
  price of 89, 90, 91, 144, 165–7, 174, 362
    in Burdwan 164
    fluctuation in 57
    of high-yielding 164
    in Katwa 164
    in Memari 164
    wholesale 92, 94
  processing 73, 235, 340, 264, 339–50
    capital and technology in 228–34
    labour process in 234–9
  procurement of 196, 197
  price for 129
  production 5, 17–18, 47, 62, 214–15, 217, 219
    in Bardhaman district 61
    growth rate in 10
    in Katwa 199
  retail price of 94
  retailers 75, 135
  self-sufficiency in 9
  smuggling 242
  storage of 94
  as subsistence crop in Bolpur and Sainthia blocks 342
  system, taxing of 34
  West Bengal as largest producing State for 41
  yields 8
  see also agro-commerce, grain, paddy
Rice Control and Levy Order 1960 194
rice markets 41, 57, 65–6
  in Bardhaman District 64–5, 79, 147, 152–3
  in Birbhum District 48, 49, 52–5, 64–5
  caste distribution in 110
  in early 1980s 72ff
  dynamics and politics of 126ff
  deregulation of 213
  in Katwa town 68, 167, 169
  in Kolkata 241–51
  in 1980–2 141–5
  political activities in 127
  in Sainthia Block 82
  social structures and labour process in 107–11

Index

state finance to 294
structure of 75–82
sub-system in 143–4
trust and power regulating 247
see also agro-commerce, markets, prices, trade
rice mill owners 81, 87, 88, 97, 106, 142, 208
investment by 105, 191
membership of organizations 136–7
Rice Mill Owners' Association 140, 240, 241
rice mills, in Bardhaman District 91, 187
in Bhirbhum District 54
in Bolpur block 61, 113
dominant elements in 26–7, 106, 228–34
entry barriers to 231
expansion of 221–2, 231–3
family labour in 234
and Forest Department 276–7
inspection of 130
investments in 231
lobby 272
modernization of 128, 136, 142, 143, 293
oligopoly 311
ownership of 252, 350
permanent labour force in 112, 118
procedural rigidity for 265–6
registration under Factories Act 132, 236–7
role of 91
state protection to 276–7, 291, 337, 346
state regulations on 130–2, 194, 196
technology 54, 152, 232–3, 342–7
in West Bengal 54–5, 77–80, 86, 101
see also paddy
rice retailing firms 136, 361
rice wholesalers/ brokers for 67–8, 78, 80, 81, 98–9, 101, 120, 131–2, 134–5, 224, 225, 244–6
investment portfolios of 357
regulations on 194, 277
risk 192
Rural Credit Survey 1951 22
rural development 7, 10, 189, 316–18
see agro-commerce
rural non-farm economy 189, 316–18
ryots 56

Sadgop caste 110
Santal labourers 116

Scheduled Castes, employment in markets 297
in Kalna 235
land distribution to 6
Scheduled Tribes, employment in markets 297
income of, in Birbhum 234
from Jharkhand in husking mills 235
land distribution to 6
seasonal livelihoods 2, 119, 292
self-employment, in markets 26, 36, 234, 297
self-organization, in systems of market 239–41
see also collective action
shallow tube wells, development of 8
sharecropping/ sharecroppers 4–5, 49, 56, 63, 215
in Bardhaman district 63
security of 311
share-rents 38
'Small Scale Industry', rice mills as 262, 346, 347
small-scale traders 189, 210
see also petty trade
social exclusion, in rice markets 23–33, 110–11
social institutions, and market system 305–6
see also institutions
social regulation 13, 202–7, 303–6, 322
social security, absence of, for labour 159
Solvent Oil Extractors Association 377
spatial flows 55–6, 79–81, 160–64, 226–28, 379–80
see also trade
'Special Rights of Ownership' 249
staple food markets 70n, 290–303
in Bardhaman 290, 294–7
in Birbhum 290–4
see also grain, mustard oil, oil paddy, rice, sugar, wheat
state, administered price, and market price 301
incentives to markets 33
interventions 126–8, 135–6, 142, 167, 295, 322
markets and 33–8, 303
1991–2002 258ff
participation, in rice business 128–31, 261
policy 145

protection to rice mills 142
regulations 33, 131–5, 188, 192, 194–5, 195–202, 207, 284
  and de- and re-regulation 300–3
  in Kolkata's retail markets 249–51
  'parametric' 33
  'participatory' 33
  -subsidies 188, 346
  -trading institutions 26
  and wholesalers in Kolkata 286
  see also Left Front Government, Policy
State Electricity Board 133, 262
Storage/hoarding 82, 132, 135, 170, 172–3, 250, 263, 274
straw, as cattle feed 74
street traders 244, 245
subsidies 33, 38, 267–71
  on credit 127
  on issue price 269–70
sugar distribution, through PDS 275
Supreme Court 139
  on licensed husking mills 139
surplus appropriation/extraction 21, 38, 39, 252
  marketed s. 54, 186, 215–6, 228, 298
  see also market

'targeted PDS' 273, 288n
  wheat and rice for 282
Tata, industrial companies of 43n
tax/taxation 199
  on paddy purchased by mills 128
  rural 37
  in Uttar Pradesh 128–9
technology, in rice processing 49–56, 59–60, 73, 132–3, 145, 198, 223, 228–41, 306, 229–50
  automation 233
  change 328, 342–50
  see also parboiling, labour displacement, processing
tenurial relations 128
  reforms in 295
  semi-feudal 21
  see also land
'total factor productivity effect' 187
trade 20
  associations 126, 127, 206 – see collective action, philanthropy

castes/ communities 28, 29, 155, 244, 248
diaspora 32
flows 55–6, 78–84, 160–64, 226–8, 379–80
restrictions, removal of 118
  see also exports, imports, inter-regional t.
transport, costs of 80–1, 122n
market 153–4
Trinamool Congress 283

Ugrokhhatriyas, in rice trade 155
underemployment 53
  see labour displacement
Unilever 74
unions, in Bardhaman district 159–60, 236–39
  FCI u. 275–6
  See also labour
United Front rule, and land reforms 6
urbanization 78

value chains 90.221.223.291.303
vaisya caste 110
Vegetable Market Committee 377
village industries 59
Visva Bharati xviii, 66, 316

wage(s), in agriculture 8, 9
  of coolie and casual labour 114
  labour 26, 226, 251, 266
  salaried 107, 112–13
  of permanent labour force 112–13
  in rice firms 117, 125n
  see also agricultural labourer , labour
water, control for agriculture 4, 214
  markets 8, 47, 62
  see also groundwater, irrigation
wealth – see accumulation, profit, income
West Bengal Cold Storage (Licensing and Regulation) Act and Rule 1966–7 192
West Bengal Cold Stores Owners' Association 375
West Bengal Commercial Taxes Department 128
West Bengal Co-operative Federation 194
West Bengal Finance Corporation 128, 194, 210, 233

Index

West Bengal Human Development Report 14n
wheat, consumption in Kolkata 273
  lobby 273
  producers 273
  through PDS 273
wholesale trade, delicensing of 258, 265
  prices 92–3
  see also agricultural commodity market, agro commerce, firms, prices, rice wholesalers, trade
women, control in family business 27
  itinerant traders 244
  labour 111, 114, 239, 240, 292, 300
  in Bardhaman district 158
  participation rate 14n
  unpaid 339
  wages for 159
  in patriarchal business 308
  subordination of, in market system 118–19
  traders 245
  in Kolkata 226
  see also gender
World Bank 1, 194

zamindars/zamindari class 5, 56, 142
  abolition of 5

Name Index

Ahluwalia, D. 287
Appadurai, A. 27

Banaji, J. 22, 63, 336, 337
Bandhyopadhyay, D. 6, 128, 280
Banerjee, H.K.S 4
Banerjee, N. 31
Bardhan, P.K. 63, 308
Basile, E. 160, 206, 240
Basu, J. 7, 165, 213, 214, 309
Basu, Jyoti 316
Bates, Robert 36
Bhaduri, Amit 21, 155, 313, 336
Bharadwaj, Krishna 20, 21
Bhattacharjee, J.P. 54
Bhattacharya, D. 9
Bhattacharyya, Sudipto 217
Bose, S. 63
Bottomore, T. 279, 334
Boyce, James 4
Burawoy, Michael 206
Byres, T.J. 4, 63
Caille, A. 19
Chandrasekhar, C.P. 187
Chatterjee, Dilip 323
Chatterjee, Partha 293
Chattopadhyay, B. 2, 22, 49, 65, 241, 307, 313, 336
Chattopadhyay, K. 217
Chaudhuri, K.N. 52
Choudhury, S. 268, 277, 324, 326

Chibber, Vivek 33
Choudhury, S. 214
Chowdury, S.K. 62, 64, 65
Clay, E. 37
Colatei, D. 32, 171
Crow, B. 19, 20, 21, 63, 89, 164, 304

Das, P.K. 8, 62
Dasgupta, B. 215
Dasgupta, Nandini 246, 247, 248, 249
Datta, S. 28, 317
Dobbin, Christine 28
Drèze, Jean xvii
Dutt, K. 49, 54

Ellis, F. 303
Engels 336
Epstein, Scarlett 109
Evers, H.D. 109

Fine, B. 334
Fukuyama, F. 28

Gandhi, M. xviii
Gandhi, Rajeev 287n
Gazdar, S. 4, 5, 315
Geertz, Clifford 187
Ghosh, A. 49, 54
Ghosh, Madan (M.G.) 11, 54, 64, 217, 234, 239
Ghosh, P.K. 2, 213, 215, 324

Index

Grant, Lewis 53
Gulati, A. 11, 280

Hansen, T.B. 269
Hardgrove, A. 29, 30
Harriss, B. 34, 37, 58, 59, 65, 106, 135, 165, 249, 278, 281, 291, 341
Harriss, J. 5, 22, 181
Harriss-White, B. 22, 26, 32, 36, 38, 59, 127, 130, 136, 160, 165, 171, 177, 181, 194, 206, 215, 240, 244, 248, 249, 262, 265, 291, 299, 313, 325, 327, 340
Hodgson, G. 19, 25, 32, 185, 334

Jadav, Devendra Prasad 289n
Jaffrelot, C. 269
Jagganathan 26
Janakarajan, S. 22
Jha, R. 294
Jomo, K.S. 267

Kalecki, Michal 36
Kaur, R. 213
Kaviraj, S. 38
Kelly, C. 59, 341
Khan, M. 262, 267
Kohli, A. 7, 63, 309, 311, 312, 313, 315
Kundu 4

Laidlow, J. 27, 29
Lambert, H. 308
Landy, F. 10
Lele, Uma 52, 53, 57, 58, 60, 65

Majid, N. 4
Mallick, Ross 312
Marx, Karl 19, 312, 313, 334-8
Mitra, S. 213
Moitra, B. 8, 62
Mooji, J. 39, 250, 261
Mukherjee, B. 8
Mukherjee, P. 54, 55, 116, 323
Mukherjee, S. 56
Mukherjee, Saumik xvii
Mukhopadhyay, S. 8, 214
Murshid, Firdous 89

Narayanan, S. 11, 280
Natarajan, H.K. 294

North, D.C. 185

Olsen, W.K. xvi, 64

Palaskas, T.B. 130, 165, 327
Patnaik, Utsa 22, 49

Rafiq, A. 7, 215
Ram, S.A. 110, 111
Ramachandran, V.K. 7, 10, 209
Ramasamy, C. 7
Rawal, V. 8, 217, 337
Ray, S.S. 198
Robinson, Joan 19
Rogaly, B. 7, 159, 215, 308, 337
Roy, R. 268
Rudra, Ashok 20, 21, 63, 115, 308, 313, 323
Rukmani, R. 308
Ruud, A. 9

Saad-Filho, A. 334
Saha, A. 5, 9
Saha, N.C. 30, 31
Sarkar, A. 8, 213, 314
Sarkar, Suman 20, 217
Sarkar, S. 64
Schrader, H. 109
Sebastian, G. 313
Sen, Amartya (A.K.) xvi, xvii, 2, 56, 66
Sen, Abhijit 10, 297
Sen, A. 62, 65
Sengupta, A. 36
Sengupta, Sunil xvi-xvii, 4, 5, 126, 315, 325
Shams, Kalimuddin 271
Singh, G. 31
Spitz, P. 65
Subrahmanyam, S. 337
Sudarshan, R. 2
Sudarshan, R.M. 213
Swaminathan, M. 5, 7, 8, 9, 10, 38, 268, 270

Tagore, R. 66
Taknet, D.K. 29, 30
Thorlind, R. 7, 314

Vaidyanathan, A. 187
Vakulabharanam, V. 11
Vidal, D. 27

Vyas, V.S. 271

Wanmali, S. 7
Webster, Neil 8, 63, 172, 295

Westergaard, 7
Williams, G. 9, 63

Zedong, Mao 241

Place Index

Ahmadpur 52, 74, 78, 80, 101, 140, 323
Alipur 244
Andhra Pradesh 79, 147, 161, 228
Assam 161, 188, 228, 280

Bangladesh 20, 89, 240, 272, 280, 281, 297, 304
  See East Bengal
Bardhaman district 9, 40, 41, 47, 48, 49, 50, 51, 56, 61–70, 74, 79, 89, 91, 146ff, 185ff, 209, 213, 218–28, 231, 234, 236, 238, 240, 241, 244, 290, 294–7, 323, 324, 371
Bhutan 224
Bihar 80, 116, 147, 161, 277, 279, 297, 280
Birbhum district 48, 49, 50, 51, 52–5, 56, 58, 64–5, 72ff, 93, 103, 109, 110, 112, 120, 146, 182, 185, 213, 218–28, 228, 231, 234, 236, 238, 241, 244, 271, 277, 290, 322, 340, 342, 349, 352, 359–61, 371
Bolpur 49, 52, 53, 55, 61, 66, 74, 78, 80, 82, 100, 101, 107, 113, 135, 136, 138, 222, 223, 226, 241, 266, 290, 323, 324, 342, 352–7,
Boro(Bura)Bazaar 30, 244, 277, 298, 319,
Burdwan city 69, 363
  see also Bardhaman
Burma 54, 56, 297

Calcutta 30, 31, 47, 120, 134, 161
  See Kolkata
China 28, 317
Coimbatore 106
Cooch Behar 31

Darjeeling 31, 317
Dhakuria 244
Doludighi 235
Durgapur 74

East Bengal 31, 105, 109, 240
  See Bangladesh
Europe 28, 228, 299

Garia 244
Gulsi village 68, 69, 154, 158, 170, 174, 324
Gujarat 277, 280
Guskara 58
Guwahati 161

Haryana 273, 280
Hooghly district 49, 65, 213

India 33, 194, 278
Ilambazar 115

Jalpaiguri 31
Japan 28, 228
Jharkhand 235, 279, 281

Kalna 235, 264, 363
Karnataka 80
Kasba 244
Katwa town 67–8, 70, 153, 154, 160, 164–8, 170, 173, 174, 199, 208, 235, 324, 362
Kerala 280
Kolkata 12, 40, 47, 55, 74, 75, 78, 80, 87, 111, 173, 199, 214, 224, 226, 228, 241–51, 273, 277, 286, 293, 295, 297, 298, 302, 324
  see also Calcutta
Konnagar 74
Korea 28, 33
Kuchli village xvii

Lake Market 244
London 194

Madhya Pradesh 280
Madras 54
Mozambique 317
Memari town 66, 67, 153, 158, 161, 164, 165, 173, 174, 176, 324
Middle East 224
Midnapur 74, 89
Murshidabad 74
Myanmar 280
    see also Burma

Nadia 161, 228
Nalhati 52
New Delhi 293
North East India 8
North Bengal 228

Orissa 116, 158, 279, 281

Punjab 61, 80, 147, 188, 198, 199, 273, 280

Rajasthan 80, 109, 147, 271, 294
Russia 335

Sahajapur village xvii, 54
Sainthia block 52, 82, 107, 113, 136, 138, 323, 342, 354–7
Santiniketan xi, xvi
Sian 115
Silguri 161
South Asia 2, 11, 20, 21
South East Asia 11
Sri Lanka 224
Suri 52

Tamil Nadu 106, 188, 291, 325, 347
24 Parganas 161, 214, 244

United Kingdom 28
United States of America 11, 28
Uttar Pradesh 79, 116, 128–9, 161, 271, 273, 280

Vietnam 280, 317